The book is dedicated to my lovely and talented wife, Angela Walker.

ABOUT THE AUTHOR

Matt Walker is currently working as a member of the Cyber Defense and Security Strategy team within Hewlett-Packard Enterprise. An IT security and education professional for more than 20 years, he has served as the director of the Network Training Center and curriculum lead/senior instructor for Cisco Networking Academy on Ramstein AB, Germany, and as a network engineer for NASA's Secure Network Systems (NSS), designing and maintaining secured data, voice, and video networking for the agency. Matt also worked as an instructor supervisor and senior instructor at Dynetics, Inc., in Huntsville, Alabama, providing on-site certification-awarding classes for ISC2, Cisco, and CompTIA, and after two years he came right back to NASA as an IT security manager for UNITeS, SAIC, at Marshall Space Flight Center. He has written and contributed to numerous technical training books for NASA, Air Education and Training Command, and the U.S. Air Force, as well as commercially, and he continues to train and write certification and college-level IT and IA security courses.

About the Technical Editor

Brad Horton currently works as an information security specialist with the U.S. Department of Defense. Brad has worked as a security engineer, commercial security consultant, penetration tester, and information systems researcher in both the private and public sectors.

This has included work with several defense contractors, such as General Dynamics C4S, SAIC, and Dynetics, Inc. Brad currently holds the Certified Information Systems Security Professional (CISSP), the CISSP – Information Systems Security Management Professional (CISSP-ISSMP), the Certified Ethical Hacker (CEH), and the Certified Information Systems Auditor (CISA) trade certifications. Brad holds a bachelor's degree in Commerce and Business Administration from the University of Alabama, a master's degree in Management of Information Systems from the University of Alabama in Huntsville (UAH), and a graduate certificate in Information Assurance from UAH. When not hacking, Brad can be found at home with his family or on a local golf course.

CONTENTS

ACKNOWLEDGMENTS

I, like most of you, had hardly ever read the acknowledgment portion of a book before. When I bought a book, I just wanted to get to the meat of the thing and see what I could drag out of it—either intellectually or entertainment-wise—and couldn't give a care about what the author thought about those who helped put it all together. Then, of all things, I *wrote* a book.

Now, I read the acknowledgment of *every* book I purchase. Why? Because having gone through the trials and tribulations of writing, editing, arguing, planning, researching, rewriting, screaming at a monitor, and restarting the whole thing all over again, I understand why they're so important. I know what it means when the writer says they "couldn't have done it without *fill-in-the-blank*." Trust me, if it's written there, then the author truly means they *couldn't have done it without them*. My *fill-in-the-blanks* deserve more than just a mention in an acknowledgments section, though, because they really did make it all possible, and I most assuredly couldn't have done it without them.

My undying gratitude and heartfelt thanks go out to the entire team at McGraw-Hill Education. Tim Green originally roped me into this a few years back, and without him I'd never even have thought of it. Amy Stonebraker provided the rubber-hose beating that every author needs to finish a product like this (okay, maybe not every author, but I sure needed it) and had a great sense of humor during the whole ordeal. Claire Yee, Rinki Kaur, Dipika Rungta, Bart Reed, Jody McKenzie, and I'm sure a bunch more all deserve a vacation somewhere warm and beachy—I'll get the first round of cold adult beverages. Once again, they all provided me with the chance to do something I dearly love and were very patient with me in putting this all together.

Lastly, I can't thank our technical editor, Brad Horton, enough. Brad makes a difficult process—technically scrubbing everything to make sure it's all in good order—not only bearable but downright fun. His edits were spot on and were always designed to make this project the absolute best it could be. He not only pointed out corrections when I messed something up but added immeasurably to the real-world aspects of this book. I simply could not, *would not,* have done this without him. It's an honor to work with him and a great blessing in my life to call him a friend.

INTRODUCTION

Hello there, Dear Reader, and welcome to the practice exams for Certified Ethical Hacker, now in version 9. If you're the proud owner of previous editions of this book or its companion All-in-One book, *CEH™ Certified Ethical Hacker All-in-One Exam Guide*, welcome back! If not and you're just picking this book up for the first time to see whether it's for you, settle in for a moment and let's cover a few really important items.

Some of you may be curious about what a "hacking" study guide looks like, or you may be thinking about attempting a new certification or career choice. Some of you may have already taken that decisive leap and started down the path, now looking for the next resource to help you along the journey. And some of you reading this may even be simply looking for some credentials for your career—most in this group are true professionals who already know how to do this job and are just finally ready to get the certification knocked out, while a small few are simply looking for a résumé bullet (one more certification you can put on your e-mail signature line to impress others).

Regardless of where you stand in your career or your desire for this certification, there are a couple of things I need to clear the air about—right up front before you commit to purchasing and reading this book. First (before I get to the bad stuff), I firmly believe this book will assist you in attaining your CEH certification. The entire team involved in this effort has spent a lot of time, energy, thought, research, and bourbon on producing what we think is the best companion resource guide on the market. I'm proud of it and proud to have been associated with the professionals who helped put it together.

That said, if you're looking for a silver bullet—a virtual copy of the exam so you can simply memorize, go take the test, and forget about it—please stop reading now and go take your chances elsewhere. Part of the ethics of attaining, and maintaining, a CEH credential is the nondisclosure agreement all candidates sign before attempting the exam. I, and everyone else involved in this project, have taken great pains to provide you with examples of questions designed to test your knowledge of the subject at hand, not to provide you with questions to memorize. Those who are looking for that, and use that method to attain the certification, belittle and cheapen the hard work the community puts into this, and I would be sickened to know of anyone using this work for that purpose.

If you want to pass this exam and have the respect and benefits that come along with holding the certification, then you better damn well know how to do the job. The memorization/test-taking junkies out there may get an interview or two with this certification on their résumé, but trust me—they'll be discovered as frauds before they ever get to round 2. This community knows the difference between a contender and a pretender, so don't try to take shortcuts. Learn the material. Become an expert in it. Then go take the exam. If you're not willing to put in the effort, maybe you should pick up another line of study. Like professional dodge ball. Or the janitorial arts. To quote a really bad 1980s testosterone movie, "There's always barber college."

With all that out of the way—and now that I'm talking to the *real* candidates for this certification—once again I firmly believe this book will help you in your attempt to attain the certification. As always, however, I must provide a word of caution: relying on a single book—*any* single book—to pass this exam is a recipe for disaster. Yes, this is a great resource, and you should definitely buy it (*right now—don't wait!*). However, you simply will not pass this exam without the time and benefit that can come only from experience. As a matter of fact, EC-Council requires candidates sitting for the exam to have at least two years of IT security–related experience. Bolster your study in this book with practice, practice, and more practice. You'll thank me for it later.

Lastly, keep in mind this certification isn't a walk in the park. Certified Ethical Hacker (CEH) didn't gain the reputation and value it has by being easy to attain. Its worth has elevated it as one of the top certifications a technician can attain and is now part of DoD 8570's call for certification on DoD networks. In short, this certification *actually means something* to employers because they know the effort it takes to attain it.

The exam itself is a four-hour, 125-question grueling marathon that will leave you exhausted when you click the Finish button. EC-Council has provided a handbook on the certification and exam (as of this writing, located at https://cert.eccouncil.org/images/doc/CEH-Handbook-v1.8.pdf) that provides all you'll need to know about qualifications, content, and other information about the exam and certification. I've included some highlights in the following sections, detailing the exam and what you'll need.

Training and Preparation

There are two ways for a candidate to attain CEH certification: with training or using only self-study. Per the site (http://iclass.eccouncil.org/?p=719), training options include the following:

- **Live, online, instructor-led**   These courses are offered by many affiliates EC-Council has certified to provide the training. They offer the official courseware in one of two methods: a standard classroom setting or via an "online-live" training class you can view from anywhere. Both offerings have an ECC-certified instructor leading the way, and as of this writing costs $2,895 per seat.

- **Client site**   EC-Council can also arrange for a class at your location, provided you're willing to pay for it, of course. Costs for that depend on your organization.

As for doing it on your own, there are a couple methods available:

- **i-Learn**   With this option, you pay for the official courseware and prerecorded offerings, along with the labs used for the class. This allows you to work through the stuff on your own, without an instructor. Cost as of this writing is $1,899.

- **Self-Study**   If you want to study on your own and don't care about the class at all (that is, you've been doing this for a while and don't see the value of going to a class to have someone teach you what you already know), you can simply buy the courseware for $870 and study on your own.

The Examination

The exam is a four-hour proctored test (in other words, it's taken in person at an authorized testing facility). It's computer based and allows you to skip and mark questions to revisit at the end of each section. Your exam score is tabulated immediately after completion, so be sure to review everything before clicking Finish. A passing score is 70 percent, which means you need to answer at least 88 questions out of 125 correctly. You can find authorized VUE test facilities at their website (http://www.vue.com/eccouncil). Here are some key points to keep in mind:

- **Test content**   Version 9 of the CEH exam, per EC-Council, tests 20 domains, cobbled together in seven different categories. Each section is tested individually and has a weighted value, with an appropriate number of questions offered to cover the material (for example, per the breakdown from the site, you'll see three questions on ethics). Most of the exam points and weighting come from system attacks, tool knowledge, and networking knowledge.

- **Eligibility**   Per EC-Council, you must either attend their official training—official CEH instructor-led training (ILT), computer-based training (CBT), or online live training—or submit an exam eligibility form (along with a $100 nonrefundable fee) proving you've been in the security field for at least two years. In either case, once you've been approved to sit for the exam, EC-Council will forward a code to you that must be presented at the Authorized VUE Testing Center on the date of the exam.

- **Forms**   Before sitting for the exam, you'll be required to sign nondisclosure forms and candidate agreement forms (indicating you promise to be ethical in your hacking). If you're taking the exam without attending training, you'll also need to submit the CEH eligibility form to certmanager@eccouncil.org. The eligibility form requires your colleagues' and boss's signatures, and you'll need to include a copy of a valid government-approved identification. EC-Council will contact your boss for a follow-up interview to complete the process and verify your eligibility. All forms and submission instructions (fax numbers and e-mail addresses) are available within the handbook.

- **Test retake policy**   If a candidate fails on the first attempt, there is no waiting period—in other words, you can immediately retake the exam if you want. On the second, third, and fourth failures, you must wait 14 days before a reattempt. The only other restriction on this is you are not allowed to attempt the exam five times within a 12-month period.

- **Getting your certification**   Per the handbook, after successfully attaining at least a minimum score, you will be issued your CEH credential and will receive your CEH welcome kit within four to eight weeks. The CEH credential is valid for three-year periods but can be renewed each period by successfully earning EC-Council Continued Education (ECE) credits. All EC-Council correspondence will be sent to the e-mail address provided during your exam registration. If your e-mail address changes, it is your responsibility to notify certadmin@eccouncil.org; failing that, you will not be able to receive ECE credits for your work.

Best of luck to you, Dear Reader. I sincerely hope your exam goes well for you and your career is filled with great experiences. Be honest, do a good job, and make every day and action work toward a better world.

In This Book

I've organized this book so that each chapter consists of a battery of practice exam questions representing part of the knowledge and skills you need to know to pass the Certified Ethical Hacker exam. This book was designed to mirror the organization of *CEH Certified Ethical Hacker All-in-One Exam Guide, Third Edition*, and it serves as an excellent companion.

Pre-assessment Test

This book features a pre-assessment test as Appendix A. The pre-assessment test will gauge your areas of strength and weakness and allow you to tailor your studies based on your needs. I recommend you take this pre-assessment test before starting the questions in Chapter 1.

Practice Exams

In addition to the practice questions included in this book, 300 practice questions are provided in an electronic test engine. You can create custom exams by chapter, or you can take multiple timed, full-length practice exams. For more information, please see Appendix B.

Getting Started: Essential Knowledge

This chapter includes questions from the following topics:
- Identify components of TCP/IP computer networking
- Understand basic elements of information security
- Understand incident management steps
- Identify fundamentals of security policies
- Identify essential terminology associated with ethical hacking
- Define ethical hacker and classifications of hackers
- Describe the five stages of ethical hacking
- Define the types of system attacks
- Identify laws, acts, and standards affecting IT security

In one of my earliest memories, I'm sitting at the table on Thanksgiving, staring lovingly at a hot apple pie being sliced into pieces and doled out onto plates. I remember watching an ice cream bowl chase the pie slices around the table, and each person scooping out delicious vanilla goodness for the top of their pie. And I remember looking at that flaky crust and the sugary, syrupy insides and thinking how great it was going to be when I got mine. But then I remember my mom looking right at me and saying, "Looks good, doesn't it? All you've got to do is finish your vegetables and you can have some."

I dearly love apple pie à la mode. It's my favorite dessert on the planet—my ambrosia, if you will. I love it so much that aggressively displacing toddlers out of my way to get to dessert nirvana isn't out of the question (okay, maybe just sternly threatening them, but you get the idea). But I absolutely *despised* most of the veggies I was forced to eat as a kid. Greens, peas, carrots, asparagus? Might as well have been kryptonite for Superman. Why not just ask me to stab my eyes out with a fork—or, worse yet, ask me to wear Auburn colors, Mom?

But when push came to shove, I ate the vegetables. Not because I liked them or because I wanted to, but because I had to in order to get what I *really* wanted.

Welcome to your veggie plate, dear reader. No, it's not the exciting dessert you're drooling over—all those sexy hacking questions come later—but this is stuff you just have to get out of the way first. The good news with this part of your exam is that this is the easy stuff. It's almost pure memorization and definitions—with no wacky formulas or script nuances to figure out. And don't worry, it's not nearly as bad as you think it's going to be. At least I'm not making you put on blue and orange.

 STUDY TIPS   When it comes to studying this chapter, where mostly definitions and rote memorization is all that is required for the exam, repetition is the key. Tables with words on one side and corresponding definitions on the other can be pretty effective—and don't discount the old-school flash cards either. When studying, try to find some key words in each definition you can associate with the term. That way, when you're looking at a weird test question on the exam, a key word will pop out and help provide the answer for you. And for goodness sake, please try not to confuse the real world with the exam—trust what you get out of this book and your other study material, and don't read too much into the questions.

Some of the most confusing questions for you in this section will probably come from security policies, laws and standards, and security control mechanisms. All these questions can get really weird, and I'd love to offer help with them, but I can't—you just have to memorize the data. Especially when it comes to laws and standards questions—they will sometimes be maddening. My best advice is to concentrate on key words and remember that the process of elimination can sometimes be more helpful in narrowing the options down to the correct answer than trying to memorize everything in the first place.

Also, and at the risk of generating derision from the "Thank you, Captain Obvious" crowd, here's another piece of advice I have for you: spend your time on the things you don't already know (trust me, I'm on to something here). Many exam prospects and students spend way too much valuable time repeating portions they already know instead of concentrating on the things they don't. If you understand the definitions regarding white hat and black hat, don't bother reviewing them. Instead, spend your time concentrating on areas that aren't so "common sense" to you.

And, finally, keep in mind that this certification is provided by an international organization. Therefore, you will sometimes see some fairly atrocious grammar on test questions here and there, especially in this section of the exam. Don't worry about it—just keep focused on the main point of the question and look for your key words.

1. A security team is implementing various security controls across the organization. After several configurations and applications, a final agreed-on set of security controls are put into place; however, not all risks are mitigated by the controls. Of the following, which is the next best step?

   A. Continue applying controls until all risk is eliminated.

   B. Ignore any remaining risk as "best effort controlled."

   C. Ensure that any remaining risk is residual or low and accept the risk.

   D. Remove all controls.

2. A Certified Ethical Hacker (CEH) follows a specific methodology for testing a system. Which step comes after footprinting in the CEH methodology?

   A. Scanning

   B. Enumeration

   C. Reconnaissance

   D. Application attack

3. Your organization is planning for the future and is identifying the systems and processes critical for their continued operation. Which of the following best describes this effort?

   A. BCP

   B. BIA

   C. DRP

   D. ALE

4. Which of the following describes security personnel who act in defense of the network during attack simulations?

   A. Red team

   B. Blue team

   C. Black hats

   D. White hats

5. You've been hired as part of a pen test team. During the brief, you learn the client wants the pen test attack to simulate a normal user who finds ways to elevate privileges and create attacks. Which test type does the client want?

   A. White box

   B. Gray box

   C. Black box

   D. Hybrid

6. Which of the following is defined as ensuring the enforcement of organizational security policy does not rely on voluntary user compliance by assigning sensitivity labels on information and comparing this to the level of security a user is operating at?

   A. Mandatory access control

   B. Authorized access control

   C. Role-based access control

   D. Discretionary access control

7. Which of the following statements is true regarding the TCP three-way handshake?

   A. The recipient sets the initial sequence number in the second step.

   B. The sender sets the initial sequence number in the third step.

   C. When accepting the communications request, the recipient responds with an acknowledgement and a randomly generated sequence number in the second step.

   D. When accepting the communications request, the recipient responds with an acknowledgement and a randomly generated sequence number in the third step.

8. Your network contains certain servers that typically fail once every five years. The total cost of one of these servers is $1000. Server technicians are paid $40 per hour, and a typical replacement requires two hours. Ten employees, earning an average of $20 per hour, rely on these servers, and even one of them going down puts the whole group in a wait state until it's brought back up. Which of the following represents the ARO for a server?

   A. $296

   B. $1480

   C. $1000

   D. 0.20

9. An ethical hacker is given no prior knowledge of the network and has a specific framework in which to work. The agreement specifies boundaries, nondisclosure agreements, and a completion date definition. Which of the following statements is true?

   A. A white hat is attempting a black-box test.

   B. A white hat is attempting a white-box test.

   C. A black hat is attempting a black-box test.

   D. A black hat is attempting a gray-box test.

10. Which of the following is a detective control?

   A. Audit trail

   B. CONOPS

   C. Procedure

   D. Smartcard authentication

   E. Process

11. As part of a pen test on a U.S. government system, you discover files containing Social Security numbers and other sensitive personally identifiable information (PII) information. You are asked about controls placed on the dissemination of this information. Which of the following acts should you check?

   A. FISMA

   B. Privacy Act

   C. PATRIOT Act

   D. Freedom of Information Act

12. Four terms make up the Common Criteria process. Which of the following contains seven levels used to rate the target?

   A. ToE

   B. ST

   C. PP

   D. EAL

13. Organization leadership is concerned about social engineering and hires a company to provide training for all employees. How is the organization handling the risk associated with social engineering?

   A. They are accepting the risk.

   B. They are avoiding the risk.

   C. They are mitigating the risk.

   D. They are transferring the risk.

14. In which phase of the ethical hacking methodology would a hacker be expected to discover available targets on a network?

   A. Reconnaissance

   B. Scanning and enumeration

   C. Gaining access

   D. Maintaining access

   E. Covering tracks

15. Which of the following was created to protect shareholders and the general public from corporate accounting errors and fraudulent practices, and to improve the accuracy of corporate disclosures?

   A. GLBA

   B. HIPAA

   C. SOX

   D. FITARA

16. Which of the following best defines a logical or technical control?

    A. Air conditioning

    B. Security tokens

    C. Fire alarms

    D. Security policy

17. Which of the following was created to protect credit card data at rest and in transit in an effort to reduce fraud?

    A. TCSEC

    B. Common Criteria

    C. ISO 27002

    D. PCI DSS

18. As part of the preparation phase for a pen test you are participating in, the client relays their intent to discover security flaws and possible remediation. They seem particularly concerned about internal threats from the user base. Which of the following best describes the test type the client is looking for?

    A. Gray box

    B. Black box

    C. White hat

    D. Black hat

19. In which phase of the attack would a hacker set up and configure "zombie" machines?

    A. Reconnaissance

    B. Covering tracks

    C. Gaining access

    D. Maintaining access

20. Which of the following should not be included in a security policy?

    A. Policy exceptions

    B. Details on noncompliance disciplinary actions

    C. Technical details and procedures

    D. Supporting document references

21. Which of the following is best defined as a set of processes used to identify, analyze, prioritize, and resolve security incidents?

    A. Incident management

    B. Vulnerability management

C. Change management

D. Patch management

22. During an assessment, your pen test team discovers child porn on a system. Which of the following is the appropriate response?

    A. Continue testing and report findings at out-brief.

    B. Continue testing but report findings to the business owners.

    C. Cease testing immediately and refuse to continue work for the client.

    D. Cease testing immediately and contact authorities.

23. Which of the following best describes an intranet zone?

    A. It has few heavy security restrictions.

    B. A highly secured zone, usually employing VLANs and encrypted communication channels.

    C. A controlled buffer network between public and private.

    D. A very restricted zone with no users.

24. A machine in your environment uses an open X-server to allow remote access. The X-server access control is disabled, allowing connections from almost anywhere and with little to no authentication measures. Which of the following are true statements regarding this situation? (Choose all that apply.)

    A. An external vulnerability can take advantage of the misconfigured X-server threat.

    B. An external threat can take advantage of the misconfigured X-server vulnerability.

    C. An internal vulnerability can take advantage of the misconfigured X-server threat.

    D. An internal threat can take advantage of the misconfigured X-server vulnerability.

25. While performing a pen test, you find success in exploiting a machine. Your attack vector took advantage of a common mistake—the Windows 7 installer script used to load the machine left the administrative account with a default password. Which attack did you successfully execute?

    A. Application level

    B. Operating system

    C. Shrink wrap

    D. Social engineering

    E. Misconfiguration

1. C	10. A	19. D
2. A	11. B	20. C
3. B	12. D	21. A
4. B	13. C	22. D
5. B	14. B	23. A
6. A	15. C	24. B, D
7. C	16. B	25. B
8. D	17. D	
9. A	18. A	

1. A security team is implementing various security controls across the organization. After several configurations and applications, a final agreed-on set of security controls are put into place; however, not all risks are mitigated by the controls. Of the following, which is the next best step?

   A. Continue applying controls until all risk is eliminated.

   B. Ignore any remaining risk as "best effort controlled."

   C. Ensure that any remaining risk is low and accept the risk.

   D. Remove all controls.

   ☑ **C.** Remember at the beginning of this chapter when I said the process of elimination may be your best bet in some cases? Well, even if you aren't well-versed in risk management and security control efforts, you could narrow this down to the correct answer. It is impossible to remove all risk from any system and still have it usable. I'm certain there are exceptions to this rule (maybe super-secret machines in underground vaults buried deep within the earth, running on geothermal-powered batteries, without any network access at all and operated by a single operator who hasn't seen daylight in many years), but in general the goal of security teams has always been to reduce risk to an acceptable level.

   ☒ **A** is incorrect because, as I just mentioned, it's impossible to reduce risk to absolute zero and still have a functional system. Remember the Security, Functionality, and Usability triangle? As you move toward more Security, you move further away from Functionality and Usability.

   ☒ **B** is incorrect because it's just silly. If you're a security professional and your response to a risk—any risk—is to ignore it, I can promise you won't be employed for long. Sure, you can point out that it's low or residual and that the chance for actual exploitation is next to nonexistent, but you can't ignore it. Best effort is for kindergarten trophies and IP packet delivery.

   ☒ **D** is incorrect because removing all controls is worse than ignoring the risk. If you remove everything, then *all* risks remain. Remember, the objective is to balance your security controls to cover as much risk as possible, while leaving the system as usable and functional as possible.

2. A Certified Ethical Hacker (CEH) follows a specific methodology for testing a system. Which step comes after footprinting in the CEH methodology?

   A. Scanning

   B. Enumeration

   C. Reconnaissance

   D. Application attack

☑ **A.** CEH methodology is laid out this way: reconnaissance (footprinting), scanning and enumeration, gaining access, escalating privileges, maintaining access, and covering tracks. While you may be groaning about scanning and enumeration both appearing as answers, they're placed here in this way on purpose. This exam is not only testing your rote memorization of the methodology but also how the methodology actually works. Remember, after scoping out the recon on your target, your next step is to scan it. After all, you have to know what targets are there first before enumerating information about them.

☒ **B** is incorrect because, although it is mentioned as part of step 2, it's actually secondary to scanning. Enumerating is used to gather more in-depth information about a target you already discovered by scanning. Things you might discover in scanning are IPs that respond to a ping. In enumerating each "live" IP, you might find open shares, user account information, and other goodies.

☒ **C** is incorrect because *reconnaissance* and *footprinting* are interchangeable in CEH parlance. An argument can be made that footprinting is a specific portion of an overall recon effort; however, in all CEH documentation, these terms are used interchangeably.

☒ **D** is incorrect because it references an attack. As usual, there's almost always one answer you can throw out right away, and this is a prime example. We're talking about step 2 in the methodology, where we're still figuring out what targets are there and what vulnerabilities they may have. Attacking, at this point, is folly.

3. Your organization is planning for the future and is identifying the systems and processes critical for their continued operation. Which of the following best describes this effort?

   A. BCP

   B. BIA

   C. DRP

   D. ALE

☑ **B.** A business impact analysis (BIA) best matches this description. In a BIA, the organization looks at all the systems and processes in use and determines which ones are absolutely critical to continued operation. Additionally, the assessor (the person or company conducting the analysis) will look at all the existing security architecture and make an evaluation on the likelihood of any system or resource being compromised. Part of this is assigning values to systems and services, determining the maximum tolerable downtime (MTD) for any, and identifying any overlooked vulnerabilities.

☒ **A** is incorrect because a business continuity plan (BCP) contains all the procedures that should be followed in the event of an organizational outage—such as a natural disaster or a cyberattack. BCPs include the order in which steps should be taken and which system should be returned to service first. BCPs include DRPs (disaster recovery plans).

☒ **C** is incorrect because a disaster recovery plan (DRP) contains steps and procedures for restoring a specific resource (service, system, and so on) after an outage. Usually DRPs are part of a larger BCP.

☒ **D** is incorrect because the annualized loss expectancy (ALE) is a mathematical measurement of the cost of replacing or repairing a specific resource. ALE is calculated by multiplying the single loss expectancy (SLE) by the annualized rate of occurrence (ARO). For example, if the total cost of a single loss of a resource is calculated at $1000 and you calculate there is a 10 percent chance it will fail in any given year, your ALE would be $100.

4. Which of the following describes security personnel who act in defense of the network during attack simulations?

   A. Red team

   B. Blue team

   C. Black hats

   D. White hats

   ☑ **B.** If you run an Internet search on "red versus blue," you'll come across some pretty entertaining comics spoofing first-person shooter gamers, but not much on IT warfare. The military runs these quite often—a security assessment where one team (red) acts as aggressors while the other (blue) acts in a defensive posture. The idea is to improve security overall because we're all supposed to be working toward the same goal. In any case, if you're a defense person, you're blue team.

   ☒ **A** is incorrect because the red team acts as aggressors during an IT warfare simulation.

   ☒ **C** is incorrect because "black hat" refers to the bad guys in the world—the crackers out there who operate without prior permission and attack for their own reasons.

   ☒ **D** is incorrect because "white hat'" refers to us—the ethical hackers of the world. We operate under permission, carrying out penetration testing to help improve the security of an organization. True, the members of red and blue teams during an exercise are technically white hat to begin with—after all, despite the competition we're all still on the same team—but it's not the best answer here.

5. You've been hired as part of a pen test team. During the brief, you learn the client wants the pen test attack to simulate a normal user who finds ways to elevate privileges and create attacks. Which test type does the client want?

   A. White box

   B. Gray box

   C. Black box

   D. Hybrid

   ☑ **B.** A gray-box test is designed to replicate an inside attacker. Otherwise known as the *partial knowledge* attack (don't forget this term), the idea is to simulate a user on the inside who might know a little about the network, directory structure, and other goodies in your enterprise. You'll probably find this one to be the most enlightening attack in out-briefing your clients in the real world—it's amazing what you can get to when you're a trusted, inside user. As an aside, you'll often find in the real world that *gray-box testing* can also refer to a test where *any* inside information is given to a pen tester—you don't necessarily need to be a fully knowledgeable inside user. In other words, if you have usable information handed to you about your client, you're performing gray-box testing.

☒ **A** is incorrect because a white-box test provides all knowledge to the pen tester up front and is designed to simulate an admin on your network who, for whatever reason, decides to go on the attack. For most pen testers, this test is really just unfair. It's tantamount to sending him into the Roman Colosseum armed with a .50-caliber automatic weapon to battle a gladiator who is holding a knife.

☒ **C** is incorrect because black-box testing indicates no knowledge at all. And if you think about it, the name is easy to correlate and remember: black = no light. Therefore, you can't "see" anything. This is the test most people think about when it comes to hacking. You know nothing and are (usually) attacking from the outside.

☒ **D** is incorrect because, as far as I can tell from the EC-Council's documentation, there is no terminology for a "hybrid-box" test. This is a little tricky because the term *hybrid* is used elsewhere—for attacks and other things. If you apply a little common sense here, this answer is easy to throw out. If you know everything about the target, it's white. If you know nothing, it's black. If you're in the middle, it's gray. See?

6. Which of the following is defined as ensuring the enforcement of organizational security policy does not rely on voluntary user compliance by assigning sensitivity labels on information and comparing this to the level of security a user is operating at?

   A. Mandatory access control

   B. Authorized access control

   C. Role-based access control

   D. Discretionary access control

   ☑ **A.** Access control is defined as the selective restraint of access to a resource, and there are several overall mechanisms to accomplish this goal. Mandatory access control (MAC) is one type that constrains the ability of a subject to access or perform an operation on an object by assigning and comparing "sensitivity labels." Suppose a person (or a process) attempts to access or edit a file. With MAC, a label is placed on the file indicating its security level. If the entity attempting to access it does not have that level, or higher, then access is denied. With mandatory access control, security is centrally controlled by a security policy administrator, and users do not have the ability to override security settings.

   This should not be confused with role-based access control (RBAC) systems, which may actually use MAC to get the job done. The difference is in whether the information itself has a labeled description or whether the person accessing it has their own label. For example, in a classified area, the information classified as Top Secret will have a label on it identifying it as such, while you, as an auditor, will have your own clearance and need-to-know label allowing you to access certain information. MAC is a property of an object; RBAC is a property of someone accessing an object.

☒ **B** is incorrect because while authorized access control may sound great, it's not a valid term.

☒ **C** is incorrect because role-based access control can use MAC or discretionary access control to get the job done. With RBAC, the goal is to assign a role, and any entity holding that role can perform the duties associated with it. Users are not assigned permissions directly; they acquire them through their role (or roles). The roles are assigned to the user's account, and each additional role provides its own unique set of permissions and rights.

☒ **D** is incorrect because discretionary access control (DAC) allows the data owner, the user, to set security permissions for the object. If you're on a Windows machine right now, you can create files and folders and then set sharing and permissions on them as you see fit. MAC administrators in the Department of Defense may shudder at that thought now.

7. Which of the following statements is true regarding the TCP three-way handshake?

   A. The recipient sets the initial sequence number in the second step.

   B. The sender sets the initial sequence number in the third step.

   C. When accepting the communications request, the recipient responds with an acknowledgement and a randomly generated sequence number in the second step.

   D. When accepting the communications request, the recipient responds with an acknowledgement and a randomly generated sequence number in the third step.

   ☑ **C.** The three-way handshake will definitely show up on your exam, and in much trickier wording than this. It's easy enough to memorize "SYN, SYN/ACK, ACK," but you'll need more than that for the exam.

   In step 1, the host sends a segment to the server, indicating it wants to open a communications session. Inside this segment, the host turns on the SYN flag and sets an initial sequence number (any random 32-bit number). When the recipient gets the segment, it crafts a segment in response to let the host know it's open and ready for the communications session. It does this by turning on the SYN and ACK flags, acknowledging the initial sequence number by incrementing it, and adding its own unique sequence number. Lastly, when the host gets this response back, it sends one more segment before the comm channel opens. In this segment, it sets the ACK flag and acknowledges the other's sequence number by incrementing it.

   For example, suppose Host A is trying to open a channel with Server B. In this example, Host A likes the sequence number 2000, while the Server likes 5000.

The first segment would look like this: SYN=1, ACK=0, ISN=2000. The response segment would look like this: SYN=1, ACK=1, ISN=5000, ACK NO=2001. The third and final segment would appear this way: SYN=0, ACK=1, SEQ NO=2001, ACK NO=5001.

☒ **A** is incorrect because the initial sequence number is set in the first step.

☒ **B** is incorrect for the same reason—the ISN is set in the first step.

☒ **D** is incorrect because this activity occurs in the second step.

8. Your network contains certain servers that typically fail once every five years. The total cost of one of these servers is $1000. Server technicians are paid $40 per hour, and a typical replacement requires two hours. Ten employees, earning an average of $20 per hour, rely on these servers, and even one of them going down puts the whole group in a wait state until it's brought back up. Which of the following represents the ARO for a server?

   A. $296

   B. $1480

   C. $1000

   D. 0.20

   ☑ **D.** When performing business impact analysis (or any other value analysis for that matter), the annualized loss expectancy (ALE) is an important measurement for every asset. To compute the ALE, multiply the annualized rate of occurrence (ARO) by the single loss expectancy (SLE). The ARO is the frequency at which a failure occurs on an annual basis. In this example, servers fail once every five years, so the ARO would be 1 failure/5 years = 20 percent.

   ☒ **A** is incorrect because this value equates to the ALE for the example. ALE = ARO × SLE. In this example, the ARO is 20 percent and the SLE is $1480: cost of a server ($1000) plus the cost of technician work to replace it ($80) plus lost time for workers (10 employees × 2 hours × $20 an hour, which works out to $400). Therefore, ALE = 20 percent × $1480, or $296.

   ☒ **B** is incorrect because this value corresponds to the SLE for this scenario. The SLE is the total cost for a single loss, so we need to count the cost of the server, plus the cost of the technician's hours, plus any downtime measurements for other workers. In this case, SLE = $1000 (cost of server) + $80 (server tech hours) + $400 (10 employees × 2 hours × $20 an hour), or $1480.

   ☒ **C** is incorrect because this number doesn't match the ARO for the sample.

9. An ethical hacker is given no prior knowledge of the network and has a specific framework in which to work. The agreement specifies boundaries, nondisclosure agreements, and a completion date definition. Which of the following statements is true?

   A. A white hat is attempting a black-box test.

   B. A white hat is attempting a white-box test.

C. A black hat is attempting a black-box test.

D. A black hat is attempting a gray-box test.

☑ **A.** I love these types of questions. Not only is this a two-for-one question, but it involves identical but confusing descriptors, causing all sorts of havoc. The answer to attacking such questions—and you *will* see them, by the way—is to take each section one at a time. Start with what kind of hacker he is. He's hired under a specific agreement, with full knowledge and consent of the target, thus making him a white hat. That eliminates C and D right off the bat. Second, to address what kind of test he's performing, simply look at what he knows about the system. In this instance, he has no prior knowledge at all, thus making it a black-box test.

☒ **B** is incorrect because although the attacker is one of the good guys (a white hat, proceeding with permission and an agreement in place), he is not provided with full knowledge of the system. In fact, it's quite the opposite—according to the question he knows absolutely nothing about it, making this particular "box" as black as it can be. A white-box target indicates one that the attacker already knows everything about. It's lit up and wide open.

☒ **C** is incorrect right off the bat because it references a black hat. Black-hat attackers are the bad guys—the ones proceeding without the target's knowledge or permission. They usually don't have inside knowledge of their target, so their attacks often start "black box."

☒ **D** is incorrect for the same reason just listed: because this attacker has permission to proceed and is operating under an agreement, he can't be a black-box attacker. Additionally, this answer went the extra mile to convince you it was wrong—and missed on both swings. Not only is this a white-hat attacker, but the attack itself is black box. A gray-box attack indicates at least some inside knowledge of the target.

10. Which of the following is a detective control?

A. Audit trail

B. CONOPS

C. Procedure

D. Smartcard authentication

E. Process

☑ **A.** A detective control is an effort used to identify problems, errors, or (in the case of post-attack discovery) cause or evidence of an exploited vulnerability—and an audit log or trail is a perfect example. Ideally, detective controls should be in place and working such that errors can be corrected as quickly as possible. Many compliance laws and standards (the Sarbanes–Oxley Act of 2002 is one example) mandate the use of detective controls.

☒ **B** is incorrect because a concept of operations (CONOPS) isn't detective in nature. A CONOPS defines what a system is and how it is supposed to be used.

☒ **C** is incorrect because a procedure is a document the spells out specific step-by-step instructions for a given situation or process.

☒ **D** is incorrect because smartcard authentication is a preventive control, not a detective one. It's designed to provide strong authentication, ideally preventing a problem in the first place.

☒ **E** is incorrect because a process can refer to a lot of different things, depending on your definition and viewpoint, but is not detective in nature as a control. A process, in general, refers to a set of steps or actions directed at accomplishing a goal.

11. As part of a pen test on a U.S. government system, you discover files containing Social Security numbers and other sensitive personally identifiable information (PII) information. You are asked about controls placed on the dissemination of this information. Which of the following acts should you check?

   A. FISMA

   B. Privacy Act

   C. PATRIOT Act

   D. Freedom of Information Act

   ☑ **B.** The Privacy Act of 1974 protects information of a personal nature, including Social Security numbers. The Privacy Act defines exactly what "personal information" is, and it states that government agencies cannot disclose any personal information about an individual without that person's consent. It also lists 12 exemptions for the release of this information (for example, information that is part of a law enforcement issue may be released). In other questions you see, keep in mind that the Privacy Act generally will define the information that is *not* available to you in and after a test. Dissemination and storage of privacy information needs to be closely controlled to keep you out of hot water. As a side note, how you obtain PII is oftentimes just as important as how you protect it once discovered. In your real-world adventures, keep the Wiretap Act (18 U.S. Code Chapter 119—Wire and Electronic Communications Interception and Interception of Oral Communications) and others like it in mind.

   ☒ **A** is incorrect because the Federal Information Security Management Act (FISMA) isn't designed to control the dissemination of PII or sensitive data. Its primary goal is to ensure the security of government systems by promoting a standardized approach to security controls, implementation, and testing. The act requires government agencies to create a security plan for their systems and to have it "accredited" at least once every three years.

   ☒ **C** is incorrect because the PATRIOT Act is not an effort to control personal information. Its purpose is to aid the U.S. government in preventing terrorism by increasing the government's ability to monitor, intercept, and maintain records on almost every imaginable form of communication. As a side effect, it has also served to increase observation and prevention of hacking attempts on many systems.

☒ **D** is incorrect because the Freedom of Information Act wasn't designed to tell you what to do with information. Its goal is to define how you can get information—specifically information regarding how your governments work. It doesn't necessarily help you in hacking, but it does provide a cover for a lot of information. Anything you uncover that could have been gathered through the Freedom of Information Act is considered legal and should be part of your overall test.

12. Four terms make up the Common Criteria process. Which of the following contains seven levels used to rate the target?

  A. ToE

  B. ST

  C. PP

  D. EAL

☑ **D.** Common Criteria is an international standard of evaluation of Information Technology (IT) products. Per the website (https://www.commoncriteriaportal.org/), Common Criteria ensures evaluations and ratings "are performed to high and consistent standards and are seen to contribute significantly to confidence in the security of those products and profiles."

Four terms within Common Criteria make up the process. The EAL (Evaluation Assurance Level) is made up of seven levels, which are used to rate a product after it has been tested. The current EAL levels are as follows:

- EAL1: Functionally tested
- EAL2: Structurally tested
- EAL3: Methodically tested and checked
- EAL4: Methodically designed, tested, and reviewed
- EAL5: Semi-formally designed and tested
- EAL6: Semi-formally verified, designed, and tested
- EAL7: Formally verified, designed, and tested

☒ **A** is incorrect because ToE is the target of evaluation—the system or product actually being tested.

☒ **B** is incorrect because ST is the security target—the documentation describing the target of evaluation and any security requirements.

☒ **C** is incorrect because PP is the protection profile—a set of security requirements for the product type being tested.

13. Organization leadership is concerned about social engineering and hires a company to provide training for all employees. How is the organization handling the risk associated with social engineering?

   A. They are accepting the risk.

   B. They are avoiding the risk.

   C. They are mitigating the risk.

   D. They are transferring the risk.

   ☑ **C.** When it comes to risks, there are four different methods of dealing with them. In risk mitigation, steps are taken to reduce the chance that the risk even will occur, and in this example that's exactly what's happening. Training on social engineering should help reduce the likelihood an employee will fall victim (real-life concerns on this notwithstanding—we are talking about test questions here).

   ☒ **A** is incorrect because the acceptance of risk means the organization understands the risk is there, but they don't do anything about it. Why would a company take this action? Perhaps the chance a threat agent will (or even can) exploit the risk is so low it makes the effort to mitigate it pointless. Or it could be the cost to mitigate simply costs more than any damage or recovery from exploitation in the first place. In any case, if the organization does nothing, they're accepting risk.

   ☒ **B** is incorrect because avoidance of risk means the organization takes steps to eliminate the service, action, or technology altogether. In other words, the risk is deemed so great the company would rather do without the asset or service in the first place. In the case of social engineering, unless the organization can work without employees, avoiding this risk is nearly impossible.

   ☒ **D** is incorrect because transferring risk occurs when the organization puts the burden of risk on another party. For example, the company might hire an insurance company to pay off in the event a risk is exploited.

14. In which phase of the ethical hacking methodology would a hacker be expected to discover available targets on a network?

   A. Reconnaissance

   B. Scanning and enumeration

   C. Gaining access

   D. Maintaining access

   E. Covering tracks

   ☑ **B.** The scanning and enumeration phase is where you'll use things such as ping sweeps to discover available targets on the network. This step occurs *after* reconnaissance. In this step, tools and techniques are actively applied to information gathered during recon to obtain more in-depth information on the targets. For example, reconnaissance may show a network subnet to have 500 or so machines connected inside a single building, whereas scanning and enumeration would discover which ones are Windows machines and which ones are running FTP.

☒ **A** is incorrect because the reconnaissance phase is nothing more than the steps taken to gather evidence and information on the targets you want to attack. Activities that occur in this phase include dumpster diving and social engineering. Another valuable tool in recon is the Internet. Look for any of these items as key words in answers on your exam. Of course, in the real world you may actually gather so much information in your recon you'll already be way ahead of the game in identifying targets and whatnot, but when it comes to the exam, stick with the hard-and-fast boundaries they want you to remember and move on.

☒ **C** is incorrect because the gaining access phase is all about attacking the machines themselves. You've already figured out background information on the client and have enumerated the potential vulnerabilities and security flaws on each target. In this phase, you break out the big guns and start firing away. Key words you're looking for here are the attacks themselves: accessing an open and nonsecured wireless access point, manipulating network devices, writing and delivering a buffer overflow, and performing SQL injection against a web application are all examples.

☒ **D** is incorrect because this phase is all about back doors and the steps taken to ensure you have a way back in. For the savvy readers out there who noticed I skipped a step here (escalating privileges), well done. Key words you'll look for on this phase (maintaining access) are back doors, zombies, and rootkits.

☒ **E** is incorrect because this phase is all about cleaning up when you're done and making sure no one can see where you've been. Clearing tracks involves steps to conceal success and avoid detection by security professionals. Steps taken here consist of removing or altering log files, hiding files with hidden attributes or directories, and even using tunneling protocols to communicate with the system.

15. Which of the following was created to protect shareholders and the general public from corporate accounting errors and fraudulent practices, and to improve the accuracy of corporate disclosures?

    A. GLBA

    B. HIPAA

    C. SOX

    D. FITARA

    ☑ **C.** The Sarbanes-Oxley Act (SOX; https://www.sec.gov/about/laws.shtml#sox2002) introduced major changes to the regulation of financial practice and corporate governance in 2002 and is arranged into 11 titles. SOX mandated a number of reforms to enhance corporate responsibility, enhance financial disclosures, and combat corporate and accounting fraud, and it created the "Public Company Accounting Oversight Board," also known as the PCAOB, to oversee the activities of the auditing profession.

☒ **A** is incorrect because the Gramm-Leach-Bliley Act (GLBA; https://www.ftc.gov/tips-advice/business-center/privacy-and-security/gramm-leach-bliley-act) requires financial institutions—companies that offer consumers financial products or services such as loans, financial or investment advice, or insurance—to explain their information-sharing practices to their customers and to safeguard sensitive data. Under the Safeguards Rule, financial institutions must protect the consumer information they collect. GLBA protects the confidentiality and integrity of personal information collected by financial institutions.

☒ **B** is incorrect because the Health Insurance Portability and Accountability Act (HIPAA; http://www.hhs.gov/hipaa/) was designed to protect the confidentiality of private health information. HIPAA contains privacy and security requirements, and provides steps and procedures for handling and protecting private health data.

☒ **D** is incorrect because the Federal Information Technology Acquisition Reform Act (FITARA; https://www.congress.gov/bill/113th-congress/house-bill/1232) didn't actually pass in full, but did contain sections that were eventually added as part of the National Defense Authorization Act (NDAA) for fiscal year 2015.

16. Which of the following best defines a logical or technical control?

    A. Air conditioning

    B. Security tokens

    C. Fire alarms

    D. Security policy

    ☑ **B.** A logical (or technical) control is one used for identification, authentication, and authorization. It can be embedded inside an operating system, application, or database management system. A security token (such as RSA's SecureID) can provide a number that changes on a recurring basis that a user must provide during authentication, or it may provide a built-in number on a USB device that must be attached during authentication. A physical control is something, well, physical in nature, such as a lock or key or maybe a guard.

    ☒ **A** and **C** are incorrect because air conditioning and fire alarms both fall into the category of physical control.

    ☒ **D** is incorrect because a security policy isn't a logical or technical control.

17. Which of the following was created to protect credit card data at rest and in transit in an effort to reduce fraud?

    A. TCSEC

    B. Common Criteria

    C. ISO 27002

    D. PCI DSS

☑ **D.** The Payment Card Industry Data Security Standard (PCI DSS) is a security standard for organizations that handle credit cards. A council including American Express, JCB, Discover, MasterCard, and Visa developed standards for the protection and transmission of card data to reduce credit card fraud. It's administered by the Payment Card Industry Security Standards Council. Validation of compliance is performed annually. The standard is composed of 12 requirements:

1. Install and maintain a firewall configuration to protect cardholder data.

2. Do not use vendor-supplied defaults for system passwords and other security parameters.

3. Protect stored cardholder data.

4. Encrypt transmission of cardholder data across open, public networks.

5. Use and regularly update antivirus software on all systems commonly affected by malware.

6. Develop and maintain secure systems and applications.

7. Restrict access to cardholder data by business need-to-know.

8. Assign a unique ID to each person with computer access.

9. Restrict physical access to cardholder data.

10. Track and monitor all access to network resources and cardholder data.

11. Regularly test security systems and processes.

12. Maintain a policy that addresses information security.

☒ **A** is incorrect because the Trusted Computer System Evaluation Criteria (TCSEC), also known as the Orange Book, was created by the Department of Defense (DoD) and defines and provides guidance on evaluating access controls within a system. TCSEC defines four levels of validation: verified protection, mandatory protection, discretionary protection, and minimal protection.

☒ **B** is incorrect because Common Criteria (http://www.commoncriteriaportal.org/) is an international standard to test and evaluate IT products. Per the website, CC is a "framework in which computer system users can specify their security requirements through the use of Protection Profiles (PPs), vendors can then *implement* and/or make claims about the security attributes of their products, and testing laboratories can *evaluate* the products to determine if they actually meet the claims. In other words, Common Criteria provides assurance that the process of specification, implementation and evaluation of a computer security product has been conducted in a rigorous and standard and repeatable manner at a level that is commensurate with the target environment for use."

☒ **C** is incorrect because the International Organization for Standardization (ISO) 27002 (http://www.iso27001security.com/html/27002.html) is an "information security standard published by ISO and the International Electrotechnical Commission (IEC) that recommends security controls based on industry best practices." This standard includes 13 objectives, ranging from structure, risk assessment, and policy to access controls, human resources security, and compliance.

18. As part of the preparation phase for a pen test you are participating in, the client relays their intent to discover security flaws and possible remediation. They seem particularly concerned about internal threats from the user base. Which of the following best describes the test type the client is looking for?

   A. Gray box

   B. Black box

   C. White hat

   D. Black hat

   ☑ **A.** Once again, this is a play on words the exam will throw at you. Note the question is asking about a *test type*, not the attacker. Reviewing CEH documentation, you'll see there are three types of tests—white, black, and gray—with each designed to test a specific threat. White tests the internal threat of a knowledgeable systems administrator or an otherwise elevated privilege level user. Black tests external threats with no knowledge of the target. Gray tests the average internal user threat to expose potential security problems inside the network.

   ☒ **B** is incorrect because black-box testing is designed to simulate the external threat. Black-box testing takes the most amount of time to complete because it means a thorough romp through the five stages of an attack (and removes any preconceived notions of what to look for) and is usually the most expensive option. Another drawback to this type of test is that it focuses solely on the threat *outside* the organization and does not take into account any trusted users on the inside.

   ☒ **C** is incorrect because a hat color refers to the attacker himself. True, the client is hiring a white hat in this instance to perform the test; however, the hat does not equate to the test. White hats are the "good guys"—ethical hackers hired by a customer for the specific goal of testing and improving security. White hats don't use their knowledge and skills without prior consent.

   ☒ **D** is incorrect because this question refers to the test itself, not the type of attacker. Black hats are the "bad guys" and are otherwise known as *crackers*. They illegally use their skills either for personal gain or for malicious intent, seeking to steal or destroy data or to deny access to resources and systems. Black hats do *not* ask for permission or consent.

19. In which phase of the attack would a hacker set up and configure "zombie" machines?

   A. Reconnaissance

   B. Covering tracks

   C. Gaining access

   D. Maintaining access

☑ **D.** Zombies are basically machines the hacker has confiscated to do his work for him. If the attacker is really good, the owners of the zombie machines don't even know their machines have been drafted into the war. There are a bajillion methods for maintaining access on a machine you've already compromised, and maintaining that access does not necessarily mean the system will be used as a zombie—you could, for example, simply want to check in from time to time to see what new juicy information the user has decided to leave in a file or folder for you, or to check on new logins, credentials, etc. However, configuring zombie systems definitely belongs in this phase.

☒ **A** is incorrect because the reconnaissance phase is all about gaining knowledge and information on a target. In reconnaissance, you're learning about the target itself—for example, what system types they may have in use, what their operating hours are, whether they use a shredder, and what personal information about their employees is available. Think of reconnaissance as the background information on a good character in a novel; it may not be completely necessary to know before you read the action scenes, but it sure makes it easier to understand why the character behaves in a certain manner during the conflict phase of the book. Setting up zombie systems goes far beyond the boundaries of gathering information.

☒ **B** is incorrect because this phase is where attackers attempt to conceal their success and avoid detection by security professionals. This can involve removing or altering log files, hiding files with hidden attributes or directories, and using tunneling protocols to communicate with the system.

☒ **C** is incorrect because in this phase attacks are leveled against the targets enumerated during the scanning and enumeration phase. Key words to look for in identifying this phase are the attacks themselves (such as buffer overflow and SQL injection). Finally, be careful about questions relating to elevating privileges. Sometimes this is counted as its own phase, so pay close attention to the question's wording in choosing your answer.

20. Which of the following should not be included in a security policy?

    A. Policy exceptions

    B. Details on noncompliance disciplinary actions

    C. Technical details and procedures

    D. Supporting document references

☑ **C.** The whole policy/standard/procedure/guideline thing can get confusing sometimes. Policy is a high-level document that doesn't get down and dirty into specifications and is intended to improve awareness. Policies are mandatory, generally short, and easy to understand, providing everyone with the rules of the road. Standards are mandatory rules designed to support a policy, and must include one or more specifications for hardware, software, or behavior. Procedures are step-by-step instructions for completing a task. Guidelines are not mandatory, but rather are recommendations for accomplishing a goal or on how to act in a given situation.

☒ **A**, **B**, and **D** are incorrect because all these are perfectly acceptable security policy entries. Exceptions to the policy and what happens to you should you decide not to follow the policy are expected entries. And supporting documents—such as various procedures, standards, and guidelines—are always referenced in the policy.

21. Which of the following is best defined as a set of processes used to identify, analyze, prioritize, and resolve security incidents?

    A. Incident management

    B. Vulnerability management

    C. Change management

    D. Patch management

    ☑ **A.** Admittedly, this one is fairly easy—or at least it should be. Incident management is a process of dealing with incidents and generally always has the same features/ steps—identify the problem or root cause, analyze and research the issue, contain the malicious effort, eradicate the effort, and resolve any damage caused. ECC defines the process as having eight steps: 1. Preparation, 2. Detection and Analysis, 3. Classification/Prioritization, 4. Notification, 5. Containment, 6. Forensic Investigation, 7. Eradication and Recovery, and 8. Post-incident Activities. The Incident Response Team is charged with handling this process.

    ☒ **B** is incorrect because vulnerability management isn't about responding to incidents; it's about identifying and eradicating vulnerabilities before an incident can occur.

    ☒ **C** is incorrect because change management involves implementing procedures or technologies to identify and implement required changes within a computer system.

    ☒ **D** is incorrect because patch management is designed to manage the identification, installations, and tracking of security patches necessary within the environment.

22. During an assessment, your pen test team discovers child porn on a system. Which of the following is the appropriate response?

    A. Continue testing and report findings at out-brief.

    B. Continue testing but report findings to the business owners.

    C. Cease testing immediately and refuse to continue work for the client.

    D. Cease testing immediately and contact authorities.

    ☑ **D.** I hesitated to add this question, for reasons that are obvious and some that aren't, but in the interest of covering everything, I felt I must. First and foremost, in the real world, discovery of something that you think might be illegal activity puts you and your team in a very, very tricky spot. Should you accuse *fill-in-the-blank* of a crime and involve the authorities, you could be setting yourself up for lawsuits and all sorts of trouble. On the other hand, if you ignore it, you might be found complicit, and at the very least negligent. In the real world, the answer is to make sure your scope agreement advises you and the client of your duty regarding potential criminal activity found during the scope of your investigation. No guessing is allowed—it better be iron-clad evidence, obvious to all, or you're in a world of hurt.

In this example, however, the choices present make this relatively easy. ECC wants ethical hackers to report any illegal activity they find. Period. Possession of child porn is a crime no matter what, so again in this particular case, stop your testing and report to the authorities.

☒ **A** and **B** are incorrect because regardless of reporting, you should immediately stop testing. Anything you do after discovery not only could destroy evidence but actually put you at risk. Who's to say *you* didn't put *fill-in-the-blank* there on the system, or by your action cause it to be there? Rest assured the defense attorney will posit that argument, should it come to that.

☒ **C** is incorrect because you've already agreed to perform this work and refusing to speak with the client isn't helping anything at all. Again, this needs to be addressed in the scope agreement up front, so there should be no surprises. It may well be that Employee Joe has illegal stuff on his system, but that doesn't necessarily mean the organization is complicit.

23. Which of the following best describes an intranet zone?

   A. It has few heavy security restrictions.

   B. A highly secured zone, usually employing VLANs and encrypted communication channels.

   C. A controlled buffer network between public and private.

   D. A very restricted zone with no users.

   ☑ **A.** The intranet can be thought of, for testing purposes, as your own happy little networking safe space. It's protected from outside attacks and interference by the DMZ and all the layers of security on the outside. Internally, you don't assign loads of heavy security restrictions, because, as you'll remember from the security versus usability discussion in the *All-in-One* book, as security increases usability and functionality decrease. If your organization users are on the intranet, you want them as productive as possible, right?

   ☒ **B** is incorrect because this describes the management network zone. This zone is usually cordoned off specifically for infrastructure and management traffic. For obvious reasons, it's highly secured. Look for "VLAN" and "IPSec" as keywords for this zone.

   ☒ **C** is incorrect because this describes the DMZ. The demilitarized zone in military parlance refers to a section of land between two adversarial parties where there are no weapons and no fighting. The idea is you could see an adversary coming across and have time to work up a defense. In networking the idea is the same: it's a controlled, buffer network between you and the uncontrolled chaos of the Internet. And keep in mind DMZs aren't just between the Internet and a network; they can be anywhere an organization decides they want or need a buffer—inside or outside various in*ter* and intra nets. DMZ networks provide great opportunity for good security measures, but can also sometimes become an Achilles' heel when too much trust is put into their creation and maintenance.

☒ **D** is incorrect because this describes the production network zone. The PNZ is a very restricted zone that strictly controls direct access from uncontrolled zones. The PNZ supports functions and actions that must have strict access control. As an aside, the PNZ is not designed to hold users.

24. A machine in your environment uses an open X-server to allow remote access. The X-server access control is disabled, allowing connections from almost anywhere and with little to no authentication measures. Which of the following are true statements regarding this situation? (Choose all that apply.)

   A. An external vulnerability can take advantage of the misconfigured X-server threat.

   B. An external threat can take advantage of the misconfigured X-server vulnerability.

   C. An internal vulnerability can take advantage of the misconfigured X-server threat.

   D. An internal threat can take advantage of the misconfigured X-server vulnerability.

   ☑ **B, D.** This is an easy one because all you have to understand are the definitions of threat and vulnerability. A *threat* is any agent, circumstance, or situation that could potentiality cause harm or loss to an IT asset. In this case, the implication is the threat is an individual (hacker) either inside or outside the network. A *vulnerability* is any weakness, such as a software flaw or logic design, that could be exploited by a threat to cause damage to an asset. In both these answers, the vulnerability—the access controls on the X-server are not in place—can be exploited by the threat, whether internal or external.

   ☒ **A** and **C** are both incorrect because they list the terms backward. Threats take advantage of vulnerabilities and exploit them, not the other way around.

25. While performing a pen test, you find success in exploiting a machine. Your attack vector took advantage of a common mistake—the Windows 7 installer script used to load the machine left the administrative account with a default password. Which attack did you successfully execute?

   A. Application level

   B. Operating system

   C. Shrink wrap

   D. Social engineering

   E. Misconfiguration

   ☑ **B.** Operating system (OS) attacks target common mistakes many people make when installing operating systems—accepting and leaving all the defaults. Examples usually include things such as administrator accounts with no passwords, ports left open, and guest accounts left behind. Another OS attack you may be asked about deals with versioning. Operating systems are never released fully secure and are consistently upgraded with hotfixes, security patches, and full releases. The potential for an old vulnerability within the enterprise is always high.

☒ **A** is incorrect because application-level attacks are centered on the actual programming codes of an application. These attacks are usually successful in an overall pen test because many people simply discount the applications running on their OS and network, preferring to spend their time hardening the OSs and network devices. Many applications on a network aren't tested for vulnerabilities as part of their creation and, as such, have many vulnerabilities built in.

☒ **C** is incorrect because shrink-wrap attacks take advantage of the built-in code and scripts most *off-the-shelf applications* come with. These attacks allow hackers to take advantage of the very things designed to make installation and administration easier. These shrink-wrapped snippets make life easier for installation and administration, but they also make it easier for attackers to get in.

☒ **D** is incorrect because social engineering isn't relevant at all in this question. There is no human element here, so this one can be thrown out.

☒ **E** is incorrect because misconfiguration attacks take advantage of systems that are, on purpose or by accident, not configured appropriately for security. For example, suppose an administrator wants to make things as easy as possible for the users and, in keeping with security and usability being on opposite ends of the spectrum, leaves security settings at the lowest possible level, enabling services, opening firewall ports, and providing administrative privileges to all users. It's easier for the users but creates a target-rich environment for the hacker.

Reconnaissance: Information Gathering for the Ethical Hacker

This chapter includes questions from the following topics:

- Define active and passive footprinting
- Identify methods and procedures in information gathering
- Understand the use of social networking, search engines, and Google hacking in information gathering
- Understand the use of whois, ARIN, and nslookup in information gathering
- Describe DNS record types

Criminology (the study of the nature, causes, control, and prevention of criminal behavior) is a fascinating subject, and although we're concentrating on the virtual world in this book, it's amazing how much footprinting is done in the *physical* criminal world as well. Most of us have already heard a million times the standard things we're supposed to do to make our homes less desirable as a target for the bad guys. Things such as keeping the house well lit, installing timers on lights and TVs to make the house appear "lived in" all the time, and installing a good alarm system are so common in these discussions that we tend to nod off in boredom when a security expert starts talking about them. But did you know most common burglars prefer to work during the daytime, when it's most likely you're not at home at all? Did you know most don't give a rip about your alarm system because they plan on being inside for eight to ten minutes or less? And did you further know that most timer systems for lights don't change a thing in the bad guy's mind because there's usually *sound* associated with people being home?

For the sake of example, take an imaginary ride with me around my subdivision here in Melbourne, Florida, and we'll try thinking like a criminal footprinting a neighborhood for targets. Maybe we'll start by just driving around the neighborhood to ascertain who the nosy neighbors are and what houses make the most promising opportunities. This house on our right is in a cul-de-sac and provides more privacy and less police patrol traffic than those on the main drag. Oh, what about that house over there? Yeah, it looks like the yard hasn't been mowed for a while, so maybe they aren't home—or they just don't pay as close attention to home details as the other homeowners do. The owners of that two-story over there have a dog, so we'll probably avoid that one.

But look just there: that house has a giant box leaning against the garbage can for the brand-new 65-inch LED TV the owner just purchased. We should probably write this address down for a closer look later. And the house across the pond there with the sliding glass door? It definitely has potential.

As fascinating as footprinting a building might seem, were you aware that *you*, as a person, could be footprinted in the physical world as well? According to several studies on the matter, criminals are good at sensing weakness based just on *the way you walk*. In one such study, 47 inmates at a maximum-security prison were surveyed, and the findings showed that social predators are very good at picking victims based on their gait, posture, and stride. The study provided the inmates with a film of 12 people (eight women and four men, some of whom had been attacked before) walking down a street and asked them to rate each person as a potential victim. The ratings were then compared against each person's actual history. Surprisingly (or maybe not so surprisingly), the people who the criminals picked as likely victims were usually the same ones who had been victimized in the past. Inmates described the men and women they saw as targets as "walking like an easy target... slow, with short strides." What distinguished the likely victims from the rest of the pedestrians? Things such as posture, body language, pace, length of stride, and awareness of their environment. Nonverbal communication works wonderfully well, and a person's level of self-confidence can be identified just by the style of walk. Walk with your head down at a slow or unorganized, meandering pace, and you're screaming to the world you lack self-confidence. Walk fast, fluidly, and with a purpose, and you're less likely to be a target.

I could go on and on here (I really like this subject and could chat about it forever), but this book is about the virtual world, and I'm prepping you to be an ethical hacker, not a policeman working a beat. This chapter is also all about reconnaissance and footprinting—in the virtual world—and is all about the methods and tools to gather information about your targets before you even try to attack them.

 STUDY TIPS   There will be plenty of questions from this particular segment of hacking, namely because it's so important to gather good intelligence before starting an attack. Sure, you can sometimes get lucky and strike quickly, but oftentimes he who puts in the work during footprinting reaps the biggest rewards.

What will be the biggest area of focus you'll see on your actual exam? A couple of versions ago, it was all things DNS, but now it's much more varied. You are just as likely to see questions on active versus passive reconnaissance as you are Google hacking, OS fingerprinting, and DNS subtleties. EC-Council has definitely broadened the horizons when it comes to recon and footprinting questions so, while I hate to say memorize everything, memorize everything.

Tips on the tricky questions here are the same as you'll hear me say in every other chapter—they're nit-picky, in-the-weeds, specific-knowledge questions designed to trip you up. Know your e-mail headers and DNS records, of course, but you'll also see questions on specific tools and how they act. And by all means start practicing your Google hacking right now—you'll definitely need it since most Google hacking questions will require you to know exact syntax.

1. You are attempting to find out the operating system and CPU type of systems in your target organization. The DNS server you wish to use for lookup is named ADNS_Server, and the target machine you want the information on is ATARGET_SYSTEM. Which of the following nslookup command series is the best choice for discovering this information? (The output of the commands is redacted.)

   A.

   ```
   > server ADNS_SERVER
   ...
   > set type=HINFO
   > ATARGET_SYSTEM
   ...
   ```

   B.

   ```
   > server ATARGET_SYSTEM
   ...
   > set type=HINFO
   > ADNS_SERVER
   ...
   ```

   C.

   ```
    > server ADNS_SERVER
   ...
   > set ATARGET_SYSTEM
   > type=HINFO
   ...
   ```

   D.

   ```
    > server type=HINFO
   ...
   > set ADNS_SERVER
   > ATARGET_SYSTEM
   ...
   ```

2. A pen test team member sends an e-mail to an address that she knows is not valid inside an organization. Which of the following is the best explanation for why she took this action?

   A. To possibly gather information about internal hosts used in the organization's e-mail system

   B. To start a denial-of-service attack

   C. To determine an e-mail administrator's contact information

   D. To gather information about how e-mail systems deal with invalidly addressed messages

3. From the partial e-mail header provided, which of the following represents the true originator of the e-mail message?

   Return-path: <SOMEONE@anybiz.com>

   Delivery-date: Wed, 13 Apr 2011 00:31:13 +0200

Received: from mailexchanger.anotherbiz.com([220.15.10.254])

by mailserver.anotherbiz.com running ExIM with esmtp

id xxxxx-xxxxxx-xxx; Wed, 13 Apr 2011 01:39:23 +0200

Received: from mailserver.anybiz.com ([158.190.50.254] helo=mailserver.anybiz.com)

by mailexchanger.anotherbiz.com with esmtp id xxxxxx-xxxxxx-xx

for USERJOE@anotherbiz.com; Wed, 13 Apr 2011 01:39:23 +0200

Received: from SOMEONEComputer [217.88.53.154] (helo=[SOMEONEcomputer])

by mailserver.anybiz.com with esmtpa (Exim x.xx)

(envelope-from <SOMEONE@anybiz.com) id xxxxx-xxxxxx-xxxx

for USERJOE@anotherbiz.com; Tue, 12 Apr 2011 20:36:08 -0100

Message-ID: <xxxxxxxx.xxxxxxx@anybiz.com>

Date: Tue, 12 Apr 2011 20:36:01 -0100

X-Mailer: Mail Client

From: SOMEONE Name <SOMEONE@anybiz.com>

To: USERJOE Name <USERJOE@anotherbiz.com>

Subject: Something to consider

...

- **A.** 220.15.10.254.
- **B.** 158.190.50.254.
- **C.** 217.88.53.154.
- **D.** The e-mail header does not show this information.

4. You are looking for pages with the terms *CEH* and *V9* in their title. Which Google hack is the appropriate one?

- **A.** inurl:CEHinurl:V9
- **B.** allintitle:CEH V9
- **C.** intitle:CEHinurl:V9
- **D.** allinurl:CEH V9

5. You are on a Cisco router and wish to identify the path a packet travels to a specific IP. Which of the following is the best command choice for this?

- **A.** ping
- **B.** ifconfig
- **C.** tracert
- **D.** traceroute

6. Which of the following activities are *not* considered passive footprinting? (Choose two.)

  A. Dumpster diving

  B. Reviewing financial sites for company information

  C. Clicking links within the company's public website

  D. Calling the company's help desk line

  E. Employing passive sniffing

7. Examine the following command sequence:

```
C:\> nslookup
Default Server:  ns1.anybiz.com
Address:  188.87.99.6
> set type=HINFO
> someserver
Server:  resolver.anybiz.com
Address:  188.87.100.5
Someserver.anybiz.com CPU=Intel Quad Chip OS=Linux 2.8
```

Which of the following best describes the intent of the command sequence?

  A. The operator is enumerating a system named someserver.

  B. The operator is attempting DNS poisoning.

  C. The operator is attempting a zone transfer.

  D. The operator is attempting to find a name server.

8. An organization has a DNS server located in the DMZ and other DNS servers located on the intranet. What is this implementation commonly called?

  A. Dynamic DNS

  B. DNSSEC

  C. Split DNS

  D. Auto DNS

9. You are setting up DNS for your enterprise. Server A is both a web server and an FTP server. You want to advertise both services for this machine as name references your customers can use. Which DNS record type would you use to accomplish this?

  A. NS

  B. SOA

  C. MX

  D. PTR

  E. CNAME

10. A company has a publicly facing web application. Its internal intranet-facing servers are separated and protected by a firewall. Which of the following choices would be helpful in protecting against unwanted enumeration?

   A. Allowing zone transfers to ANY

   B. Ensuring there are no A records for internal hosts on the public-facing name server

   C. Changing the preference number on all MX records to zero

   D. Not allowing any DNS query to the public-facing name server

11. Within the DNS system, a primary server (SOA) holds and maintains all records for the zone. Secondary servers will periodically ask the primary if there have been any updates, and if updates have occurred, they will ask for a zone transfer to update their own copies. Under what conditions will the secondary name server request a zone transfer from a primary?

   A. When the primary SOA record serial number is higher than the secondary's

   B. When the secondary SOA record serial number is higher than the primary's

   C. Only when the secondary reboots or restarts services

   D. Only when manually prompted to do so

12. Examine the following SOA record:

```
@   IN  SOARTDNSRV1.somebiz.com.  postmaster.somebiz.com. (
200408097    ; serial number
                            3600        ; refresh   [1h]
                            600         ; retry     [10m]
                            86400       ; expire    [1d]
7200 )       ; min TTL   [2h]
```

If a secondary server in the enterprise is unable to check in for a zone update within an hour, what happens to the zone copy on the secondary?

   A. The zone copy is dumped.

   B. The zone copy is unchanged.

   C. The serial number of the zone copy is decremented.

   D. The serial number of the zone copy is incremented.

13. Which protocol and port number combination is used by default for DNS zone transfers?

   A. UDP 53

   B. UDP 161

   C. TCP 53

   D. TCP 22

14. Examine the following command-line entry:

```
C:\>nslookup
   Default Server:  ns1.somewhere.com
   Address:   128.189.72.5
> set q=mx
>mailhost
```

Which statements are true regarding this command sequence? (Choose two.)

- **A.** Nslookup is in noninteractive mode.
- **B.** Nslookup is in interactive mode.
- **C.** The output will show all mail servers in the zone somewhere.com.
- **D.** The output will show all name servers in the zone somewhere.com.

15. Joe accesses the company website, www.anybusi.com, from his home computer and is presented with a defaced site containing disturbing images. He calls the IT department to report the website hack and is told they do not see any problem with the site—no files have been changed, and when accessed from their terminals (inside the company), the site appears normally. Joe connects over VPN into the company website and notices the site appears normally. Which of the following might explain the issue?

- **A.** DNS poisoning
- **B.** Route poisoning
- **C.** SQL injection
- **D.** ARP poisoning

16. One way to mitigate against DNS poisoning is to restrict or limit the amount of time records can stay in cache before they're updated. Which DNS record type allows you to set this restriction?

- **A.** NS
- **B.** PTR
- **C.** MX
- **D.** CNAME
- **E.** SOA

17. Which of the following may be a security concern for an organization?

- **A.** The internal network uses private IP addresses registered to an Active Directory–integrated DNS server.
- **B.** An external DNS server is Active Directory integrated.
- **C.** All external name resolution requests are accomplished by an ISP.
- **D.** None of the above.

18. Which of the following is a good footprinting tool for discovering information on a publicly traded company's founding, history, and financial status?

- **A.** SpiderFoot
- **B.** EDGAR Database
- **C.** Sam Spade
- **D.** Pipl.com

19. What method does traceroute use to map routes traveled by a packet?

    A. By carrying a hello packet in the payload, forcing the host to respond

    B. By using DNS queries at each hop

    C. By manipulating the Time-To-Live (TTL) parameter

    D. By using ICMP Type 5, Code 0 packets

20. Brad is auditing an organization and is asked to provide suggestions on improving DNS security. Which of the following would be valid options to recommend? (Choose all that apply.)

    A. Implementing a split-horizon operation

    B. Restricting zone transfers

    C. Obfuscating DNS by using the same server for other applications and functions

    D. Blocking all access to the server on port 53

21. A zone file consists of which records? (Choose all that apply.)

    A. PTR

    B. MX

    C. SN

    D. SOA

    E. DNS

    F. A

    G. AX

22. Examine the following SOA record:

```
@   IN  SOARTDNSRV1.somebiz.com.  postmaster.somebiz.com.  (
200408097    ; serial number
                          3600           ; refresh    [1h]
                          600            ; retry      [10m]
                          86400          ; expire     [1d]
7200 )       ; min TTL    [2h]
```

    How long will the secondary server wait before asking for an update to the zone file?

    A. One hour

    B. Two hours

    C. Ten minutes

    D. One day

23. A colleague enters the following into a Google search string:

```
intitle:intranetinurl:intranet+intext:"human resources"
```

Which of the following is most correct concerning this attempt?

  A. The search engine will not respond with any result because you cannot combine Google hacks in one line.

  B. The search engine will respond with all pages having the word *intranet* in their title and *human resources* in the URL.

  C. The search engine will respond with all pages having the word *intranet* in the title and in the URL.

  D. The search engine will respond with only those pages having the word *intranet* in the title and URL and with *human resources* in the text.

24. Amanda works as senior security analyst and overhears a colleague discussing confidential corporate information being posted on an external website. When questioned on it, he claims about a month ago he tried random URLs on the company's website and found confidential information. Amanda visits the same URLs but finds nothing. Where can Amanda go to see past versions and pages of a website?

  A. Search.com

  B. Google cache

  C. Pasthash.com

  D. Archive.org

25. Which of the following is a primary service of the U.S. Computer Security Incident Response Team (CSIRT)?

  A. CSIRT provides an incident response service to enable a reliable and trusted single point of contact for reporting computer security incidents worldwide.

  B. CSIRT provides a computer security surveillance service to supply a government with important intelligence information on individuals traveling abroad.

  C. CSIRT provides a penetration testing service to support exception reporting on incidents worldwide by individuals and multinational corporations.

  D. CSIRT provides a vulnerability assessment service to assist law enforcement agencies with profiling an individual's property or company's asset.

26. Your client's business is headquartered in Japan. Which regional registry would be the best place to look for footprinting information?

  A. APNIC

  B. RIPE

  C. ASIANIC

  D. ARIN

  E. LACNIC

1. A	**10.** B	**19.** C
2. A	**11.** A	**20.** A, B
3. C	**12.** B	**21.** A, B, D, F
4. B	**13.** C	**22.** A
5. D	**14.** B, C	**23.** D
6. D, E	**15.** A	**24.** D
7. A	**16.** E	**25.** A
8. C	**17.** B	**26.** A
9. E	**18.** B	

1. You are attempting to find out the operating system and CPU type of systems in your target organization. The DNS server you wish to use for lookup is named ADNS_Server, and the target machine you want the information on is ATARGET_SYSTEM. Which of the following nslookup command series is the best choice for discovering this information? (The output of the commands is redacted.)

A.

```
> server ADNS_SERVER
...
> set type=HINFO
> ATARGET_SYSTEM
...
```

B.

```
> server ATARGET_SYSTEM
...
> set type=HINFO
> ADNS_SERVER
...
```

C.

```
 > server ADNS_SERVER
...
> set ATARGET_SYSTEM
> type=HINFO
...
```

D.

```
 > server type=HINFO
...
> set ADNS_SERVER
> ATARGET_SYSTEM
...
```

☑ **A.** This question gets you on two fronts. One regards knowledge on HINFO, and the other is nslookup use. First, the DNS record HINFO (per RFC 1035) is a resource type that identifies values for CPU type and operating system. Are you absolutely required to include an HINFO record for each host in your network? No, not at all. Should you? I'm sure there's some reason, somewhere and sometime, that adding HINFO makes sense, but I certainly can't think of one. In other words, this is a great record type to remember for your exam, but your chances of seeing it in use in the real world rank somewhere between seeing Lobster on the menu at McDonald's and catching a Leprechaun riding a unicorn through your back yard.

Nslookup syntax is the second portion of this question, and you'll definitely need to know it. The syntax for the tool is fairly simple:

```
nslookup [-options] {hostname | [-server]}
```

The command can be run as a single instance, providing information based on the options you choose, or you can run it in interactive mode, where the command runs as a tool, awaiting input from you. For example, on a Microsoft Windows machine, if you simply type **nslookup** at the prompt, you'll see a display showing your default DNS server and its associated IP address. From there, nslookup sits patiently, waiting for you to ask whatever you want (as an aside, this is known as *interactive mode*). Typing a question mark shows all the options and switches you have available.

☒ **B, C,** and **D** are incorrect because the syntax does not match.

2. A pen test team member sends an e-mail to an address that she knows is not valid inside an organization. Which of the following is the best explanation for why she took this action?

   A. To possibly gather information about internal hosts used in the organization's e-mail system

   B. To start a denial-of-service attack

   C. To determine an e-mail administrator's contact information

   D. To gather information about how e-mail systems deal with invalidly addressed messages

   ☑ **A.** The thought process behind this is a lot like banner grabbing or any of a hundred different forced error situations in hacking: lots of information can be gleaned from responses to an error situation. A bogus internal address has the potential to provide more information about the internal servers used in the organization, including IP addresses and other pertinent details.

   ☒ **B** is incorrect because a bogus e-mail doesn't necessarily indicate the beginning of a DoS attack.

   ☒ **C** is incorrect because the e-mail administrator's contact information is not sent on invalid e-mail responses.

   ☒ **D** is incorrect because the pen tester would already know how systems deal with bogus e-mail addresses—what she wouldn't know is what servers inside this particular organization carry out those steps.

3. From the partial e-mail header provided, which of the following represents the true originator of the e-mail message?

   Return-path: <SOMEONE@anybiz.com>

   Delivery-date: Wed, 13 Apr 2011 00:31:13 +0200

   Received: from mailexchanger.anotherbiz.com([220.15.10.254])

   by mailserver.anotherbiz.com running ExIM with esmtp

   id xxxxxx-xxxxxx-xxx; Wed, 13 Apr 2011 01:39:23 +0200

   Received: from mailserver.anybiz.com ([158.190.50.254] helo=mailserver.anybiz.com) by mailexchanger.anotherbiz.com with esmtp id xxxxxx-xxxxxx-xx

for USERJOE@anotherbiz.com; Wed, 13 Apr 2011 01:39:23 +0200

Received: from SOMEONEComputer [217.88.53.154] (helo=[SOMEONEcomputer])

by mailserver.anybiz.com with esmtpa (Exim x.xx)

(envelope-from <SOMEONE@anybiz.com) id xxxxx-xxxxxx-xxxx

for USERJOE@anotherbiz.com; Tue, 12 Apr 2011 20:36:08 -0100

Message-ID: <xxxxxxxx.xxxxxxxx@anybiz.com>

Date: Tue, 12 Apr 2011 20:36:01 -0100

X-Mailer: Mail Client

From: SOMEONE Name <SOMEONE@anybiz.com>

To: USERJOE Name <USERJOE@anotherbiz.com>

Subject: Something to consider

...

- **A.** 220.15.10.254.
- **B.** 158.190.50.254.
- **C.** 217.88.53.154.
- **D.** The e-mail header does not show this information.

☑ **C.** E-mail headers are packed with information showing the entire route the message has taken, and I can guarantee you'll see at least one question on your exam about them. You'll most likely be asked to identify the true originator—the machine (person) who sent it in the first place (even though in the real world with proxies and whatnot to hide behind, it may be impossible). This is clearly shown in line 9: Received: from SOMEONEComputer [217.88.53.154] (helo=[SOMEONEcomputer]). But don't just study and rely on that one section. Watch the entire trek the message takes and make note of the IPs along the way.

☒ **A** and **B** are incorrect because these IPs do not represent the true originator of the message. They show e-mail servers that are passing/handling the message.

☒ **D** is incorrect because the e-mail header definitely shows the true originator.

4. You are looking for pages with the terms *CEH* and *V9* in their title. Which Google hack is the appropriate one?

- **A.** inurl:CEHinurl:V9
- **B.** allintitle:CEH V9
- **C.** intitle:CEHinurl:V9
- **D.** allinurl:CEH V9

☑ **B.** The Google search operator *allintitle* searches for pages that contain the string, or strings, you specify. It also allows for the combination of strings in the title, so you can search for more than one term within the title of a page.

☒ **A** is incorrect because the operator *inurl* looks only in the URL of the site, not the page title. In this example, the search might bring you to a page like this: http://anyplace.com/apache_Version/pdfs.html.

☒ **C** is incorrect because the *inurl* operator isn't looking in the page title. Yes, you can combine operators, but these two just won't get this job done.

☒ **D** is incorrect because *allinurl* does not look at page titles; it's concerned only with the URL itself. As with the title searches, this allinurl operator allows you to combine search strings.

5. You are on a Cisco router and wish to identify the path a packet travels to a specific IP. Which of the following is the best command choice for this?

   A. ping

   B. ifconfig

   C. tracert

   D. traceroute

   ☑ **D.** You probably knew, right up front, this was a traceroute question, but the kicker comes when deciding *which* traceroute command to use. Traceroute, of course, uses ICMP packets and the TTL ("time to live") value to map out a path between originator and destination. The first packet sent uses a TTL of 1, to show the first hop. The next packet sets to 2, and so on, and so on, until the destination is found. Each ICMP response provides information on the current hop (unless ICMP is being filtered). On a Windows machine, you'd use the command *tracert*. On Linux (and Cisco for that matter), you'd use *traceroute*.

   ☒ **A** is incorrect because the ping command simply tests for connectivity and to see if the system is "live." ICMP Echo Request packets are sent to the destination, and ICMP Echo Reply packets are returned with information on the system. Of course, ICMP is often filtered at the host (or firewall) level, so a negative ping response doesn't necessarily mean the system is down.

   ☒ **B** is incorrect because the ifconfig command is used in Linux systems to display information about the system's network interfaces. Ifconfig allows for configuring, controlling, and querying TCP/IP network interface parameters—for example, setting the IP address and subnet mask (netmask) on a NIC.

   ☒ **C** is incorrect because the tracert command will work on a Windows system, but not on a Cisco device.

6. Which of the following activities are *not* considered passive footprinting? (Choose two.)

   A. Dumpster diving

   B. Reviewing financial sites for company information

C. Clicking links within the company's public website

D. Calling the company's help desk line

E. Employing passive sniffing

☑ **D** and **E.** This one may be a little tricky, but only because we live and work in the real world and this is an exam question. EC-Council has several questionable takes on things regarding real-world application and what they say you should remember for your exam, and this is one of those examples. Just remember ECC wants you to know active and passive footprinting can be defined by two things: what you touch and how much discovery risk you put yourself in. Social engineering in and of itself is not all passive or active in nature. In the case of dumpster diving, it's also considered passive (despite the real-world risk of discovery and the action you have to take to pull it off) according to ECC.

However, pick up a phone and call someone inside the company or talk to people in the parking lot, and you've exposed yourself to discovery and are now practicing active footprinting. As far as "passive" sniffing goes, sniffing isn't a footprinting action at all. The term "passive sniffing" concerns the act of simply plugging in and watching what comes by, without any packet interjection or other naughtiness required on your part.

☒ **A, B,** and **C** are incorrect because these are all examples of passive reconnaissance. Other examples might include checking out DNS records (DNS is publicly available and, per ECC, you can passively footprint an organization by using freely available DNS records) and checking job listings for the company.

7. Examine the following command sequence:

```
C:\> nslookup
Default Server:  ns1.anybiz.com
Address:  188.87.99.6
> set type=HINFO
> someserver
Server:  resolver.anybiz.com
Address:  188.87.100.5
Someserver.anybiz.com CPU=Intel Quad Chip OS=Linux 2.8
```

Which of the following best describes the intent of the command sequence?

A. The operator is enumerating a system named someserver.

B. The operator is attempting DNS poisoning.

C. The operator is attempting a zone transfer.

D. The operator is attempting to find a name server.

☑ **A.** The HINFO record type is one of those really great ideas that was designed to make life easier on everyone yet turned out to be a horrible idea. Defined in RFC 1035, Host Information (HINFO) DNS records were originally intended to provide the type of computer and operating system a host uses (back in the day, you could also put things in like room numbers and other descriptions in the record, too).

However, to avoid publicly advertising that information (for obvious reasons), this record type simply is not used much anymore. And if you find one on a public-facing machine, it's a sure sign of incompetence on the part of the server administrators. In this example, the type is set to HINFO, and a machine name—someserver— is provided. The attacker can use the information contained in the record as an enumeration source.

☒ **B** is incorrect because DNS poisoning is not carried out this way. In this command sequence, the operator is asking for information, not pushing up false entries to a name server.

☒ **C** is incorrect because this is not how nslookup is used to perform a zone transfer. To do that, you would use the **set type=any** command and then **ls –d anybiz.com**. You'll more than likely see that on your exam, too.

☒ **D** is incorrect because checking for name servers in the domain would require the **set type=NS** command.

8. An organization has a DNS server located in the DMZ and other DNS servers located on the intranet. What is this implementation commonly called ?

   A. Dynamic DNS

   B. DNSSEC

   C. Split DNS

   D. Auto DNS

   ☑ **C.** The idea behind split DNS is pretty simple: create two zones for the same domain, with one just for the internal network while the other is used by any external networks. Internal hosts are directed to the internal domain name server. Separating the domain servers greatly restricts the footprinting an attacker can perform from the outside.

   ☒ **A** is incorrect because dynamic DNS doesn't work this way. In "regular" DNS, a name is tied to a static IP address; however, for any number of reasons, a hosted device may need or wish to change its IP address often. In dynamic DNS, a service provider uses a program that runs on the system, contacting the DNS service each time the IP address changes and subsequently updating the DNS database to reflect the change in IP address. That way, even though a domain name's IP address changes, users don't have to do anything out of the ordinary to continue service—the dynamic DNS service will ensure they're pointed in the right direction.

   ☒ **B** is incorrect because Domain Name System Security Extensions (DNSSEC) is a suite of IETF specifications for securing certain kinds of information provided by DNS. Dan Kaminsky made DNS vulnerabilities widely known back around 2010, and most service providers roll this out to ensure that DNS results are cryptographically protected. It's designed to provide origin authentication of DNS data and data integrity.

   ☒ **D** is incorrect because this term simply doesn't exist. It's here purely as a distractor.

9. You are setting up DNS for your enterprise. Server A is both a web server and an FTP server. You want to advertise both services for this machine as name references your customers can use. Which DNS record type would you use to accomplish this?

A. NS

B. SOA

C. MX

D. PTR

E. CNAME

☑ **E.** We all know—or should know by now—that a hostname can be mapped to an IP using an A record within DNS. CNAME records provide for aliases within the zone on that name. For instance, your server might be named mattserver1.matt.com. A sample DNS zone entry to provide HTTP and FTP access might look like this:

```
NAME                     TYPE    VALUE
--------------------------------------------------
ftp.matt.com.            CNAME   mattserver.matt.com
www.matt.com             CNAME   mattserver.matt.com
mattserver1.matt.com.      A        202.17.77.5
```

☒ **A** is incorrect because a name server (NS) record shows the name servers within your zone. These servers are the ones that respond to your client's requests for name resolution.

☒ **B** is incorrect because the Start of Authority (SOA) entry identifies the primary name server for the zone. The SOA record contains the hostname of the server responsible for all DNS records within the namespace, as well as the basic properties of the domain.

☒ **C** is incorrect because the Mail Exchange (MX) record identifies the e-mail servers within your domain.

☒ **D** is incorrect because a pointer record (PTR) works opposite to an A record. The pointer maps an IP address to a hostname and is generally used for reverse lookups.

10. A company has a publicly facing web application. Its internal intranet-facing servers are separated and protected by a firewall. Which of the following choices would be helpful in protecting against unwanted enumeration?

A. Allowing zone transfers to ANY

B. Ensuring there are no A records for internal hosts on the public-facing name server

C. Changing the preference number on all MX records to zero

D. Not allowing any DNS query to the public-facing name server

☑ **B.** If your company has a publicly facing website, it follows that a name server somewhere has to answer lookups in order for your customers to find the site. That name server, however, does not need to provide lookup information to internal machines. Of the choices provided, as silly as it seems to point out, ensuring there are no A records (those used to map hostnames to an IP address) on the external name server is a good start.

☒ **A** is incorrect because allowing a zone transfer to anyone asking for it is just plain dumb. It may or may not help an attacker enumerate your internal network (maybe you don't have anything in there to worry about), but it's just a horrendously bad idea.

☒ **C** is incorrect because changing the preference number on an MX record doesn't have a thing to do with enumeration. The preference number (a lower number means first used) determines only which server handles e-mail first.

☒ **D** is incorrect because if your customers can't query for the IP associated with the hostname, how are they supposed to find your website?

11. Within the DNS system, a primary server (SOA) holds and maintains all records for the zone. Secondary servers will periodically ask the primary if there have been any updates, and if updates have occurred, they will ask for a zone transfer to update their own copies. Under what conditions will the secondary name server request a zone transfer from a primary?

    A. When the primary SOA record serial number is higher than the secondary's

    B. When the secondary SOA record serial number is higher than the primary's

    C. Only when the secondary reboots or restarts services

    D. Only when manually prompted to do so

    ☑ **A.** Occasionally you'll get a question like this. It's not necessarily hacking in nature but more about how the DNS system works in general. The serial number on an SOA record is incremented each time the zone file is changed. So, when the secondary checks in with the primary, if the serial number is higher than its own, the secondary knows there has been a change and asks for a full zone transfer.

    ☒ **B** is incorrect because the serial number increments with each change, not decrements. If the secondary checked in and the numbers were reversed—in other words, the secondary had a serial number higher than the primary—it would either leave its own record unchanged or most likely dump the zone altogether.

    ☒ **C** is incorrect because a zone transfer does not occur on startup. Additionally, and this is a free test-taking tip here, any time you see the word "only" in an answer, it's usually wrong. In this case, that's definitely true because the servers are configured to check in with each other on occasion to ensure the zone is consistent across the enterprise.

    ☒ **D** is incorrect because this is just a ridiculous answer. Could you imagine having to manually update every DNS server? I can think of worse jobs, but this one would definitely stink.

12. Examine the following SOA record:

```
@   IN  SOARTDNSRV1.somebiz.com.  postmaster.somebiz.com. (
200408097   ; serial number
                            3600        ; refresh    [1h]
                            600         ; retry      [10m]
                            86400       ; expire     [1d]
7200 )      ; min TTL    [2h]
```

If a secondary server in the enterprise is unable to check in for a zone update within an hour, what happens to the zone copy on the secondary?

A. The zone copy is dumped.

B. The zone copy is unchanged.

C. The serial number of the zone copy is decremented.

D. The serial number of the zone copy is incremented.

☑ **B.** You will definitely see questions about the SOA record. In this question, the key portion you're looking for is the TTL ("time to live") value at the bottom, which is currently two hours (7,200 seconds). This sets the time a secondary server has to verify its records are good. If it can't check in, this TTL for zone records will expire, and they'll all be dumped. Considering, though, this TTL is set to two hours and the question states it has been only one hour since update, the zone copy on the secondary will remain unchanged.

☒ **A** is incorrect because the secondary is still well within its window for verifying the zone copy it holds. It dumps the records only when TTL is exceeded.

☒ **C** is incorrect because, first, serial numbers are never decremented; they're always incremented. Second, the serial number of the zone copy is changed only when a connection to the primary occurs and a copy is updated.

☒ **D** is incorrect because while serial numbers are incremented on changes (the secondary copies the number from the primary's copy when transferring records), the serial number of the zone copy is changed only when a connection to the primary occurs and a copy is updated. That has not occurred here.

13. Which protocol and port number combination is used by default for DNS zone transfers?

A. UDP 53

B. UDP 161

C. TCP 53

D. TCP 22

☑ **C.** TCP 53 is the default protocol and port number for zone transfers. DNS actually uses both TCP and UDP to get its job done, and if you think about what it's doing, they make sense in particular circumstances. A name resolution request and reply? Small and quick, so use port 53 on UDP. A zone transfer, which could potentially be large and requires some insurance it all gets there? Port 53 on TCP is the answer.

☒ **A**, **B**, and **D** are incorrect because they do not represent the default port and protocol combination for a zone transfer.

14. Examine the following command-line entry:

```
C:\>nslookup
    Default Server:  ns1.somewhere.com
    Address:  128.189.72.5
> set q=mx
>mailhost
```

Which statements are true regarding the following command sequence? (Choose two.)

A. Nslookup is in noninteractive mode.

B. Nslookup is in interactive mode.

C. The output will show all mail servers in the zone somewhere.com.

D. The output will show all name servers in the zone somewhere.com.

☑ **B** and **C.** Nslookup runs in one of two modes—interactive and noninteractive. Noninteractive mode is simply the use of the command followed by an output. For example, **nslookup www.google.com** will return the IP address your server can find for Google. Interactive mode is started by simply typing **nslookup** and pressing ENTER. Your default server name will display, along with its IP address, and a caret (>) will await entry of your next command. In this scenario, we've entered interactive mode and set the type to MX, which we all know means "Please provide me with all the mail exchange servers you know about."

☒ **A** is incorrect because we are definitely in interactive mode.

☒ **D** is incorrect because type was set to MX, not NS.

15. Joe accesses the company website, www.anybusi.com, from his home computer and is presented with a defaced site containing disturbing images. He calls the IT department to report the website hack and is told they do not see any problem with the site—no files have been changed, and when accessed from their terminals (inside the company), the site appears normally. Joe connects over VPN into the company website and notices the site appears normally. Which of the following might explain the issue?

A. DNS poisoning

B. Route poisoning

C. SQL injection

D. ARP poisoning

☑ **A.** DNS poisoning makes the most sense here. In many cases (such as mine right here in my own work-from-home office), a VPN connection back to the company forces you to use the company DNS instead of your local resolution. In this example, Joe's connection from home uses a different DNS server for lookups than that of the business network. It's entirely possible someone has changed the cache entries in his local server to point to a different IP than the one hosting the real website—one that the hackers have set up to provide the defaced version. The fact the web files haven't changed and it seems to be displaying just fine from inside the network also bears this out. If it turns out Joe's DNS modification is the only one in place, there is a strong likelihood that Joe is being specifically targeted for exploitation—something Joe should take very seriously. Lastly, the HOSTS and LMHOSTS files can also play a big role in this kind of scenario—however, if an attacker already has that kind of access to Joe's computer, he has bigger problems than the corporate website.

☒ **B** is incorrect because route poisoning has nothing to do with this. Route poisoning is used in distance vector routing protocols to prevent route loops in routing tables.

☒ **C** is incorrect because although SQL injection is, indeed, a hacking attack, it's not relevant here. The fact the website files remain intact and unchanged prove that access to the site through an SQL weakness isn't what occurred here.

☒ **D** is incorrect because ARP poisoning is relevant inside a particular subnet, not outside it (granted, you can have ARP forwarded by a router configured to do so, but it simply isn't the case for this question). ARP poisoning will redirect a request from one machine to another inside the same subnet and has little to do with the scenario described here.

16. One way to mitigate against DNS poisoning is to restrict or limit the amount of time records can stay in cache before they're updated. Which DNS record type allows you to set this restriction?

   A. NS

   B. PTR

   C. MX

   D. CNAME

   E. SOA

   ☑ **E.** The SOA record holds all sorts of information, and when it comes to DNS poisoning, the TTL is of primary interest. The shorter the TTL, the less time records are held in cache. While it won't prevent DNS poisoning altogether, it can limit the problems a successful cache poisoning attack causes.

   ☒ **A** is incorrect because an NS record shows the name servers found in the domain.

   ☒ **B** is incorrect because a PTR record provides for reverse lookup capability—an IP-address-to-hostname mapping.

   ☒ **C** is incorrect because an MX record shows the mail exchange servers in the zone.

   ☒ **D** is incorrect because a CNAME record is used to provide alias entries for your zone (usually for multiple services or sites on one IP address).

17. Which of the following may be a security concern for an organization?

    A. The internal network uses private IP addresses registered to an Active Directory–integrated DNS server.

    B. An external DNS server is Active Directory integrated.

    C. All external name resolution requests are accomplished by an ISP.

    D. None of the above.

    ☑ **B.** If you have a Windows Active Directory (AD) network, having AD-integrated DNS servers has some great advantages. For example (and directly from Microsoft, I might add), "with directory-integrated storage, dynamic updates to DNS are conducted based upon a multimaster update model. In this model, any authoritative DNS server, such as a domain controller running a DNS server, is designated as a primary source for the zone. Because the master copy of the zone is maintained in the Active Directory database, which is fully replicated to all domain controllers, the zone can be updated by the DNS servers operating at any domain controller for the domain." Zones are also replicated and synchronized to new domain controllers automatically whenever a new one is added to an Active Directory domain, and directory replication is faster and more efficient than standard DNS replication. But having an Active Directory server facing externally is a horrible idea.

    ☒ **A** is incorrect because having AD-integrated DNS servers inside your network, with all private IP addresses, is just fine. Actually, it's a pretty good idea if you think about it for a bit.

    ☒ **C** is incorrect because having an external ISP answer all name resolution requests for your public-facing servers isn't a bad idea at all. Even if the ISP's DNS is subject to attack, nothing is there but the public-facing hosts anyway.

    ☒ **D** is incorrect because there is a correct answer provided.

18. Which of the following is a good footprinting tool for discovering information on a publicly traded company's founding, history, and financial status?

    A. SpiderFoot

    B. EDGAR Database

    C. Sam Spade

    D. Pipl.com

    ☑ **B.** The EDGAR Database—https://www.sec.gov/edgar.shtml—holds all sorts of competitive intelligence information on businesses and is an old favorite of EC-Council. Per the website, "All companies, foreign and domestic, are required to file registration statements, periodic reports, and other forms electronically through EDGAR. Anyone can access and download this information for free. Here you'll find links to a complete list of filings available through EDGAR and instructions for searching the EDGAR database." Finally, one more note on EDGAR and the SEC: They have purview only over publicly traded companies. Privately held companies are not regulated or obligated to put information in EDGAR. Additionally, even publicly traded companies might not provide information about privately owned subsidiaries, so be careful and diligent.

☒ **A** is incorrect because SpiderFoot is a free, open source, domain footprinting tool. According to the site, "it will scrape the websites on that domain, as well as search Google, Netcraft, Whois and DNS to build up information."

☒ **C** is incorrect because Sam Spade is a DNS footprinting tool.

☒ **D** is incorrect because pipl.com is a site used for "people search." For footprinting, pipl.com can use so-called "deep web searching" for loads of information you can use. The following is from the site: "Also known as 'invisible web,' the term 'deep web' refers to a vast repository of underlying content, such as documents in online databases that general-purpose web crawlers cannot reach. The deep web content is estimated at 500 times that of the surface web, yet has remained mostly untapped due to the limitations of traditional search engines."

19. What method does traceroute use to map routes traveled by a packet?

   A. By carrying a hello packet in the payload, forcing the host to respond

   B. By using DNS queries at each hop

   C. By manipulating the Time-To-Live (TTL) parameter

   D. By using ICMP Type 5, Code 0 packets

   ☑ **C.** Traceroute (at least on Windows machines) tracks a packet across the Internet by incrementing the TTL on each packet it sends by one after each hop is hit and returns, ensuring the response comes back explicitly from that hop and returns its name and IP address. This provides route path and transit times. It accomplishes this by using ICMP ECHO packets to report information on each "hop" (router) from the source to destination. As an aside, Linux machines use a series of UDP packets by default to carry out the same function in traceroute.

   ☒ **A** is incorrect because ICMP simply doesn't work that way. A hello packet is generally used between clients and servers as a check-in/health mechanism, not a route-tracing method.

   ☒ **B** is incorrect because a DNS lookup at each hop is pointless and does you no good. DNS isn't for route tracing; it's for matching hostnames and IP addresses.

   ☒ **D** is incorrect because an ICMP Type 5, Code 0 packet is all about message redirection and not about a ping request (Type 8).

20. Brad is auditing an organization and is asked to provide suggestions on improving DNS security. Which of the following would be valid options to recommend? (Choose all that apply.)

   A. Implementing a split-horizon operation

   B. Restricting zone transfers

C. Obfuscating DNS by using the same server for other applications and functions

D. Blocking all access to the server on port 53

☑ **A, B.** Split-horizon DNS (also known as split-view or split DNS) is a method of providing different answers to DNS queries based on the source address of the DNS request. It can be accomplished with hardware or software solutions and provides one more step of separation between you and the bad guys. Restricting zone transfers to only those systems you desire to have them is always a good idea. If you leave it open for anyone to grab, you're just asking for trouble. DNSSEC should also be included, but isn't an option listed.

☒ **C** is incorrect because you generally should not put DNS services on a machine performing other tasks or applications. Does it happen in the real world? Sure it does, and just like it's not too far-fetched to find a stray Windows 2000 machine in any given organization's network, it's probably more common than we'd like to guess.

☒ **D** is incorrect because restricting all port 53 access to the server means it's not acting as a DNS server anymore: no one can query for name lookups, and no zone transfers are going to happen. I guess in some weird way the DNS side of it is *really* secure, but its functionality has dropped to nothing.

21. A zone file consists of which records? (Choose all that apply.)

    A. PTR

    B. MX

    C. SN

    D. SOA

    E. DNS

    F. A

    G. AX

    ☑ **A, B, D, F.** A zone file contains a list of all the resource records in the namespace zone. Valid resource records are as follows:

SRV	**Service**	This record defines the hostname and port number of servers providing specific services, such as a Directory Services server.
SOA	**Start of Authority**	This record identifies the primary name server for the zone. The SOA record contains the hostname of the server responsible for all DNS records within the namespace, as well as the basic properties of the domain.
PTR	**Pointer**	This record maps an IP address to a hostname (providing for reverse DNS lookups). You don't absolutely need a PTR record for every entry in your DNS namespace, but PTR records are usually associated with e-mail server records.
NS	**Name Server**	This record defines the name servers within your namespace. These servers are the ones that respond to your client's requests for name resolution.
MX	**Mail Exchange**	This record identifies your e-mail servers within your domain.

CNAME   **Canonical Name**   This record provides for domain name aliases within your zone. For example, you may have an FTP server and a web service running on the same IP address. CNAME records could be used to list both within DNS for you.

A   **Address**   This record maps an IP address to a hostname and is used most often for DNS lookups.

☒ **C, E,** and **G** are incorrect because they are not valid DNS resource records.

22. Examine the following SOA record:

```
@   IN  SOARTDNSRV1.somebiz.com.  postmaster.somebiz.com. (
200408097    ; serial number
                              3600        ; refresh   [1h]
                              600         ; retry     [10m]
                              86400       ; expire    [1d]
7200 )         ; min TTL    [2h]
```

How long will the secondary server wait before asking for an update to the zone file?

A. One hour

B. Two hours

C. Ten minutes

D. One day

☑ **A.** The refresh interval defines the amount of time a secondary will wait before checking in to see whether it needs a zone update.

☒ **B** is incorrect because the refresh interval is set to 3600 seconds (one hour). If you chose this because the TTL interval appealed to you, note that the TTL interval is the minimum time to live for all records in the zone (if it's not updated by a zone transfer, the records will perish).

☒ **C** is incorrect because the refresh interval is set to 3600 seconds (one hour). If you chose this because the retry interval appealed to you, note that the retry interval is the amount of time a secondary server will wait to retry *if the zone transfer fails.*

☒ **D** is incorrect because the refresh interval is set to 3600 seconds (one hour). If you chose this because the expire interval appealed to you, note the expire interval is the maximum amount of time a secondary server will spend trying to complete a zone transfer.

23. A colleague enters the following into a Google search string:

```
intitle:intranet inurl:intranet +intext:"finance"
```

Which of the following is most correct concerning this attempt?

A. The search engine will not respond with any result because you cannot combine Google hacks in one line.

B. The search engine will respond with all pages having the word *intranet* in their title and *finance* in the URL.

C. The search engine will respond with all pages having the word *intranet* in the title and in the URL.

D. The search engine will respond with only those pages having the word *intranet* in the title and URL and with *finance* in the text.

☑ **D.** This is a great Google hack that's listed on several websites providing Google hacking examples. Think about what you're looking for here—an internal page (*intranet* in title and URL) possibly containing finance data. Don't you think that would be valuable? This example shows the beauty of combining Google hacks to really burrow down to what you want to grab. Granted, an intranet being available from the Internet, indexed by Google and open enough for you to touch it, is unlikely, but these are questions concerning syntax, not reality.

☒ **A** is incorrect because Google hack operators *can* be combined. In fact, once you get used to them, you'll spend more time combining them to narrow an attack than launching them one by one.

☒ **B** is incorrect because the operator does not say to look for *human resources* in the URL. It specifically states that should be looked for in the text of the page.

☒ **C** is incorrect because there is more to the operation string than just *intranet* in the URL and title. Don't just glaze over the **intext:"finance"** operator—it makes Answer D more correct.

24. Amanda works as a senior security analyst and overhears a colleague discussing confidential corporate information being posted on an external website. When questioned on it, he claims about a month ago he tried random URLs on the company's website and found confidential information. Amanda visits the same URLs but finds nothing. Where can Amanda go to see past versions and pages of a website?

A. Search.com

B. Google cache

C. Pasthash.com

D. Archive.org

☑ **D.** The Internet Archive (http://archive.org) is a nonprofit organization "dedicated to build an Internet library. Its purposes include offering permanent access for researchers, historians, scholars, people with disabilities, and the general public to historical collections that exist in digital format." The good-old Wayback Machine has been used for a long time to pull up old copies of websites, for good and maybe not-so-good purposes. Archive.org includes "snapshots of the World Wide Web," which are archived copies of pages taken at various points in time dating back to 1996. As an additional note, Archive.org is only going to pull and store pages that were linked, shared, or commonly available, so don't assume every page ever put up by anyone anywhere will always be available.

☒ **A** is incorrect because Search.com is simply another search engine at your disposal. It does not hold archived copies.

☒ **B** is incorrect because Google cache holds a copy of the site only from the latest "crawl"—usually nothing older than a couple to few days.

☒ **C** is incorrect because, as far as I know, Pasthash.com doesn't even exist.

25. Which of the following is a primary service of the U.S. Computer Security Incident Response Team (CSIRT)?

    A. CSIRT provides an incident response service to enable a reliable and trusted single point of contact for reporting computer security incidents worldwide.

    B. CSIRT provides computer security surveillance to governments, supplying important intelligence information on individuals traveling abroad.

    C. CSIRT provides pen testing services to individuals and multinational corporations.

    D. CSIRT provides vulnerability assessment services to law enforcement agencies.

    ☑ **A.** EC-Council *loves* CSIRT, and I promise you'll see it mentioned somewhere on the exam. Per its website (http://www.csirt.org/), the Computer Security Incident Response Team (CSIRT) "provides 24x7 Computer Security Incident Response Services to any user, company, government agency or organization. CSIRT provides a reliable and trusted single point of contact for reporting computer security incidents worldwide. CSIRT provides the means for reporting incidents and for disseminating important incident-related information." A privately held company that started in 2001, CSIRT seeks "to raise awareness among its customers of computer security issues, and provides information for secure protection of critical computing infrastructure and equipment against potential organized computer attacks."

    ☑ **B, C,** and **D** are incorrect because these statements do not match CSIRT's purpose or actions.

26. Your client's business is headquartered in Japan. Which regional registry would be the best place to look for footprinting information?

    A. APNIC

    B. RIPE

    C. ASIANIC

    D. ARIN

    E. LACNIC

    ☑ **A.** This one is easy as pie and should be a free one if you see it on the test. There are five regional Internet registries that provide overall management of the public IP address space within a given geographic region. APNIC handles Asia and Pacific realms.

    ☒ **B** is incorrect because RIPE handles Europe, Middle East, and parts of Central Asia/ Northern Africa. If you're wondering, the name is French and stands for Réseaux IP Européens.

☒ **C** is incorrect because ASIANIC is not a regional registry. It's purely a distractor here.

☒ **D** is incorrect because the ARIN service region includes Canada, many Caribbean and North Atlantic islands, and the United States. Caribbean islands falling under ARIN include Puerto Rico, the Bahamas, Antigua, American and British Virgin Islands, Turks and Caicos Islands, and the Cayman Islands (among others).

☒ **E** is incorrect because LACNIC handles Latin America and parts of the Caribbean. It stands for Latin America and Caribbean Network Information Center. LACNIC coverage includes most of South America, Guatemala, French Guiana, Dominican Republic, and Cuba (among others). This one and ARIN most often get confused.

Scanning and Enumeration

This chapter includes questions from the following topics:
- Understand EC-Council's scanning methodology
- Describe scan types and the objectives of scanning
- Understand the use of various scanning and enumeration tools
- Describe TCP communication (three-way handshake and flag types)
- Understand basic subnetting
- Understand enumeration and enumeration techniques
- Describe vulnerability scanning concepts and actions
- Describe the steps involved in performing enumeration

I love fishing. Scratch that—a better statement is that I am *addicted* to fishing. I dream about it. I think about it during my workday, I plan my weekends around it—heck, I even decorated my office with fishing paraphernalia, and occasionally catch myself staring at that sea trout picture over there to my right and sighing mournfully. And, on days like today where the lake behind my house looks like a mirror that God is using to comb his hair in as He looks down from above, it's all I can do not to grab the rods and race out of the house. Instead, I'm sitting here in my little home office dedicating my morning to you and your needs, dear reader. You're welcome.

All fishing is good, and I've tried most of it. I'm not really wild about catching fish with my hands (those noodling guys don't have all the cheese on their crackers), and ice fishing isn't a favorite of mine because I hate the cold—not to mention it just seems so dang boring, sitting there looking at a little hole and hoping you've drilled in just the right spot—but I *love* kayak fishing. Don't get me wrong—I still really enjoy going out on a deep-sea boat or riding along in someone's bass boat, flying across the top of the water—but being in a kayak just seems more *personal*. Sitting right on top of the water, sneaking up to fish, and watching them eat the bait is just short of a religious experience, and it cannot be beat.

Here on the flats of East-Central Florida, you can certainly catch fish just by paddling around and casting blindly all around you. But if you want to catch good fish and catch them with more regularity, you have to learn how to read the water, and since I can't bring you all here and paddle around to give a hands-on lesson, we'll have to run a little thought experiment instead. Sit back in our little virtual kayak, and we'll paddle around to see what we can find. Look around in your mind's eye with me and scan the water around us. See that little ripple over there? Those are mullet swimming around in lazy circles. Nothing is after them, or they'd be darting and running into the shallows, so there's no point in paddling that way yet. That heavy wake over there that kind of looks like a small submarine underwater? That's a redfish, and he's definitely after something. We should definitely take a shot his way. And those things that look like tiny brooms poking out of the water over there? Yeah, that's a bunch of redfish, nosed down into the muck eating crabs or shrimp. If we watch the school for a bit, it'll make it easier to map out an approach and figure out the best casting opportunities without spooking them.

Much like the signs we can see by scanning the surface of the water here on the flats, your scanning and enumeration efforts in the virtual world will point you in the right direction and, once you get some experience with what you're looking at, will improve your hook-up percentage. As stated in the companion book to this study guide, you know how to footprint your client; now it's time to learn how to dig around what you found for relevant, salient information. After footprinting, you'll need to scan for basics; then when you find a machine up and about, you'll need to get to know it really well, asking some rather personal questions.

 STUDY TIPS   In previous versions of the exam, EC-Council focused a lot of attention on scanning and enumeration. I'm not saying it's not the same in the current version, I'm just saying it's… different. The new exam focuses a little more on network knowledge, how tools actually work, and in-the-weeds questions. Sure, you'll still find a few freebies from this section, but most will be very focused.

First and foremost, get your network knowledge down pat. Know your port numbers, protocols, and communications handshakes like the back of your hand. Learn how routing/switching basics can affect your efforts: for example, knowing that a *routing* protocol (such as OSPF and BGP) determines how routers communicate with each other and make decisions on moving packets, and that *routed* protocols (such as IP) are the ones providing network layer addressing, will help you out. There won't be a ton of them, but questions on subnetting will make an appearance, so know your math well.

When it comes to scanning, know your scanning tools very well. EC-Council absolutely *adores* nmap, so know syntax, responses, results, switches… all of it. You'll be quizzed on use, output, syntax, and lots of scanning tools, so prep by practicing—it's the absolute best way to prepare for this exam.

Lastly, Windows and Linux architecture basics aren't going to make up the majority of your exam, but rest assured you will be tested on them—especially on anything that's different between the two. For example, some tools will work with and on Windows, but not on Linux, and vice versa. Each has built-in tools and services (for example, know net command usage in Windows very well) that may work differently on the other, so be sure to focus on those for study.

1. Your team is hired to test a business named Matt's Bait 'n Tackle Shop (domain name mattsBTshop.com). A team member runs the following command:

```
metagoofil -d mattsBTshop.com -t doc,docx -l 50 -n 20 -f results.html
```

   Which of the following best describes what the team member is attempting to do?

   A. Extract metadata info from web pages in mattsBTshop.com, outputting results in Microsoft Word format.

   B. Extract metadata info from the results.html page in mattsBTshop.com, outputting results in Microsoft Word format.

   C. Extract metadata info from Microsoft Word documents found in mattsBTshop.com, outputting results in an HTML file.

   D. Uploading results.html as a macro attachment to any Microsoft Word documents found in mattsBTshop.com.

2. Which of the following is true regarding the p0f tool?

   A. It is an active OS fingerprinting tool.

   B. It is a passive OS fingerprinting tool.

   C. It is designed to extract metadata for Microsoft files.

   D. It is designed for remote access.

3. You have a zombie system ready and begin an IDLE scan. As the scan moves along, you notice that fragment identification numbers gleaned from the zombie machine are incrementing randomly. What does this mean?

   A. Your IDLE scan results will not be useful to you.

   B. The zombie system is a honeypot.

   C. There is a misbehaving firewall between you and the zombie machine.

   D. This is an expected result during an IDLE scan.

4. You want to perform a ping sweep of a subnet within your target organization. Which of the following nmap command lines is your best option?

   A. nmap 192.168.1.0/24

   B. nmap -sT 192.168.1.0/24

   C. nmap -sP 192.168.1.0/24

   D. nmap -P0 192.168.1.0/24

5. A team member runs an Inverse TCP scan. What is the expected return for an open port?

   A. Open ports respond with a SYN/ACK.

   B. Open ports respond with a RST.

   C. Open ports respond with a FIN.

   D. Open ports do not respond at all.

6. You are examining traffic to see if there are any network-enabled printers on the subnet. Which of the following ports should you be monitoring for?

   A. 53

   B. 88

   C. 445

   D. 514

   E. 631

7. A colleague enters the following command:

   ```
   root@mybox: # hping3 -A 192.168.2.x -p 80
   ```

   What is being attempted here?

   A. An ACK scan using hping3 on port 80 for a single address

   B. An ACK scan using hping3 on port 80 for a group of addresses

   C. Address validation using hping3 on port 80 for a single address

   D. Address validation using hping3 on port 80 for a group of addresses

8. You are examining traffic between hosts and note the following exchange:

   ```
   Source            Prot  Port  Flag          Destination
   192.168.5.12      TCP   4082  FIN/URG/PSH   192.168.5.50
   192.168.5.12      TCP   4083  FIN/URG/PSH   192.168.5.50
   192.168.5.12      TCP   4084  FIN/URG/PSH   192.168.5.50
   192.168.5.50      TCP   4083  RST/ACK       192.168.5.12
   192.168.5.12      TCP   4085  FIN/URG/PSH   192.168.5.50
   ```

   Which of the following statements are true regarding this traffic? (Choose all that apply.)

   A. It appears to be part of an ACK scan.

   B. It appears to be part of an XMAS scan.

   C. It appears port 4083 is open.

   D. It appears port 4083 is closed.

9. You are examining traffic and notice an ICMP Type 3, Code 13 response. What does this normally indicate?

   A. The network is unreachable.

   B. The host is unknown.

   C. Congestion control is enacted for traffic to this host.

   D. A firewall is prohibiting connection.

10. Which port-scanning method presents the most risk of discovery but provides the most reliable results?

    A. Full-connect

    B. Half-open

C. Null scan

D. XMAS scan

11. As a pen test on a major international business moves along, a colleague discovers an IIS server and a mail exchange server on a DMZ subnet. You review a ping sweep accomplished earlier in the day on that subnet and note neither machine responded to the ping. What is the most likely reason for the lack of response?

   A. The hosts might be turned off or disconnected.

   B. ICMP is being filtered.

   C. The destination network might be down.

   D. The servers are Linux based and do not respond to ping requests.

12. A team member is using nmap and asks about the "scripting engine" in the tool. Which option switches can be used to invoke the nmap scripting engine? (Choose two.)

   A. --script

   B. -z

   C. -sA

   D. -sC

13. Which of the following commands is the best choice to use on a Linux machine when attempting to list processes and the UIDs associated with them in a reliable manner?

   A. ls

   B. chmod

   C. pwd

   D. lsof

14. You want to display active and inactive services on a Windows Server machine. Which of the following commands best performs this service?

   A. sc query

   B. sc query type=all

   C. sc query type=service

   D. sc query state= all

15. An administrator enters the following command on a Linux system:

   `iptables -t nat -L`

   Which of the following best describes the intent of the command entered?

   A. The administrator is attempting a port scan.

   B. The administrator is configuring IP masquerading.

   C. The administrator is preparing to flood a switch.

   D. The administrator is preparing a DoS attack.

16. What is being attempted with the following command?

    ```
    nc -u -v -w2 192.168.1.100 1-1024
    ```

    A. A full connect scan on ports 1–1024 for a single address

    B. A full connect scan on ports 1–1024 for a subnet

    C. A UDP port scan of ports 1–1024 on a single address

    D. A UDP scan of ports 1–1024 on a subnet

17. You are told to monitor a packet capture for any attempted DNS zone transfer. Which port should you focus your search on?

    A. TCP 22

    B. TCP 53

    C. UDP 22

    D. UDP 53

18. A team member issues the **nbtstat.exe -c** command. Which of the following best represents the intent of the command?

    A. It displays the IP route table for the machine.

    B. It displays the NetBIOS name cache.

    C. It displays active and inactive services.

    D. It puts a NIC into promiscuous mode for sniffing.

19. Consider the ports shown in the nmap output returned on an IP scanned during footprinting:

    ```
    PORT STATE SERVICE 21/tcp open ftp 23/tcp open telnet 80/tcp open http
    139/tcp open netbios-ssn 515/tcp open 631/tec open ipp 9100/tcp
    open MAC Address: 01:2A:48:0B:AA:81
    ```

    Which of the following is true regarding the output?

    A. The host is most likely a router or has routing enabled.

    B. The host is most likely a printer or has a printer installed.

    C. The host is definitely a Windows Server.

    D. The host is definitely a Linux Server.

20. The following results are from an nmap scan:

    ```
    Starting nmap V. 3.10A ( www.insecure.org/nmap/
    <http://www.insecure.org/nmap/> )
    Interesting ports on 192.168.15.12:
    (The 1592 ports scanned but not shown below are in state: filtered)
    Port State Service
    21/tcp open ftp
    25/tcp open smtp
    53/tcp closed domain
    80/tcp open http
    443/tcp open https
    ```

```
Remote operating system guess: Too many signatures match to
    reliably guess the OS.
Nmap run completed -- 1 IP address (1 host up) scanned in 263.47 seconds
```

Which of the following is the best option to assist in identifying the operating system?

A. Attempt an ACK scan.

B. Traceroute to the system.

C. Run the same nmap scan with the -vv option.

D. Attempt banner grabbing.

21. You want to run a scan against a target network. You're concerned about it being a reliable scan, with legitimate results, but want to take steps to ensure it is as stealthy as possible. Which scan type is best in this situation?

   A. nmap -sN targetIPaddress

   B. nmap -sO targetIPaddress

   C. nmap -sS targetIPaddress

   D. nmap -sT targetIPaddress

22. What is the second step in the TCP three-way handshake?

   A. SYN

   B. ACK

   C. SYN/ACK

   D. ACK-SYN

   E. FIN

23. You are enumerating a subnet. While examining message traffic, you discover SNMP is enabled on multiple targets. If you assume default settings in setting up enumeration tools to use SNMP, which community strings should you use?

   A. Public (read-only) and Private (read/write)

   B. Private (read-only) and Public (read/write)

   C. Read (read-only) and Write (read/write)

   D. Default (both read and read/write)

24. Nmap is a powerful scanning and enumeration tool. What does the following nmap command attempt to accomplish?

   ```
   nmap -sA -T4 192.168.15.0/24
   ```

   A. A serial, slow operating system discovery scan of a Class C subnet

   B. A parallel, fast operating system discovery scan of a Class C subnet

   C. A serial, slow ACK scan of a Class C subnet

   D. A parallel, fast ACK scan of a Class C subnet

25. You are examining a packet capture of all traffic from a host on the subnet. The host sends a segment with the SYN flag set in order to set up a TCP communications channel. The destination port is 80, and the sequence number is set to 10. Which of the following statements are *not* true regarding this communications channel? (Choose all that apply.)

   A. The host will be attempting to retrieve an HTML file.

   B. The source port field on this packet can be any number between 1024 and 65535.

   C. The first packet from the destination in response to this host will have the SYN and ACK flags set.

   D. The packet returned in answer to this SYN request will acknowledge the sequence number by returning 10.

26. Which TCP flag instructs the recipient to ignore buffering constraints and immediately send all data?

   A. URG

   B. PSH

   C. RST

   D. BUF

27. You receive a RST-ACK from a port during a SYN scan. What is the state of the port?

   A. Open

   B. Closed

   C. Filtered

   D. Unknown

1. A	**10.** A	**19.** B
2. B	**11.** B	**20.** D
3. A	**12.** A, D	**21.** C
4. C	**13.** D	**22.** C
5. D	**14.** D	**23.** A
6. E	**15.** B	**24.** D
7. B	**16.** C	**25.** A, D
8. B, C	**17.** B	**26.** B
9. D	**18.** B	**27.** B

1. Your team is hired to test a business named Matt's Bait 'n Tackle Shop (domain name mattsBTshop.com). A team member runs the following command:

   ```
   metagoofil –d mattsBTshop.com –t doc,docx –l 50 –n 20 –f results.html
   ```

   Which of the following best describes what the team member is attempting to do?

   A. Extract metadata info from web pages in mattsBTshop.com, outputting results in Microsoft Word format.

   B. Extract metadata info from the results.html page in mattsBTshop.com, outputting results in Microsoft Word format.

   C. Extract metadata info from Microsoft word documents found in mattsBTshop.com, outputting results in an HTML file.

   D. Uploading results.html as a macro attachment to any Microsoft Word documents found in mattsBTshop.com.

   ☑ **A.** This is an example of good tool knowledge and use. Metgoofil (http://www .edge-security.com/metagoofil.php) "is an information gathering tool designed for extracting metadata of public documents (pdf, doc, xls, ppt, docx, pptx, xlsx) belonging to a target company. It performs a search in Google to identify and download the documents to local disk and then will extract the metadata with different libraries like Hachoir, PdfMiner? and others. With the results it will generate a report with usernames, software versions and servers or machine names that will help Penetration testers in the information gathering phase."

   In the syntax above, metagoofil will search mattsBTshop.com for up to 50 results (the -l switch determine the number of results) of any Microsoft Word documents (in both doc and docx format) it can find. It will then attempt to download the first 20 found (the -n switch handles that), and the -f switch will send the results where you want (in this case, to an HTML file).

   And just what will those results be? Well that's where the fun comes in. Remember, metagoofil tries to extract metadata from publicly available Microsoft Word documents available on the site. You might find e-mail addresses, document paths, software versions, and even user names in the results.

   ☒ **B, C,** and **D** are incorrect because they do not match the syntax provided.

2. Which of the following is true regarding the p0f tool?

   A. It is an active OS fingerprinting tool.

   B. It is a passive OS fingerprinting tool.

   C. It is designed to extract metadata for Microsoft files.

   D. It is designed for remote access.

   ☑ **B.** p0f, per http://lcamtuf.coredump.cx/p0f3/, "is a tool that utilizes an array of sophisticated, purely passive traffic fingerprinting mechanisms to identify the players behind any incidental TCP/IP communications (often as little as a single normal SYN) without interfering in any way. The tool can be operated in the foreground or as a daemon, and offers a simple real-time API for third-party components that wish to obtain additional information about the actors they are talking to. Common uses for p0f include reconnaissance during penetration tests; routine network monitoring; detection of unauthorized network interconnects in corporate environments; providing signals for abuse-prevention tools; and miscellaneous forensics."

When nmap scanning is blocked or otherwise unreliable, p0f can make use of a "vanilla" TCP connection to passively fingerprint. It can provide measurement of system uptime and network hookup, distance (including topology behind NAT or packet filters), and user language preferences. It also provides automated detection of connection sharing (NAT), load balancing, and application-level proxying setups.

☒ **A, C,** and **D** are incorrect because these do not describe p0f. Active fingerprinting involves sending traffic in an effort to read responses and determine open ports and other goodies (like nmap does). p0f does not read metadata from available files for information purposes (like metagoofil does), and it's definitely not a remote access tool (like netcat).

3. You have a zombie system ready and begin an IDLE scan. As the scan moves along, you notice that fragment identification numbers gleaned from the zombie machine are incrementing randomly. What does this mean?

   A. Your IDLE scan results will not be useful to you.

   B. The zombie system is a honeypot.

   C. There is a misbehaving firewall between you and the zombie machine.

   D. This is an expected result during an IDLE scan.

   ☑ **A.** An IDLE scan makes use of a zombie machine and IP's knack for incrementing fragment identifiers (IPIDs). However, it is absolutely essential the zombie remain idle to all other traffic during the scan. The attacker will send packets to the target with the (spoofed) source address of the zombie. If the port is open, the target will respond to the SYN packet with a SYN/ACK, but this will be sent to the zombie. The zombie system will then craft a RST packet in answer to the unsolicited SYN/ACK, and the IPID will increase. If this occurs randomly, then it's probable your zombie is not, in fact, idle, and your results are moot. See, if it's not idle, it's going to increment haphazardly because communications from the device will be shooting hither and yon with wild abandon. You're banking on the fact the machine is quietly doing your bidding—and nothing else.

   ☒ **B** is incorrect because there is not enough information here to identify the zombie machine as anything at all—much less a machine set up as a "honeypot."

   ☒ **C** is incorrect because a firewall between you and the zombie won't have any effect at all on the zombie's IPIDs.

☒ **D** is incorrect because this is definitely *not* expected behavior during an IDLE scan. Expected behavior is for the IPID to increase regularly with each discovered open port, not randomly, as occurs with traffic on an active system.

4. You want to perform a ping sweep of a subnet within your target organization. Which of the following nmap command lines is your best option?

   A. nmap 192.168.1.0/24

   B. nmap -sT 192.168.1.0/24

   C. nmap -sP 192.168.1.0/24

   D. nmap -P0 192.168.1.0/24

   ☑ **C.** The -sP switch within nmap is designed for a ping sweep. Nmap syntax is fairly straightforward: nmap<scan options><target>. If you don't define a switch, nmap performs a basic enumeration scan of the targets. The switches, though, provide the real power with this tool.

   ☒ **A** is incorrect because this syntax will not perform a ping sweep. This syntax will run a basic scan against the entire subnet.

   ☒ **B** is incorrect because the -sT switch does not run a ping sweep. It stands for a TCP Connect scan, which is the slowest—but most productive and loud—scan option.

   ☒ **D** is incorrect because this syntax will not perform a ping sweep. The -P0 switch actually runs the scan without ping (ICMP). This is a good switch to use when you don't seem to be getting responses from your targets. It forces nmap to start the scan even if it thinks that the target doesn't exist (which is useful if the computer is blocked by a firewall).

5. A team member runs an inverse TCP scan. What is the expected return for an open port?

   A. Open ports respond with a SYN/ACK.

   B. Open ports respond with a RST.

   C. Open ports respond with a FIN.

   D. Open ports do not respond at all.

   ☑ **D.** ECC can get infuriating at times with nomenclature and semantics. Versions of the Inverse TCP Flag scan used to be called the FIN scan or the NULL scan. Stealth scans used to be known as SYN scans. Why? Well, other than the fact that EC-Council can do whatever they want with the certification, the reasoning for the Inverse scan name comes down to the way it behaves: it's the inverse of all the other scans. This scan uses the FIN, URG or PSH flags (or, in one version, no flags at all) to poke at system ports. If the port is open, there will be no response at all. If the port is closed, a RST/ACK will be sent in response—you know, the inverse of the TCP connect scan.

   In case you're wondering, this scan is closely related to the so-called XMAS scan. A Christmas scan is so named because all flags are turned on, so the packet is "lit up" like a Christmas tree. Port responses are the same as with an Inverse TCP scan. XMAS scans do not work against Microsoft Windows machines due to Microsoft's TCP/IP stack implementation (Microsoft TCP/IP is not RFC 793 compliant).

☒ **A** is incorrect because this response for open ports would be seen in a TCP Connect (Full) or SYN (Half-Open) scan. In these scans, open ports will respond with a SYN/ACK, and closed ports will respond with a RST.

☒ **B** is incorrect because this is the response for closed ports on TCP Connect and SYN scans.

☒ **C** is incorrect because the FIN flag is used to bring a communications session to an orderly close.

6. You are examining traffic to see if there are any network-enabled printers on the subnet. Which of the following ports should you be monitoring for?

   A. 53

   B. 88

   C. 445

   D. 514

   E. 631

   ☑ **E.** You will probably see 3–5 questions on port numbering alone. So just exactly how do you commit 1024 port numbers (0–1023 is the well-known range) to memory when you have all this other stuff to keep track of? You probably won't, and maybe you can't. The best advice I can give you is to memorize the really important ones— the ones you know beyond a shadow of a doubt you'll see on the exam somewhere, and then use the process of elimination to get to the right answer.

   For example, suppose you had no idea that TCP port 631 was used for by Internet Printing Protocol (IPP), but you did know what 53, 88, and 445 were for. Suddenly it's not that difficult (now down to a 50/50 chance). By the way, 631 won't be the only thing you'll be monitoring for, but of the answers provided, it is the best choice.

   ☒ **A** is incorrect because 53 is the port number used by DNS (TCP and UDP). The TCP side will be used for across-Internet traffic, where the loss of speed due to connection-oriented traffic is worth it to ensure delivery, and UDP will be mostly internal.

   ☒ **B** is incorrect because 88 is the port number used by Kerberos.

   ☒ **C** is incorrect because 445 is used for Microsoft SMB file sharing. You'll definitely see SMB file sharing and this port somewhere on the exam, usually as part of a scenario like the one in this question.

   ☒ **D** is incorrect because 514 is the (UDP) port number used by syslog—and trust me, you need to know this one. EC Council *loves* syslog. You'll definitely see it a couple of times on the exam.

7. A colleague enters the following command:

```
root@mybox: # hping3 -A 192.168.2.x -p 80
```

What is being attempted here?

A. An ACK scan using hping3 on port 80 for a single address

B. An ACK scan using hping3 on port 80 for a group of addresses

C. Address validation using hping3 on port 80 for a single address

D. Address validation using hping3 on port 80 for a group of addresses

☑ **B.** Hping is a great tool providing all sorts of options. You can craft packets with it, audit and test firewalls, and do all sorts of crazy man-in-the-middle stuff with it. In this example, you're simply performing a basic ACK scan (the -A switch) using port 80 (-p 80) on an entire Class C subnet (the *x* in the address runs through all 254 possibilities). Hping3, the latest version, is scriptable (TCL language) and implements an engine that allows a human-readable description of TCP/IP packets.

☒ **A** is incorrect because the syntax is for an entire subnet (or, I guess to be technically specific, all 254 addresses that start with 192.168.2). The *x* in the last octet tells hping to fire away at all those available addresses.

☒ **C** and **D** are both incorrect because "address validation" is not a scan type.

8. You are examining traffic between hosts and note the following exchange:

```
Source            Prot  Port  Flag          Destination
192.168.5.12      TCP   4082  FIN/URG/PSH   192.168.5.50
192.168.5.12      TCP   4083  FIN/URG/PSH   192.168.5.50
192.168.5.12      TCP   4084  FIN/URG/PSH   192.168.5.50
192.168.5.50      TCP   4083  RST/ACK       192.168.5.12
192.168.5.12      TCP   4085  FIN/URG/PSH   192.168.5.50
```

Which of the following statements are true regarding this traffic? (Choose all that apply.)

A. It appears to be part of an ACK scan.

B. It appears to be part of an XMAS scan.

C. It appears port 4083 is open.

D. It appears port 4083 is closed.

☑ **B, C.** The exam will ask you to define scan types in many, many ways. It may be a simple definition match; sometimes it'll be some crazy Wireshark or tcpdump listing. In this example, you see a cleaned-up traffic exchange showing packets from one host being sent one after another to the second host, indicating a scan attempt. The packets have the FIN, URG, and PSH flags all set, which tells you it's an XMAS scan. If the destination port is open, you should receive a RST/ACK response; if it's closed, you get nothing. This tells you port 4083 looks like it's open. As an addendum, did you know there are two reasons why it's called an XMAS scan? The first is because it lights up an IDS like a Christmas tree, and the second is because the flags themselves are all lit. As an aside, you probably won't see this much out in the real world because it just really doesn't have much applicability. But on your exam? Oh yes—it'll be there.

⊠ **A** is incorrect because there is no indication this is an ACK scan. An ACK scan has only the ACK flag set and is generally used in firewall filter tests: no response means a firewall is present, and RST means the firewall is not there (or the port is not filtered).

⊠ **D** is incorrect because you did receive an answer from the port (a RST/ACK was sent in the fourth line of the capture).

9. You are examining traffic and notice an ICMP Type 3, Code 13 response. What does this normally indicate?

   A. The network is unreachable.

   B. The host is unknown.

   C. Congestion control is enacted for traffic to this host.

   D. A firewall is prohibiting connection.

   ☑ **D.** ICMP types will be covered in depth on your exam, so know them well. Type 3 messages are all about "destination unreachable," and the code in each packet tells you why it's unreachable. Code 13 indicates "communication administratively prohibited," which indicates a firewall filtering traffic. Granted, this occurs only when a network designer is nice enough to configure the device to respond in such a way, and you'll probably never get that nicety in the real world, but the definitions of what the "type" and "code" mean are relevant here.

   ⊠ **A** is incorrect because "network unreachable" is Type 3, Code 0. It's generated by a router to inform the source that the destination address is unreachable; that is, it does not have an entry in the route table to send the message to.

   ⊠ **B** is incorrect because "host unknown" is Type 3, Code 7. There's a route to the network the router knows about, but that host is not there (this sometimes refers to a naming or DNS issue).

   ⊠ **C** is incorrect because "congestion control" ICMP messaging is Type 4.

10. Which port-scanning method presents the most risk of discovery but provides the most reliable results?

    A. Full-connect

    B. Half-open

    C. Null Scan

    D. XMAS scan

    ☑ **A.** A full-connect scan runs through an entire TCP three-way handshake on all ports you aim at. It's loud and easy to see happening, but the results are indisputable. As an aside, the -sT switch in nmap runs a full-connect scan (you should go ahead and memorize that one).

☒ **B** is incorrect because a half-open scan involves sending only the SYN packet and watching for responses. It is designed for stealth but may be picked up on IDS sensors (both network and most host-based IDSs).

☒ **C** is incorrect because a null scan sends packets with no flags set at all. Responses will vary, depending on the OS and version, so reliability is spotty. As an aside, null scans are designed for Unix/Linux machines and don't work on Windows systems.

☒ **D** is incorrect because although an XMAS scan is easily detectable (as our celebrated technical editor put it, "a fairly well-trained monkey would see it"), the results are oftentimes sketchy. The XMAS scan is great for test questions but won't result in much more than a derisive snort and an immediate disconnection in the real world.

11. As a pen test on a major international business moves along, a colleague discovers an IIS server and a mail exchange server on a DMZ subnet. You review a ping sweep accomplished earlier in the day on that subnet and note neither machine responded to the ping. What is the most likely reason for the lack of response?

   A. The hosts might be turned off or disconnected.

   B. ICMP is being filtered.

   C. The destination network might be down.

   D. The servers are Linux based and do not respond to ping requests.

☑ **B.** Admittedly, this one is a little tricky, and, yes, I purposefully wrote it this way (mainly because I've seen questions like this before). The key here is the "most likely" designator. It's entirely possible—dare I say, even *expected*—that the systems administrator for those two important machines would turn off ICMP. Of the choices provided, this one is the most likely explanation.

☒ **A** is incorrect, but only because there is a better answer. This is a major firm that undoubtedly does business at all times of day and with customers and employees around the world (the question did state it was an international business). Is it possible that both these servers are down? Sure, you might have timed your ping sweep so poorly that you happened to hit a maintenance window or something, but it's highly unlikely.

☒ **C** is incorrect because, frankly, the odds of an entire DMZ subnet being down while you're pen testing are very slim. And I can promise you if the subnet did drop while you were testing, your test is over.

☒ **D** is incorrect because this is simply not true.

12. A team member is using nmap and asks about the "scripting engine" in the tool. Which option switches can be used to invoke the nmap scripting engine? (Choose two.)

   A. --script

   B. -z

   C. -sA

   D. -sC

☑ **A, D.** Nmap is a great scanning tool, providing all sorts of options, and you'll need to know the syntax very well. The NSE (Nmap Scripting Engine) is a portion of the tool that allows the use of scripts in scanning. Directly from nmap's site (https://nmap.org/book/nse.html), "NSE is activated with the -sC option (or --script if you wish to specify a custom set of scripts) and results are integrated into Nmap normal and XML output."

I've also seen mentioned in other study material that the -A switch is also considered as an NSE function. -A turns on "aggressive" scanning, which reports on version detection, operating system fingerprinting, and all sorts of other goodies. A pretty good wrap-up of nmap switches can be found on linuxcommand.org (http://linuxcommand.org/man_pages/nmap1.html).

☒ **B** is incorrect because -z isn't an nmap switch.

☒ **C** is incorrect because the -sA switch runs an ACK scan (ACK segments are sent to ports to determine their state).

13. Which of the following commands is the best choice to use on a Linux machine when attempting to list processes and the PIDs associated with them in a reliable manner?

    A. ls

    B. chmod

    C. pwd

    D. lsof

    ☑ **D.** Supported in most Unix-like flavors, the "list open files" command (lsof) provides a list of all open files and the processes that opened them. The lsof command describes, among other things, the identification number of the process (PID) that has opened the file, the command the process is executing, and the owner of the process. With optional switches, you can also receive all sorts of other information.

    ☒ **A** is incorrect because ls (list) simply displays all the files and folders in your current directory. Its counterpart in the PC world is dir.

    ☒ **B** is incorrect because chmod is used to set permissions on files and objects in Linux.

    ☒ **C** is incorrect because pwd (print working directory) is a command used to display the directory you are currently working in.

14. You want to display active and inactive services on a Windows Server. Which of the following commands best performs this service?

    A. sc query

    B. sc query type=all

    C. sc query type=service

    D. sc query state= all

    ☑ **D.** The sc command will definitely make an appearance or two somewhere on the exam. Per Microsoft, SC.exe retrieves and sets control information about services.

You can use SC.exe for testing and debugging service programs. Service properties stored in the registry can be set to control how service applications are started at boot time and run as background processes. SC.exe parameters can configure a specific service, retrieve the current status of a service, as well as stop and start a service.

A sampling of uses for the sc command follows:

- **sc config**   Determines the status of a service at system startup, and sets a service to run automatically, manually or not at all.

- **sc query**   Displays information about services, drivers, and types of both. Without parameters, it returns a list of all running services and associated information. To create a list of all services, use **sc query state= all**.

- **sc start**   Starts a service that is not running.

- **sc stop**   Stops a running service.

- **sc pause**   Pauses a service.

- **sc continue**   Resumes a paused service.

- **sc enumdepend**   Lists the services that cannot run unless the specified service is running.

- **sc qc**   Displays the configuration of a particular service.

And finally, one more quick note: Remember there is always a space *after* the equals sign. Syntax is important, and ECC will probably spring that on you.

☒ **A, B,** and **C** all use incorrect syntax for the question asked.

15. An administrator enters the following command on a Linux system:

```
iptables -t nat -L
```

Which of the following best describes the intent of the command entered?

A. The administrator is attempting a port scan.

B. The administrator is configuring IP masquerading.

C. The administrator is preparing to flood a switch.

D. The administrator is preparing a DoS attack.

☑ **B.** Do you remember Network Address Translation? It's a neat little technology that allows lots of internal hosts, using nonroutable private addressing, to access the Internet by borrowing and using a single address (or a group of addresses) managed by a router or other system. IP masquerading is much the same thing; it's just accomplished through a Linux host. In short, a Linux machine can act as a NAT translator by employing proper routing configuration, using one NIC to communicate with the internal network and one for the external, and enabling IP Masquerade.

Looking over the man page for the command (one copy can be found at http://ipset.netfilter.org/iptables.man.html), we see that iptables is an administration tool for IPv4 packet filtering and NAT. Per the man page, "Iptables is used to set up, maintain, and inspect the tables of IPv4 packet filter rules in the Linux kernel. Several different tables may be defined. Each table contains a number of built-in chains and may also contain user-defined chains." Syntax is **iptables -t *tablename* -*switch***, where *tablename* is filter, nat, mangle, raw, or security, and *switch* equates to the option you wish to enable. For example, -A appends rules, -D deletes rules, and -R replaces rules.

☒ **A, C,** and **D** are incorrect because they do not accurately represent what is being attempted.

16. What is being attempted with the following command?

    ```
    nc –u –v –w2 192.168.1.100 1-1024
    ```

    A. A full connect scan on ports 1–1024 for a single address

    B. A full connect scan on ports 1–1024 for a subnet

    C. A UDP port scan of ports 1–1024 on a single address

    D. A UDP scan of ports 1–1024 on a subnet

    ☑ **C.** In this example, netcat is being used to run a scan on UDP ports (the -u switch gives this away) from 1 to 1024. The address provided is a single address, not a subnet. Other switches in use here are -v (for verbose) and -w2 (defines the two-second timeout for connection, where netcat will wait for a response).

    ☒ **A** is incorrect because the -u switch shows this as a UDP scan. By default (that is, no switch in place), netcat runs in TCP.

    ☒ **B** is incorrect because the -u switch shows this as a UDP scan. Additionally, this is aimed at a single address, not a subnet.

    ☒ **D** is incorrect because this is aimed at a single address, not a subnet.

17. You are told to monitor a packet capture for any attempted DNS zone transfer. Which port should you focus your search on?

    A. TCP 22

    B. TCP 53

    C. UDP 22

    D. UDP 53

    ☑ **B.** DNS uses port 53 in both UDP and TCP. Port 53 over UDP is used for DNS lookups. Zone transfers are accomplished using port 53 over TCP. Considering the reliability and error correction available with TCP, this makes perfect sense.

    ☒ **A** is incorrect because TCP port 22 is for SSH, not DNS.

    ☒ **C** is incorrect because UDP port 22 simply doesn't exist (SSH is TCP based).

    ☒ **D** is incorrect because UDP port 53 is used for DNS lookups. Because lookups are generally a packet or two and we're concerned with speed on a lookup, UDP's fire-and-forget speed advantage is put to use here.

18. A team member issues the **nbtstat.exe -c** command. Which of the following best represents the intent of the command?

A. It displays the IP route table for the machine.

B. It displays the NetBIOS name cache.

C. It displays active and inactive services.

D. It puts a NIC into promiscuous mode for sniffing.

☑ **B.** Per Microsoft, regarding the nbtstat command: "Nbtstat is designed to help troubleshoot NetBIOS name resolution problems. When a network is functioning normally, NetBIOS over TCP/IP (NetBT) resolves NetBIOS names to IP addresses. It does this through several options for NetBIOS name resolution, including local cache lookup, WINS server query, broadcast, LMHOSTS lookup, Hosts lookup, and DNS server query. The nbtstat command removes and corrects preloaded entries using a number of case-sensitive switches." Syntax for the command includes the following:

- **nbtstat - a <name>** Performs a NetBIOS adapter status command on the computer name specified by <name>. The adapter status command returns the local NetBIOS name table for that computer as well as the MAC address of the adapter card.

- **nbtstat -A <IP address>** Performs the same function as the -a switch, but using a target IP address rather than a name.

- **nbtstat - c** Shows the contents of the NetBIOS name cache, which contains NetBIOS-name-to-IP-address mappings.

- **nbtstat -n** Displays the names that have been registered locally on the system by NetBIOS applications such as the server and redirector.

- **nbtstat -r** Displays the count of all NetBIOS names resolved by broadcast and by querying a WINS server.

- **nbtstat -R** Purges the name cache and reloads all #PRE entries from the LMHOSTS file (#PRE entries are the LMHOSTS name entries that are preloaded into the cache).

- **nbtstat -RR** Sends name release packets to the WINS server and starts a refresh, thus re-registering all names with the name server without a reboot being required.

- **nbtstat -S** Lists current NetBIOS sessions and their status, including statistics.

☒ **A, C,** and **D** are incorrect because they do not match the command usage. If you wish to see the route table on a Windows system, use the **route print** command. The **sc query state= all** command will show all the active and inactive services on the system. To put the NIC in promiscuous mode, you'd need the WinPcap driver installed.

19. Consider the ports shown in the nmap output returned on an IP scanned during footprinting:

```
PORT STATE SERVICE 21/tcp open ftp 23/tcp open telnet 80/tcp open http
139/tcp open netbios-ssn 515/tcp open 631/tec open ipp 9100/tcp
open MAC Address: 01:2A:48:0B:AA:81
```

Which of the following is true regarding the output?

A. The host is most likely a router or has routing enabled.

B. The host is most likely a printer or has a printer installed.

C. The host is definitely a Windows server.

D. The host is definitely a Linux server.

☑ **B.** So this output is pretty interesting, huh? There's some FTP, Telnet, and HTTP open, and a little NetBIOS action going on there, too. The TCP ports 515 and 631, however, are the ones to note here. 515 corresponds to the Line Printer Daemon protocol/Line Printer Remote protocol (or LPD, LPR), which is used for submitting print jobs to a remote printer. Port 631 corresponds to the Internet Printing Protocol (IPP). Both of which point to printing.

☒ **A** is incorrect because none of these ports show anything related to routing.

☒ **C** and **D** are incorrect because there is simply not enough information to definitively identify the operating system in use. Yes, it is true that the Line Printer Daemon protocol was originally in the BSD UNIX operating system; however, it is used regardless of OS.

20. The following results are from an nmap scan:

```
Starting nmap V. 3.10A ( www.insecure.org/nmap/
<http://www.insecure.org/nmap/> )
Interesting ports on 192.168.15.12:
(The 1592 ports scanned but not shown below are in state: filtered)
Port State Service
21/tcp open ftp
25/tcp open smtp
53/tcp closed domain
80/tcp open http
443/tcp open https
Remote operating system guess: Too many signatures match to reliably
guess the OS.
Nmap run completed -- 1 IP address (1 host up) scanned in 263.47 seconds
```

Which of the following is the best option to assist in identifying the operating system?

A. Attempt an ACK scan.

B. Traceroute to the system.

C. Run the same nmap scan with the -vv option.

D. Attempt banner grabbing.

☑ **D.** Of the options presented, banner grabbing is probably your best bet. In fact, it's a good *start* for operating system fingerprinting. You can telnet to any of these active ports or run an nmap banner grab. Either way, the returning banner may help in identifying the OS.

☒ **A** is incorrect because an ACK scan isn't necessarily going to help here. For that matter, it may have already been run.

☒ **B** is incorrect because traceroute does not provide any information on fingerprinting. It will show you a network map, hop by hop, to the target, but it won't help tell you whether it's a Windows machine.

☒ **C** is incorrect because the -vv switch provides only more (verbose) information on what nmap already has. Note that the original run presented this message on the OS fingerprinting effort: "Remote operating system guess: Too many signatures match to reliably guess the OS."

21. You want to run a scan against a target network. You're concerned about it being a reliable scan, with legitimate results, but want to take steps to ensure it is as stealthy as possible. Which scan type is best in this situation?

    A. nmap -sN targetIPaddress

    B. nmap -sO targetIPaddress

    C. nmap -sS targetIPaddress

    D. nmap -sT targetIPaddress

    ☑ **C.** A half-open scan, as defined by this nmap command line, is the best option in this case. The SYN scan was created with stealth in mind because the full connect scan was simply too noisy (or created more entries in an application-level logging system, whichever your preference). As far as the real world is concerned, it's a fact that most IDSs can pick up a SYN scan just as easily as a full connect, but if you go slow enough, both a SYN and a full connect can be almost invisible. A connect scan is indistinguishable from a real connection, whereas a SYN scan can be. In other words, the full connect will look like any other conversation—just bunches of them all at once—where a SYN scan will show a lot of systems answering a conversation starter only to be met with rude silence. The lesson is any scan can and probably will be seen in the real world by a monitoring IDS, however the slower you go the less chance you'll have of being seen, all things being equal.

    ☒ **A** is incorrect because a null scan may not provide the reliability you're looking for. Remember, this scan won't work on a Windows host at all.

    ☒ **B** is incorrect because the -sO switch tells you this is an operating system scan. Fingerprinting scans are not stealthy by anyone's imagination, and they won't provide the full information you're looking for here.

    ☒ **D** is incorrect because the -sT option indicates a full connect scan. Although this is reliable, it is noisy, and you will most likely be discovered during the scan.

22. What is the second step in the TCP three-way handshake?

    A. SYN

    B. ACK

    C. SYN/ACK

    D. ACK/SYN

    E. FIN

    ☑ **C.** Admittedly, this is an easy one, but I'd bet dollars to doughnuts you see it in some form on your exam. It's such an important part of scanning and enumeration because, without understanding this basic principle of communication channel setup, you're almost doomed to failure. A three-way TCP handshake has the originator forward a SYN. The recipient, in step 2, sends a SYN and an ACK. In step 3, the originator responds with an ACK. The steps are referred to as SYN, SYN/ACK, ACK.

    ☒ **A** is incorrect because SYN is the first step (flag set) in the three-way handshake.

    ☒ **B** is incorrect because ACK is the last step (flag set) in the three-way handshake.

    ☒ **D** is incorrect because of the order listed. True, both these flags are the flags set in the three-way handshake. However, in the discussion of this step-by-step process, at least as far as your exam is concerned, it's SYN/ACK, not the other way around. And, yes, this distractor, in some form, will most likely be on your exam. You won't care about the order in the real world since flags are a mathematical property of the packet and not some ridiculous order, but for your exam you'll need to know it this way.

    ☒ **E** is incorrect because the FIN flag brings an orderly close to a communication session.

23. You are enumerating a subnet. While examining message traffic you discover SNMP is enabled on multiple targets. If you assume default settings in setting up enumeration tools to use SNMP, which community strings should you use?

    A. Public (read-only) and Private (read/write)

    B. Private (read-only) and Public (read/write)

    C. Read (read-only) and Write (read/write)

    D. Default (both read and read/write)

    ☑ **A.** SNMP uses a community string as a form of a password. The read-only version of the community string allows a requester to read virtually anything SNMP can drag out of the device, whereas the read/write version is used to control access for the SNMP SET requests. The read-only default community string is *public,* whereas the read/write string is *private.* If you happen upon a network segment using SNMPv3, though, keep in mind that SNMPv3 can use a hashed form of the password in transit versus the clear text.

    ☒ **B** is incorrect because the community strings are listed in reverse here.

☒ **C** is incorrect because Read and Write are not community strings.

☒ **D** is incorrect because Default is not a community string in SNMP.

24. Nmap is a powerful scanning and enumeration tool. What does this nmap command attempt to accomplish?

    ```
    nmap -sA -T4 192.168.15.0/24
    ```

    A. A serial, slow operating system discovery scan of a Class C subnet

    B. A parallel, fast operating system discovery scan of a Class C subnet

    C. A serial, slow ACK scan of a Class C subnet

    D. A parallel, fast ACK scan of a Class C subnet

    ☑ **D.** You are going to need to know nmap switches well for your exam. In this example, the -A switch indicates an ACK scan (the only scan that returns no response on a closed port), and the -T4 switch indicates an "aggressive" scan, which runs fast and in parallel.

    ☒ **A** is incorrect because a slow, serial scan would use the -T, -T0, or -T! switch. Additionally, the OS detection switch is -O, not -A.

    ☒ **B** is incorrect because although this answer got the speed of the scan correct, the operating system detection portion is off.

    ☒ **C** is incorrect because although this answer correctly identified the ACK scan switch, the -T4 switch was incorrectly identified.

25. You are examining a packet capture of all traffic from a host on the subnet. The host sends a segment with the SYN flag set in order to set up a TCP communications channel. The destination port is 80, and the sequence number is set to 10. Which of the following statements are *not* true regarding this communications channel? (Choose all that apply.)

    A. The host will be attempting to retrieve an HTML file.

    B. The source port field on this packet can be any number between 1024 and 65535.

    C. The first packet from the destination in response to this host will have the SYN and ACK flags set.

    D. The packet returned in answer to this SYN request will acknowledge the sequence number by returning "10."

    ☑ **A, D.** Yes, it is true that port 80 traffic is generally HTTP; however, there are two problems with this statement. The first is all that is happening here is an arbitrary connection to something on port 80. For all we know, it's a listener, Telnet connection, or anything at all. Second, assuming it's actually an HTTP server, the sequence described here would do nothing but make a connection—not necessarily transfer anything. Sure, this is picky, but it's the truth. Next, sequence numbers are acknowledged between systems during the three-way handshake by incrementing by 1. In this example, the source sent an opening sequence number of 10 to the recipient. The recipient, in crafting the SYN/ACK response, will first acknowledge the opening sequence number by incrementing it to 11. After this, it will add its own sequence number to the packet (a random number it will pick) and send both off.

☒ **B** is incorrect because it's a true statement. Source port fields are dynamically assigned using anything other than the "well-known" port range (0–1023). IANA has defined the following port number ranges: ports 1024 to 49151 are the registered ports (assigned by IANA for specific service upon application by a requesting entity), and ports 49152 to 65535 are dynamic or private ports that cannot be registered with IANA.

☒ **C** is incorrect because it's a true statement. The requesting machine has sent the first packet in the three-way handshake exchange—a SYN packet. The recipient will respond with a SYN/ACK and wait patiently for the last step—the ACK packet.

26. Which TCP flag instructs the recipient to ignore buffering constraints and immediately send all data?

   A. URG

   B. PSH

   C. RST

   D. BUF

   ☑ **B.** This answer normally gets mixed up with the URG flag because we all read it as urgent. However, just remember the key word with PSH is "buffering." In TCP, buffering is used to maintain a steady, harmonious flow of traffic. Every so often, though, the buffer itself becomes a problem, slowing things down. A PSH flag tells the recipient stack that the data should be pushed up to the receiving application immediately.

   ☒ **A** is incorrect because the URG flag is used to inform the receiving stack that certain data within a segment is urgent and should be prioritized. As an aside, URG isn't used much by modern protocols.

   ☒ **C** is incorrect because the RST flag forces a termination of communications (in both directions).

   ☒ **D** is incorrect because BUF isn't a TCP flag at all.

27. You receive a RST-ACK from a port during a SYN scan. What is the state of the port?

   A. Open

   B. Closed

   C. Filtered

   D. Unknown

☑ **B.** Remember, a SYN scan occurs when you send a SYN packet to all open ports. If the port is open, you'll obviously get a SYN/ACK back. However, if the port is closed, you'll get a RST-ACK.

☒ **A** is incorrect because an open port would respond differently (SYN/ACK).

☒ **C** is incorrect because a filtered port would likely not respond at all. (The firewall wouldn't allow the packet through, so no response would be generated.)

☒ **D** is incorrect because you know exactly what state the port is in because of the RST-ACK response.

Sniffing and Evasion

This chapter includes questions from the following topics:

- Describe sniffing concepts, including active and passive sniffing and protocols susceptible to sniffing
- Describe ethical hacking techniques for Layer 2 traffic
- Describe sniffing tools and understand their output
- Describe sniffing countermeasures
- Learn about intrusion detection system (IDS), firewall, and honeypot types, use, and placement
- Describe signature analysis within Snort
- Describe IDS, firewall, and honeypot evasion techniques

Overhearing a conversation, whether intentionally or via eavesdropping, is just part of our daily lives. Sometimes we sniff conversations without even meaning or trying to—it just happens. Anyone who has worked in a cube-farm office environment knows how easy it is to overhear conversations even when we don't want to. Or, if you have kids in your house who don't yet understand that sound travels, eavesdropping is a constant part of your day.

Sometimes our very nature makes it impossible not to listen in. A study in *Psychological Science* explored a "paradox of eavesdropping": it's harder to *not* listen to a conversation when someone is talking on the phone (we hear only one side of the dialogue) than when two physically present people are talking to each other. Although the phone conversation contains much less information, we're much more curious about what's being said. That means we're hardwired to want to listen in. We can't help it.

But come on, admit it—you enjoy it sometimes too. Overhearing a juicy piece of information just makes us happy and, for the gossip crowd, provides lots of ammunition for the next water-cooler session. And we all really like secrets. In fact, I think the thrill of learning and knowing a secret is matched only by the overwhelming desire to share it. For those working in the classified arena, this paradox of human nature is something that has to be guarded against every single day of their working lives.

Eavesdropping in the virtual world is almost always not accidental—there's purpose involved. You don't necessarily need to put a whole lot of effort into it, but it almost never happens on its own without your purposeful manipulation of something. Sniffing provides all sorts of information to the ethical hacker and is a skill all should be intimately familiar with. Just know that the secrets you overhear on your job as a pen tester might be really exciting, and you might *really* want to tell *somebody* about them, but you may find yourself *really* in jail over it too.

 STUDY TIPS   The good news is, there hasn't been very much updated from the last version regarding sniffing and evasion—so any study you'd put in previously will still apply. The bad news is, it's still tough stuff, and sometimes picky questioning. Just as with the previous chapter, review your basic network knowledge thoroughly. You'll see lots of questions designed to test your knowledge on how networking devices handle traffic, how addressing affects packet flow, what layers sniffing concentrates in (Layers 2 and 3), and which protocols are susceptible to sniffing.

Additionally, learn Wireshark *very* well. Pay particular attention to filters within Wireshark—how to set them up and what syntax they follow—and how to read a capture (not to mention the "follow TCP stream" option). If you haven't already, download Wireshark and start playing with it—right now, before you even read the questions that follow. On any exam questions that show a Wireshark screen capture, pay close attention to the flags set in the segment, the source and destination addresses, and the protocols listed. These items are easy to pick out for almost anyone who can spell and will answer 99 percent of the questions you'll see.

IDS types and ways to get around them won't make up a gigantic portion of your test, but they'll definitely be there. These will most likely come in the form of scenario questions, as opposed to straight definitions. While ECC loves fragmentation, session splicing (with something like Whisker), and tunneling (HTTP or even TCP over DNS), just remember there are other ways to get around an IDS, including generating "cover fire" (that is, tons of false positives) and, of course, the ultimate in evasion—encryption. If the traffic is encrypted, the IDS sees nothing.

Snort is another tool you'll need to know well. You won't see a ton of SNORT questions, but those you do see will probably revolve around configuring rules and reading output from a Snort capture/alert. When it comes to those captures, by the way, oftentimes you can peruse an answer just by pulling out port numbers and such, so don't panic when you see them.

Lastly, don't forget your firewall types—you won't see many questions on identifying a definition, but you'll probably see at least a couple of scenario questions where this knowledge comes in handy—in particular, how stateful firewalls work and what they do.

1. Given the following Wireshark filter, what is the attacker attempting to view?

```
((tcp.flags == 0x02) || (tcp.flags == 0x12) ) ||
((tcp.flags == 0x10) && (tcp.ack==1) && (tcp.len==0) )
```

   A. SYN, SYN/ACK, ACK

   B. SYN, FIN, URG, and PSH

   C. ACK, ACK, SYN, URG

   D. SYN/ACK only

2. A target machine (with a MAC of 12:34:56:AB:CD:EF) is connected to a switch port. An attacker (with a MAC of 78:91:00:ED:BC:A1) is attached to a separate port on the same switch with a packet capture running. There is no spanning of ports or port security in place. Two packets leave the target machine. Message 1 has a destination MAC of E1:22:BA:87:AC:12. Message 2 has a destination MAC of FF:FF:FF:FF:FF:FF. Which of the following statements is true regarding the messages being sent?

   A. The attacker will see message 1.

   B. The attacker will see message 2.

   C. The attacker will see both messages.

   D. The attacker will see neither message.

3. You have successfully tapped into a network subnet of your target organization. You begin an attack by learning all significant MAC addresses on the subnet. After some time, you decide to intercept messages between two hosts. You begin by sending broadcast messages to Host A showing your MAC address as belonging to Host B. Simultaneously, you send messages to Host B showing your MAC address as belonging to Host A. What is being accomplished here?

   A. ARP poisoning to allow you to see all messages from either host without interrupting their communications process

   B. ARP poisoning to allow you to see messages from Host A to Host B

   C. ARP poisoning to allow you to see messages from Host B to Host A

   D. ARP poisoning to allow you to see messages from Host A destined to any address

   E. ARP poisoning to allow you to see messages from Host B destined to any address

4. Your target subnet is protected by a firewalled DMZ. Reconnaissance shows the external firewall passes some traffic from external to internal, but blocks most communications. HTTP traffic to a web server in the DMZ, which answers to www.somebiz.com, is allowed, along with standard traffic such as DNS queries. Which of the following may provide a method to evade the firewall's protection?

   A. An ACK scan

   B. Firewalking

   C. False positive flooding

   D. TCP over DNS

5. Which of the following is the best choice in setting an NIDS tap?

    A. Connect directly to a server inside the DMZ.

    B. Connect directly to a server in the intranet.

    C. Connect to a SPAN port on a switch.

    D. Connect to the console port of a router.

6. You have a large packet capture file in Wireshark to review. You want to filter traffic to show all packets with an IP address of 192.168.22.5 that contain the string HR_admin. Which of the following filters would accomplish this task?

    A. ip.addr==192.168.22.5 &&tcp contains HR_admin

    B. ip.addr 192.168.22.5 && "HR_admin"

    C. ip.addr 192.168.22.5 &&tcp string ==HR_admin

    D. ip.addr==192.168.22.5 + tcp contains tide

7. Which of the following techniques can be used to gather information from a fully switched network or to disable some of the traffic isolation features of a switch? (Choose two.)

    A. DHCP starvation

    B. MAC flooding

    C. Promiscuous mode

    D. ARP spoofing

8. Which of the following is true regarding the discovery of sniffers on a network?

    A. To discover the sniffer, ping all addresses and examine latency in responses.

    B. To discover the sniffer, send ARP messages to all systems and watch for NOARP responses.

    C. To discover the sniffer, configure the IDS to watch for NICs in promiscuous mode.

    D. It is almost impossible to discover the sniffer on the network.

9. Which of the following could provide useful defense against ARP spoofing? (Choose all that apply.)

    A. Use ARPWALL.

    B. Set all NICs to promiscuous mode.

    C. Use private VLANs.

    D. Use static ARP entries.

10. Examine the following Snort rule:

```
alerttcp !$HOME_NET any -> $HOME_NET 23 (content:
"admin";msg:"Telnet attempt..admin access";)
```

Which of the following are true regarding the rule? (Choose all that apply.)

    A. This rule will alert on packets coming from the designated home network.

    B. This rule will alert on packets coming from outside the designated home address.

C. This rule will alert on packets designated for any port, from port 23, containing the "admin" string.

D. This rule will alert on packets designated on port 23, from any port, containing the "admin" string.

11. You want to begin sniffing, and you have a Windows 7 laptop. You download and install Wireshark but quickly discover your NIC needs to be in "promiscuous mode." What allows you to put your NIC into promiscuous mode?

   A. Installing lmpcap

   B. Installing npcap

   C. Installing WinPcap

   D. Installing libPcap

   E. Manipulating the NIC properties through Control Panel | Network and Internet | Change Adapter Settings

12. A network and security administrator installs an NIDS. After a few weeks, a successful intrusion into the network occurs and a check of the NIDS during the timeframe of the attack shows no alerts. An investigation shows the NIDS was not configured correctly and therefore did not trigger on what should have been attack alert signatures. Which of the following best describes the actions of the NIDS?

   A. False positives

   B. False negatives

   C. True positives

   D. True negatives

13. A pen test member has gained access to an open switch port. He configures his NIC for promiscuous mode and sets up a sniffer, plugging his laptop directly into the switch port. He watches traffic as it arrives at the system, looking for specific information to possibly use later. What type of sniffing is being practiced?

   A. Active

   B. Promiscuous

   C. Blind

   D. Passive

   E. Session

14. Which of the following are the best preventive measures to take against DHCP starvation attacks? (Choose two.)

   A. Block all UDP port 67 and 68 traffic.

   B. Enable DHCP snooping on the switch.

   C. Use port security on the switch.

   D. Configure DHCP filters on the switch.

15. What does this line from the Snort configuration file indicate?

```
var RULE_PATH c:\etc\snort\rules
```

    A. The configuration variable is not in the proper syntax.

    B. It instructs the Snort engine to write rule violations in this location.

    C. It instructs the Snort engine to compare packets to the rule set named "rules."

    D. It defines the location of the Snort rules.

16. Which of the following tools is the best choice to assist in evading an IDS?

    A. Nessus

    B. Nikto

    C. Libwhisker

    D. Snort

17. Examine the Snort output shown here:

```
08/28-12:23:13.014491 01:10:BB:17:E3:C5 ->A5:12:B7:55:57:AB type:0x800 len:0x3C
190.168.5.12:33541 ->213.132.44.56:23 TCP TTL:128 TOS:0x0 ID:12365

IpLen:20 DgmLen:48 DF
***A**S* Seq: 0xA153BD Ack: 0xA01657 Win: 0x2000 TcpLen: 28
TCP Options (4) => MSS: 1460 NOP NOPSackOK
0x0000: 00 02 B3 87 84 25 00 10 5A 01 0D 5B 08 00 45 00  .%..Z..[..E.
0x0010: 00 30 98 43 40 00 80 06 DE EC C0 A8 01 04 C0 A8  .0.C@...
0x0020: 01 43 04 DC 01 BB 00 A1 8B BD 00 00 00 00 70 02  .C....p.
0x0030: 20 00 4C 92 00 00 02 04 05 B4 01 01 04 02        .L.....
```

Which of the following is true regarding the packet capture?

    A. The capture indicates a NOP sled attack.

    B. The capture shows step 2 of a TCP handshake.

    C. The packet source is 213.132.44.56.

    D. The packet capture shows an SSH session attempt.

18. Your IDS sits on the network perimeter and has been analyzing traffic for a couple of weeks. On arrival one morning, you find the IDS has alerted on a spike in network traffic late the previous evening. Which type of IDS are you using?

    A. Stateful

    B. Snort

    C. Passive

    D. Signature based

    E. Anomaly based

19. You are performing an ACK scan against a target subnet. You previously verified connectivity to several hosts within the subnet but want to verify all live hosts on the subnet. Your scan, however, is not receiving any replies. Which type of firewall is most likely in use at your location?

    A. Packet filtering

    B. IPS

    C. Stateful

    D. Active

20. You are separated from your target subnet by a firewall. The firewall is correctly configured and allows requests only to ports opened by the administrator. In firewalking the device, you find that port 80 is open. Which technique could you employ to send data and commands to or from the target system?

    A. Encrypt the data to hide it from the firewall.

    B. Use session splicing.

    C. Use MAC flooding.

    D. Use HTTP tunneling.

21. Which of the following tools can be used to extract application layer data from TCP connections captured in a log file into separate files?

    A. Snort

    B. Netcat

    C. TCPflow

    D. Tcpdump

22. Examine the Wireshark filter shown here:

    ```
    ip.src == 192.168.1.1 &&tcp.srcport == 80
    ```

    Which of the following correctly describes the capture filter?

    A. The results will display all traffic from 192.168.1.1 destined for port 80.

    B. The results will display all HTTP traffic to 192.168.1.1.

    C. The results will display all HTTP traffic from 192.168.1.1.

    D. No results will display because of invalid syntax.

23. You need to put the NIC into listening mode on your Linux box, capture packets, and write the results to a log file named my.log. How do you accomplish this with tcpdump?

    A. tcpdump -i eth0 -w my.log

    B. tcpdump -l eth0 -c my.log

    C. tcpdump /i eth0 /w my.log

    D. tcpdump /l eth0 /c my.log

24. Which of the following tools can assist with IDS evasion? (Choose all that apply.)

    A. Whisker

    B. Fragroute

    C. Capsa

    D. Wireshark

    E. ADMmutate

    F. Inundator

25. Which command puts Snort into packet logger mode?

    A. ./snort -dev -l ./log

    B. ./snort –v

    C. ./snort -dev -l ./log -h 192.168.1.0/24 -c snort.conf

    D. None of the above

26. A security administrator is attempting to "lock down" her network and blocks access from internal to external on all external firewall ports except for TCP 80 and TCP 443. An internal user wants to make use of other protocols to access services on remote systems (FTP, as well as some nonstandard port numbers). Which of the following is the most likely choice the user could attempt to communicate with the remote systems over the protocol of her choice?

    A. Use HTTP tunneling.

    B. Send all traffic over UDP instead of TCP.

    C. Crack the firewall and open the ports required for communication.

    D. MAC flood the switch connected to the firewall.

1. A
2. B
3. B
4. D
5. C
6. A
7. B, D
8. D
9. A, C, D

10. B, D
11. C
12. B
13. D
14. B, C
15. D
16. C
17. B
18. E

19. C
20. D
21. C
22. C
23. A
24. A, B, E, F
25. A
26. A

1. Given the following Wireshark filter, what is the attacker attempting to view?

```
((tcp.flags == 0x02) || (tcp.flags == 0x18) ) ||
((tcp.flags == 0x16) && (tcp.ack==1) && (tcp.len==0) )
```

A. SYN, SYN/ACK, ACK

B. SYN, FIN, URG, and PSH

C. ACK, ACK, SYN, URG

D. SYN/ACK only

☑ **A.** You'll see bunches of Wireshark questions on your exam—it's probably the subject EC-Council loves the most regarding this chapter—and syntax will be the key to answering all of them. For this particular question subject, remember Wireshark has the ability to filter based on a decimal numbering system assigned to TCP flags. The assigned flag decimal numbers are FIN = 1, SYN = 2, RST = 4, PSH = 8, ACK = 16, and URG = 32. Adding these numbers together (for example, SYN + ACK = 18) allows you to simplify a Wireshark filter. For example, **tcp.flags == 0x2** looks for SYN packets, **tcp.flags == 0x16** looks for ACK packets, and **tcp.flags == 0x18** looks for both (the attacker here will see all SYN packets, all SYN/ACK packets, and all ACK packets). In this example, the decimal numbers were used, just not in a simplified manner.

As far as the rest of Wireshark filtering syntax goes, there are a couple key points to remember. First, be sure to remember it uses double "equals" signs (==) in the expression (**ip.addr = 10.10.10.0/24** won't work, but **ip addr == 10.10.10.0/24** will). Next, know the difference between the definitions for "and" and "or." An "and" in the filter means both expressions will be queried and displayed, but only if *both* are true. (In other words, "show me all packets containing this source address and headed toward this destination IP. If it's from this source but going somewhere else, ignore it. If it's headed to this destination but is not from this source, ignore it.") An "or" in the filter means *either* of the expressions can be true (that is, "show me all packets containing this source address *and* any packets going to this destination IP, no matter the destination or source address, respectively, for the two").

☒ **B, C,** and **D** are incorrect because these do not match the decimals provided in the capture (2 for SYN, 18 for SYN/ACK, and 16 for ACK).

2. A target machine (with a MAC of 12:34:56:AB:CD:EF) is connected to a switch port. An attacker (with a MAC of 78:91:00:ED:BC:A1) is attached to a separate port on the same switch with a packet capture running. There is no spanning of ports or port security in place. Two packets leave the target machine. Message 1 has a destination MAC of E1:22:BA:87:AC:12. Message 2 has a destination MAC of FF:FF:FF:FF:FF:FF. Which of the following statements is true regarding the messages being sent?

A. The attacker will see message 1.

B. The attacker will see message 2.

C. The attacker will see both messages.

D. The attacker will see neither message.

☑ **B.** *This question is all about how a switch works*, with a little MAC knowledge thrown in. Remember that switches are designed to filter unicast messages but to flood multicast and broadcast messages (filtering goes to only one port, whereas flooding sends to all). Broadcast MAC addresses in the frame are easy to spot—they're always all *F*s, indicating all 48 bits turned on in the address. In this case, message 1 is a unicast address and went off to its destination, whereas message 2 is clearly a broadcast message, which the switch will gladly flood to all ports, including the attacker's.

Other versions of this same question will center on the efforts an attacker can use to see that packet. Should the attacker desire to see all messages, a MAC flood could turn the switch into a hub, effectively flooding all packets to all ports. Another option is to span a port (break into the configuration of the switch and tell it to send all traffic destined for a specific port to that port *and* to the attacker's). Lastly, *port stealing* (a new and totally fun memorization term from EC-Council) allows an attacker to take advantage of the "race condition" (where the switch is constantly updating MAC address bindings for ports) during a MAC flood attempt to effectively steal a port and sniff all traffic aimed for the target machine.

☒ **A** is incorrect because the unicast destination MAC does not match the attacker's machine. When the frame is read by the switch and compared to the internal address list (CAM table), it will be filtered and sent to the appropriate destination port.

☒ **C** is incorrect because the switch will not flood both messages to the attacker's port—it floods only broadcast and multicast.

☒ **D** is incorrect because the broadcast address will definitely be seen by the attacker.

3. You have successfully tapped into a network subnet of your target organization. You begin an attack by learning all significant MAC addresses on the subnet. After some time, you decide to intercept messages between two hosts. You send broadcast messages to Host A showing your MAC address as belonging to Host B. What is being accomplished here?

A. ARP poisoning to allow you to see all messages from either host without interrupting their communications process

B. ARP poisoning to allow you to see messages from Host A to Host B

C. ARP poisoning to allow you to see messages from Host B to Host A

D. ARP poisoning to allow you to see messages from Host A destined to any address

E. ARP poisoning to allow you to see messages from Host B destined to any address

☑ **B.** ARP poisoning is a relatively simple way to place yourself as the "man in the middle" and spy on traffic (by the way, be careful with the term *man in the middle* because it usually refers to a position where you are not interrupting traffic).

The ARP cache is updated whenever your machine does a name lookup or when ARP (a broadcast protocol) receives an unsolicited message advertising a MAC-to-IP match. In this example, you've told Host A that you hold the MAC address for Host B. Host A will update its cache, and when a message is being crafted by the OS, it will happily put the spoofed address in its place. Just remember that ARP poisoning is oftentimes noisy and may be easy to discover if port security is enabled: the port will lock (or *amber* in nerd terminology) when an incorrect MAC tries to use it or when multiple broadcasts claiming different MACs are seen. Additionally, watch out for denial-of-service side effects of attempting ARP poisoning—you may well bring down a target without even trying to, not to mention Host B is eventually going to find out it's not receiving anything from Host A. As a side note, detection of ARP poisoning can be done with a tool called xARP (http://www.chrismc.de).

☒ **A** is incorrect for a couple reasons. First, you won't receive messages from each host addressed to anywhere in the world—you'll only receive messages addressed from Host A to Host B. Second, the communications flow between the two hosts will be affected by this. As a matter of fact, Host A can never talk to Host B: the ARP poisoning has all messages going to you, the hacker.

☒ **C** is incorrect because you didn't poison Host B's cache—Host A was the target.

☒ **D** is incorrect because you didn't poison Host A's mapping to the default gateway or anything like that—you will only receive messages intended for Host B.

☒ **E** is incorrect because you did not poison Host B at all.

4. Your target subnet is protected by a firewalled DMZ. Reconnaissance shows the external firewall passes some traffic from external to internal, but blocks most communications. HTTP traffic to a web server in the DMZ, which answers to www.somebiz.com, is allowed, along with standard traffic such as DNS queries. Which of the following may provide a method to evade the firewall's protection?

   A. An ACK scan

   B. Firewalking

   C. False positive flooding

   D. TCP over DNS

   ☑ **D.** Of the choices provided, TCP over DNS is the only one that makes any sense. TCP over DNS is exactly what it sounds like—sending TCP traffic that would otherwise use a different port number in packets using port 53. Because the firewall usually allows DNS requests to pass, hiding traffic under port 53 is convenient and fairly easy. The whole thing does require a special DNS server and DNS client setup, but it's really not rocket science. While TCP over DNS *will* allow you to evade the firewall and send traffic internally, it will *not* provide you instant access to machines or anything like that—it simply allows you to send traffic unnoticed through a firewall.

TCP over DNS tools include Iodine (http://code.kryo.se/iodine/), DNS Tunnel (http://dnstunnel.de), and Netcross (https://**sourceforge**.net/projects/**netcross**).

Another very common option for passing traffic through a firewall is HTTP tunneling. The same principle applies, except in HTTP tunneling you abuse port 80 instead of port 53. HTTP tunneling tools include HTTPort (http://www.targeted.org), SuperNetwork Tunnel (http://www.networktunnel.net), and HTTP-Tunnel (http://www.http-tunnel.com).

☒ **A** is incorrect because an ACK scan does nothing to hide traffic or evade the firewall. The scan itself would be loud and noisy, and would not affect the firewall at all.

☒ **B** is incorrect because firewalking is a great technique to discover which ports are open (that is, which ports the firewall is allowing to pass) and which are closed. However, it does nothing to hide traffic or evade any suspicion.

☒ **C** is incorrect because while false positive flooding does provide good "cover fire" for an attacker in an IDS, it does nothing to affect the firewall in any way—traffic to other ports will be blocked because that's just what a firewall does.

5. Which of the following is the best choice in setting an NIDS tap?

   A. Connect directly to a server inside the DMZ.

   B. Connect directly to a server in the intranet.

   C. Connect to a SPAN port on a switch.

   D. Connect to the console port of a router.

☑ **C.** A network intrusion detection system (NIDS) only works well if it can see all the network traffic, and placement obviously makes a huge difference. One common implementation is to connect via a SPAN (Switched Port Analyzer) port on a switch. The configuration for a SPAN port ensures all traffic from a defined range of ports is also sent to the SPAN port. This makes the best option for your NIDS tap, at least as far as this question goes: in the real world, you would most likely set up a passive tap, positioned in the correct location to see everything coming across the wire.

☒ **A** is incorrect because connecting directly to a single server would give you only the traffic sent to that server (or that server's subnet, provided the server is watching promiscuously and is configured appropriately). In this case, the DMZ's traffic is all you'd see.

☒ **B** is incorrect because connection directly to a single server would give you only the traffic sent to that server (or that server's subnet, provided the server is watching promiscuously and is configured appropriately). In this case, the intranet's traffic is all you'd see.

☒ **D** is incorrect because connection to the console port on a router would provide access to no traffic at all. The console port on the router is used specifically for configuration and management of the router.

6. You have a large packet capture file in Wireshark to review. You want to filter traffic to show all packets with an IP address of 192.168.22.5 that contain the string HR_admin. Which of the following filters would accomplish this task?

   A. ip.addr==192.168.22.5 &&tcp contains HR_admin

   B. ip.addr 192.168.22.5 && "HR_admin"

   C. ip.addr 192.168.22.5 &&tcp string ==HR_admin

   D. ip.addr==192.168.22.5 + tcp contains tide

   ☑ **A.** This is a perfect example of a typical Wireshark question on your exam regarding syntax. Answer A is the only one that sticks to Wireshark filter syntax. Definitely know the ip.addr, ip.src, and ip.dst filters; the "tcp contains" filter is another favorite of test question writers. When you combine filters in one search, use the && designator, and don't forget the use of double equals signs. Another fun version of this same question involves reading the output from Wireshark. A tool that can help you out with the raw files—including output from other tools like tcpdump—is tcptrace (http://www.tcptrace.org/).

   ☒ **B, C,** and **D** are all incorrect because the syntax is wrong for Wireshark filters. As an aside, a great way to learn the syntax of these filters is to use the expression builder directly beside the filter entry box. It's self-explanatory and contains thousands of possible expression builds.

7. Which of the following techniques can be used to gather information from a fully switched network or to disable some of the traffic isolation features of a switch? (Choose two.)

   A. DHCP starvation

   B. MAC flooding

   C. Promiscuous mode

   D. ARP spoofing

   ☑ **B, D.** Switches filter all traffic—unless you tell them otherwise, make them behave differently, or the traffic is broadcast or multicast. If you can gain administrative access to the IOS, you can tell it to behave otherwise by configuring a span port (which sends copies of messages from all ports to yours). Legitimate span ports are designed for things such as network IDS. To make the switch behave differently (at least on older switches, because newer ones don't allow this much anymore), send more MAC addresses to the switch than it can handle. This fills the CAM and turns the switch, effectively, into a hub (sometimes called a *fail open* state). Using a tool such as MacOF or Yersinia, you can send thousands and thousands of fake MAC addresses to the switch's CAM table. ARP spoofing doesn't really involve the switch much at all—it continues to act and filter traffic just as it was designed to do. The only difference is you've lied to it by faking a MAC address on a connected port. The poor switch, believing those happy little ARP messages, will forward all packets destined for that MAC address to you instead of the intended recipient. How fun!

☒ **A** is incorrect because DHCP starvation is a form of a DoS attack, where the attacker "steals" all the available IP addresses from the DHCP server, which prevents legitimate users from connecting.

☒ **C** is incorrect because the term *promiscuous* applies to the way a NIC processes messages. Instead of tossing aside all messages that are not addressed specifically for the machine (or broadcast/multicast), promiscuous mode says, "Bring 'em all in so we can take a look at them using our handy sniffing application."

8. Which of the following is true regarding the discovery of sniffers on a network?

A. To discover the sniffer, ping all addresses and examine latency in responses.

B. To discover the sniffer, send ARP messages to all systems and watch for NOARP responses.

C. To discover the sniffer, configure the IDS to watch for NICs in promiscuous mode.

D. It is almost impossible to discover the sniffer on the network.

☑ **D.** This question is more about active versus passive sniffing than anything else. I'm not saying it's impossible, because almost nothing is, but discovering a passive sniffer on your network is very difficult. When a NIC is set to promiscuous mode, it just blindly accepts any packet coming by and sends it up the layers for further processing (which is what allows Wireshark and other sniffers to analyze the traffic). Because sniffers are sitting there pulling traffic and not sending anything in order to get it, they're difficult to detect. Active sniffing is another thing altogether. If a machine is ARP spoofing or MAC flooding in order to pull off sniffing, it's much easier to spot it.

☒ **A** is incorrect because the premise is absolutely silly. Thousands of things can affect latency in response to a ping, but running a sniffer on the box isn't necessarily one of them, nor an indicator of one being present.

☒ **B** is incorrect because NOARP is a Linux kernel module that filters and drops unwanted ARP requests. It's not a response packet we can discover sniffers with.

☒ **C** is incorrect because it's impossible to watch for NICs in promiscuous mode. The NIC is simply doing the same job every other NIC is doing—it's sitting there pulling traffic. The network IDS wouldn't know, or care, about it.

9. Which of the following could provide useful defense against ARP spoofing? (Choose all that apply.)

A. Use ARPWALL.

B. Set all NICs to promiscuous mode.

C. Use private VLANs.

D. Use static ARP entries.

☑ **A, C, D.** ARPWALL (http://sourceforge.net/projects/arpwall/) is an application available for download from SourceForge. It gives an early warning when an ARP attack occurs and simply blocks the connection. Virtual LANs (VLANs) provide a means to create multiple broadcast domains within a single network. Machines on the same switch are in different networks, and their traffic is isolated. Since ARP works on broadcast, this can help prevent large-scale ARP spoofing. Static ARP entries are a great idea and probably the only true way to fix all ARP poisoning, since no matter what is banging around out on the network, the system uses the static mapping you configured. An IDS may also be helpful in spotting ARP naughtiness starting but wouldn't necessarily do anything about it.

☒ **B** is incorrect because setting NICs to promiscuous mode wouldn't do a thing to prevent a broadcast message (ARP) from being received.

10. Examine the following Snort rule:

```
alerttcp !$HOME_NET any -> $HOME_NET 23 (content:
"admin";msg:"Telnet attempt..admin access";)
```

Which of the following are true regarding the rule? (Choose all that apply.)

A. This rule will alert on packets coming from the designated home network.

B. This rule will alert on packets coming from outside the designated home address.

C. This rule will alert on packets designated for any port, from port 23, containing the "admin" string.

D. This rule will alert on packets designated on port 23, from any port, containing the "admin" string.

☑ **B, D.** Snort rules, logs, entries, and configuration files will definitely be part of your exam. This particular rule takes into account a lot of things you'll see. First, note the exclamation mark (!) just before the HOME_NET variable. Any time you see this, it indicates the opposite of the following variable—in this case, any packet from an address *not* in the home network and using any source port number, intended for any address that is within the home network. Following that variable is a spot for a port number, and the word *any* indicates we don't care what the source port is. Next, we spell out the destination information: anything in the home network and destined for port 23. Lastly, we add one more little search before spelling out the message we want to receive: the "content" designator allows us to spell out strings we're looking for.

☒ **A** and **C** are incorrect because these statements are polar opposite to what the rule is stating.

11. You want to begin sniffing, and you have a Windows 7 laptop. You download and install Wireshark but quickly discover your NIC needs to be in "promiscuous mode." What allows you to put your NIC into promiscuous mode?

A. Installing lmpcap

B. Installing npcap

C. Installing WinPcap

D. Installing libPcap

E. Manipulating the NIC properties through Control Panel | Network and Internet | Change Adapter Settings

☑ **C.** To understand this, you have to know how a NIC is designed to work. The NIC "sees" lots of traffic but pulls in only the traffic it knows belongs to you. It does this by comparing the MAC address of each frame against its own: if they match, it pulls the frame in and works on it; if they don't match, the frame is ignored. If you plug a sniffer into a NIC that looks only at traffic designated for the machine you're on, you've kind of missed the point, wouldn't you say? Promiscuous mode tells the NIC to pull in *everything*. This allows you to see all those packets moving to and fro inside your collision domain. WinPcap is a library that allows NICs on Windows machines to operate in promiscuous mode.

☒ **A** is incorrect because lmpcap does not exist.

☒ **B** is incorrect because npcap does not exist.

☒ **D** is incorrect because libPcap is used on Linux machines for the same purpose—putting cards into promiscuous mode.

☒ **E** is incorrect because accessing the Change Adapter Setting window does not allow you to put the card into promiscuous mode—you still need WinPcap for this.

12. A network and security administrator installs an NIDS. After a few weeks, a successful intrusion into the network occurs and a check of the NIDS during the timeframe of the attack shows no alerts. An investigation shows the NIDS was not configured correctly and therefore did not trigger on what should have been attack alert signatures. Which of the following best describes the actions of the NIDS?

A. False positives

B. False negatives

C. True positives

D. True negatives

☑ **B.** When it comes to alerting systems, false negatives are much more concerning than false positives. A false negative occurs when there is traffic and circumstances in place for an attack signature, but the IDS does not trigger an alert. In other words, if your system is firing a lot of false negatives, the security staff may feel like they're secure when, in reality, they're really under successful attack. Keep in mind a false negative is different from your IDS simply not seeing the traffic. For example, if you tell your IDS to send an alert for Telnet traffic and it simply didn't see those packets (for whatever reason), that may be a false negative for exam purposes but in the real world is probably more of a configuration issue. A better example of a false negative in the real world would be for the attacker to encrypt a portion of payload so that the IDS doesn't recognize it as naughty. In other words, the IDS sees the traffic, it just doesn't recognize anything bad about it.

☒ **A** is incorrect because false positives occur when legitimate traffic is alerted on as if there were something wrong with it. Keeping false positives to a minimum is a concern when choosing and configuring IDS.

☒ **C** and **D** are incorrect because these are not legitimate terms.

13. A pen test member has gained access to an open switch port. He configures his NIC for promiscuous mode and sets up a sniffer, plugging his laptop directly into the switch port. He watches traffic as it arrives at the system, looking for specific information to possibly use later. What type of sniffing is being practiced?

    A. Active

    B. Promiscuous

    C. Blind

    D. Passive

    E. Session

    ☑ **D.** This is one of those weird CEH definitions that drive us all crazy on the exam. Knowing the definition of *passive* versus *active* isn't really going to make you a better pen tester, but it may save you a question on the test. When it comes to sniffing, if you are not injecting packets into the stream, it's a passive exercise. Tools such as Wireshark are passive in nature. A tool such as Ettercap, though, has built-in features to trick switches into sending all traffic their way, and all sorts of other sniffing hilarity. This type of sniffing, where you use packet interjection to force a response, is active in nature. As a quick aside here for you real-world preppers out there, true passive sniffing with a laptop is pretty difficult to pull off. As soon as you attach a Windows machine, it'll start broadcasting all kinds of stuff (ARP and so on) which is, technically, putting packets on the wire. The real point is that passive sniffing is a mindset where you are not *intentionally* putting packets on a wire.

    ☒ **A** is incorrect because in the example given, no packet injection is being performed. The pen tester is simply hooking up a sniffer and watching what comes by. The only way this can be more passive is if he has a hammock nearby.

    ☒ **B** is incorrect because the term *promiscuous* is not a sniffing type. Instead, it refers to the NIC's ability to pull in frames that are not addressed specifically for it.

    ☒ **C** is incorrect because the term *blind* is not a sniffing type. This is included as a distractor.

    ☒ **E** is incorrect because the term *session* is not a sniffing type. This is included as a distractor.

14. Which of the following are the best preventive measures to take against DHCP starvation attacks? (Choose two.)

    A. Block all UDP port 67 and 68 traffic.

    B. Enable DHCP snooping on the switch.

C. Use port security on the switch.

D. Configure DHCP filters on the switch.

☑ **B, C.** DHCP starvation is a denial-of-service attack EC-Council somehow slipped into the sniffing section. The attack is pretty straightforward: the attacker requests all available DHCP addresses from the server, so legitimate users cannot pull an address and connect or communicate with the network subnet. DHCP snooping on a Cisco switch (using the **ip dhcp snooping** command) creates a whitelist of machines that are allowed to pull a DHCP address. Anything attempting otherwise can be filtered. Port security, while not necessarily directly related to the attack, can be a means of defense as well. By limiting the number of MACs associated with a port, as well as whitelisting which specific MACs can address it, you could certainly reduce an attacker's ability to drain all DHCP addresses.

As a side note, you may also see a question relating to how DHCP works in the first place. An easy way to remember it all is the acronym DORA: Discover, Offer, Request, and Acknowledge. Additionally, packets in DHCPv6 have different names than those of DHCPv4. DHCPDISCOVER, DHCPOFFER, DHCPREQUEST, and DHCPACK are known as Solicit, Advertise, Request (or Confirm/Renew), and Reply, respectively.

☒ **A** is incorrect because blocking all UDP 67 and 68 traffic would render the entire DHCP system moot because no one could pull an address.

☒ **D** is incorrect because DHCP filtering is done on the server and not the switch. DHCP filtering involves configuring the whitelist on the server itself.

15. What does this line from the Snort configuration file indicate?

```
var RULE_PATH c:\etc\snort\rules
```

A. The configuration variable is not in proper syntax.

B. It instructs the Snort engine to write rule violations in this location.

C. It instructs the Snort engine to compare packets to the rule set named "rules."

D. It defines the location of the Snort rules.

☑ **D.** The **var RULE_PATH** entry in the config file defines the path to the rules for the IDS—in this case, they will be located in C:\etc\snort\rules. The rules container will hold tons of rule sets, with each available for you to "turn on." If you were configuring Snort to watch for fantasy football traffic, for example, you would tell it to look for all the rules in this container and then turn on the rule set you defined for fantasy football connection attempts.

While this question is aimed at the config file itself, another fun thing you'll see regarding Snort deals the rules themselves. You may need to remember that Snort evaluates rules in Pass, Drop, Alert, and then Log order, by default.

☒ **A** is incorrect because this configuration line is in proper syntax.

☒ **B** is incorrect because this variable is not designed for that purpose. The rule violations will be written to a log file that you designate when starting the Snort engine. For example, the command

```
snort -l c:\snort\log\ -c c:\snort\etc\snort.conf
```

starts Snort and has the log file located at c:\snort\log.

☒ **C** is incorrect because the "include" variable is the one used for this purpose. Within this same configuration file, for example, you may have a rule set named fantasy.rules. To get Snort to alert on these rules, you point the configuration files to where all the rules are (accomplished by the variable RULE_PATH) and then you tell it which of the rule sets to bring into play:

```
include $RULE_PATH/fantasy.rules
```

16. Which of the following tools is the best choice to assist in evading an IDS?

   A. Nessus

   B. Nikto

   C. Libwhisker

   D. Snort

   ☑ **C.** It's a hallmark of EC-Council certification exams to have a few off-the-wall, tool-specific questions, and this is a great example. Libwhisker (https://sourceforge.net/projects/whisker/) is a full-featured Perl library used for all sorts of things, including HTTP-related functions, vulnerability scanning, exploitation, and IDS evasion. In fact, some scanners actually use libwhisker for session splicing in order to scan without being seen.

   ☒ **A** is incorrect because Nessus is a vulnerability scanner and, on its own, is not designed to evade IDS detection.

   ☒ **B** is incorrect because Nikto, like Nessus, is a vulnerability scanner and, on its own, is not designed to evade IDS detection.

   ☒ **D** is incorrect because Snort is an IDS itself. Snort is also a perfectly acceptable sniffer.

17. Examine the Snort output shown here:

```
08/28-12:23:13.014491 01:10:BB:17:E3:C5 ->A5:12:B7:55:57:AB type:0x800 len:0x3C
190.168.5.12:33541 ->213.132.44.56:23 TCP TTL:128 TOS:0x0 ID:12365

IpLen:20 DgmLen:48 DF
***A**S* Seq: 0xA153BD Ack: 0xA01657 Win: 0x2000 TcpLen: 28
TCP Options (4) => MSS: 1460 NOP NOPSackOK
0x0000: 00 02 B3 87 84 25 00 10 5A 01 0D 5B 08 00 45 00  .%..Z..[..E.
0x0010: 00 30 98 43 40 00 80 06 DE EC C0 A8 01 04 C0 A8  .0.C@...
0x0020: 01 43 04 DC 01 BB 00 A1 8B BD 00 00 00 00 70 02  .C....p.
0x0030: 20 00 4C 92 00 00 02 04 05 B4 01 01 04 02        .L.....
```

Which of the following is true regarding the packet capture?

A. The capture indicates a NOP sled attack.

B. The capture shows step 2 of a TCP handshake.

C. The packet source is 213.132.44.56.

D. The packet capture shows an SSH session attempt.

☑ **B.** You'll probably see at least one or two Snort capture logs on the exam, and most of them are just this easy. If you examine the capture log, it shows a TCP port 23 packet from 190.168.5.12 headed toward 213.132.44.56. The TCP flags are clearly shown in line 5 as ***A**S*, indicating the SYN and ACK flags are set. Because the three-way handshake is SYN, SYN/ACK, and ACK—*voilà!*—we've solved another one!

☒ **A** is incorrect because this is a single packet that is not attempting a NOP sled in any shape or form.

☒ **C** is incorrect because this answer has it in reverse—the source is 190.168.5.12.

☒ **D** is incorrect because the port number shown in the capture is 23 (Telnet), not 22 (SSH).

18. Your IDS sits on the network perimeter and has been analyzing traffic for a couple of weeks. On arrival one morning, you find the IDS has alerted on a spike in network traffic late the previous evening. Which type of IDS are you using?

A. Stateful

B. Snort

C. Passive

D. Signature based

E. Anomaly based

☑ **E.** The scenario described here is precisely what an anomaly- or behavior-based system is designed for. The system watches traffic and, over time, develops an idea of what "normal" traffic looks like—everything from source and destinations, ports in use, and times of higher data flows. In one sense, it's better than a plain signature-based system because it can find things heuristically based on behavior; however, anomaly-based systems are notorious for the number of false positives they spin off—especially early on.

☒ **A** is incorrect because *stateful* refers to a firewall type, not an IDS.

☒ **B** is incorrect because Snort is a signature-based IDS.

☒ **C** is incorrect because the term *passive* isn't associated with IDS. Now, an IDS *can* react to an alert by taking action to stop or prevent an attack, but this is referred to as an *intrusion prevention system (IPS)*, not active or passive.

☒ **D** is incorrect because a signature-based IDS isn't going to care about the amount of traffic going by, or what time it occurs. A signature-based IDS simply compares each packet against a list (signature file) you configure it to look at. If nothing matches in the signature file, then no action is taken.

19. You are performing an ACK scan against a target subnet. You previously verified connectivity to several hosts within the subnet but want to verify all live hosts on the subnet. Your scan, however, is not receiving any replies. Which type of firewall is most likely in use at your location?

   A. Packet filtering

   B. IPS

   C. Stateful

   D. Active

   ☑ **C.** Most people think of a firewall as a simple packet filter, examining packets as they are coming in against an access list—if the port is allowed, let the packet through. However, the stateful inspection firewall has the ability to examine the session details regarding the packet and make a determination on its state. For a common (dare I say, textbook) example, if a stateful firewall receives an ACK packet, it's smart enough to know whether there is an associated SYN packet that originated from inside the network to go along with it. If there isn't not—that is, if communications did not start from inside the subnet—it'll drop the packet.

   ☒ **A** is incorrect because a packet-filtering firewall wouldn't bother with the flags. It would be concerned about what port the packet was headed to. If, for instance, you host a web page out of that subnet but not an FTP server, your firewall should be set up to allow port 80 in but not port 21.

   ☒ **B** is incorrect because an intrusion prevention system (IPS) isn't a firewall at all. It's a network-monitoring solution that has the capability of recognizing malicious traffic and taking action to prevent or stop the attack.

   ☒ **D** is incorrect because the term *active* is not associated with a firewall type. This is included as a distractor.

20. You are separated from your target subnet by a firewall. The firewall is correctly configured and allows requests only to ports opened by the administrator. In firewalking the device, you find that port 80 is open. Which technique could you employ to send data and commands to or from the target system?

   A. Encrypt the data to hide it from the firewall.

   B. Use session splicing.

   C. Use MAC flooding.

   D. Use HTTP tunneling.

☑ **D.** HTTP tunneling is a successful "hacking" technique, but it's hardly new. Microsoft makes use of HTTP tunneling for lots of things, and it has been doing so for years. The tactic is fairly simple: because port 80 is almost never filtered by a firewall, you can craft port 80 segments to carry a payload for protocols the firewall may have otherwise blocked. Of course, you'll need something on the other end to pull the payload out of all those port 80 packets that IIS is desperately wanting to answer, but that's not altogether difficult.

☒ **A** is incorrect because encryption won't do a thing for you here. The firewall isn't looking necessarily at content/payload—it's looking at the packet/frame header and port information. Encryption is a good choice to get around an IDS, not a firewall.

☒ **B** is incorrect because session splicing is a technique for evading an IDS, not a firewall. Again, the firewall is interested in the packet and frame header, not what fragments of code you've hidden in the payload.

☒ **C** is incorrect because MAC flooding is a technique for sniffing switches. The idea is to fill the CAM table to the brim with thousands of useless MAC addresses. This effectively turns the switch into a hub, because it is too confused to filter and just begins flooding all traffic to all ports.

21. Which of the following tools can be used to extract application layer data from TCP connections captured in a log file into separate files?

A. Snort

B. Netcat

C. TCPflow

D. Tcpdump

☑ **C.** TCPflow (https://github.com/simsong/tcpflow/wiki/tcpflow-%E2%80%94-A-tcp-ip-session-reassembler) is "a program that captures data transmitted as part of TCP connections (flows), and stores the data in a way that is convenient for protocol analysis and debugging. Each TCP flow is stored in its own file. Thus, the typical TCP flow will be stored in two files, one for each direction. tcpflow can also process stored 'tcpdump' packet flows. tcpflow is similar to 'tcpdump', in that both process packets from the wire or from a stored file. But it's different in that it reconstructs the actual data streams and stores each flow in a separate file for later analysis."

☒ **A** is incorrect because Snort is a great IDS, sniffer, and packet logger, but it isn't so great about separating TCP streams for application layer analysis.

☒ **B** is incorrect because netcat (the Swiss Army knife of hacking, as it's called) isn't designed for sniffing and packet analysis.

☒ **D** is incorrect because tcpdump will certainly pull everything for you but does not reconstruct the actual data streams or store each flow in a separate file for later analysis.

22. Examine the Wireshark filter shown here:

```
ip.src == 192.168.1.1 &&tcp.srcport == 80
```

Which of the following correctly describes the capture filter?

A. The results will display all traffic from 192.168.1.1 destined for port 80.

B. The results will display all HTTP traffic to 192.168.1.1.

C. The results will display all HTTP traffic from 192.168.1.1.

D. No results will display because of invalid syntax.

☑ **C.** Wireshark filters will be covered quite a bit on your exam, and, as stated earlier, these are easy questions for you. The preceding syntax designates the source IP and combines it with a source TCP port. This is effectively looking at all answers to port 80 requests by 192.168.1.1. As another important study tip, watch for the period (.) between "ip" and "src" on the exam because they'll drop it or change it to a dash (-) to trick you. And lastly, for real-world application, it's important to note that Wireshark considers certain friendly terms such as HTTP as simple placeholders for the actual port. This means in Wireshark, HTTP and 80 are more or less identical. As a budding ethical hacker, you should know by now that even though something is traveling on port 80, it may or may not be HTTP traffic.

☒ **A** is incorrect because port 80 is defined as the *source* port, not the destination. 192.168.1.1 is answering a request for an HTML page.

☒ **B** is incorrect because 192.168.1.1 is defined as the *source* address, not the destination.

☒ **D** is incorrect because the syntax is indeed correct.

23. You need to put the NIC into listening mode on your Linux box, capture packets, and write the results to a log file named my.log. How do you accomplish this with tcpdump?

A. tcpdump -i eth0 -w my.log

B. tcpdump -l eth0 -c my.log

C. tcpdump/i eth0 /w my.log

D. tcpdump/l eth0 /c my.log

☑ **A.** Tcpdump syntax is simple: tcpdump *flag(s) interface*. The -i flag specifies the interface (in this example, eth0) for tcpdump to listen on, and the -w flag defines where you want your packet log to go. For your own study, be aware that many study references—including EC-Council's official reference books—state that the -i flag "puts the interface into listening mode." It doesn't actually modify the interface at all, so this is a little bit of a misnomer—it just identifies to tcpdump which interface to listen on for traffic. Lastly, be aware that the -w flag dumps traffic in binary format. If you want the traffic to be readable, you'll need to have it display onscreen. Better yet, you can dump it to a file using the | designator and a filename.

☒ **B** is incorrect because the -l flag does not put the interface in listening mode; it actually has to do with line buffering.

☒ **C** and **D** are incorrect for the same reason; flags are designated with a dash (-) not a slash (/).

24. Which of the following tools can assist with IDS evasion? (Choose all that apply.)

    A. Whisker

    B. Fragroute

    C. Capsa

    D. Wireshark

    E. ADMmutate

    F. Inundator

    ☑ **A, B, E, F.** IDS evasion comes down to a few methods: encryption, flooding, and fragmentation (session splicing). Whisker is an HTTP scanning tool but also has the ability to craft session-splicing fragments. Fragroute intercepts, modifies, and rewrites egress traffic destined for the specified host and can be used to fragment an attack payload over multiple packets. ADMmutate can create multiple scripts that won't be easily recognizable by signature files, and Inundator is a flooding tool that can help you hide in thc cover fire.

    ☒ **C** and **D** are incorrect because both Capsa (Colasoft) and Wireshark are sniffers.

25. Which command puts Snort into packet logger mode?

    A. ./snort -dev -l ./log

    B. ./snort -v

    C. ./snort -dev -l ./log -h 192.168.1.0/24 -c snort.conf

    D. None of the above

    ☑ **A.** This is the proper syntax to start Snort in packet logger mode. Assuming you have the /log folder created, Snort will start happily logging packets as it captures them. Here are some flags of note within this command:

    - **-d** Includes the application layer information, when used with the -v argument
    - **-e** Includes the data link layer information with the packet
    - **-v** Puts Snort in verbose mode, to look at all packets

    When put altogether, the -dev arguments tell Snort to display all packet data, including the headers.

    ☒ **B** is incorrect because this syntax starts Snort in sniffer mode, meaning packet headers will be displayed directly to the screen.

☒ **C** is incorrect because this syntax starts Snort in network intrusion detection mode. Yes, the -l switch logs files, but the bigger issue for you here is the addition of the -c switch, indicating the configuration file the NIDS needs.

☒ **D** is incorrect because the correct syntax is indeed displayed.

26. A security administrator is attempting to "lock down" her network and blocks access from internal to external on all external firewall ports except for TCP 80 and TCP 443. An internal user wants to make use of other protocols to access services on remote systems (FTP, as well as some nonstandard port numbers). Which of the following is the most likely choice the user could attempt to communicate with the remote systems over the protocol of her choice?

    A. Use HTTP tunneling.

    B. Send all traffic over UDP instead of TCP.

    C. Crack the firewall and open the ports required for communication.

    D. MAC flood the switch connected to the firewall.

    ☑ **A.** If you happen to own the companion book to this practice exams tome, you're undoubtedly aware by now I harp on protocols not necessarily being tied to a given port number in the real world. Sure, FTP is supposed to be on TCP port 21, SMTP is supposed to ride on 25, and Telnet is supposed to be on 23, but the dirty little truth is *they don't have to*. An HTTP tunnel is a brilliant example of this. To the firewall and everyone else watching, traffic from your machine is riding harmless little old port 80—nothing to see here folks, just plain-old, regular HTTP traffic. But a peek inside that harmless little tunnel shows you can run *anything you want*. Typically you connect to an external server over port 80, and it will unwrap and forward your other protocol traffic for you, once you've gotten it past your pesky firewall.

    ☒ **B** is incorrect because, well, this is just a ridiculous answer. UDP ports are filtered by a firewall just like TCP ports, so sending only UDP would be useless.

    ☒ **C** is incorrect because while it would certainly allow the communication, it wouldn't be for very long. Every sensor on the network would be screaming, and the happy little security admin would lock it back down ASAP. Not to mention, you'd get fired.

    ☒ **D** is incorrect because MAC flooding refers to active sniffing on a switch, not bypassing a firewall.

Attacking a System

This chapter includes questions from the following topics:

- Describe the CEH Hacking Methodology and System Hacking steps
- Describe methods used to gain access to systems
- Describe methods used to escalate privileges
- Describe methods used to maintain access to systems
- Describe methods of evidence erasure
- Identify rootkit function and types
- Identify basics of Windows and Linux file structure, directories, and commands

I hope nobody reading this will ever find themselves in this situation, but have you ever given any thought at all to what you would do if challenged to a fight? I'm not talking about the free-for-all brawls in elementary and middle school, surrounded by a circle of cheering, but ignorant, children; I'm talking about an actual street confrontation you cannot get out of. In almost every situation, most people are taught to leave the situation and protect themselves, and that's absolutely the right way to go. But every once in a while, good law-abiding folks are put in a situation they can't get out of, and a physical confrontation is inevitable.

Did you know there's a science to hand-to-hand combat? Pugilism (*pygmachia* in Greek, made into an Olympic sport in 688 BC) is the hand-to-hand combat sport better known as boxing. Despite the circus it has become in modern times, boxing was a well-respected and carefully studied art for thousands of years. It's not just simply putting two guys in a ring and having them beat on each other; it's about crafting a strategy to accentuate strengths and exploit weaknesses. Sound familiar?

And we're not talking about just boxing here—hand-to-hand combat takes on many forms. Professional boxers, for example, might tell you that light punches are faster, require less energy, and leave you less vulnerable. They might also advise you that deception and speed in combat are much more valuable than strength and the "knockout punch." Self-defense experts might point out areas of the human anatomy that disable an attacker, providing you a means of escape. They might also point out things like the value of a knife versus a gun in defense situations and that one cleverly executed strike, set up and thrown with quickness (sometimes not even with power), may be all it takes to frustrate and confuse an attacker. The science of carrying out a physical attack on an individual, and protecting yourself against such an attack, is founded on the principles of distance, leverage, and timing. It's fascinating stuff, even if you don't ever plan on being in a situation requiring the knowledge.

You may be sitting there having no idea what kind of virtual damage you can do with the knowledge you've gained so far. Who knows if, put in the right situation, you'd knock out virtual targets with ease? I can see you now, looking down at your keyboard in awe and answering the "How did you do that?" question with, "I don't know—the training just kicked in." Granted, we still have a lot of training to do, and I doubt you'll be punching any virtual targets outside an agreed-upon scope (after all, you are an ethical hacker, right?). However, this chapter will help hone your skills. Here, we'll talk all about system attacks and putting to use some of the training and knowledge you already have in place.

 STUDY TIPS   System attacks come in many forms, but EC-Council *really* likes the password attacks. Know your password rules, attacks, and tools well. You will definitely see loads of questions about passwords—the use, storage, and hashing of passwords, as well as attacks against them, will be covered *ad nauseam* on your exam. Pull some of these tools down and play with them because you'll need to know what they look like, how they operate, and what capabilities they have.

Next, when it comes to this chapter, you really need to get to know Linux better. Questions regarding Linux will most likely revolve around kernel modules, file structures, storage locations, and the command-line interface. Again, the easiest way to learn all this is to download a Linux distro and run it in a VM on your machine. Take advantage of the thousands of Linux how-to videos and articles you can find on the Internet: it's one thing to read it in a book, but you'll learn far more if you actually perform it yourself.

1. You are examining test logs from the day's pen test activities and note the following entries on a Windows 8 machine:

```
C:\> net user
User accounts for \\ANYPC

-------------------------------------------------------------------------------
Administrator          Backup                   DefaultAccount
Guest                  USER1
The command completed successfully.
C:\> net user USER1 user2
```

Which of the following is true regarding the code listing?

A. The team member added a user account.

B. The team member switched his login to that of a different user.

C. The team member changed the password of a user.

D. The team member renamed a user account.

2. Amanda works as a security administrator for a large organization. She discovers some remote tools installed on a server and has no record of a change request asking for them. After some investigation, she discovers an unknown IP address connection that was able to access the network through a high-level port that was not closed. The IP address is first traced to a proxy server in Mexico. Further investigation shows the connection bounced between several proxy servers in many locations. Which of the following is the most likely proxy tool used by the attacker to cover his tracks?

A. ISA proxy

B. IAS proxy

C. TOR proxy

D. Netcat

3. The following HOSTS file was pulled during an incident response:

Copyright (c) 1993-2009 Microsoft Corp.

#

This is a sample HOSTS file used by Microsoft TCP/IP for Windows.

This file contains the mappings of IP addresses to host names. Each

entry should be kept on an individual line. The IP address should

be placed in the first column followed by the corresponding host name.

The IP address and the host name should be separated by at least one

space.

Additionally, comments (such as these) may be inserted on individual

lines or following the machine name denoted by a '#' symbol.

#

For example:

```
#     102.54.94.97    rhino.acme.com        # source server
#     38.25.63.10     x.acme.com          # x client host
220.181.0.16         mybank.com
220.181.0.16         amazon.com
220.181.0.16         google.com
220.181.0.16         gmail.com
220.181.0.16         facebook.com
# localhost name resolution is handled within DNS itself.
#127.0.0.1     localhost
#::1           localhost
```

Which of the following best describes the HOSTS file?

A. A user on the machine attempting to go to check their bank account at mybank.com will be directed to a Chinese IP address instead.

B. A user on the machine attempting to go to google.com will receive an HTTP return code of 400.

C. A user on the machine attempting to go to gmail.com will redirect to the local host.

D. Any DNS resolution to IP 220.181.0.16 will be redirected to one of the five sites listed in round-robin fashion.

4. Which of the following opens the Computer Management MMC in a Windows command line?

A. compmgmt.mmc

B. compmgmt.msc

C. compmgmt.exe

D. computermgmt.exe

5. Which of the following will extract an executable file from NTFS streaming?

A. c:\> cat file1.txt:hidden.exe > visible.exe

B. c:\> more file1.txt | hidden.exe > visible.exe

C. c:\> type notepad.exe > file1.txt:hidden.exe

D. c:\> list file1.txt$hidden.exe > visible.exe

6. Which command is used to allow all privileges to the user, read-only to the group, and read-only for all others to a particular file, on a Linux machine?

A. chmod 411 file1

B. chmod 114 file1

C. chmod 117 file1

D. chmod 711 file1

E. chmod 744 file1

7. Examine the following passwd file:

```
root:x:0:0:root:/root:/bin/bash
mwalk:x:500:500:Matt Walker,Room 2238,email:/home/mwalk:/bin/sh
jboll:x:501:501:Jason Bollinger,Room 2239,email:/home/jboll:/bin/sh
rbell:x:502:502:Rick Bell,Room 1017,email:/home/rbell:/bin/sh
afrench:x:503:501:Alecia French,Room 1017,email:/home/afrench:/bin/sh
```

Which of the following statements are true regarding this passwd file? (Choose all that apply.)

A. None of the user accounts has passwords assigned.

B. The system makes use of the shadow file.

C. The root account password is root.

D. The root account has a shadowed password.

E. Files created by Alecia will initially be viewable by Jason.

8. You are attempting to hack a Windows machine and want to gain a copy of the SAM file. Where can you find it? (Choose all that apply.)

A. /etc/passwd

B. /etc/shadow

C. c:\windows\system32\config

D. c:\winnt\config

E. c:\windows\repair

9. Which of the following statements are true concerning Kerberos? (Choose all that apply.)

A. Kerberos uses symmetric encryption.

B. Kerberos uses asymmetric encryption.

C. Clients ask for authentication tickets from the KDC in clear text.

D. KDC responses to clients never include a password.

E. Clients decrypt a TGT from the server.

10. What is the difference between a dictionary attack and a hybrid attack?

A. Dictionary attacks are based solely on word lists, whereas hybrid attacks make use of both word lists and rainbow tables.

B. Dictionary attacks are based solely on whole word lists, whereas hybrid attacks can use a variety of letters, numbers, and special characters.

C. Dictionary attacks use predefined word lists, whereas hybrid attacks substitute numbers and symbols within those words.

D. Hybrid and dictionary attacks are the same.

11. Which of the following contains a listing of port numbers for well-known services defined by IANA?

    A. %windir%\etc\lists

    B. %windir%\system32\drivers\etc\lmhosts

    C. %windir%\system32\drivers\etc\services

    D. %windir%\system32\drivers\etc\hosts

12. Which of the following SIDs indicates the true administrator account?

    A. S-1-5-21-1388762127-2960977290-773940301-1100

    B. S-1-5-21-1388762127-2960977290-773940301-1101

    C. S-1-5-21-1388762127-2960977290-773940301-500

    D. S-1-5-21-1388762127-2960977290-773940301-501

13. In which step of EC-Council's system hacking methodology would you find steganography?

    A. Cracking passwords

    B. Escalating privileges

    C. Executing applications

    D. Hiding files

    E. Covering tracks

14. A review of the command history on a Linux box shows the following command entered:

    `env x= '(){ :;};echo exploit ' bash -c 'cat/etc/passwd`

    Which of the following is the best description of what the attacker is attempting to accomplish?

    A. Add a user to the system.

    B. Elevate current login privileges.

    C. Change passwords for users.

    D. Display password file contents.

15. You are examining LM password hashes and see the following:

    3A02DF5289CF6EEFAAD3B435B51404EE

    Which of the following passwords is most likely to have created the hash?

    A. 123456789

    B. CEHISHARD

    C. c3HisH@RD!

    D. CEHhard

16. You are examining history logs on a Linux machine and note the attacker added an ampersand (&) after a few process commands. Which of the following is true regarding this?

A. The & symbol has no effect on the process command.

B. The & symbol runs the process as a background task and closes it when the user logs off.

C. The & symbol ensures the process continues to run after the user logs off.

D. The & symbol concatenates the process to subsequent commands.

17. Which of the following are considered offline password attacks? (Choose all that apply.)

A. Using a hardware keylogger

B. Brute-force cracking with Cain and Abel on a stolen SAM file

C. Using John the Ripper on a stolen passwd file

D. Shoulder surfing

18. If a rootkit is discovered on the system, which of the following is the *best* alternative for recovery?

A. Replacing all data files from a good backup

B. Installing Tripwire

C. Reloading the entire system from known-good media

D. Deleting all data files and rebooting

19. Examine the following portion of a log file, captured during a hacking attempt:

```
[matt@localhost]#rm -rf /tmp/mykit_headers
[matt@localhost]#rm -rf /var/log/messages
[matt@localhost]#rm -rf /root/.bash_history
```

What was the attacker attempting to do?

A. Copy files for later examination

B. Cover his tracks

C. Change the shell to lock out other users

D. Upload a rootkit

20. You suspect a hack has occurred against your Linux machine. Which command will display all running processes for you to review?

A. ls -d

B. ls -l

C. su

D. ps -ef

E. ifconfig

21. An organization wants to control network traffic and perform stateful inspection of traffic going into and out of their DMZ. Which built-in functionality of Linux can achieve this?

   A. iptables

   B. ipchains

   C. ipsniffer

   D. ipfirewall

22. Which of the following best describes Cygwin?

   A. Cygwin is a Unix subsystem running on top of Windows.

   B. Cygwin is a Windows subsystem running on top of Unix.

   C. Cygwin is a C++ compiler.

   D. Cygwin is a password-cracking tool.

23. Which folder in Linux holds administrative commands and daemons?

   A. /sbin

   B. /bin

   C. /dev

   D. /mnt

   E. /usr

24. Which of the following is the appropriate means to pivot within a Metasploit attack session?

   A. Use the pivot exploit outside meterpreter.

   B. Reconfigure network settings in meterpreter.

   C. Set the payload to propagate.

   D. Create a route statement in the meterpreter.

25. You are examining files on a Windows machine and note one file's attributes include "h." What does this indicate?

   A. The file is flagged for backup.

   B. The file is part of the help function.

   C. The file is fragmented because of size.

   D. The file has been quarantined by an antivirus program.

   E. The file is hidden.

26. An attacker has gained access to an internal system. Using Metasploit, he accesses and attacks other internal systems. Which of the following terms best describe the action taken?

   A. Attack splitting

   B. Pivoting

C. Attack swinging

D. Hinging

27. Which of the following tools can assist in discovering the use of NTFS file streams? (Choose all that apply.)

  A. LADS

  B. ADS Spy

  C. Sfind

  D. Snow

28. Which authentication method uses DES for encryption and forces 14-character passwords for hash storage?

  A. NTLMv1

  B. NTLMv2

  C. LAN Manager

  D. Kerberos

1. C	11. C	21. A
2. C	12. C	22. A
3. A	13. D	23. A
4. B	14. D	24. D
5. A	15. D	25. E
6. D	16. B	26. B
7. B, D, E	17. A, B, C	27. A, B, C
8. C, E	18. C	28. C
9. A, B, C, D, E	19. B	
10. C	20. D	

1. You are examining test logs from the day's pen test activities and note the following entries on a Windows 8 machine:

```
C:\> net user
User accounts for \\ANYPC
-------------------------------------------------------------------------------
Administrator          Backup                    DefaultAccount
Guest                  USER1
The command completed successfully.
C:\> net user USER1 user2
```

Which of the following is true regarding the code listing?

A. The team member added a user account.

B. The team member switched his login to that of a different user.

C. The team member changed the password of a user.

D. The team member renamed a user account.

☑ **C.** The NET commands in Windows will definitely make an appearance on your exam, and it's impossible to tell which syntax or command structure they'll throw at you. So learn them all. In this example, the **net user** command lists all users on the machine. Next, the team member used the **net user** *USERNAME PASSWORD* command—where *USERNAME* equates to the user to update and *PASSWORD* is the password to set for the user. In this example, the user—USER1—had his password updated to user2. Other **net user** options include ADD, DELETE, TIMES, and ACTIVE. Net commands run in the security context you are logged on as, so ensure you're actually an administrator on the machine before attempting many of them.

Net commands can also be used for loads of other things. For just a few examples, **net view** will display systems in the workgroup, **net use** lets you create, connect to, and display information on shared resources, **net share** will list all the shares the user has access to, and **net start** allows you to start a service.

☒ **A** is incorrect because this does not match the syntax provided. If the team member wanted to add a user, he'd first ensure he had administrative privileges, and would then use the **net user /ADD** *USERNAME* command (where *USERNAME* is the name of the user to be created).

☒ **B** is incorrect because this command or syntax would not accomplish this action.

☒ **D** is incorrect because this command or syntax would not accomplish this action.

2. Amanda works as a security administrator for a large organization. She discovers some remote tools installed on a server and has no record of a change request asking for them. After some investigation, she discovers an unknown IP address connection that was able to access the network through a high-level port that was not closed. The IP address is first traced to a proxy server in Mexico. Further investigation shows the connection bounced

between several proxy servers in many locations. Which of the following is the most likely proxy tool used by the attacker to cover his tracks?

A. ISA proxy

B. IAS proxy

C. TOR proxy

D. Netcat

☑ **C.** I've mentioned it before, and I'll mention it again here: sometimes the CEH exam and real life just don't match up. Yes, this question may be, admittedly, a little on the "hokey" side, but it's valid insofar as EC-Council is concerned. The point here is that TOR (The Onion Routing; https://www.torproject.org/) provides a quick, easy, and really groovy way to hide your true identity when performing almost anything online. From the site, "Tor protects you by bouncing your communications around a distributed network of relays run by volunteers all around the world: it prevents somebody watching your Internet connection from learning what sites you visit, and it prevents the sites you visit from learning your physical location." (For the real-world folks out there, just know that without law enforcement and some serious network visibility, you'd probably be successful in tracking to the first hop, but that'd be it.) TOR is, by nature, dynamic, and a hacker can simply use a different path for each attack. Just remember the question is really about identifying TOR as a means of covering tracks and not necessarily a treatise on how it *really* works. Were this a reality discussion, we'd be more interested in how Amanda would determine the connection was bouncing around proxies in the first place: more realistically, she might detect several similar connections leveraging the same access that were coming from several different countries.

☒ **A** is incorrect because an Internet Security and Acceleration (ISA) server isn't designed to bounce between multiple proxies to obscure the original source. Per Microsoft, ISA "is the successor to Microsoft's Proxy Server 2.0 (see proxy server) and provides the two basic services of an enterprise firewall and a Web proxy/cache server. ISA Server's firewall screens all packet-level, circuit-level, and application-level traffic. The Web cache stores and serves all regularly accessed Web content in order to reduce network traffic and provide faster access to frequently-accessed Web pages. ISA Server also schedules downloads of Web page updates for non-peak times."

☒ **B** is incorrect because Internet Authentication Service (IAS) is a component of servers that allows you to provide a Remote Authentication Dial-In User Service (RADIUS) connection to clients. It's not designed as an obfuscating proxy—its purpose is in authentication.

☒ **D** is incorrect because while you can set up a single proxy using Netcat and it may even be possible to chain several together, it's simply not designed to work that way (and that's what this question was all about to begin with). You can set up a listening port with it, but it's not designed to act as a proxy, and setting one up as a chain of proxies would be insanely complicated and unnecessary with the myriad other options available.

3. The following HOSTS file was pulled during an incident response:

```
# Copyright (c) 1993-2009 Microsoft Corp.
#
# This is a sample HOSTS file used by Microsoft TCP/IP for Windows.
# This file contains the mappings of IP addresses to host names. Each
# entry should be kept on an individual line. The IP address should
# be placed in the first column followed by the corresponding host name.
# The IP address and the host name should be separated by at least one
# space.
# Additionally, comments (such as these) may be inserted on individual
# lines or following the machine name denoted by a '#' symbol.
#
# For example:
#      102.54.94.97    rhino.acme.com        # source server
#       38.25.63.10    x.acme.com           # x client host
220.181.0.16          mybank.com
220.181.0.16          amazon.com
220.181.0.16          google.com
220.181.0.16          gmail.com
220.181.0.16          facebook.com
# localhost name resolution is handled within DNS itself.
#127.0.0.1     localhost
#::1           localhost
```

Which of the following best describes the HOSTS file?

A. A user on the machine attempting to go to check their bank account at mybank.com will be directed to a Chinese IP address instead.

B. A user on the machine attempting to go to google.com will receive an HTTP return code of 400.

C. A user on the machine attempting to go to gmail.com will redirect to the local host.

D. Any DNS resolution to IP 220.181.0.16 will be redirected to one of the five sites listed in round-robin fashion.

☑ **A.** The hosts file is a thing of beauty or an instrument of horror and terror, depending on how you look at it. Before any Windows system even bothers to check DNS for an IP matching a name request, it checks the hosts file first. For example, when the user types **www.mybank.com** in their browser and presses ENTER, Windows checks the hosts file to see if there is a mapping for mybank.com. If there is one, that's where the user will go. If there's not, Windows will ask DNS for an IP to use. Therefore, if you edit your own hosts file, you can save yourself from lots of ad stream sites (just redirect them to localhost) and ensure your kids don't accidentally go somewhere they're not supposed to. If you get a hold of your target's hosts file, you can send them anywhere you want.

In this example, it appears someone has gotten a hold of this particular machine's hosts file and has edited it to send some common URL requests to a Chinese IP. Maybe they've set up fake versions of these sites in order to grab credentials. Or maybe they just want to DoS the user. In any case, any attempt to go to mybank .com, google.com, gmail.com, amazon.com, or facebook.com will immediately get redirected to the Chinese IP listed. The only way the user could avoid this is to use IP addresses instead of named URL.

☒ **B** is incorrect because it is impossible to tell if the 400 return code (which means the server cannot or will not process the request due to an apparent client error, such as a malformed request syntax, invalid request message framing, or deceptive request routing) would appear. If the request is valid (it should be) and the server is capable of registering the request as valid (again, that depends on what the bad guy set up on that particular IP), then Code 400 will not be returned.

☒ **C** and **D** are incorrect because neither matches the action taken in a hosts file entry.

4. Which of the following opens the Computer Management MMC in a Windows command line?

   A. compmgmt.mmc

   B. compmgmt.msc

   C. compmgmt.exe

   D. computermgmt.exe

   ☑ **B.** Admittedly this one is an easy pick—assuming, of course, you've studied and know your MMCs in Windows. You have studied them, right? Because if you had, you'd know that the Microsoft Management Consoles can be used for all sorts of things. These MMCs include but are not limited to Computer Management, Device Management, Event Viewer, Group Policy Editor, and Active Directory Users and Computers. While you can create your own custom MMC, by typing **mmc** in the command line and then using Add/Remove Snap in from the menu line, you can also just open the individual consoles themselves by using their "msc" command-line option. For example, Computer Management can be a snap-in for a custom MMC, or you can open it by itself using the compmgmt.msc command. Others you may want to know for future reference include AD Users and Computers (dsa.msc), Device Manager (devmgmt.msc), Event Viewer (eventvwr.msc), Local Group Policy Editor (gpedit.msc), and Local Security Settings Manager (secpol.msc).

A, C, and **D** are all incorrect because they do not match the syntax for opening Computer Management.

5. Which of the following will extract an executable file from NTFS streaming?

   A. c:\> cat file1.txt:hidden.exe > visible.exe

   B. c:\> more file1.txt | hidden.exe > visible.exe

   C. c:\> type notepad.exe > file1.txt:hidden.exe

   D. c:\> list file1.txt$hidden.exe > visible.exe

   ☑ **A.** This is the correct syntax. The cat command will extract the executable directly into the folder you execute the command from. NTFS file steaming allows you to hide virtually any file behind any other file, rendering it invisible to directory searches. The file can be a text file, to remind you of steps to take when you return to the target, or even an executable file you can run at your leisure later. Alternate Data Streams (ADS) in the form of NTFS file streaming is a feature of the Windows-native NTFS file systems to ensure compatibility with Apple file systems (called HFS). Be careful on the exam—you will see ADS and NTFS file streaming used interchangeably. As an aside, the cat command isn't available on Windows 7 and Windows 10 machines (you'll need a Linux emulator or something like it to use the cat command on these). As a gift from our beloved technical editor, you can use **c:\> (more<file1.txt:hidden.exe) > output.txt** as another option. This will read the output of the hidden stream and write it to the output.txt file without having to use cat.

   ☒ **B** is incorrect because this is not the correct syntax. There is no pipe (|) function in extracting a file, and the more command is used to display the contents of a text file, not extract an executable from ADS.

   ☒ **C** is incorrect because this is not the correct syntax. This option would display the contents of a hidden text file—maybe one you've stowed away instructions in for use later.

   ☒ **D** is incorrect because the syntax is not correct by any stretch of the imagination. This is included as a distractor.

6. Which command is used to allow all privileges to the user, read-only to the group, and read-only for all others to a particular file, on a Linux machine?

   A. chmod 411 file1

   B. chmod 114 file1

   C. chmod 117 file1

   D. chmod 711 file1

   E. chmod 744 file1

   ☑ **D.** You're going to need to know some basic Linux commands to survive this exam, and one command I can guarantee you'll see a question on is chmod. File permissions in Linux are assigned via the use of the binary equivalent for each rwx group: read is equivalent to 4, write to 2, and execute to 1. To accumulate permissions, you add the number: 4 is read-only, 6 is read and write, and adding execute to the bunch means a 7. As an aside, if you think in binary, the numbers are just as easy to define: 111 equates to 7 in decimal, and each bit turned on gives read, write, and execute. Setting the bits to 101 turns on read, turns off write, and turns on execute; and its decimal equivalent is 5.

☒ **A**, **B**, **C**, and **E** are all incorrect syntax for what we're trying to accomplish here: 411 equates to read-only, execute, and execute (with 114 being the reverse of that), and 117 equates to execute, execute, full permissions, with 711 being the reverse.

7. Examine the following passwd file:

```
root:x:0:0:root:/root:/bin/bash
mwalk:x:500:500:Matt Walker,Room 2238,email:/home/mwalk:/bin/sh
jboll:x:501:501:Jason Bollinger,Room 2239,email:/home/jboll:/bin/sh
rbell:x:502:502:Rick Bell,Room 1017,email:/home/rbell:/bin/sh
afrench:x:503:501:Alecia French,Room 1017,email:/home/afrench:/bin/sh
```

Which of the following statements are true regarding this passwd file? (Choose all that apply.)

A. None of the user accounts has passwords assigned.

B. The system makes use of the shadow file.

C. The root account password is root.

D. The root account has a shadowed password.

E. Files created by Alecia will initially be viewable by Jason.

☑ **B, D, E.** If there are not two to four questions on your exam regarding the Linux passwd file, I'll eat my hat. Every exam and practice exam I've ever taken references this file—a lot—and it's included here to ensure you pay attention. Fields in the passwd file, from left to right, are as follows:

- **User Name**   This is what the user types in as the login name. Each user name must be unique.

- **Password**   If a shadow file is being used, an *x* will be displayed here. If not, you'll see the password in clear text. As an aside, setting this to an asterisk (*) is a method to deactivate an account.

- **UID**   The user identifier is used by the operating system for internal purposes. It is typically incremented by 1 for each new user added.

- **GID**   The group identifier identifies the primary group of the user. All files that are created by this user will normally be accessible to this group, unless a chmod command prevents it (which is the reason for the "initial" portion of the question).

- **Gecos**   This is a descriptive field for the user, generally containing contact information separated by commas.

- **Home Directory**   This is the location of the user's home directory.

- **Startup Program**   This is the program that is started every time the user logs in. It's usually a shell for the user to interact with the system.

☒ **A** is incorrect because the *x* indicates a shadowed password, not the absence of one.

☒ **C** is incorrect because the *x* indicates that root does indeed have a password, but it is shadowed. Could it actually be root? Sure, but there's no way to tell that from this listing.

8. You are attempting to hack a Windows machine and want to gain a copy of the SAM file. Where can you find it? (Choose all that apply.)

A. /etc/passwd

B. /etc/shadow

C. c:\windows\system32\config

D. c:\winnt\config

E. c:\windows\repair

☑ **C, E.** Per Microsoft's definition, the Security Account Manager (SAM) is a database that stores user accounts and security descriptors for users on the local computer. The SAM file can be found in c:\windows\system32\config. If you're having problems getting there, try pulling a copy from system restore (c:\windows\repair).

☒ **A** and **B** are both incorrect because /etc is a dead giveaway this is a Linux folder (note the forward slash instead of the Windows backward slash). The /etc folder contains all the administration files and passwords on a Linux system. Both the password and shadow files are found here.

☒ **D** is incorrect because this is not the correct location of the SAM. It's included as a distractor.

9. Which of the following statements are true concerning Kerberos? (Choose all that apply.)

A. Kerberos uses symmetric encryption.

B. Kerberos uses asymmetric encryption.

C. Clients ask for authentication tickets from the KDC in clear text.

D. KDC responses to clients never include a password.

E. Clients decrypt a TGT from the server.

☑ **A, B, C, D, E.** All answers are correct. Kerberos makes use of both symmetric and asymmetric encryption technologies to securely transmit passwords and keys across a network. The entire process consists of a key distribution center (KDC), an authentication service (AS), a ticket granting service (TGS), and the ticket granting ticket (TGT). A basic Kerberos exchange starts with a client asking the KDC, which holds the AS and TGS, for a ticket, which will be used to authenticate throughout the network. This request is in clear text. The server will respond with a secret key, which is hashed by the password copy kept on the server (passwords are never sent—only hashes and keys). This is known as the TGT. The client decrypts the message, since it knows the password, and the TGT is sent back to the server requesting a TGS service ticket. The server responds with the service ticket, and the client is allowed to log on and access network resources.

10. What is the difference between a dictionary attack and a hybrid attack?

    A. Dictionary attacks are based solely on word lists, whereas hybrid attacks make use of both word lists and rainbow tables.

    B. Dictionary attacks are based solely on whole word lists, whereas hybrid attacks can use a variety of letters, numbers, and special characters.

    C. Dictionary attacks use predefined word lists, whereas hybrid attacks substitute numbers and symbols within those words.

    D. Hybrid and dictionary attacks are the same.

    ☑ **C.** A hybrid attack is a variant on a dictionary attack. In this effort, you still have a word list; however, the cracker is smart enough to replace letters and characters within those words. For example, both attacks might use a list containing the word Password. To have multiple variants on it, the dictionary attack would need to have each variant added to the list individually (P@ssword, Pa$$word, and so on). A hybrid attack would require the word list only to include Password because it would swap out characters and letters to find different versions of the same word.

    ☒ **A** is incorrect because hybrid attacks don't use rainbow tables.

    ☒ **B** is incorrect because dictionary attacks can use all sorts of variants of a whole word; they just need to be listed separately in the list.

    ☒ **D** is incorrect because hybrid and dictionary attacks are most definitely different.

11. Which of the following contains a listing of port numbers for well-known services defined by IANA?

    A. %windir%\etc\lists

    B. %windir%\system32\drivers\etc\lmhosts

    C. %windir%\system32\drivers\etc\services

    D. %windir%\system32\drivers\etc\hosts

    ☑ **C.** I've sat back many times in writing these books struggling to determine why certain specific but not very useful things seem to be so near and dear to the test makers at EC-Council, but I can't find any particular rhyme or reason. Sometimes, Dear Reader, you just have to memorize and move on, and this example is no exception. If you happen to be out on your real job and completely forget every well-known port number, you'd probably just look up the list on an Internet search. If you're bored or really nerdy, though, you can pull up a list of them by visiting the services file. It's sitting right there beside the hosts and lmhosts files.

☒ **A, B**, and **D** are incorrect because these locations do not hold the services file.

12. Which of the following SIDs indicates the true administrator account?

   A. S-1-5-21-1388762127-2960977290-773940301-1100

   B. S-1-5-21-1388762127-2960977290-773940301-1101

   C. S-1-5-21-1388762127-2960977290-773940301-500

   D. S-1-5-21-1388762127-2960977290-773940301-501

   ☑ **C.** The security identifier (SID) in Windows is used to identify a "security principle." It's unique to each account and service and is good for the life of the principle. Everything else associated with the account is simply a property of the SID, allowing accounts to be renamed without affecting their security attributes. In a Windows system, the true administrator account always has an RID (relative identifier) of 500.

   ☒ **A** and **B** are incorrect because neither 1100 nor 1101 is the RID associated with the administrator account. RID values between 1000 and 1500 indicate a standard user account.

   ☒ **D** is incorrect because 501 is the RID for the guest account.

13. In which step of EC-Council's system hacking methodology would you find steganography?

   A. Cracking passwords

   B. Escalating privileges

   C. Executing applications

   D. Hiding files

   E. Covering tracks

   ☑ **D.** Yes, sometimes you get a question that's relatively easy, and this is a prime example. Hiding files is exactly what it sounds like—find a way to hide files on the system. There are innumerable ways to accomplish this, but steganography (which includes hiding all sorts of stuff inside images, video, and such) and NTFS file streaming are the two you'll most likely see referenced on the exam.

   ☒ **A, B, C**, and **E** are incorrect because you do not hide files in these steps. Cracking passwords is self-explanatory. Escalating privileges refers to the means taken to elevate access to administrator level. Executing applications is exactly what it sounds like, and you'll probably see remote execution tools referenced (and, for some bizarre reason, keyloggers and spyware). Covering tracks deals with proxies, log files, and such.

14. A review of the command history on a Linux box shows the following command entered:

```
env x= '(){ :;};echo exploit ' bash -c 'cat/etc/passwd
```

Which of the following is the best description of what the attacker is attempting to accomplish?

A. Add a user to the system.

B. Elevate current login privileges.

C. Change passwords for users.

D. Display password file contents.

☑ **D.** Ever heard of Bashdoor (a.k.a. the Shellshock vulnerability)? Of course you have, and that's what's being attempted here. Vulnerable versions of the Bash shell (commonly used to process requests) allow an attacker to execute arbitrary commands concatenated to the end of function definitions stored in environment variables. In this case, the attacker is trying to read the contents of the password file using the **cat** command.

☒ **A, B**, and **C** are incorrect because they do not match the command syntax.

15. You are examining LM password hashes and see the following:

3A02DF5289CF6EEFAAD3B435B51404EE

Which of the following passwords is most likely to have created the hash?

A. 123456789

B. CEHISHARD

C. c3HisH@RD!

D. CEHhard

☑ **D.** You will certainly see LM hashes on your exam at least once or twice, and usually in this type of scenario. EC-Council isn't just going to come out and ask you if you knew the last half of the LM hash is always the same if the password is seven characters or less—they're going to throw it in a scenario and see if you remember it in the stress of test time. For review purposes, LM splits any password into two seven-character pieces and hashes each piece. If the password is seven characters or less, the last half of the hash is always the value of a hash of nothing (which equates to AAD3B435B51404EE, by the way). In this question, apply the LM "splitting" of passwords into two separate groups of seven characters, and it's easy to see the answer: the first seven characters are CEHhard and the second seven do not exist, so the hash of CEHhard equals 3A02DF5289CF6EEF, and the hash of the blank characters equals AAD3B435B51404EE.

On a final note, because it's related here, don't get hung up on password complexity unless it is explicitly noted in the question. Most people are in a rush during the exam and may not read things carefully. Glancing at the answers, these folks might pick the complex password by mistake. Therefore, use caution in reading the questions—take time to fully understand what they're asking for before just pressing the choice and moving on.

☒ **A** is incorrect because this password has nine characters; therefore, the second half of the hash would be different (LM would hash 1234567 and then 89).

☒ **B** is incorrect because this password also has nine has characters; therefore, the second half of the hash would be different (LM would hash CEHISHA and then RD).

☒ **C** is incorrect because this password has ten characters; therefore, the second half of the hash would be different (LM would hash c3HisH@ and then RD!).

16. You are examining history logs on a Linux machine and note the attacker added an ampersand (&) after a few process commands. Which of the following is true regarding this?

   A. The & symbol has no effect on the process command.

   B. The & symbol runs the process as a background task and closes it when the user logs off.

   C. The & symbol ensures the process continues to run after the user logs off.

   D. The & symbol concatenates the process to subsequent commands.

   ☑ **B.** Okay, so this one is a little picky, I admit it, but lots of questions on your exam will be picky, so I'm not apologizing. The ampersand (&) is not only one of the coolest sounding character symbols of all time, but it's also used in the Linux command line to place a process in the background and cause it to close at user logoff. As an aside, you can use the bg and fg commands to move processes to the background and foreground, respectively.

   ☒ **A** is incorrect because it does have an effect on the command.

   ☒ **C** is incorrect because the process will not continue to run after logoff.

   ☒ **D** is incorrect because it does not concatenate anything.

17. Which of the following are considered offline password attacks? (Choose all that apply.)

   A. Using a hardware keylogger

   B. Brute-force cracking with Cain and Abel on a stolen SAM file

   C. Using John the Ripper on a stolen passwd file

   D. Shoulder surfing

   ☑ **A, B, C.** An offline password attack occurs when you take the password file (or the passwords themselves) offline for work. A common method involves stealing the SAM or passwd (shadow) file and then running a dictionary, hybrid, or brute-force attack against it (using a password-cracking tool such as Cain and Abel or John the Ripper). Keyloggers are also considered offline attacks because you examine the contents off network.

⊠ **D** is incorrect because shoulder surfing is considered another form of attack altogether—a nonelectronic attack. No, I'm not making this up; it's actually a term in CEH lingo and refers to social engineering methods of obtaining a password. Shoulder surfing is basically standing behind someone and watching their keystrokes.

18. If a rootkit is discovered on the system, which of the following is the *best* alternative for recovery?

   A. Replacing all data files from a good backup

   B. Installing Tripwire

   C. Reloading the entire system from known-good media

   D. Deleting all data files and reboot

   ☑ **C.** Sometimes a good old wipe and reload is not only faster than a clean effort but is just flat out better. When it comes to rootkits, it's really your only option. If it's an off-the-shelf rootkit that has been documented, it's likely that good instructions on how to fully remove it are available somewhere. However, just remember that while you *think* you may have it removed by following removal instructions, you *know* it's gone if you blow the system away and reload it.

   ⊠ **A** and **D** are incorrect because nearly anything you're doing with the data files themselves isn't going to help in getting rid of a rootkit. The device has been rooted, so all data should be treated as suspect.

   ⊠ **B** is incorrect because while Tripwire is a great tool, it isn't really useful to you once the machine has been infected.

19. Examine the following portion of a log file, captured during a hacking attempt:

```
[matt@localhost]#rm -rf /tmp/mykit_headers
[matt@localhost]#rm -rf /var/log/messages
[matt@localhost]#rm -rf /root/.bash_history
```

   What was the attacker attempting to do?

   A. Copy files for later examination

   B. Cover his tracks

   C. Change the shell to lock out other users

   D. Upload a rootkit

   ☑ **B.** You'll definitely see basic Linux commands on your test, and this is one example of how you'll be asked about them. In this example, the rm command is used to remove (delete) files on a Linux system. Looking at what the hacker is attempting to remove, it seems logical to assume—even without seeing the rest of the log—that the hacker is covering his tracks.

   ⊠ **A** is incorrect because the command for copy in Linux is cp.

   ⊠ **C** is incorrect because the shell is not being tampered with. This answer is included as a distractor.

☒ **D** is incorrect because there is no evidence in this capture that anything is being uploaded; all commands are for removal of files (using the rm command). Granted, it's highly likely something was uploaded before this portion, but we're not privy to that information here.

20. You suspect a hack has occurred against your Linux machine. Which command will display all running processes for you to review?

   A. ls -d

   B. ls -l

   C. su

   D. ps -ef

   E. ifconfig

   ☑ **D.** The ps command is used in Linux to display processes. The -e switch selects all processes, running or not, and the -f switch provides a full listing. A couple of other options you might see include -r (restrict output to running processes), -u (select by effective user ID; supports names), and -p (select by process ID).

   ☒ **A** and **B** are incorrect because the ls command in Linux lists files inside a storage directory. A couple switches of note include -d (list directory entries instead of contents), -h (print sizes in human readable format), -l (use a long listing format), and -p (file type).

   ☒ **C** is incorrect because the su command in Linux is for "switch user." Assuming you have permission/authentication to do so, this allows you to change the effective user ID and group ID to whatever you want.

   ☒ **E** is incorrect because ifconfig is used to configure a network interface in Linux. It looks, and works, very much like the ipconfig command in Windows, which makes it an easy target for test question writers, so pay close attention to the OS when asked about configuring your NIC.

21. An organization requires an option to control network traffic and perform stateful inspection of traffic going into and out of the DMZ. Which built-in functionality of Linux can achieve this?

   A. iptables

   B. ipchains

   C. ipsniffer

   D. ipfirewall

   ☑ **A.** iptables is a built-in "user space" application in Linux that allows you to configure the tables used by the Linux kernel firewall. It must be executed with root privileges and allows for stateful inspection. On most Linux systems, iptables is installed as /usr/sbin/iptables.

☒ **B** is incorrect because ipchains won't allow for stateful inspection.

☒ **C** and **D** are incorrect because as far as I know there's no such thing as ipsniffer or ipfirewall.

22. Which of the following best describes Cygwin?

    A. Cygwin is a Unix subsystem running on Windows.

    B. Cygwin is a Windows subsystem running on top of Unix.

    C. Cygwin is a C++ compiler.

    D. Cygwin is a password-cracking tool.

    ☑ **A.** Cygwin (http://www.cygwin.com/) provides a Linux-like environment for Windows. It's a large collection of GNU and open source tools that provide functionality similar to a Linux distribution on Windows, as well as a DLL (cygwin1.dll) that provides substantial POSIX API functionality, according to the website. The Cygwin DLL currently works with all recent, commercially released x86 32-bit and 64-bit versions of Windows, starting with Windows XP SP3.

    ☒ **B, C,** and **D** are incorrect descriptions of Cygwin.

23. Which folder in Linux holds administrative commands and daemons?

    A. /sbin

    B. /bin

    C. /dev

    D. /mnt

    E. /usr

    ☑ **A.** The system binaries folder holds most administrative commands (/etc holds others) and is the repository for most of the routines Linux runs (known as *daemons*).

    ☒ **B** is incorrect because this folder holds all sorts of basic Linux commands (a lot like the C:\Windows\System32 folder in Windows).

    ☒ **C** is incorrect because this folder contains the pointer locations to the various storage and input/output systems you will need to mount if you want to use them, such as optical drives and additional hard drives or partitions. By the way, everything in Linux is a file. Everything.

    ☒ **D** is incorrect because this folder holds the access locations you've actually mounted.

    ☒ **E** is incorrect because this folder holds most of the information, commands, and files unique to the users.

24. Which of the following is the appropriate means to pivot within a Metasploit attack session?

    A. Use the pivot exploit outside meterpreter.

    B. Reconfigure network settings in meterpreter.

C. Set the payload to propagate.

D. Create a route statement in the meterpreter.

☑ **D.** To answer this, you have to know what *pivot* means and what the meterpreter is, and the best explanations for both are found right on the Offensive Security website (http://www.offensive-security.com/): "Pivoting is the unique technique of using an instance (also referred to as a *plant* or *foothold*) to be able to 'move' around inside a network. Basically using the first compromise to allow and even aid in the compromise of other otherwise inaccessible systems. Metasploit has an autoroute meterpreter script that allows an attack into a secondary network through a first compromised machine. Meterpreter is an advanced, dynamically extensible payload that uses in-memory DLL injection stagers and is extended over the network at runtime. Meterpreter resides entirely in memory and writes nothing to disk." Adding a route statement inside the dynamic meterpreter environment allows the attack to "pivot" to a new target. Neat, eh?

☒ **A, B,** and **C** are incorrect because they are neither legitimate nor accurate statements regarding a pivot attack.

25. You are examining files on a Windows machine and note one file's attributes include "h." What does this indicate?

A. The file is flagged for backup.

B. The file is part of the help function.

C. The file is fragmented because of size.

D. The file has been quarantined by an antivirus program.

E. The file is hidden.

☑ **E.** The hidden attribute can be set on any file to hide it from standard directory searches. You can accomplish this with the command line

```
attrib +h filename
```

or by right-clicking, choosing Properties, and selecting the Hidden attribute check box at the bottom of the dialog.

☒ **A, B, C,** and **D** are all incorrect definitions of the hidden attribute.

26. An attacker has gained access to an internal system. Using Metasploit, he accesses and attacks other internal systems. Which of the following terms best describe the action taken?

A. Attack splitting

B. Pivoting

C. Attack swinging

D. Hinging

☑ **B.** I love definition questions on the exam—they're simple and easy. Pivoting refers to attackers using a compromised system to access systems they'd otherwise not be able to get to. You can use the route statement meterpreter attack session and—voilà—you are pivoting from the compromised system onto others. Offensive Security (https://www.offensive-security.com/metasploit-unleashed/pivoting/) has a great write-up on using the autoroute meterpreter script for the same purpose.

☒ **A, C**, and **D** are incorrect because these answers do not match any action taken from Metasploit.

27. Which of the following tools can assist in discovering the use of NTFS file streams? (Choose all that apply.)

    A. LADS

    B. ADS Spy

    C. Sfind

    D. Snow

    ☑ **A, B, C.** NTFS streaming (alternate data streaming) isn't a huge security problem, but it is something many security administrators concern themselves with. If you want to know where it's going on, you can use any of these tools: LADS and ADS Spy are freeware tools that list all alternate data streams of an NTFS directory. ADS Spy can also remove alternate data streams (ADS) from NTFS file systems. Sfind, probably the oldest one here, is a Foundstone forensic tool you can use for finding ADS. As an aside, **dir /R** on Windows systems does a great job of pointing these out.

    ☒ **D** is incorrect because Snow is a steganography tool used to conceal messages in ASCII text by appending whitespace to the end of lines.

28. Which authentication method uses DES for encryption and forces 14-character passwords for hash storage?

    A. NTLMv1

    B. NTLMv2

    C. LAN Manager

    D. Kerberos

    ☑ **C.** LAN Manager is an older authentication model that burst onto the scene around the Windows 95 launch. It uses DES as an encryption standard (a 56-bit key DES, to be technical) and, as covered before, has a quirky habit of capitalizing passwords and splitting them into two seven-character halves. Believe it or not, this is still in use in the field. It's most often found in places where backward compatibility was needed for something and, eventually, it was just forgotten or overlooked.

☒ **A** is incorrect because NTLMv1 (NT LAN Manager) improved upon LM methods. It stopped crazy practices such as padding passwords to 14 characters, and it supported stronger encryption.

☒ **B** is incorrect because NTLMv2 also did not follow the encryption methods used by LM. In addition to the improvements from version 1, NTLMv2 made use of 128-bit MD5 hashing.

☒ **D** is incorrect because Kerberos is a strong and secure authentication method that does not work like LM. Kerberos makes use of a key distribution center (KDC) and grants tickets to properly authenticated clients to access resources on the network.

Web-Based Hacking: Servers and Applications

This chapter includes questions from the following topics:

- Identify features of common web server architecture
- Identify web application function and architecture points
- Describe web server and web application attacks
- Identify web server and application vulnerabilities
- Identify web application hacking tools

In the Spring of 1863, a mismatch was shaping up on the battlefield. General Robert E. Lee and Stonewall Jackson had amassed a sizeable Confederate force of around 60,000 men in and around Chancellorsville, Virginia, after the recent victory in Fredericksburg. Major General Joseph Hooker, however, commanded a Union army of around 130,000 men and was under direct orders from President Lincoln to annihilate the Confederate army. He thus decided upon a plan of action, well based in current military strategy, to apply his vastly superior forces and march against the enemy. By any measure, this was shaping up as an easy victory for the North.

General Lee, however, wasn't well known for following strict rules of battle. While Hooker amassed forces for a front-on attack, Lee did something that, at the time, was considered either the dumbest move in history or brilliant strategy: He split his already outnumbered army into three groups. He left a paltry 10,000 men to meet the head-on charge, but sent the other 50,000 men in two groups to surround and flank the Union troops. Through a series of improbable victories on the Confederate side and utterly tentative and puzzling decision making by their Northern counterparts, the battle became a treatise on victory against all odds, and the power of mind and strategy on the battlefield.

And what is the relevance here for us, you may ask? By changing the focus of his attack, General Lee succeeded in pulling off one of the most unbelievable military victories in history. You can do the same in your pen testing by focusing your efforts on those areas the strong defenses of your target may overlook: their web applications and servers (yes, I know it's corny, just go with it). Businesses and corporations are like that Union army, with so many defenses arrayed against you they seem impenetrable. But most of them can be outflanked, via their public-facing web fronts (which may or may not have proper security included) and their customized, internal web applications. This chapter is all about web servers and applications and how you can exploit them. After all, if the target is going to trust them, why not have a look?

 STUDY TIPS   Web server and web application attack questions are a little more focused, and difficult, in this version. I wish I could tell you memorization of terminology and key words would be enough to make it through them, but that's simply not the case anymore. ECC wants to make sure you know web servers and applications pretty thoroughly, so they've upped the ante in question offerings. Some will be more in the form of a scenario where you may need to pull from multiple areas of study in order to derive the correct answer. A couple of very specific questions may even involve scripting and will appear really difficult; however, if you'll simply remember protocols, ports, and basic networking, you can usually work your way through them.

Know your attacks well, including CSRF, CSPP, HTTP response splitting, and of course XSS, SQL injection, and URL tampering (among all the others). Be sure to spend some time in HTTP, and know it well. Another must-know for the exam is OWASP—know what it is, what it does, and its Top 10 lists well.

1. In nmap, the http-methods script can be used to test for potentially risky HTTP options supported by a target. Which of the following methods would be considered risky per the script?

    A. CONNECT

    B. GET

    C. POST

    D. HEAD

2. OWASP, an international organization focused on improving the security of software, produced a "Top Ten Security Priorities" for web applications. Which item is the primary concern on the list?

    A. XSS

    B. Injection

    C. SQL injection

    D. Broken authentication

3. A web application developer wishes to test a new application for security flaws. Which of the following is a method of testing input variations by using randomly generated invalid input in an attempt to crash the program?

    A. Insploit

    B. Finglonger

    C. Metasplation

    D. Fuzzing

4. Which of the following uses HTML entities properly to represent <script>?

    A. <script>

    B. (script)

    C. &script&

    D. "script"

5. An attacker tricks a user into visiting a malicious website via a phishing e-mail. The user clicks the e-mail link and visits the malicious website while maintaining an active, authenticated session with his bank. The attacker, through the malicious website, then instructs the user's web browser to send requests to the bank website. Which of the following best describes this attack?

    A. CSPP

    B. XSS

    C. CSRF

    D. Hidden form field

6. Which of the following is used by SOAP services to format information?

   A. Unicode

   B. HTML entities

   C. NTFS

   D. XML

7. A web application developer is discussing security flaws discovered in a new application prior to production release. He suggests to the team that they modify the software to ensure users are not allowed to enter HTML as input into the application. Which of the following is most likely the vulnerability the developer is attempting to mitigate against?

   A. Cross-site scripting

   B. Cross-site request forgery

   C. Connection string parameter pollution

   D. Phishing

8. Which of the following is a common SOA vulnerability?

   A. SQL injection

   B. XSS

   C. XML denial of service

   D. CGI manipulation

9. The source code of software used by your client seems to have a large number of gets() alongside sparsely used fgets(). What kind of attack is this software potentially susceptible to?

   A. SQL injection

   B. Buffer overflow

   C. Parameter tampering

   D. Cookie manipulation

10. Which of the following would be the best choice in the prevention of XSS?

   A. Challenge tokens

   B. Memory use controls

   C. HttpOnly flag in cookies

   D. Removing hidden form fields

11. You are examining log files and come across this URL:

    ```
    http://www.example.com/script.ext?template%2e%2e%2e%2e%2e%2f%2e%2f%65%
    74%63%2f%70%61%73%73%77%64
    ```

Which of the following best describes this potential attack?

A. This is not an attack but a return of SSL handshakes.

B. An attacker appears to be using Unicode.

C. This appears to be a buffer overflow attempt.

D. This appears to be an XSS attempt.

12. Which MSFconsole command allows you to connect to a host from within the console?

A. pivot

B. connect

C. get

D. route

13. Which character is your best option in testing for SQL injection vulnerability?

A. The @ symbol

B. A double dash

C. The + sign

D. A single quote

14. An angry former employee of the organization discovers a web form vulncrable to SQL injection. Using the injection string **SELECT * FROM Orders_Pend WHERE Location_City = 'Orlando'**, he is able to see all pending orders from Orlando. If he wanted to delete the Orders_Pend table altogether, which SQL injection string should be used?

A. SELECT * FROM Orders_Pend WHERE Location_City = Orlando';DROP TABLE Orders_Pend --

B. SELECT * FROM Orders_Pend WHERE 'Orlando';DROP_TABLE --

C. DROP TABLE Orders_Pend WHERE 'Orlando = 1' --

D. WHERE Location_City = Orlando'1 = 1': DROP_TABLE --

15. Efforts to gain information from a target website have produced the following error message:

```
Microsoft OLE DB Provider for ODBC Drivers error '80040e08'
[Microsoft]{OBDC SQL Server Driver}
```

Which of the following best describes the error message?

A. The site may be vulnerable to XSS.

B. The site may be vulnerable to buffer overflow.

C. The site may be vulnerable to SQL injection.

D. The site may be vulnerable to a malware injection.

16. An attacker discovers a legitimate username (user1) and enters the following into a web form authentication window:

Which of the following is most likely the attack being attempted?

A. SQL injection

B. LDAP injection

C. URL tampering

D. DHCP amplification

17. Which of the following is a standard method for web servers to pass a user's request to an application and receive data back to forward to the user?

A. SSI

B. SSL

C. CGI

D. CSI

18. An attacker performs a SQL injection attack but receives nothing in return. She then proceeds to send multiple SQL queries, soliciting TRUE or FALSE responses. Which attack is being carried out?

A. Blind SQL injection

B. SQL denial of service

C. SQL code manipulation

D. SQL replay

19. A tester is attempting a CSPP attack. Which of the following is she most likely to use in conjunction with the attack?

A. ;

B. :

C. '

D. "

E. --

F. ~

20. An attacker is attempting to elevate privileges on a machine by using Java or other functions, through nonvalidated input, to cause the server to execute a malicious piece of code and provide command-line access. Which of the following best describes this action?

   A. Shell injection

   B. File injection

   C. SQL injection

   D. URL injection

21. An attacker is successful in using a cookie, stolen during an XSS attack, during an invalid session on the server by forcing a web application to act on the cookie's contents. How is this possible?

   A. A cookie can be replayed at any time, no matter the circumstances.

   B. Encryption was accomplished at the application layer, using a single key.

   C. Authentication was accomplished using XML.

   D. Encryption was accomplished at the network layer.

22. HTML forms include several methods for transferring data back and forth. Inside a form, which of the following encodes the input into the Uniform Resource Identifier (URI)?

   A. HEAD

   B. PUT

   C. GET

   D. POST

23. An attacker is looking at a target website and is viewing an account from the store on URL http://www.anybiz.com/store.php?id=2. He next enters the following URL:

   http://www.anybiz.com/store.php?id=2 and 1=1

   The web page loads normally. He then enters the following URL:

   http://www.anybiz.com/store.php?id=2 and 1=2

   A generic page noting "An error has occurred" appears.

   Which of the following is a correct statement concerning these actions?

   A. The site is vulnerable to cross-site scripting.

   B. The site is vulnerable to blind SQL injection.

   C. The site is vulnerable to buffer overflows.

   D. The site is not vulnerable to SQL injection.

24. Which of the following is not true regarding WebGoat?

   A. WebGoat is maintained and made available by OWASP.

   B. WebGoat can be installed on Windows systems only.

   C. WebGoat is based on a black-box testing mentality.

   D. WebGoat can use Java or .NET.

25. An attacker is viewing a blog entry showing a news story and asking for comments. In the comment field, the attacker enters the following:

```
Nice post and a fun read
<script>onload=window.location='http://www.badsite.com'</script>
```

   What is the attacker attempting to perform?

   A. A SQL injection attack against the blog's underlying database

   B. A cross-site scripting attack

   C. A buffer overflow DoS attack

   D. A file injection DoS attack

26. Which of the following is one of the most common methods for an attacker to exploit the Shellshock vulnerability?

   A. SSH brute force

   B. CSRF

   C. Form field entry manipulation

   D. Through web servers utilizing CGI (Common Gateway Interface)

27. You are examining website files and find the following text file:

```
# robots.txt for http://www.anybiz.com/
User-agent: Googlebot
Disallow: /tmp/
User-agent: *
Disallow: /
Disallow: /private.php
Disallow: /listing.html
```

   Which of the following is a true statement concerning this file?

   A. All web crawlers are prevented from indexing the listing.html page.

   B. All web crawlers are prevented from indexing all pages on the site.

   C. The Googlebot crawler is allowed to index pages starting with /tmp/.

   D. The Googlebot crawler can access and index everything on the site except for pages starting with /tmp/.

1. A	**10.** C	**19.** A
2. B	**11.** B	**20.** A
3. D	**12.** B	**21.** B
4. A	**13.** D	**22.** C
5. C	**14.** A	**23.** B
6. D	**15.** C	**24.** B
7. A	**16.** B	**25.** B
8. C	**17.** C	**26.** D
9. B	**18.** A	**27.** D

1. In nmap, the http-methods script can be used to test for potentially risky HTTP options supported by a target. Which of the following methods would be considered risky per the script?

   A. CONNECT

   B. GET

   C. POST

   D. HEAD

   ☑ **A.** The http-methods script usage syntax is **nmap --script http-methods <target>**, where <target> is the IP of the system you're after. From nmap's support pages (https://nmap.org/nsedoc/scripts/http-methods.html), this script "finds out what options are supported by an HTTP server by sending an OPTIONS request and lists potentially risky methods. It tests those methods not mentioned in the OPTIONS headers individually and sees if they are implemented. Any output other than 501/405 suggests that the method is not in the range 400 to 600. If the response falls under that range then it is compared to the response from a randomly generated method. In this script, 'potentially risky' methods are anything except GET, HEAD, POST, and OPTIONS. If the script reports potentially risky methods, they may not all be security risks, but you should check to make sure." You can also use additional parameters, such as url-path, to further hone your results. For example, output from the preceding syntax showing PUT as a risky method might look like this:

   ```
   PORT STATE SERVICE REASON
   80/tcp open http syn-ack
   | http-methods:
   |_ Supported Methods: GET PUT HEAD POST OPTIONS
   .....
   ```

   Quite obviously, there is a lot of information tested in this one question—and many, many ways you might see it on the exam. The HTTP options themselves will show up somewhere, so knowing the difference, for example, between HTTP POST (submits data to be processed, normally allowable) and HTTP PUT (allows a client to upload new files on the web server, normally shouldn't be allowed) will become very important to your success. From OWASP (https://www.owasp.org/index.php/ Test_HTTP_Methods_%28OTG-CONFIG-006%29), the following options are important to know:

   - **PUT**   This method allows a client to upload new files on the web server. An attacker can exploit it by uploading malicious files (for example, an .asp file that executes commands by invoking cmd.exe) or by simply using the victim's server as a file repository.

   - **DELETE**   This method allows a client to delete a file on the web server. An attacker can exploit it as a very simple and direct way to deface a website or to mount a DoS attack.

- **CONNECT**   This method could allow a client to use the web server as a proxy.

- **TRACE**   This method simply echoes back to the client whatever string has been sent to the server, and it's used mainly for debugging purposes. This method, originally assumed harmless, can be used to mount an attack known as *cross-site tracing*.

☒ **B, C,** and **D** are incorrect because these are not considered "risky" options.

2. OWASP, an international organization focused on improving the security of software, produced a "Top Ten Security Priorities" for web applications. Which item is the primary concern on the list?

   A. XSS

   B. Injection

   C. SQL injection

   D. Broken authentication

   ☑ **B.** I know you're thinking there is no way something this specific and picky will be on the exam, but I promise you will see something like this on your exam (not verbatim of course, but you get my drift). OWASP's Top 10 Security Priorities was released in 2013, and ECC loves it. If nothing else, memorize the top five items on the list:

   - **Number 1: Injection**   OWASP lumps several attacks into this one (SQL injections, OS injections, LDAP injections, and so on).

   - **Number 2: Broken Authentication and Session Management**   This one deals with problems in authentication and session management (allowing attackers to compromise passwords, encryption keys, session tokens, and so on).

   - **Number 3: XSS**   *Cross-site scripting* (XSS) happens when an attacker injects code (a script) into the web page of a legitimate company or user—usually into input fields on a web form.

   - **Number 4: Insecure Direct Object References**   This occurs when an application references an internal object without appropriate access controls.

   - **Number 5: Security Misconfiguration**   This one is all about insecure default settings in applications and systems.

   ☒ **A** is incorrect because XSS is number 3 on the list.

   ☒ **C** is incorrect because SQL injection falls into the Injection topic: on its own, it's not listed as a separate topic. Yes, technically you can argue this topic with me, and you can be as outraged as you wish, but you need to know it is *not* a topic on its own per the Top 10 list.

   ☒ **D** is incorrect because Broken Authentication and Session Management is number 2 on the list.

3. A web application developer wishes to test a new application for security flaws. Which of the following is a method of testing input variations by using randomly generated invalid input in an attempt to crash the program?

   A. Insploit

   B. Finglonger

   C. Metasplation

   D. Fuzzing

   ☑ **D.** Even if you didn't know what "fuzzing" meant, you probably could've whittled this down by eliminating the known wrong answers. Per OWASP (https://www .owasp.org/index.php/Fuzzing), "*Fuzz testing* or *fuzzing* is a Black Box software testing technique, which basically consists in finding implementation bugs using malformed/semi-malformed data injection in an automated fashion." In other words, fuzzing sends tons of weird inputs into fields to see what the application will do.

   As an aside, you would find fuzzing in the Verification phase of Microsoft's Security Development Lifecycle (SDL). The entire SDL consists of Training, Requirements, Design, Implementation, Verification, Release, and Response.

   ☒ **A**, **B**, and **C** are incorrect because none of these are legitimate terms as far as testing is concerned. Insploit and Metasplation are not real terms. Finglonger isn't either, but it did make an appearance in a fantastic episode of *Futurama*.

4. Which of the following uses HTML entities properly to represent <script>?

   A. <script>

   B. (script)

   C. &script&

   D. "script"

   ☑ **A.** Cross-site scripting generally relies on web pages not properly validating user input, and HTML entities can be used to take the place of certain characters. In this case, the less-than sign (<) and the greater-than sign (>) surround the word *script*. The appropriate HTML entity for each is < and > (the *lt* and *gt* should give that one away).

   ☒ **B** is incorrect because (and) stand for the open and close parentheses, respectively. For example, **(hello)** would read **(hello)** using HTML entities.

   ☒ **C** is incorrect because & stands for the ampersand character (&).

   ☒ **D** is incorrect because " stands for the quote character (").

5. An attacker tricks a user into visiting a malicious website via a phishing email. The user clicks the email link and visits the malicious website while maintaining an active, authenticated session with his bank. The attacker, through the malicious website,

then instructs the user's web browser to send requests to the bank website. Which of the following best describes this attack?

A. CSPP

B. XSS

C. CSRF

D. Hidden form field

☑ **C.** There are few truisms in life, but here's one: you will definitely be asked about CSRF on your exam. Cross-site request forgery (CSRF) attacks are exactly what's being described here—an attacker takes advantage of an open, active, authenticated session between the victim and a trusted site, sending message requests to the trusted site as if they are from the victim's own browser. Usually this involves phishing, or maybe an advertisement, but the principle is always the same. CSRF attacks can be prevented by configuring random challenge tokens, which allow the server to verify user requests.

As an aside, a similar attack is known as *session fixation*. The attacker logs in to a legitimate site, pulls a session ID, and then sends an e-mail with a link containing the fix session ID. When the user clicks it and logs in to the same legitimate site, the hacker now logs in and runs with the user's credentials.

☒ **A** is incorrect because this does not describe a CSPP attack. A connection string parameter pollution attack exploits web applications that use semicolons to separate parameters during communications.

☒ **B** is incorrect because this does not describe a cross-site scripting attack. An XSS attack attempts to interject a script into input fields.

☒ **D** is incorrect because a hidden form field attack occurs when an attacker manipulates the values of a hidden form field and resubmits to the server.

6. Which of the following is used by SOAP services to format information?

A. Unicode

B. HTML entities

C. NTFS

D. XML

☑ **D.** Simple Object Access Protocol (SOAP) is a protocol designed for exchanging structured information within web services across multiple variant systems. In other words, it's a way for a program running in one kind of operating system (let's say Windows Server 2008) to communicate with a program on another (such as Linux). It uses HTTP and XML to exchange information and specifies how to encode HTTP headers and XML files so that applications can talk to each other. One great advantage to this is also a great detriment, security-wise: because HTTP is generally allowed through most firewalls, applications using SOAP can generally communicate at will throughout networks.

SOAP injection attacks allow you to inject malicious query strings (much like SQL injection, as a matter of fact) that might give you the means to bypass authentication and access databases behind the scenes. SOAP is compatible with HTTP and SMTP, and messages are typically one way in nature.

☒ **A** is incorrect because Unicode is not used by SOAP in this manner. It's a standard for representing text in computing.

☒ **B** is incorrect because HTML entities are not used by SOAP in this manner. They're used to represent characters in HTML code.

☒ **C** is incorrect because NTFS is a file system and has nothing to do with SOAP.

7. A web application developer is discussing security flaws discovered in a new application prior to production release. He suggests to the team that they modify the software to ensure users are not allowed to enter HTML as input into the application. Which of the following is most likely the vulnerability the developer is attempting to mitigate against?

A. Cross-site scripting

B. Cross-site request forgery

C. Connection string parameter pollution

D. Phishing

☑ **A.** XSS flaws occur whenever an application takes untrusted data and sends it to a web browser without proper validation or escaping. The basics of this attack revolve around website (or web application on that site) design, dynamic content, and invalidated input data. Usually when a web form pops up, the user inputs something, and then some script dynamically changes the appearance or behavior of the website based on what has been entered. XSS occurs when the bad guys take advantage of that scripting (Java, for instance) and have it perform something other than the intended response. For example, suppose instead of entering what you're supposed to enter in a form field, you enter an actual script. The server then does what it's supposed to—it processes the code sent from an authorized user. The best defense against this is proper design and good input validation before the app ever sees production in the first place.

☒ **B** is incorrect because the fix actions being suggested would not necessarily affect CSRF attacks. In CSRF, an attacker takes advantage of an open, active, authenticated session between the victim and a trusted site, sending message requests to the trusted site as if they are from the victim's own browser.

☒ **C** is incorrect because the fix actions being suggested would not necessarily affect CSPP attacks. A connection string parameter pollution attack exploits web applications that use semicolons to separate parameters during communications.

☒ **D** is incorrect because the fix action being recommended would not necessarily affect any social engineering effort.

8. Which of the following is a common SOA vulnerability?

A. SQL injection

B. XSS

C. XML denial of service

D. CGI manipulation

☑ **C.** Service-oriented architecture (SOA) is a software design idea that is based on specific pieces of software providing functionality as services between applications. The idea is to define how two applications can interact so that one can perform a piece of work for the other (better said, on behalf of the other). Each interaction is independent of any other and is self-contained. SOA programmers make extensive use of XML to carry all this out, and that leaves it vulnerable to crafty XML tampering. If an attacker can somehow pass an XML message with a large payload, or any of a number of other bad content, they can DoS an SOA application. This isn't to imply it's the only DoS available or that SOA is uniquely vulnerable (for instance, the only thing a specifically crafted XML attack can affect). It's just a question, so don't read too much into it.

☒ **A, B,** and **D** are incorrect because these attacks don't necessarily apply here with SOA in this context.

9. The source code of software used by your client seems to have a large number of gets() alongside sparsely used fgets(). What kind of attack is this software potentially susceptible to?

A. SQL injection

B. Buffer overflow

C. Parameter tampering

D. Cookie manipulation

☑ **B.** A buffer overflow is an attempt to write more data into an application's prebuilt buffer area in order to overwrite adjacent memory, execute code, or crash a system (application). By inputting more data than the buffer is allocated to hold, you may be able to crash the application or machine or alter the application's data pointers. gets() is a common source of buffer overflow vulnerabilities because it reads a line from standard input into a buffer until a terminating EOF is found. It performs no check for buffer overrun and is largely replaced by fgets().

☒ **A** is incorrect because SQL injection has nothing to do with this scenario. No evidence is presented that this software even interacts with a database.

☒ **C** is incorrect because parameter tampering deals with manipulating a URL.

☒ **D** is incorrect because cookie manipulation has nothing to do with this software. A cookie is a small file used to provide a more consistent web experience for a web visitor. Because it holds all sorts of information, though, it can be manipulated for nefarious purposes (using the Firefox add-on Cookie Editor, for instance).

10. Which of the following would be the best choice in the prevention of XSS?

   A. Challenge tokens

   B. Memory use controls

   C. HttpOnly flag in cookies

   D. Removing hidden form fields

☑ **C.** In addition to input validation controls (always good for bunches of vulnerability mitigations), setting the HttpOnly flag in cookies can be used in mitigation against some XSS attacks. Cross-site scripting occurs when an attacker interjects code into a web page form field that does not have appropriate input validation configured. The HttpOnly cookie flag can stop any injected code from being accessible by a client-side script.

Per OWASP, if the HttpOnly flag is included in the HTTP response header, the cookie cannot be accessed through client-side script. As a result, even if a cross-site scripting flaw exists, and a user accidentally accesses a link that exploits this flaw, the browser (primarily Internet Explorer) will not reveal the cookie to a third party.

☒ **A** is incorrect because challenge tokens are used in mitigation of CSRF.

☒ **B** is incorrect because memory use control configurations wouldn't necessarily affect XSS vulnerabilities at all.

☒ **D** is incorrect because removing hidden form fields would not necessarily do anything to mitigate XSS.

11. You are examining log files and come across this URL:

```
http://www.example.com/script.ext?template%2e%2e%2e%2e%2e%2f%2e%2f%65%
74%63%2f%70%61%73%73%77%64
```

Which of the following best describes this potential attack?

   A. This is not an attack but a return of SSL handshakes.

   B. An attacker appears to be using Unicode.

   C. This appears to be a buffer overflow attempt.

   D. This appears to be an XSS attempt.

☑ **B.** Unicode is just another way to represent text, so why not use it to try to get past an IDS? Of course, in the real world every IDS would probably be looking for weird Unicode requests anyway (it isn't ciphered or encrypted and really does nothing more than provide a cursory obfuscation), but let's just stick with EC-Council and the CEH exam here for now. This request appears to be attempting a grab of some passwords:

```
%2e%2e%2f%2e%2e%2f%2e%2f% = ../../../
%65%74%63 = etc
%2f = /
%70%61%73%73%77%64 = passwd
```

☒ **A, C,** and **D** are all incorrect because this URL does not necessarily indicate any of these attacks and is quite clearly a Unicode attempt.

12. Which MSFconsole command allows you to connect to a host from within the console?

    A. pivot

    B. connect

    C. get

    D. route

    ☑ **B.** Questions on Metasploit can be very generalized, or—like this question—pretty darn specific. MSFconsole, opened with the msfconsole command, is a common method of interfacing with Metasploit. As put by Offensive Security, it provides an "all-in-one" centralized console and allows you efficient access to virtually all of the options available in the MSF, and is the only supported way to access most of the features within Metasploit. Commands used in the interface are listed and discussed pretty well on Offensive Security's site (https://www.offensive-security.com/metasploit-unleashed/msfconsole-commands/). The connect command acts like a miniature netcat clone, supporting SSL, proxies, pivoting, and file sends. By issuing the connect command with an IP address and port number, you can connect to a remote host from within MSFconsole the same as you would with netcat or telnet.

    In addition to MSFconsole, you should also know Metasploit architecture holds five modules: Exploits, Payloads, Encoders, NOPS, and Auxiliary. Exploits is the basic module, used to encapsulate (and configure behaviors for) an exploit. Payloads establishes a communication channel between Metasploit and the target. Auxiliary is used to run things like port scanning and fuzzing.

    ☒ **A** is incorrect because there is no pivot command in MSFconsole. Pivoting does refer to connecting to other machines from a compromised system, but is not accomplished with a pivot command.

    ☒ **C** is incorrect because the get command gets the value of a context-specific variable.

    ☒ **D** is incorrect because the route command is used to route traffic through a session (and is generally seen, question-wise, in regard to pivoting).

13. Which character is your best option in testing for SQL injection vulnerability?

    A. The @ symbol

    B. A double dash

    C. The + sign

    D. A single quote

    ☑ **D.** SQL injection is all about entering queries and commands into a form field (or URL) to elicit a response, gain information, or manipulate data. On a web page, many times entries into a form field are inserted into a SQL command. When you enter your username and information into the fields and click the button, the SQL command in the background might read something like this:

```
SELECT OrderID, FirstName, Lastname FROM Orders
```

In SQL, a single quote is used to indicate an upcoming character string. Once SQL sees that open quote, it starts parsing everything behind it as string input. If there's no close quote, an error occurs because SQL doesn't know what to do with it. If the web page is configured poorly, that error will return to you and let you know it's time to start injecting SQL commands.

☒ **A**, **B**, and **C** are incorrect characters to use as part of a *SQL* injection test. The @ symbol is used to designate a variable in SQL (you'll need to define the variable, of course). The + sign is used to combine strings (as in Matt+Walker). A double dash indicates an upcoming comment in the line.

14. An angry former employee of the organization discovers a web form vulnerable to SQL injection. Using the injection string **SELECT * FROM Orders_Pend WHERE Location_City = 'Orlando'**, he is able to see all pending orders from Orlando. If he wanted to delete the Orders_Pend table altogether, which SQL injection string should be used?

    A. SELECT * FROM Orders_Pend WHERE Location_City = 'Orlando';DROP TABLE Orders_Pend; --

    B. SELECT * FROM Orders_Pend WHERE 'Orlando';DROP_TABLE; --

    C. DROP TABLE Orders_Pend WHERE ' Orlando = 1'; --

    D. WHERE Location_City = Orlando'1 = 1': DROP_TABLE; --

    ☑ **A.** SQL queries usually read pretty straightforward, although they can get complicated pretty quickly. In this case you're telling the database, "Can you check the table Orders_Pend and see whether there's a city called Orlando? Oh, by the way, since you're executing any command I send anyway, just go ahead and drop the table called Orders_Pend while you're at it." The only thing missing from SQL queries is a thank-you at the end.

    ☒ **B**, **C**, and **D** are incorrect because these are not proper syntax.

15. Efforts to gain information from a target website have produced the following error message:

```
Microsoft OLE DB Provider for ODBC Drivers error '80040e08'
[Microsoft]{OBDC SQL Server Driver}
```

Which of the following best describes the error message?

    A. The site may be vulnerable to XSS.

    B. The site may be vulnerable to buffer overflow.

C. The site may be vulnerable to SQL injection.

D. The site may be vulnerable to a malware injection.

☑ **C.** Once again, you will get a few "gimme" questions on the exam. The error message clearly displays a SQL error, telling us there's an underlying SQL database to contend with and it's most likely not configured correctly (or we wouldn't be getting an error message like this—through a web interface and telling us exactly what's there—in the first place).

☒ **A**, **B**, and **D** are all incorrect for the same reason: the error message simply doesn't provide enough information to make those leaps. There is nothing here indicating cross-site scripting or buffer overflow on either side of the ledger. Although it's true the error may indicate which kinds of malware may increase your odds of success, there's nothing there to indicate, by itself, that the site is vulnerable.

16. An attacker discovers a legitimate username (user1) and enters the following into a web form authentication window:

Which of the following is most likely the attack being attempted?

A. SQL injection

B. LDAP injection

C. URL tampering

D. DHCP amplification

☑ **B.** LDAP injection works a lot like SQL injection—you enter code that is passed by the application to something behind it for processing. With LDAP injection, if the input is not validated, you can enter direct LDAP queries into the form and watch for results. In this case, the attacker logs in without any password. The actual LDAP query from a legitimate login would have appeared like this: **(&(user=user1)(password=meh))**. The addition of the **)(&)** characters turns the expression to this **(&(user=user1)(&))(password=meh))**, which processes only the username portion of the query. And since that's always true, *voilà*—the attacker is in.

LDAP injection questions may also center on the Boolean operators used in syntax. The operators to remember are summarized in the following table:

OPERATOR	SYNTAX
=	(objectclass=user)
>=	(mdbStorageQuota>=10000)
<=	(mdbStorageQuota<=10000)
~=	(displayName~=Jones)
*	(displayName=*Jon*)
AND (&)	(&(objectclass=user) (displayName=Jones)
OR (|)	(|(objectclass=user) (displayName=Jones)
NOT (!)	(!(objectclass=user) (displayName=Jones)

☒ **A** is incorrect because this does not indicate a SQL injection attack. SQL injection attempts make use of the open quote and SQL statements: for example, **test ') ;DROP TABLE Users;--**.

☒ **C** is incorrect because this does not show a URL tampering attack.

☒ **D** is incorrect because this does not show a DHCP amplification attack.

17. Which of the following is a standard method for web servers to pass a user's request to an application and receive data back to forward to the user?

    A. SSI

    B. SSL

    C. CGI

    D. CSI

    ☑ **C.** Common Gateway Interface (CGI) is a standardized method for transferring information between a web server and an executable (a CGI script is designed to perform some task with the data). CGI is considered a server-side solution because processing is done on the web server and not the client. Because CGI scripts can run essentially arbitrary commands on your system with the permissions of the web server user and because they are almost always wrapped so that a script will execute as the owner of the script, they can be extremely dangerous if not carefully checked. Additionally, all CGI scripts on the server will run as the same user, so they have the potential to conflict (accidentally or deliberately) with other scripts (an attacker could, for example, write a CGI script to destroy all other CGI databases).

    ☒ **A** is incorrect because server-side includes (SSIs) are directives placed in HTML pages and evaluated on the server while the pages are being served. They let you add dynamically generated content to an existing HTML page, without having to serve the entire page via a CGI program or other dynamic technology.

☒ **B** and **D** are incorrect because both are included as distractors. By now you're certainly familiar with Secure Sockets Layer (SSL) and its value as an encryption method. CSI? Well, that's just good television. Or it used to be, anyway.

18. An attacker performs a SQL injection attack but receives nothing in return. She then proceeds to send multiple SQL queries, soliciting TRUE or FALSE responses. Which attack is being carried out?

    A. Blind SQL injection

    B. SQL denial of service

    C. SQL code manipulation

    D. SQL replay

    ☑ **A.** Blind SQL injection is really kinda neat, even if you're not a nerd. Sometimes a security admin does just enough to frustrate efforts, and you don't receive the error messages or returned information you originally counted on. So, to pull out the info you want, you start asking it (the SQL database) a lot of true or false questions. For example, you could ask the database, "True or false—you have a table called USERS?" If you get a TRUE, then you know the table name and can start asking questions about it. For example, "Hey, database, got an entry in your USERS table named admin?" (SELECT * from USERS where name='admin' and 1=1;#';). Blind SQL is a long, laborious effort, but it can be done.

    ☒ **B, C,** and **D** are all incorrect because, so far as I know, none of them is a recognized attack by EC-Council. I'm sure you can find ways to perform a DoS on a SQL database, and we're manipulating SQL all over the place in these injection attacks, but these terms just aren't recognized on your exam and are here solely as distractors.

19. A tester is attempting a CSPP attack. Which of the following is she most likely to use in conjunction with the attack?

    A. ;

    B. :

    C. '

    D. "

    E. --

    F. ~

    ☑ **A.** CSPP (connection string parameter attack) is another form of an injection attack. In many web applications, communications with back-end databases make use of the semicolon to separate parameter requests. Much as with URL tampering, in CSPP you just change the communication string and see what happens: add a semicolon, type in your request, and watch to see if it was successful.

    ☒ **B, C, D, E,** and **F** are incorrect because these characters do not correspond to a CSPP attack. The single quote is most often tied to a SQL injection attempt. The other characters may show up in scripts strings and whatnot, but don't let them fool you—they're simply distractors.

20. An attacker is attempting to elevate privileges on a machine by using Java or other functions, through nonvalidated input, to cause the server to execute a malicious piece of code and provide command-line access. Which of the following best describes this action?

    A. Shell injection

    B. File injection

    C. SQL injection

    D. URL injection

    ☑ **A.** When it comes to web application attacks, there are many vectors and avenues to take. One of the more common is injecting something into an input string to exploit poor code. EC-Council defines these attacks in many ways. Also known as *command injection,* shell injection is defined as an attempt to gain shell access using Java or other functions. In short, the attacker will pass commands through a form input (or other avenue) in order to elevate privileges and open a shell for further naughtiness. It occurs when commands are entered into form fields instead of the expected entry.

    ☒ **B** is incorrect because the EC-Council defines a file injection attack as one where the attacker injects a pointer in the web form input to an exploit hosted on a remote site. Sure, this may accomplish the same thing, but it's not the best choice in this case.

    ☒ **C** is incorrect because SQL injection attacks involve using SQL queries and commands to elicit a response or action.

    ☒ **D** is incorrect because URL injection is not an attack type and is included here as a distractor.

21. An attacker is successful in using a cookie, stolen during an XSS attack, during an invalid session on the server by forcing a web application to act on the cookie's contents. How is this possible?

    A. A cookie can be replayed at any time, no matter the circumstances.

    B. Encryption was accomplished using a single key.

    C. Authentication was accomplished using XML.

    D. Encryption was accomplished at the network layer.

    ☑ **B.** Cookies can be used for all sorts of things. If you can grab all user cookies, you can see what they visited and sometimes even how long they've been there. Cookies can also hold passwords—and because most people use the same password on multiple sites, this can be a gold mine for the attacker. In this scenario, the cookie is being replayed by an attacker to gain access to goodies. If a single key is used in encryption, a replay attack is possible, because cookie authentication is carried out at the application layer. It is for this reason some organization require browsers to automatically delete cookies on termination.

☒ **A** is incorrect because a replay attack of anything—cookie, stolen authentication stream, and so on—can't necessarily be carried out at any time. Replay attacks require planning and proper setup.

☒ **C** is incorrect because XML has nothing to do with this.

☒ **D** is incorrect because encryption is not carried out at the network layer here.

22. HTML forms include several methods for transferring data back and forth. Inside a form, which of the following encodes the input into the Uniform Resource Identifier (URI)?

   A. HEAD

   B. PUT

   C. GET

   D. POST

☑ **C.** An HTTP GET is a method for returning data from a form that "encodes" the form data to the end of the URI (a character string that identifies a resource on the Web, such as a page of text, a video clip, an image, or an application). For example, if you were to enter a credit card number in a form using GET, the resulting URL might look something like https://somesite.com/creditcard .asp?c#=4013229567852219, where the long number is obviously a credit card number just sitting there waiting for anyone to use.

Generally speaking, a POST is "more secure" than a GET, although they both have their uses. If you're wondering when a GET should be used as opposed to a POST, the answer has to do with a vocabulary lesson: defining the term *idempotent*. Thrown about with HTTP GET, idempotent is a mathematical concept about an operation property: if the operation can be performed without changing results, even if it is run multiple times, it's considered idempotent. Therefore, if the input return is assured of having no lasting effect on the state of the form in total, then using a GET is perfectly reasonable. Also, a GET can usually transfer only up to 8KB, whereas a POST can usually handle up to 2GB. However, keep in mind it may wind up including sensitive information in that URI. Suppose your form returns a credit card number and a bad guy is logging URIs: if HTTP GET is in place, the attacker may be able to derive the information. In short, users can manipulate both GET and POST, but GET is simply more visible because of its reliance on something that browsers render to the screen in an editable field. A POST is meant for pushing data directly, and a GET is used when the server is expected to pull something from the data submitted in the URL.

☒ **A** is incorrect because although HEAD and GET are similar, HEAD is not used in forms. It's usually used to pull header information from a web server (for example, banner grabbing) and to test links.

☒ **B** is incorrect because HTTP PUT is not used in forms. It's used to transfer files to a web server.

☒ **D** is incorrect because POST does not include the form data in the URI request. According to the World Wide Web Consortium (http://www.w3.org/), HTML specifications define the difference between GET and POST so that GET means that form data will be encoded by a browser into a URL, whereas POST means the form data is to appear within the message body. In short, a GET can be used for basic, simple retrieval of data, and a POST should be used for most everything else (such as sending an e-mail, updating data on a database, and ordering an item).

23. An attacker is looking at a target website and is viewing an account from the store on URL http://www.anybiz.com/store.php?id=2. He next enters the following URL:

    http://www.anybiz.com/store.php?id=2 and 1=1

    The web page loads normally. He then enters the following URL:

    http://www.anybiz.com/store.php?id=2 and 1=2

    A generic page noting "An error has occurred" appears.

    Which of the following is a correct statement concerning these actions?

    A. The site is vulnerable to cross-site scripting.

    B. The site is vulnerable to blind SQL injection.

    C. The site is vulnerable to buffer overflows.

    D. The site is not vulnerable to SQL injection.

    ☑ **B.** The URLs shown here are attempting to pass a SQL query through to see what may be going on in the background. Notice the first URL entered added **and 1=1**. Because this was a true statement, the page loaded without problem. However, changing that to a false statement—**and 1=2**—caused the database to return an error. This would now be considered "blind" SQL injection because the actual error was not returned to the attacker (instead, he got a generic page most likely configured by the database administrator). As an aside, sometimes the attacker won't receive the error message or error page at all, but the site will be displayed differently—images out of place, text messed up, and so on—which also indicates blind SQL may be in order.

    ☒ **A** and **C** are incorrect because neither this attack nor the results have anything to do with cross-site scripting or buffer overflows.

    ☒ **D** is incorrect because the results indicate SQL injection is possible. Granted, it will take longer, because the attacker can't see error messaging, and will require lots of guesswork and trial and error, but it is susceptible.

24. Which of the following is not true regarding WebGoat?

    A. WebGoat is maintained and made available by OWASP.

    B. WebGoat can be installed on Windows systems only.

C. WebGoat is based on a black-box testing mentality.

D. WebGoat can use Java or .NET.

☑ **B.** WebGoat, now in version 7 (https://www.owasp.org/index.php/Category:OWASP_ WebGoat_Project), is a deliberately insecure web application maintained by OWASP designed to teach web application security lessons. In each lesson, users must demonstrate their understanding of a security issue by exploiting a real vulnerability in the WebGoat application. It's designed to teach from a black-box mentality (that is, learners aren't provided with all information up front, and must discover what they need to know to figure out each lesson, just as they'd have to do in the real world), can be installed on virtually anything, and makes use of Java and .NET.

☒ **A, C,** and **D** are incorrect because they are true statements regarding WebGoat.

25. An attacker is viewing a blog entry showing a news story and asking for comments. In the comment field, the attacker enters the following:

```
Nice post and a fun read
<script>onload=window.location='http://www.badsite.com'</script>
```

What is the attacker attempting to perform?

A. A SQL injection attack against the blog's underlying database

B. A cross-site scripting attack

C. A buffer overflow DoS attack

D. A file injection DoS attack

☑ **B.** This is a classic (an overly simplified but classic nonetheless) example of cross-site scripting. In a blog, the post entry field is intended to take text entry from a visitor and copy it to a database in the background. What's being attempted here is to have more than just the text copied—the <script> indicator is adding a nice little pointer to a naughty website. If it works, the next visitor to the site who clicks that news story will be redirected to the bad site location.

☒ **A, C,** and **D** are all incorrect because this example contains nothing to indicate a SQL injection or a buffer overflow. Additionally, the idea here is not to perform a denial of service. Actually, it's quite the opposite: the attacker wants the site up and operational so more and more users can be sent to badsite.com.

26. Which of the following is one of the most common methods for an attacker to exploit the Shellshock vulnerability?

A. SSH brute force

B. CSRF

C. Form field entry manipulation

D. Through web servers utilizing CGI (Common Gateway Interface)

☑ **D.** I would bet very large sums of cash you will see Shellshock on your exam—maybe even a couple of times. Shellshock (also known as Bashdoor) exploits a feature in bash shell designed to allow environmental variable setting configuration. Basically someone was playing around in bash back in 2014 and figured out they could add arbitrary commands to environmental variable configuration command-line submissions. If an attacker input something like

```
env val='() [ :;}; echo BADCOMMAND' bash -c "echo  REALCOMMAND"
```

on a vulnerable system, BADCOMMAND would be executed before the real command.

Per Symantec (http://www.symantec.com/connect/blogs/shellshock-all-you-need-know-about-bash-bug-vulnerability), "The most likely route of attack is through Web servers utilizing CGI (Common Gateway Interface), the widely used system for generating dynamic Web content. An attacker can potentially use CGI to send a malformed environment variable to a vulnerable Web server. Because the server uses Bash to interpret the variable, it will also run any malicious command tacked on to it." Other avenues for Shellshock exploitation include the following:

- **OpenSSH**   The "force command" function (where a fixed command is run when a user logs on, even if the user requested a different command) can be exploited in Shellshock.

- **DHCP**   Some DHCP clients have the capability of passing commands to the bash shell—for example, during connection to a Wi-Fi network. This can be exploited in Shellshock.

- **Qmail**   If bash is used to process e-mail messaging, the server processes external input in a way that can be exploited in bash.

☒ **A** is incorrect because brute-forcing an SSH session login has nothing to do with Shellshock.

☒ **B** is incorrect because cross-site request forgery is a different vulnerability altogether, dealing with web browser hijacking.

☒ **C** is incorrect because form field manipulation has nothing to do with Shellshock.

27. You are examining website files and find the following text file:

```
# robots.txt for http://www.anybiz.com/
User-agent: Googlebot
Disallow: /tmp/
User-agent: *
Disallow: /
Disallow: /private.php
Disallow: /listing.html
```

Which of the following is a true statement concerning this file?

A. All web crawlers are prevented from indexing the listing.html page.

B. All web crawlers are prevented from indexing all pages on the site.

C. The Googlebot crawler is allowed to index pages starting with /tmp/.

D. The Googlebot crawler can access and index everything on the site except for pages starting with /tmp/.

☑ **D.** The robots.txt file was created to allow web designers to control index access to their sites. There are a couple of things you need to know about this file—for your exam and the real world. The first is, no matter what the robots.txt file says, attackers using a crawler to index your site are going to ignore it anyway: it's valid only for "good-guy" crawlers. After that, the rest is easy: robots.txt is stored on the root, is available to anyone (by design), and is read in order from top to bottom, much like an ACL on a router. The format is simple: define the crawler (**User-agent :*name_of_crawler***), and then define what it does not have access to. Most robot.txt files will make use of the * variable to signify all crawlers, but you can certainly get specific with who is allowed in and what they can see.

In this example, from top to bottom, the Googlebot crawler is defined and restricted from seeing /tmp/ pages—no other restrictions are listed. After that, all other crawlers (**User-agent: ***) are restricted from seeing any page (**Disallow: /**). The last two lines are truly irrelevant because the condition to ignore all pages has been read.

For additional information here, if you think about what a robots.txt file does, you could consider it a pointer to pages you, as an attacker, really want to see. After all, if the security person on the site didn't want Google indexing it, useful information probably resides there. On the flip side, a security-minded person may get a little snippy with it and have a little fun, sending you to some truly terrible Internet locations should you try to access one of the pages listed there.

☒ **A** and **B** are incorrect because the Googlebot crawler is allowed to crawl the site.

☒ **C** is incorrect because Googlebot is instructed to ignore all /tmp/ pages.

Wireless Network Hacking

This chapter includes questions from the following topics:
- Describe wireless network architecture and terminology
- Identify wireless network types and forms of authentication
- Describe wireless encryption algorithms
- Identify wireless hacking methods and tools
- Describe mobile platform attacks
- Identify Mobile Device Management

I grew up in a time when television had only three channels, the music industry was all up in arms because of the new technology allowing anyone to tape their own music (cassette tapes), and if you needed to talk to someone about something, you had to either meet them face to face or call their one and only home phone (and hope they were there). Oh, sure, the ultra-rich had phones built into their limos (not really much more than glorified CB radio devices actually), but the idea of a cell phone didn't really hit the public consciousness until sometime in the early 1980s. In fact, the first real foray into the technology came in 1973, when a Motorola researcher created a mobile phone. The handset came in at a stealthy 8 by 5 inches, weighing approximately 2½ pounds, and offered a whopping 30 minutes of talk time.

After a decade or so of further research and attempts at bringing the technology to market, the first analog cellular network (Advanced Mobile Phone Service [AMPS]) hit the United States, and a company called DynaTAC released a device that has been ridiculed in technology circles for decades now—the bag phone. Despite the weight and bulkiness of the system and that it provided only a half hour of talk time and took nearly 10 hours to charge, demand for the thing was incredible, and people signed up on waiting lists by the thousands.

I remember quite clearly how jealous I felt seeing people driving around with those ultra-cool giant-battery phones that they could use anywhere. I even looked into buying one and can remember the first time I slung that big old bag over my head to rest the strap on my shoulder so I could heft the cord-connected handset and dial home. Looking back, it seems really silly, but that strong desire by the consumer population fueled an explosion in mobile device technology that has changed the world.

The wireless revolution touched everything in life—not just the humble phone. We looked at making everything wireless and just knew we could do it. (*Star Trek* had been showing wireless communication for decades, so why not?) Computer networks were an obvious branch to follow, and seemingly everything else followed. Our wireless technologies are now as much part of life as the light switch on the wall—we wouldn't know what to do without them, and we all just *expect* it all to work. Hence the problem.

I've said repeatedly that almost every technological implementation designed to make our lives easier and better can be, and usually has already been, corrupted by the bad guys, and wireless tech is no exception. Wireless networks are everywhere, and they're broadcasting information across the air that anyone can pick up. Cellular devices are called smartphones, even though the users of the devices aren't, and mobile malware is as common and ubiquitous as teenagers texting during family dinner. And the opportunity for co-opting wireless signals that control everything else, such as your car's built-in computer functions, your refrigerator, and maybe the turbine control at the local power plant? Let's just say that while all this wireless technology is really cool and offers us a whole lot of benefits, we better all pay attention to the security side of the whole thing. Who knows what kind of societal uproar could take place if cellular devices and computer networking were taken down and nobody could play Angry Birds?

 STUDY TIPS Depending on the pool of test questions the system pulls for your exam, you'll either grow to love the test you're taking or hate it with a fiery passion. Questions on wireless and mobile platforms are usually fairly easy and shouldn't bother you too much. Except for the ones that aren't— those will drive you insane.

Whereas EC-Council once seemed to focus on WEP, SSIDs, and weird questions on encoding methods, channel interference, and things of that nature, now they're much more focused on the mobile world. Yes, you will still see the same old stuff on wireless networking you're supposed to know—tools used in hacking wireless, encryption standards, and so on—but be prepped to see much more of a mobile-device-centric layout now. Make sure you know Bluetooth well, and check out any and all mobile device tools you can find—there will likely be a couple off-the-wall mobile tool questions along the way, and I can't possibly put them all in here. Mobile Device Management (MDM), BYOD, rooting, and jailbreaking are all topics you'll need to read up on and know well.

1. A company hires you as part of their security team. They are implementing new policies and procedures regarding mobile devices in the network. Which of the following would *not* be a recommended practice?

   A. Create a BYOD policy and ensure all employees are educated and aware of it.

   B. Whitelist applications and ensure all employees are educated and aware of them.

   C. Allow jailbroken and rooted devices on the network, as long as the employee has signed the policy.

   D. Implement MDM.

2. Which of the following is a true statement?

   A. Kismet can be installed on Windows, but not on Linux.

   B. NetStumbler can be installed on Linux, but not on Windows.

   C. Kismet cannot monitor traffic on 802.11n networks.

   D. NetStumbler cannot monitor traffic on 802.11n networks.

3. Which of the following tools would be used in a blackjacking attack?

   A. Aircrack

   B. BBCrack

   C. BBProxy

   D. Paros Proxy

4. Which of the following use a 48-bit initialization vector? (Choose all that apply.)

   A. WEP

   B. WPA

   C. WPA2

   D. WEP2

5. Which of the following are true statements? (Choose all that apply.)

   A. WEP uses shared key encryption with TKIP.

   B. WEP uses shared key encryption with RC4.

   C. WPA2 uses shared key encryption with RC4.

   D. WPA2 uses TKIP and AES encryption.

6. Which of the following tools is a vulnerability scanner for Android devices?

   A. X-ray

   B. evasi0n7

   C. Pangu

   D. DroidSheep Guard

7. Which type of jailbreaking allows user-level access but does not allow iBoot-level access?

    A. iBoot

    B. Bootrom

    C. userland

    D. iRoot

8. While on vacation, Joe receives a phone call from his identity alert service notifying him that two of his accounts have been accessed in the past hour. Earlier in the day, he did connect a laptop to a wireless hotspot at McDonald's and accessed the two accounts in question. Which of the following is the most likely attack used against Joe?

    A. Unauthorized association

    B. Honeyspot access point

    C. Rogue access point

    D. Jamming signal

9. An attacker is attempting to crack a WEP code to gain access to the network. After enabling monitor mode on wlan0 and creating a monitoring interface (mon 0), she types this command:

    ```
    aireplay -ng -0 0 -a 0A:00:2B:40:70:80 -c mon0
    ```

    What is she trying to accomplish?

    A. To gain access to the WEP access code by examining the response to deauthentication packets, which contain the WEP code

    B. To use deauthentication packets to generate lots of network traffic

    C. To determine the BSSID of the access point

    D. To discover the cloaked SSID of the network

10. Which wireless standard works at 54 Mbps on a frequency range of 2.4 GHz?

    A. 802.11a

    B. 802.11b

    C. 802.11g

    D. 802.11n

11. The team has discovered an access point configured with WEP encryption. What is needed to perform a fake authentication to the AP in an effort to crack WEP? (Choose all that apply.)

    A. A captured authentication packet

    B. The IP address of the AP

    C. The MAC address of the AP

    D. The SSID

12. Which of the tools listed here is a passive discovery tool?

    A. Aircrack

    B. Kismet

    C. NetStumbler

    D. Netsniff

13. You have discovered an access point using WEP for encryption purposes. Which of the following is the best choice for uncovering the network key?

    A. NetStumbler

    B. Aircrack

    C. John the Ripper

    D. Kismet

14. Which of the following statements are true regarding TKIP? (Choose all that apply.)

    A. Temporal Key Integrity Protocol forces a key change every 10,000 packets.

    B. Temporal Key Integrity Protocol ensures keys do not change during a session.

    C. Temporal Key Integrity Protocol is an integral part of WEP.

    D. Temporal Key Integrity Protocol is an integral part of WPA.

15. Regarding SSIDs, which of the following are true statements? (Choose all that apply.)

    A. SSIDs are always 32 characters in length.

    B. SSIDs can be up to 32 characters in length.

    C. Turning off broadcasting prevents discovery of the SSID.

    D. SSIDs are part of every packet header from the AP.

    E. SSIDs provide important security for the network.

    F. Multiple SSIDs are needed to move between APs within an ESS.

16. You are discussing WEP cracking with a junior pen test team member. Which of the following are true statements regarding the initialization vectors? (Choose all that apply.)

    A. IVs are 32 bits in length.

    B. IVs are 24 bits in length.

    C. IVs get reused frequently.

    D. IVs are sent in clear text.

    E. IVs are encrypted during transmission.

    F. IVs are used once per encryption session.

17. A pen test member has configured a wireless access point with the same SSID as the target organization's SSID and has set it up inside a closet in the building. After some time, clients begin connecting to his access point. Which of the following statements are true regarding this attack? (Choose all that apply.)

    A. The rogue access point may be discovered by security personnel using NetStumbler.

    B. The rogue access point may be discovered by security personnel using NetSurveyor.

    C. The rogue access point may be discovered by security personnel using Kismet.

    D. The rogue access point may be discovered by security personnel using Aircrack.

    E. The rogue access point may be discovered by security personnel using ToneLoc.

18. A pen test member is running the Airsnarf tool from a Linux laptop. What is she attempting?

    A. MAC flooding against an AP on the network

    B. Denial-of-service attacks against APs on the network

    C. Cracking network encryption codes from the WEP AP

    D. Stealing usernames and passwords from an AP

19. What frequency does Bluetooth operate in?

    A. 2.4–2.48 GHz

    B. 2.5 GHz

    C. 2.5–5 GHz

    D. 5 GHz

20. What is the integrity check mechanism for WPA2?

    A. CBC-MAC

    B. CCMP

    C. RC4

    D. TKIP

21. Jack receives a text message on his phone advising him of a major attack at his bank. The message includes a link to check his accounts. After clicking the link, an attacker takes control of his accounts in the background. Which of the following attacks is Jack facing?

    A. Phishing

    B. Smishing

    C. Vishing

    D. App sandboxing

22. Which of the following allows an Android user to attain privileged control of the device?

   A. DroidSheep

   B. SuperOneClick

   C. Faceniff

   D. ZitMo

23. Which of the following is a true statement regarding wireless security?

   A. WPA2 is a better encryption choice than WEP.

   B. WEP is a better encryption choice than WPA2.

   C. Cloaking the SSID and implementing MAC filtering eliminate the need for encryption.

   D. Increasing the length of the SSID to its maximum increases security for the system.

24. A pen test colleague is attempting to use a wireless connection inside the target's building. On his Linux laptop he types the following commands:

```
ifconfig wlan0 down
ifconfig wlan0 hw ether 0A:0B:0C:1A:1B:1C
ifconfig wlan0 up
```

   What is the most likely reason for this action?

   A. Port security is enabled on the access point.

   B. The SSID is cloaked from the access point.

   C. MAC filtering is enabled on the access point.

   D. Weak signaling is frustrating connectivity to the access point.

25. An individual attempts to make a call using his cell phone; however, it seems unresponsive. After a few minutes of effort, he turns it off and turns it on again. During his next phone call, the phone disconnects and becomes unresponsive again. Which Bluetooth attack is underway?

   A. Bluesmacking

   B. Bluejacking

   C. Bluesniffing

   D. Bluesnarfing

26. Which of the following is a pairing mode in Bluetooth that rejects every pairing request?

   A. Non-pairing

   B. Non-discoverable

   C. Promiscuous

   D. Bluejack

1. C	**10.** C	**19.** A
2. D	**11.** C, D	**20.** A
3. C	**12.** B	**21.** B
4. B, C	**13.** B	**22.** B
5. B, D	**14.** A, D	**23.** A
6. A	**15.** B, D	**24.** C
7. C	**16.** B, C, D	**25.** A
8. B	**17.** A, B, C	**26.** A
9. B	**18.** D	

1. A company hires you as part of their security team. They are implementing new policies and procedures regarding mobile devices in the network. Which of the following would *not* be a recommended practice?

   A. Create a BYOD policy and ensure all employees are educated and aware of it.

   B. Whitelist applications and ensure all employees are educated and aware of them.

   C. Allow jailbroken and rooted devices on the network, as long as the employee has signed the policy.

   D. Implement MDM.

   ☑ **C.** Bring Your Own Device (BYOD) and Mobile Device Management (MDM) are becoming more and more of a headache for security administrators. BYOD is the idea that employees can bring their own smartphones, tablets, and mobile devices to the workplace and use them as part of the enterprise network. Mobile Device Management (often implemented with the use of a third-party product containing management features for mobile device vendors) is an effort to administrate and secure mobile device use within the organization.

   Obviously having mobile devices roaming in and out of a network can cause all sorts of security issues, and there are lots of common-sense steps that can be taken. Allowing rooted and jailbroken devices—essentially devices that could have any number of installed (knowingly or not) issues on them—is not among the good steps to take.

   ☒ **A, B,** and **D** are incorrect choices because these are all good ideas regarding mobile device use and management. Other good ideas include, but are not limited to, ensuring all devices have a screen lockout code enabled, using encryption (in transit and for data-at-rest concerns), making sure there are clear delineations between business and personal data, implementing antivirus, and making sure the OS and patching are up to date.

2. Which of the following is a true statement?

   A. Kismet can be installed on Windows, but not on Linux.

   B. NetStumbler can be installed on Linux, but not on Windows.

   C. Kismet cannot monitor traffic on 802.11n networks.

   D. NetStumbler cannot monitor traffic on 802.11n networks.

   ☑ **D.** Not only is this question overly confusing and very tool specific, it's pretty much exactly the type of question you'll see on your exam. Kismet and NetStumbler are both wireless monitoring tools with detection and sniffing capabilities. NetStumbler is Windows specific, whereas Kismet can be installed on virtually anything. Both do a great job of monitoring 802.11a, b, and g networks, but NetStumbler can't handle 802.11n. Kismet can even be used as an IDS for your wireless network!

One last fun-fact to know in relation to this question—Kismet does a better job of pulling management packets. A lot of wireless cards on Windows systems don't support monitor mode and have a difficult time pulling management and control packets.

☒ **A, B,** and **C** are incorrect statements. Kismet can be installed on anything, NetStumbler is Windows specific and not available on Linux, and Kismet can monitor 802.11n networks.

3. Which of the following tools would be used in a blackjacking attack?

   A. Aircrack

   B. BBCrack

   C. BBProxy

   D. Paros Proxy

   ☑ **C.** This is another tool-specific question, but one that should be relatively easy. Blackjacking and BBProxy were exposed at DefCon several years ago, so this isn't anything new in terms of an attack. In short, a Blackberry device is, in effect, part of the internal network, and configuring an attack properly on the handset may provide access to resources on the internal network. BBProxy is used in part of this attack, and you can see the whole thing pulled off at this link from the original presentation in 2006: http://www.praetoriang.net/presentations/blackjack.html.

   ☒ **A, B,** and **D** are incorrect because these tools aren't used in blackjacking attempts. Aircrack is used in wireless network encryption cracking, and Paros is a proxy service, but neither is used in blackjacking. BBCrack doesn't exist.

4. Which of the following use a 48-bit initialization vector? (Choose all that apply.)

   A. WEP

   B. WPA

   C. WPA2

   D. WEP2

   ☑ **B, C.** One of the improvements from WEP to WPA involved extending the initialization vector (IV) to 48 bits from 24 bits. An initialization vector (IV) provides for confidentiality and integrity. Wireless encryption algorithms use it to calculate an integrity check value (ICV), appending it to the end of the data payload. The IV is then combined with a key to be input into an algorithm (RC4 for WEP, AES for WPA2). Therefore, because the length of an IV determines the total number of potential random values that can possibly be created for encryption purposes, doubling to 48 bits increased overall security. By itself, this didn't answer *all* security problems—it only meant it took a little longer to capture enough IV packets to crack the code—however, combined with other steps it did provide for better security.

☒ **A** is incorrect because WEP uses a 24-bit IV. In WEP, this meant there were approximately 16 million unique IV values. Although this may seem like a large number, it's really not—a determined hacker can capture enough IVs in a brute-force attack in a matter of hours to crack the key.

☒ **D** is incorrect because there is no such thing as WEP2.

5. Which of the following are true statements? (Choose all that apply.)

   A. WEP uses shared key encryption with TKIP.

   B. WEP uses shared key encryption with RC4.

   C. WPA2 uses shared key encryption with RC4.

   D. WPA2 uses TKIP and AES encryption.

   ☑ **B, D.** WEP uses a 24-bit initialization vector and RC4 to "encrypt" data transmissions, although saying that makes me shake in disgust because it's really a misnomer. WEP was designed as *basic* encryption merely to simulate the "security" of being on a wired network—hence, the "equivalent" part in Wired Equivalent Privacy. It was never intended as true encryption protection. WPA was an improvement on two fronts. First, the shared key portion of encryption was greatly enhanced by the use of Temporal Key Integrity Protocol (TKIP). In short, the key used to encrypt data was made temporary in nature and is swapped out every 10,000 packets or so. Additionally, WPA2 uses NIST-approved encryption with AES as the algorithm of choice.

   ☒ **A** is incorrect because WEP does not use TKIP. Along with the same key being used to encrypt and decrypt (shared key), it's not changed and remains throughout the communication process—which is part of the reason it's so easy to crack.

   ☒ **C** is incorrect because WPA2 does not use RC4 as an encryption algorithm.

6. Which of the following tools is a vulnerability scanner for Android devices?

   A. X-ray

   B. evasi0n7

   C. Pangu

   D. DroidSheep Guard

   ☑ **A.** Mobile tools will pop up all over the place on your exam, so do your best to get as much exposure to as many of them as possible. X-ray is an Android vulnerability scanner explicitly called out by EC-Council. It searches out unpatched vulnerabilities and automatically updates for new vulnerability signatures as they are discovered.

   ☒ **B** and **C** are incorrect because both are jailbreaking applications for iOS devices.

   ☒ **D** is incorrect because DroidSheep Guard is a tool that monitors the ARP table on your phone, alerting on suspicious entries and disabling shady Wi-Fi connections.

7. Which type of jailbreaking allows user-level access but does not allow iBoot-level access?

   A. iBoot

   B. Bootrom

   C. Userland

   D. iRoot

   ☑ **C.** I don't own an iPhone, iPod, or iAnything, and have no desire to. However, since iOS is one of the most popular mobile device operating systems, I have to have at least some working knowledge of it. And you do too, if you want to be a CEH. Jailbreaking an iPhone is the process of removing the software restrictions imposed by Apple so you can install a modified set of kernel patches, thereby allowing you to run whatever software or updates you want. EC-Council lists three main methods of jailbreaking, two of which (iBoot and Bootrom) allow something called iBoot access. iBoot access basically refers to the ability to affect the firmware itself.

   Userland is a term referring to the software running on the iOS device *after* the kernel has loaded. Therefore, a userland jailbreak, being entirely software based, can be patched by Apple after the effort. Userland jailbreaks include JailbreakMe Star, Saffron, Spirit, Absinthe, evasi0n, and Pangu.

   ☒ **A** and **B** are incorrect because both jailbreaking efforts allow iBoot access. In other words, each method allows for boot chain-of-trust and firmware update.

   ☒ **D** is incorrect because this is not a type of jailbreaking.

8. While on vacation, Joe receives a phone call from his identity alert service notifying him that two of his accounts have been accessed in the past hour. Earlier in the day, he did connect a laptop to a wireless hotspot at McDonald's and accessed the two accounts in question. Which of the following is the most likely attack used against Joe?

   A. Unauthorized association

   B. Honeyspot access point

   C. Rogue access point

   D. Jamming signal

   ☑ **B.** Sometimes EC-Council creates and uses redundant terminology, so don't blame your happy little author or publication editors for this insanely annoying jewel. In this case, Joe most likely connected to what he thought was the legitimate McDonald's free Wi-Fi while he was getting his morning coffee and checked the accounts in question. However, an attacker in (or close to) the restaurant had set up another wireless network using the same SSID as the restaurant's. This practice is known as the honeyspot attack.

   ☒ **A** is incorrect because the unauthorized association attack exploits so-called soft access points—embedded wireless LAN radios in some mobile devices that can be launched inadvertently and used by the attacker for access to the enterprise network.

☒ **C** is incorrect, but just barely so. The whole idea of a honeyspot attack is predicated on the idea that the attacker has some kind of rogue access point set up to trick people into connecting. However, this is a case of one answer being more correct than the other. Honeyspot attacks are explicitly called out as a separate type of rogue attack by EC-Council, so you'll need to remember it that way.

☒ **D** is incorrect because a jamming attack seeks to DoS the entire signal, not necessarily to steal anything from it.

9. An attacker is attempting to crack a WEP code to gain access to the network. After enabling monitor mode on wlan0 and creating a monitoring interface (mon 0), she types this command:

```
aireplay -ng -0 0 -a 0A:00:2B:40:70:80 -c mon0
```

What is she trying to accomplish?

A. To gain access to the WEP access code by examining the response to deauthentication packets, which contain the WEP code

B. To use deauthentication packets to generate lots of network traffic

C. To determine the BSSID of the access point

D. To discover the cloaked SSID of the network

☑ **B.** Within 802.11 standards, there are several different management-type frames in use: everything from a beacon and association request to something called (and I'm not making this up) a *probe request*. One of these management frames is a deauthentication packet, which basically shuts off a client from the network. The client then has to reconnect—and will do so quickly. The idea behind this kind of activity is to generate lots of traffic to capture in order to discern the WEP access code (from clients trying to re-associate to all the new ARP packets that will come flying around, since many machines will dump their ARP cache after being shut off the network). Remember that the initialization vectors within WEP are relatively short (24 bits) and are reused frequently, so any attempt to crack the code requires, in general, around 15,000 or so packets. You can certainly gather these over time, but generating traffic can accomplish it much faster. One final note on this must be brought up: this type of attack can just as easily result in a denial-of-service attack against hosts and the AP in question, so be careful.

☒ **A** is incorrect because the response to a deauth packet does not contain the WEP access code in the clear. If it did, the attacker wouldn't need to bother with all this traffic generation in the first place—one simple packet would be enough to crack all security.

☒ **C** is incorrect because the basic service set identifier (BSSID) is the MAC address of the AP. It's usually easy enough to gain from any number of methods (using airodump, for instance) and isn't a reason for sending multiple deauth packets. There are networks where the BSSID is hidden (referred to as *cloaking*), but other tools (airmon and airodump) can help with that.

☒ **D** is incorrect because even if an SSID is "cloaked," that doesn't mean it's actually hidden; all it means is that it is not *broadcast*. The SSID is still contained in every single packet sent from the AP, and discovering it is easy enough.

10. Which wireless standard is designed to work at 54 Mbps on a frequency range of 2.4 GHz?

   A. 802.11a

   B. 802.11b

   C. 802.11g

   D. 802.11n

   ☑ **C.** The 802.11 series of standards identifies all sorts of wireless goodies, such as the order imposed on how clients communicate, rules for authentication, data transfer, size of packets, how the messages are encoded into the signal, and so on. 802.11g combines the advantages of both the "a" and "b" standards without as many of the drawbacks. It's fast (at 54 Mbps), is backward compatible with 802.11b clients, and doesn't suffer from the coverage area restrictions 802.11a has to contend with. Considering it operates in the 2.4GHz range, however, there may be some interference issues to deal with. Not only are a plethora of competing networks blasting their signals (sometimes on the same channel) near and around your network, but you also have to consider Bluetooth devices, cordless phones, and even baby monitors that may cause disruption (due to interference) of wireless signals. And microwave ovens happen to run at 2.45 GHz—right smack dab in the middle of the range.

   ☒ **A** is incorrect because 802.11a operates at 54 Mbps but uses the 5GHz frequency range. The big drawback to 802.11a was the frequency range itself—because of the higher frequency, network range was limited. Whereas 802.11b clients could be spread across a relative large distance, 802.11a clients could communicate much faster but had to be closer together. Combined with the increased cost of equipment, this contributed to 802.11a not being fully accepted as a de facto standard. That said, for security purposes, it may not be a bad choice. Not as many people use it, or even look for it, and its smaller range may work to assist you in preventing spillage outside your building.

   ☒ **B** is incorrect because 802.11b operates at 11 Mbps on the 2.4GHz frequency range. It's slower than "a" and "g," but soon after its release it became the de facto standard for wireless. Price and network range contributed to this.

   ☒ **D** is incorrect because 802.11n works at 100 Mbps (+) in frequency ranges from 2.4 to 5 GHz. It achieves this rate using multiple in, multiple out (MIMO) antennas.

11. The team has discovered an access point configured with WEP encryption. What is needed to perform a fake authentication to the AP in an effort to crack WEP? (Choose all that apply.)

   A. A replay of a captured authentication packet

   B. The IP address of the AP

C. The MAC address of the AP

D. The SSID

☑ **C, D.** Cracking WEP generally comes down to capturing a whole bunch of packets and running a little math magic to crack the key. If you want to generate traffic by sending fake authentication packets to the AP, you need the AP's MAC address and the SSID to make the attempt.

☒ **A** and **B** are incorrect because this information is not needed for a fake authentication packet. Sure, you can capture and replay an entire authentication packet, but it won't do much good, and the IP is not needed at all.

12. Which of the tools listed here is a passive discovery tool?

A. Aircrack

B. Kismet

C. NetStumbler

D. Netsniff

☑ **B.** A question like this one can be a little tricky, depending on its wording; however, per the EC-Council, Kismet works as a true passive network discovery tool, with no packet interjection whatsoever. The following is from www.kismetwireless.net: "Kismet is an 802.11 layer 2 wireless network detector, sniffer, and intrusion detection system. Kismet will work with any wireless card which supports raw monitoring (rfmon) mode, and (with appropriate hardware) can sniff 802.11b, 802.11a, 802.11g, and 802.11n traffic. Kismet also supports plugins which allow sniffing other media." You might also see two other interesting notables about Kismet on your exam: First, it works by *channel hopping,* which means to discover as many networks as possible. Second, it has the ability to sniff packets and save them to a log file, readable by Wireshark or TCPDump.

☒ **A** is incorrect because Aircrack is "an 802.11 WEP and WPA-PSK keys cracking program that can recover keys once enough data packets have been captured. It implements the standard FMS attack along with some optimizations like KoreK attacks, as well as the all-new PTW attack" (http://www.aircrack-ng.org).

☒ **C** is incorrect because NetStumbler is considered an active network discovery application. NetStumbler is among the most popular wireless tools you might see in anyone's arsenal.

☒ **D** is incorrect because Netsniff is included as a distractor and is not a valid tool.

13. You have discovered an access point using WEP for encryption purposes. Which of the following is the best choice for uncovering the network key?

A. NetStumbler

B. Aircrack

C. John the Ripper

D. Kismet

☑ **B.** Aircrack is a fast tool for cracking WEP. You'll need to gather a lot of packets (assuming you've collected at least 50,000 packets or so, it'll work swimmingly fast) using another toolset, but once you have them together, Aircrack does a wonderful job cracking the key. One method Aircrack uses that you may see referenced on the exam is *KoreK implementation*, which basically involves slicing bits out of packets and replacing them with guesses—the more this is done, the better the guessing and, eventually, the faster the key is recovered. Other tools for cracking WEP include Cain (which can also use KoreK), KisMac, WEPCrack, and Elcomsoft's Wireless Security Auditor tool.

☒ **A** is incorrect because NetStumbler is a network discovery tool. It can also be used to identify rogue access points and interference and is also useful in measuring signal strength (for aiming antennas and such).

☒ **C** is incorrect because John the Ripper is a Linux-based password-cracking tool, not a wireless key discovery one.

☒ **D** is incorrect because Kismet is a passive network discovery (and other auditing) tool but does not perform key cracking.

14. Which of the following statements are true regarding TKIP? (Choose all that apply.)

    A. Temporal Key Integrity Protocol forces a key change every 10,000 packets.

    B. Temporal Key Integrity Protocol ensures keys do not change during a session.

    C. Temporal Key Integrity Protocol is an integral part of WEP.

    D. Temporal Key Integrity Protocol is an integral part of WPA.

    ☑ **A, D.** TKIP is a significant step forward in wireless security. Instead of sticking with one key throughout a session with a client and reusing it, as occurred in WEP, *Temporal* Key Integrity Protocol changes the key out every 10,000 packets or so. Additionally, the keys are transferred back and forth during an Extensible Authentication Protocol (EAP) authentication session, which makes use of a four-step handshake process in proving the client belongs to the AP, and vice versa. TKIP came about in WPA.

    ☒ **B** and **C** are simply incorrect statements. TKIP does not maintain a single key, it changes the key frequently, and it is part of WPA (and WPA2), not WEP.

15. Regarding SSIDs, which of the following are true statements? (Choose all that apply.)

    A. SSIDs are always 32 characters in length.

    B. SSIDs can be up to 32 characters in length.

    C. Turning off broadcasting prevents discovery of the SSID.

    D. SSIDs are part of every packet header from the AP.

    E. SSIDs provide important security for the network.

    F. Multiple SSIDs are needed to move between APs within an ESS.

☑ **B, D**. Service set identifiers have only one real function in life, so far as you're concerned on this exam: identification. They are not a security feature in any way, shape, or form, and they are designed solely to identify one access point's network from another's—which is part of the reason they're carried in all packets. SSIDs can be up to 32 characters in length but don't have to be that long (in fact, you'll probably discover most of them are not).

☒ **A** is incorrect because SSIDs do not *have* to be 32 characters in length. They *can* be, but they do not have to fill 32 characters of space.

☒ **C** is incorrect because "cloaking" the SSID really doesn't do much at all. It's still part of every packet header, so discovery is relatively easy.

☒ **E** is incorrect because SSIDs are not considered a security feature for wireless networks.

☒ **F** is incorrect because an extended service set (ESS; an enterprise-wide wireless network consisting of multiple APs) requires only a single SSID that all APs work with.

16. You are discussing WEP cracking with a junior pen test team member. Which of the following are true statements regarding the initialization vectors? (Choose all that apply.)

    A. IVs are 32 bits in length.

    B. IVs are 24 bits in length.

    C. IVs get reused frequently.

    D. IVs are sent in clear text.

    E. IVs are encrypted during transmission.

    F. IVs are used once per encryption session.

    ☑ **B, C, D**. Weak initialization vectors and poor encryption are part of the reason WEP implementation is not encouraged as a true security measure on wireless networks. And, let's be fair here, it was never truly designed to be, which is why it's named Wired Equivalent Privacy instead of Wireless Encryption Protocol (as some have erroneously tried to name it). IVs are 24 bits in length, are sent in clear text, and are reused a lot. Capture enough packets, and you can easily crack the code.

    ☒ **A, E,** and **F** are incorrect statements. IVs are not 32 bits in length, are not encrypted themselves, and are definitely not used once per session (that would be even worse than being reused).

17. A pen test member has configured a wireless access point with the same SSID as the target organization's SSID and has set it up inside a closet in the building. After some time, clients begin connecting to his access point. Which of the following statements are true regarding this attack? (Choose all that apply.)

    A. The rogue access point may be discovered by security personnel using NetStumbler.

    B. The rogue access point may be discovered by security personnel using NetSurveyor.

    C. The rogue access point may be discovered by security personnel using Kismet.

D. The rogue access point may be discovered by security personnel using Aircrack.

E. The rogue access point may be discovered by security personnel using ToneLoc.

☑ **A, B, C**. Rogue access points (sometimes called *evil twin attacks*) can provide an easy way to gain useful information from clueless users on a target network. However, be forewarned, security personnel can use multiple tools and techniques to discover rogue APs. NetStumbler is one of the more popular, and useful, tools available. It's a great network discovery tool that can also be used to identify rogue access points, network interference, and signal strength. Kismet, another popular tool, provides many of the same features and is noted as a "passive" network discovery tool. NetSurveyor is a free, easy-to-use Windows-based tool that provides many of the same features as NetStumbler and Kismet and works with virtually every wireless NIC in modern existence. A "professional" version of NetSurveyor is now available (you get ten uses of it before you're required to buy a license). Lastly, identifying a rogue access point requires the security staff to have knowledge of every access point owned—and its MAC. If it's known there are ten APs in the network and suddenly an 11th appears, that alone won't help find and disable the bad one. It takes some level of organization to find these things, and that plays into your hands as an ethical hacker. The longer your evil twin is left sitting there, the better chance it will be found, so keep it short and sweet.

☒ **D** is incorrect because Aircrack is used to crack network encryption codes, not to identify rogue access points.

☒ **E** is incorrect because ToneLoc is a tool used for war dialing (identifying open modems within a block of phone numbers). As an aside, this was also the moniker for a 1980s one-hit-wonder rapper, although I can promise that won't be on your exam.

18. A pen test member is running the Airsnarf tool from a Linux laptop. What is she attempting?

A. MAC flooding against an AP on the network

B. Denial-of-service attacks against APs on the network

C. Cracking network encryption codes from the WEP AP

D. Stealing usernames and passwords from an AP

☑ **D**. Identifying tools and what they do is a big part of the exam—which is easy enough because it's pure memorization, and this is a prime example. Per the website (http://airsnarf.shmoo.com/), "Airsnarf is a simple rogue wireless access point setup utility designed to demonstrate how a rogue AP can steal usernames and passwords from public wireless hotspots. Airsnarf was developed and released to demonstrate an inherent vulnerability of public 802.11b hotspots—snarfing usernames and passwords by confusing users with DNS and HTTP redirects from a competing AP." It basically turns your laptop into a competing AP in the local area and confuses client requests into being sent your way.

☒ **A** is incorrect because Airsnarf does not provide MAC flooding. You may want to MAC flood a network switch for easier sniffing, but that doesn't work the same way for an access point on a wireless network.

☒ **B** is incorrect because Airsnarf is not a DoS tool. You can make an argument the clients themselves are denied service while they're erroneously communicating with the Airsnarf laptop, but it's not the intent of the application to perform a DoS attack on the network. Quite the opposite: the longer things stay up and running, the more usernames and passwords that can be gathered.

☒ **C** is incorrect because Airsnarf is not an encryption-cracking tool. It reads a lot like "Air*crack*," so don't get confused (these will be used as distractors against one another on your exam).

19. What frequency does Bluetooth operate in?

   A. 2.4–2.48 GHz

   B. 2.5 GHz

   C. 2.5–5 GHz

   D. 5 GHz

☑ **A.** Yes, you may actually get a question this "down in the weeds" regarding Bluetooth. As an additional study note, you will commonly see a reference to Bluetooth working at 2.45 GHz (the FCC reserves certain frequency ranges for public access, and this is in the range; check http://reboot.fcc.gov/spectrumdashboard/searchSpectrum .seam?conversationId=4494.com for more details). Bluetooth is designed to work within a ten-meter range and can attach up to eight devices simultaneously. It makes use of something called *spread-spectrum frequency hopping*, which significantly reduces the chance that more than one device will use the same frequency in communicating.

Want more inane knowledge you might get quizzed on out of the blue? You may see a question regarding something called the "phase-shift key" (PSK) used in Bluetooth 2.0 (and other wireless communication methods). Bluetooth 2.0 EDR uses 8DPSK and a really weird one called π/4-DQPSK. They're both digital modulation used in transmission of data. Others in use with wireless communication include Binary PSK (BPSK; used in RFID-type cards), Quadrature PSK (QPSK; used for CDMA cellular and 802.11B communications), and Differential BPSK (DBPSK; also used in 802.11b networking).

☒ **B, C,** and **D** are incorrect frequency ranges for Bluetooth.

20. What is the integrity check mechanism for WPA2?

   A. CBC-MAC

   B. CCMP

   C. RC4

   D. TKIP

☑ **A.** If you've not done your reading and study, this one could be quite tricky. WPA2 uses CCMP as its encryption protocol, and CCMP uses CBC-MAC for authentication and integrity. Counter Mode CBC-MAC Protocol is an encryption protocol specifically designed for 802.11i wireless networking. CCMP uses CBC-MAC for authentication and integrity. As for how it exactly provides for integrity, the true techo-babble answer is very long and confusing, but the short of it is this: the message is encrypted with a block cipher, and the encryption of each block in the chain is dependent on the encryption value of the block in front of it. In other words, if block 2 is altered in any way, then decryption of blocks 3, 4, and so on becomes impossible. One final note on CCMP for your study and memory: CCMP is based on AES processing and uses a 128-bit key and a 128-bit block size, and ECC sometimes refers to it as AES-CCMP.

☒ **B** is incorrect because CCMP is the encryption protocol that makes use of CBC-MAC.

☒ **C** is incorrect because RC4 is an encryption algorithm used by WEP.

☒ **D** is incorrect because Temporal Key Integrity Protocol is used in WPA.

21. Jack receives a text message on his phone advising him of a major attack at his bank. The message includes a link to check his accounts. After clicking the link, an attacker takes control of his accounts in the background. Which of the following attacks is Jack facing?

    A. Phishing

    B. Smishing

    C. Vishing

    D. App sandboxing

    ☑ **B.** *Smishing* is the term given to a mobile device attack whereby an attacker sends an SMS text message to a target with an embedded link. If the user clicks the malicious link, the attacker gains valuable information and control. These attacks are successful for largely the same reasons phishing is so effective in the e-mail world—people just click through sometimes without pausing to think about it. Users who would otherwise ignore an e-mail with a link in it from an unknown (or even known) source sometimes don't think twice when the link is in a text message.

    ☒ **A** is incorrect because the term *phishing* refers to e-mail messaging and works in much the same way as smishing.

    ☒ **C** is incorrect because *vishing* is a term referring to the use of phone calls and voice messaging to carry out an attack.

    ☒ **D** is incorrect because app sandboxing is not an attack on its own: it's a security measure designed to limit resources an application can access on a mobile device.

22. Which of the following allows an Android user to attain privileged control of the device?

    A. DroidSheep

    B. SuperOneClick

C. Faceniff

D. ZitMo

☑ **B.** Rooting of an Android device is the same idea as jailbreaking an iOS one: allowing the user total control over the device to add applications, modify system files and actions, and (in some cases and usually risking security to do so) improve performance. Rooting can be done in a variety of methods, but some tools you can use are SuperOneClick, Superboot, One Click Root, and Kingo. In SuperOneClick, you simply connect the phone to a system over USB (ensuring it's in charge mode only), enable USB Debugging, and run the application.

☒ **A** is incorrect because DroidSheep is a tool used for session hijacking on Android devices. It can extract session IDs and sidejack on WEP, WPA, and WPA2 networks.

☒ **C** is incorrect because Faceniff is a sniffer for Android, designed to sniff and intercept web profiles.

☒ **D** is incorrect because ZitMo (Zeus-in-the-Mobile) is a banking Trojan. ZitMo can even enable bot-like control and command for attackers over the infected device.

23. Which of the following is a true statement regarding wireless security?

A. WPA2 is a better encryption choice than WEP.

B. WEP is a better encryption choice than WPA2.

C. Cloaking the SSID and implementing MAC filtering eliminate the need for encryption.

D. Increasing the length of the SSID to its maximum increases security for the system.

☑ **A.** WPA2 is, by far, a better security choice for your system. It makes use of TKIP, to change out the keys every 10,000 packets instead of using one for the entire session (as in WEP). Additionally, WPA2 uses AES for encryption and a 128-bit encryption key, as opposed to RC4 and 24-bit IVs in WEP.

☒ **B** is incorrect because WEP only provides the equivalent privacy of being on a wired network. Its "encryption" is ridiculously easy to crack and is not considered a valid security measure. It's perfectly reasonable to use it if your goal is just to frustrate casual surfers from connecting to your network (such as your neighbors), but it's not a valid encryption method.

☒ **C** is incorrect because these two options do nothing to protect the actual data being transmitted. SSID cloaking is somewhat pointless, given that SSIDs are included in every header of every packet (not to mention that SSIDs aren't designed for security). MAC filtering will frustrate casual observers; however, spoofing a MAC address on the network is relatively easy and eliminates this as a foolproof security method.

☒ **D** is incorrect because the length of an SSID has nothing whatsoever to do with security and encryption. Increasing the length of the SSID does not increase network security.

24. A pen test colleague is attempting to use a wireless connection inside the target's building. On his Linux laptop he types the following commands:

```
ifconfig wlan0 down
ifconfig wlan0 hw ether 0A:0B:0C:1A:1B:1C
ifconfig wlan0 up
```

What is the most likely reason for this action?

A. Port security is enabled on the access point.

B. The SSID is cloaked from the access point.

C. MAC filtering is enabled on the access point.

D. Weak signaling is frustrating connectivity to the access point.

☑ **C.** The sequence of the preceding commands has the attacker bringing the wireless interface down, changing its hardware address, and then bringing it back up. The most likely reason for this is MAC filtering is enabled on the AP, which is restricting access to only those machines the administrator wants connecting to the wireless network. The easy way around this is to watch traffic and copy one of the MAC addresses. A quick spoof on your own hardware and—*voilà*—you're connected. As an aside, MAC spoofing isn't just for the wireless world. The command would be slightly different (wlan0 refers to a wireless NIC; eth0 would be an example of a wired port), but the idea is the same.

☒ **A** is incorrect because port security isn't an option on wireless access points. Were this attacker connecting to a switch, this might be valid, but not on a wireless connection.

☒ **B** is incorrect because SSID cloaking has nothing to do with this scenario. The commands are adjusting a MAC address.

☒ **D** is incorrect because weak signal strength has nothing to do with this scenario. The commands are adjusting a MAC address.

25. An individual attempts to make a call using his cell phone; however, it seems unresponsive. After a few minutes of effort, he turns it off and turns it on again. During his next phone call, the phone disconnects and becomes unresponsive again. Which Bluetooth attack is underway?

A. Bluesmacking

B. Bluejacking

C. Bluesniffing

D. Bluesnarfing

☑ **A.** From the description, it appears the phone is either defective or—since it's spelled out so nicely in the question for you—there is a denial-of-service attack against the phone. Bluesmacking is a denial-of-service attack on a Bluetooth device. An attacker somewhere nearby (within ten meters or, for the real bad guys, farther away using a big enough transmitter, amplifier, and antenna) is using something like the Linux Bluez packages (http://www.bluez.org) to carry out a DoS against the phone.

☒ **B** is incorrect because bluejacking involves sending unsolicited messages—much like spam—to a Bluetooth device.

☒ **C** is incorrect because bluesniffing is a basic sniffing attempt, where the device's transmissions are sniffed for useful information.

☒ **D** is incorrect because bluesnarfing refers to the actual theft of data directly from the device. This takes advantage of the "pairing" feature of most Bluetooth devices, willingly seeking out other devices to link up with.

26. Which of the following is a pairing mode in Bluetooth that rejects every pairing request?

   A. Non-pairing

   B. Non-discoverable

   C. Promiscuous

   D. Bluejack

☑ **A.** When you get a simple question on the exam, celebrate. Bluetooth has two pairing modes and three discovery modes. Pairing—the decision to pair with another device requesting it—is either turned on (pairing mode, where every request is accepted) or off (non-pairing mode, where every request is rejected). Discovery—the decision to respond to search requests and let the inquiry know the device is live and available—can be fully on (discoverable mode, responding to everything from everyone), partially on (limited-discoverable mode, responding only during a short time span), or off altogether (never answering an inquiry).

☒ **B** is incorrect because non-discoverable is a discovery mode, not a pairing one.

☒ **C** is incorrect because promiscuous has no meaning in this context.

☒ **D** is incorrect because bluejack refers to a Bluetooth attack where an attacker can leverage the target phone's contacts, resulting in anonymous, unsolicited message transmission to targets).

Security in Cloud Computing

This chapter includes questions from the following topics:
- Identify cloud computing concepts
- Understand basic elements of cloud security
- Identify cloud security tools

A few years back my television exploded. Not like in a fiery, Michael-Bay-EXPLOSION movie scene (although that would have provided a great story and been much more entertaining than the show I was watching), but in a soft whimper of electronic death. I was immediately filled with two separate, but equally strong, emotional sentiments. First, that I was going to be out a lot of cash and would have a lot of hassle ahead of me. The second, though, was much more exhilarating: I was going to get to buy a *new* television.

Have you ever seen a perpetually tired, beaten-down parent get to go to an electronics store to actually *buy* something? It's like watching a cult member on the verge of entering their holy land, or a teenage rock fan stepping behind the curtain for backstage access. No minivans, no diapers, no recitals...nothing but pure, unadulterated fun, and I couldn't wait. When I got to the store, the sales staff must have immediately recognized the glow of purchase-ready rapture on my face, because they descended upon me in droves. I was advised about pixels, hues, sound digitalization efforts, something called "true" black, white balance, refresh rate...before I knew what was happening, I was standing in front of a $3000 TV that looked so clear and large I could just step into it. It was beyond HD, crystal clear, and according to the salesman was not only "smart" but also capable of 3D! For a brief moment, my eyes glazed over and I thought, "Yeah, *this* makes sense!"

Thankfully my phone rang and awoke me from my hypnotic stance. Did I need a TV that big? Where would I even put it? What is "smart" technology and is it something I'd even use? And what 3D programming is actually available to see in the first place? I stepped aside, cleared my head...and wound up buying a smart-enabled, 3D TV. Not because I even had any idea what the technology was, but I knew it was cool and brand new. And I wanted it.

Cloud computing isn't anywhere near as exciting as televisions (have you seen the UHD screens available now?), but it is simultaneously a big draw to those searching for enterprise growth and largely misunderstood by a lot of people. EC-Council added a brand-new chapter on the subject in their official courseware, and you can rest assured it will receive more and more attention on the exam as time passes. This chapter captures the exam information you'll need to know regarding cloud computing and security.

 STUDY TIPS   How do you provide study tips on questioning that is so brand new? By comparing the subject matter with those topics you do know about and drawing logical conclusions about what will be targeted.

EC-Council tends to focus on lists, categories, and in-the-weeds specificity in other topics, and cloud computing will be no different. Know the types and deployment models very well, and completely memorize NIST's reference architecture on cloud. Most of the attacks and threats in cloud computing are similar to everything else, but a couple are very specific, and those will likely find their way onto your exam. Lastly, there aren't a whole lot of cloud-specific tools to know, but you will definitely need to be familiar with them.

1. Which of the following statements is true regarding cloud computing?

    A. In IaaS, applications, data, middleware, virtualization, and servers are part of the service provision.

    B. In PaaS, applications, data, middleware, virtualization, and servers are part of the service provision.

    C. In SaaS, applications, data, middleware, virtualization, and servers are part of the service provision.

    D. None of the above.

2. Which of the following is a government-wide program that provides a standardized approach to security assessment, authorization, and continuous monitoring for cloud products and services?

    A. NIST Cloud Architecture

    B. FedRAMP

    C. PCI DSS Cloud Special Interest Group

    D. Cloud Security Alliance

3. A business owner is advised that inventory, storage, sales, and backup online services can be provided cheaper and more securely via a cloud service. After investigating the options, the business owner determines the best cloud service provider for his needs also happens to be the provider for several of his competitors. Should he decide to engage the same provider, which cloud service deployment model will be used?

    A. Private

    B. IaaS

    C. Community

    D. Public

4. In NIST Cloud Computing Reference Architecture, which of the following is the intermediary for providing connectivity between the cloud and the subscriber?

    A. Cloud provider

    B. Cloud carrier

    C. Cloud broker

    D. Cloud auditor

5. A company relies on a private cloud solution for most of its internal computing needs. After expanding into more online retailing, they rely on a portion of a public cloud for external sales and e-commerce offerings. Which of the following best describes the cloud deployment type in use?

   A. Private

   B. Public

   C. Hybrid

   D. Community

6. Cloud computing would be best suited for which of the following businesses?

   A. A medical practice

   B. An established rural general sales store

   C. A law enforcement agency

   D. A Christmas supply store

7. A software company has decided to build and test web applications in a cloud computing environment. Which of the following cloud computing types best describes this effort?

   A. IaaS

   B. PaaS

   C. SaaS

   D. Community

8. Which of the following statements is not true?

   A. Private cloud is operated solely for a single organization.

   B. Public cloud makes use of virtualized servers.

   C. Public cloud is operated over an intranet.

   D. Private cloud makes use of virtualized servers.

9. A company relies solely on Google Docs, Google Sheets, and other provisions for their office documentation software needs. Which of the following cloud computing types best describes this?

   A. SaaS

   B. PaaS

   C. IaaS

   D. Public

10. A subscriber purchases machine virtualization and hosting through Amazon EC2. Which of the following cloud computing types does this describe?

    A. IaaS

    B. PaaS

    C. SaaS

    D. Hybrid

11. Cloud computing faces many of the same security concerns as traditional network implementations. Which of the following are considered threats to cloud computing?

    A. Data breach or loss

    B. Abuse of services

    C. Insecure interfaces

    D. Malicious insiders

    E. All of the above

12. Which of the following attacks occurs during the translation of SOAP messages?

    A. Wrapping attack

    B. Cross-guest VM

    C. Side channel

    D. Session riding

13. Which of the following is an architectural pattern in computer software design in which application components provide services to other components via a communications protocol, typically over a network?

    A. API

    B. SOA

    C. EC2

    D. IaaS

14. In NIST Cloud Computing Reference Architecture, which entity manages cloud services and maintains the relationship between cloud providers and subscribers?

    A. Cloud broker

    B. Cloud auditor

    C. Cloud carrier

    D. Cloud consumer

15. Which of the following is not a benefit of virtualization?

    A. Allows for more efficient backup, data protection, and disaster recovery

    B. Reduces system administration work

    C. Improves operational efficiency

    D. Locks individual hardware to each individual virtual machine

16. A company acquires a cloud environment for much of its business IT needs. The environment is used and operated solely for the single organization. Which of the following represents the cloud deployment model in question?

    A. Public

    B. IaaS

    C. Sole-source

    D. Private

17. Which of the following is true regarding cloud computing?

    A. Security in the cloud is the responsibility of the provider only.

    B. Security in the cloud is the responsibility of the consumer only.

    C. Security in the cloud is the responsibility of both the consumer and the provider.

    D. None of the above.

18. Which tool offers penetration-test-like services for Amazon EC2 customers?

    A. CloudPassage Halo

    B. Core Cloud

    C. CloudInspect

    D. Panda Cloud Office Protection

19. An attacker sets up a VM on the same physical cloud host as the target's VM. He then takes advantage of the shared physical resources to steal data. Which of the following describes this attack?

    A. Side channel

    B. VM flood

    C. Session riding

    D. Cybersquatting

20. In the trusted computing model, what is a set of functions called that's always trusted by the computer's operating system?

    A. SOA

    B. RoT

    C. TCG

    D. VM

1. C	**8.** C	**15.** D
2. B	**9.** A	**16.** D
3. C	**10.** A	**17.** C
4. B	**11.** E	**18.** C
5. C	**12.** A	**19.** A
6. D	**13.** B	**20.** B
7. B	**14.** A	

ANSWERS

1. Which of the following statements is true regarding cloud computing?

   A. In IaaS, applications, data, middleware, virtualization, and servers are part of the service provision.

   B. In PaaS, applications, data, middleware, virtualization, and servers are part of the service provision.

   C. In SaaS, applications, data, middleware, virtualization, and servers are part of the service provision.

   D. None of the above.

   ☑ **C.** So there are several things EC-Council is very concerned that you know regarding cloud computing, but two in particular are right at the top of the list. The concepts of separation of duties and separation of responsibility—both of which are key aims and benefits of cloud computing—keep popping up over and over again in study materials and will be key to your success. Separation of duties is a provision of all cloud computing types, but only one of the three (Infrastructure as a Service, Platform as a Service, and Software as a Service) takes care of everything. In Software as a Service (SaaS), the service provider delivers the entirety of the span of responsibility. Everything from applications and data through middleware and OS, all the way down to the networking itself, is provided by the service provisioner. For comparison sake, in PaaS, the service provider takes care of everything except the applications and data. In IaaS, the client holds the applications, data, runtime, middleware, and OS, while the provider takes care of everything else—virtualization, servers, storage, and networking.

   ☒ **A, B,** and **D** are incorrect because these are not true statements. In IaaS, the subscriber holds applications, data, and middleware but not virtualization and servers. In PaaS, the client only holds the applications and data.

2. Which of the following is a government-wide program that provides a standardized approach to security assessment, authorization, and continuous monitoring for cloud products and services?

   A. NIST Cloud Architecture

   B. FedRAMP

   C. PCI DSS Cloud Special Interest Group

   D. Cloud Security Alliance

   ☑ **B.** EC-Council, at least as of this writing, doesn't mention one single regulatory effort in cloud computing *at all*, outside of NIST's reference architecture, in their official courseware. This does not mean you will not see any cloud computing regulatory efforts on your exam. I'm willing to bet you'll see more and more of them as time goes on, and FedRAMP is the 800-pound gorilla of cloud computing regulatory efforts you absolutely need to know about.

CEH Certified Ethical Hacker Practice Exams

The Federal Risk and Authorization Management Program (FedRAMP; http://www.fedramp.gov/) is a government-wide program that provides a standardized approach to security assessment, authorization, and continuous monitoring for cloud products and services. It not only provides an auditable framework for ensuring basic security controls for any government cloud effort, but FedRAMP also offers weekly tips for security and configuration and even has free training available on the site. FedRAMP is the result of close collaboration with cybersecurity and cloud experts from the General Services Administration (GSA), National Institute of Standards and Technology (NIST), Department of Homeland Security (DHS), Department of Defense (DOD), National Security Agency (NSA), Office of Management and Budget (OMB), the Federal Chief Information Officer (CIO) Council and its working groups, as well as private industry.

☒ **A** is incorrect because the definition provided does not match the NIST Cloud Computing Reference Architecture. NIST (National Institutes of Standards and Technology) released Special Publication 500-292: NIST Cloud Computing Reference Architecture in 2011 to provide a "fundamental reference point to describe an overall framework that can be used government wide" (http://www.nist.gov/customcf/get_pdf.cfm?pub_id=909505).

☒ **C** is incorrect because the definition provided does not match the PCI Data Security Standard (PCI DSS) Cloud Special Interest Group. PCI is not a federal government regulatory body.

☒ **D** is incorrect because the definition provided does not match the Cloud Security Alliance (CSA). CSA is the leading professional organization devoted to promoting cloud security best practices and organizing cloud security professionals.

3. A business owner is advised that inventory, storage, sales, and backup online services can be provided cheaper and more securely via a cloud service. After investigating the options, the business owner determines the best cloud service provider for his needs also happens to be the provider for several of his competitors. Should he decide to engage the same provider, which cloud service deployment model will be used?

   A. Private

   B. IaaS

   C. Community

   D. Public

   ☑ **C.** In most circumstances, it doesn't matter who else uses the cloud provider you want to use—what matters is the services provided, the costs, and the available security. A *community cloud* model is one where the infrastructure is shared by several organizations, usually with the same policy and compliance considerations. For example, multiple different state-level organizations may get together and take advantage of a community cloud for services they require. Or, in this case, even adversarial competitors may make use of the same services from the same cloud provider.

⊠ **A** is incorrect because a private cloud model is, not surprisingly, private in nature. The cloud is operated solely for a single organization (a.k.a. single-tenant environment) and is usually not a pay-as-you-go type of operation.

⊠ **B** is incorrect because Infrastructure as a Service is a type of cloud computing, not a deployment model.

⊠ **D** is incorrect because a *public cloud* model is one where services are provided over a network that is open for public use (like the Internet). Public cloud is generally used when security and compliance requirements found in large organizations isn't a major issue.

4. In NIST Cloud Computing Reference Architecture, which of the following is the intermediary for providing connectivity between the cloud and the subscriber?

   A. Cloud provider

   B. Cloud carrier

   C. Cloud broker

   D. Cloud auditor

   ☑ **B.** I can guarantee you'll see several questions from the cloud world on your exam, and many of those questions will be simply identifying portions of the NIST Cloud Computing Reference Architecture. The *cloud carrier* is defined in the architecture as the organization with the responsibility of transferring the data—akin to the power distributor for the electric grid. The cloud carrier is the intermediary for connectivity and transport between the subscriber and provider.

   ⊠ **A** is incorrect because the cloud provider is the purveyor of products and services.

   ⊠ **C** is incorrect because the cloud broker acts to manage the use, performance, and delivery of cloud services as well as the relationships between providers and subscribers. The broker acts as the intermediate between the consumer and provider and will help consumers through the complexity of cloud service offerings and may also create value-added cloud services as well.

   ⊠ **D** is incorrect because the cloud auditor is the independent assessor of cloud service and security controls.

5. A company relies on a private cloud solution for most of its internal computing needs. After expanding into more online retailing, they rely on a portion of a public cloud for external sales and e-commerce offerings. Which of the following best describes the cloud deployment type in use?

   A. Private

   B. Public

   C. Hybrid

   D. Community

☑ **C.** A hybrid cloud deployment is exactly what is sounds like—a combination of two or more deployment types together.

☒ **A** is incorrect because a private cloud deployment is operated solely for a single organization (a.k.a. single-tenant environment).

☒ **B** is incorrect because a public cloud deployment model is one where services are provided over a network that is open for public use (like the Internet).

☒ **D** is incorrect because a community cloud deployment model is one where the infrastructure is shared by several organizations, usually with the same policy and compliance considerations.

6. Cloud computing would be best suited for which of the following businesses?

   A. A medical practice

   B. An established rural general sales store

   C. A law enforcement agency

   D. A Christmas supply store

☑ **D.** Scenario questions like this will be peppered throughout your exam on multiple topics, and cloud computing is no different. In this case, the Christmas supply store is, by its very nature, seasonal in nature. This means instead of a steady flow of business and computing resources, they will need much more support during the last couple months of the year than they would in, say, July. Cloud computing provides the elasticity (another term you may see pop up) of adding or removing computing resources as you need them, which could very well save the company money.

☒ **A** is incorrect. Of the choices provided, a medical practice would not be the best choice because of the sensitive data it holds (not to mention the federally mandated protections they would have to have in place for those records).

☒ **B** is incorrect because an established storefront with steady sales and employee staff doesn't necessarily need cloud services.

☒ **C** is incorrect because law enforcement agencies also deal with highly sensitive information. Therefore, of the choices provided, this is not the best one.

7. A software company has decided to build and test web applications in a cloud computing environment. Which of the following cloud computing types best describes this effort?

   A. IaaS

   B. PaaS

   C. SaaS

   D. Community

☑ **B.** This scenario is tailor-made for Platform as a Service (PaaS). Despite also being a name brand recognized mostly during Easter for coloring eggs, PaaS is geared toward software development, as it provides a development platform that allows subscribers to develop applications without building the infrastructure it would normally take to develop and launch software. Hardware and software is hosted by the provider on its own infrastructure, so customers do not have to install or build homegrown hardware and software for development work. PaaS doesn't usually replace an organization's actual infrastructure—instead, it just offers key services the organization may not have on site.

☒ **A** is incorrect because this does not describe Infrastructure as a Service. IaaS provides virtualized computing resources over the Internet. A third-party provider hosts infrastructure components, applications, and services on behalf of its subscribers, with a hypervisor (such as VMware, Oracle VirtualBox, Xen, or KVM) running the virtual machines as guests.

☒ **C** is incorrect because this does not describe Software as a Service. SaaS is simply a software distribution model—the provider offers on-demand applications to subscribers over the Internet.

☒ **D** is incorrect because community refers to the cloud deployment model, not the type.

8. Which of the following statements is not true?

   A. Private cloud is operated solely for a single organization.

   B. Public cloud makes use of virtualized servers.

   C. Public cloud is operated over an intranet.

   D. Private cloud makes use of virtualized servers.

   ☑ **C.** Most of the time I deplore the "not" questions—they seem designed to trip candidates up more than to test their knowledge—but EC-Council (and, not surprisingly, virtually every other certification provider) makes use of them often. In this case, a private cloud is, of course, operated solely for one organization, and virtualization is used in all cloud deployment models. A public cloud, however, explicitly provides services on a network that is open for public use (like the Internet).

   ☒ **A, B,** and **D** are incorrect because these are true statements.

9. A company relies solely on Google Docs, Google Sheets, and other provisions for their office documentation software needs. Which of the following cloud computing types best describes this?

   A. SaaS

   B. PaaS

   C. IaaS

   D. Public

   ☑ **A.** This scenario aptly describes Software as a Service. SaaS is a software distribution model—the provider offers on-demand applications to subscribers over the Internet. Google Docs and Google Sheets, where word processing and spreadsheet software actions are provided online, are perfect examples.

☒ **B** is incorrect because Platform as a Service is a great choice for software development, but is not designed to provide software services in this manner.

☒ **C** is incorrect because Infrastructure as a Service is not designed for use in this manner.

☒ **D** is incorrect because *public* refers to the deployment model.

10. A subscriber purchases machine virtualization and hosting through Amazon EC2. Which of the following cloud computing types does this describe?

    A. IaaS

    B. PaaS

    C. SaaS

    D. Hybrid

    ☑ **A.** There are three types of cloud computing implementation—IaaS, PaaS, and SaaS. In the case of Amazon EC2, Infrastructure as a Service best matches the description. IaaS basically provides virtualized computing resources over the Internet. A third-party provider hosts infrastructure components, applications, and services on behalf of its subscribers, with a *hypervisor* (such as VMware, Oracle VirtualBox, Xen, or KVM) running the virtual machines as guests. Collections of hypervisors within the cloud provider exponentially increase the virtualized resources available and provide scalability of service to subscribers. As a result, IaaS is a good choice not just for day-to-day infrastructure service but also for temporary or experimental workloads that may change unexpectedly. IaaS subscribers typically pay on a per-use basis (within a certain timeframe, for instance) or sometimes by the amount of virtual machine space used.

    ☒ **B** is incorrect because Platform as a Service does not best match this description. PaaS is geared toward software development, as it provides a development platform that allows subscribers to develop applications without building the infrastructure it would normally take to develop and launch software.

    ☒ **C** is incorrect because Software as a Service does not best match this description. SaaS is probably the simplest and easiest to think about. It is simply a software distribution model—the provider offers on-demand applications to subscribers over the Internet.

    ☒ **D** is incorrect because hybrid does not best match this description. The term "hybrid" deals with the deployment method of the cloud (for example, if you had a cloud environment that was both Public and Community in nature, it would be referred to as hybrid).

11. Cloud computing faces many of the same security concerns as traditional network implementations. Which of the following are considered threats to cloud computing?

    A. Data breach or loss

    B. Abuse of services

    C. Insecure interfaces

D. Malicious insiders

E. All of the above

☑ **E.** EC-Council dedicated a lot of real estate in their official courseware to cloud threats, even though much of it is the same as it would be in traditional networking. Three are called out in particular and, because they also appear in the Cloud Security Alliance's "The Notorious Nine: Cloud Computing Top Threats in 2013" publication, it's probably important that you know data breach and loss, abuse of cloud services, and insecure interfaces/APIs. Each is exactly what it sounds like and doesn't require much in the way of explanation. However, the following explanations are for the sake of your exam:

- **Data breach/loss** In addition to data erasure, theft, and/or modification, this also deals with loss of encryption keys and misuse of the data by the Cloud Security Provider itself.

- **Abuse of cloud services** This occurs when the bad guys create anonymous access to cloud services and use the cloud's resources to carry out their activities. Why do password cracking, host exploits, or malware on your own machine when you can do it all in the cloud?

- **Insecure interfaces/APIs** These allow the bad guys to circumvent user-defined policies and perhaps reuse passwords or tokens.

There are pages and pages of cloud computing threats mentioned in the official courseware—everything from insufficient due diligence, shared technology issues, and inadequate planning, through supply chain failure, management interface compromise, and hardware failures. It's impossible to cover them all here, but they're all pretty straightforward. On your exam, you're probably more likely to have to identify which threats *aren't* specific to cloud, and that should be a piece of cake for you.

Lastly, here are the CSA's Notorious Nine: Cloud Computing Top Threats in 2013 (https://downloads.cloudsecurityalliance.org/initiatives/top_threats/The_Notorious_Nine_Cloud_Computing_Top_Threats_in_2013.pdf), listed in order from first to last:

1. Data breaches

2. Data loss

3. Account hijacking

4. Insecure APIs

5. Denial of service

6. Malicious insiders

7. Abuse of cloud services

8. Insufficient due diligence

9. Shared technology issues

☒ **A, B, C,** and **D** are incorrect because they're all cloud computing threats.

12. Which of the following attacks occurs during the translation of SOAP messages?

A. Wrapping attack

B. Cross-guest VM

C. Side channel

D. Session riding

☑ **A.** Attacks aren't necessarily specific to cloud computing, but EC-Council covers wrapping attacks here, so we'll follow suit. In a wrapping attack, the user sends a request to the server, but the SOAP response is intercepted by the attacker. He then duplicates the original message and sends it as if he is the user. In short, to pull this off, just intercept the response, change the data in the SOAP envelope, and replay.

☒ **B** and **C** are incorrect because this does not describe cross-guest VM attacks, which are also known as *side channel attacks* and deal with virtualization itself. If an attacker can somehow gain control of an existing VM (or place his own) on the same physical host as the target, he may be able to pull off lots of naughty activities.

☒ **D** is incorrect because this does not describe a session riding attack. Session riding is, in effect, simply CSRF under a different name and deals with cloud services instead of traditional data centers.

13. Which of the following is an architectural pattern in computer software design in which application components provide services to other components via a communications protocol, typically over a network?

A. API

B. SOA

C. EC2

D. IaaS

☑ **B.** In Service-Oriented Architecture (SOA), software is designed where each of its individual components works and communicates with components on different systems across the network. Each computer can run any of the services in the software, and each individual component is built so that it can exchange information with any other service in the network, without interaction or the need to make changes to the software. For example, someone might create an API that provides access to a database, which then allows third-party vendors to create their own applications to take advantage of it.

☒ **A** is incorrect because this does not define an application programming interface. APIs are sets of protocols and tools for building applications.

☒ **C** is incorrect because EC2 is a cloud service offering from Amazon.

☒ **D** is incorrect because IaaS is a cloud type.

14. In NIST Cloud Computing Reference Architecture, which entity manages cloud services and maintains the relationship between cloud providers and subscribers?

   A. Cloud broker

   B. Cloud auditor

   C. Cloud carrier

   D. Cloud consumer

   ☑ **A.** NIST Cloud Computing Reference Architecture defines the cloud broker as the entity that acts to manage use, performance, and delivery of cloud services, as well as the relationships between providers and subscribers. The broker "acts as the intermediate between consumer and provider and will help consumers through the complexity of cloud service offerings and may also create value added cloud services as well."

   ☒ **B** is incorrect because the cloud auditor is the independent assessor of cloud service provider's security controls.

   ☒ **C** is incorrect because the cloud carrier is the organization that has the responsibility of transferring the data between the provider and subscriber.

   ☒ **D** is incorrect because the cloud consumer is the individual or organization that acquires and uses cloud products and services.

15. Which of the following is not a benefit of virtualization?

   A. Allows for more efficient backup, data protection, and disaster recovery

   B. Reduces system administration work

   C. Improves operational efficiency

   D. Locks individual hardware to each individual virtual machine

   ☑ **D.** Some of you may actually work with and in a cloud, and you may disagree with at least one of the benefits listed here. However, while there may be differences between the real world and your CEH exam, for your test you really need to know virtualization benefits. The idea itself is great—run one or more operating systems *simultaneously* on the same physical box by virtualizing the hardware to each OS. Multiple companies (such as VMware, Oracle VirtualBox, and Xen) provide the hypervisor—a.k.a. virtual machine monitor (VMM): an application or hardware that creates and runs virtual machines—that allows multiple OSs to share the same physical machine hardware. Virtualizing your server can improve operational efficiency, provide for more efficient backups, offer disaster recovery and data protection, and reduce administrative work. Additionally, virtualization may have a positive effect on ensuring control and compliance throughout the network, as well as reduce overall costs.

   ☒ **A, B,** and **C** are incorrect because these are all benefits of the virtualization of servers.

16. A company acquires a cloud environment for much of its business IT needs. The environment is used and operated solely for the single organization. Which of the following represents the cloud deployment model in question?

A. Public

B. IaaS

C. Sole-source

D. Private

☑ **D.** In a private cloud model, the cloud is operated solely for a single organization (a.k.a. single-tenant environment) and is usually not a pay-as-you-go type operation. Private clouds are usually preferred by larger organizations, because the hardware is dedicated and security and compliance requirements can be more easily met.

☒ **A** is incorrect because a public cloud is for use by anyone and everyone.

☒ **B** is incorrect because IaaS is a cloud type providing virtualized computing resources over the Internet. A third-party provider hosts infrastructure components, applications, and services on behalf of its subscribers, with a hypervisor running the virtual machines as guests. IaaS is a good choice for day-to-day infrastructure service and temporary or experimental workloads that may change unexpectedly. IaaS subscribers typically pay on a per-use basis (within a certain timeframe, for instance) or sometimes by the amount of virtual machine space used.

☒ **C** is incorrect because sole-source is not a deployment method.

17. Which of the following is true regarding cloud computing?

A. Security in the cloud is the responsibility of the provider only.

B. Security in the cloud is the responsibility of the consumer only.

C. Security in the cloud is the responsibility of both the consumer and the provider.

D. None of the above.

☑ **C.** One of the biggest misconceptions about cloud computing seems to be where the lines of responsibility are drawn. However, it should come as no surprise that security is everyone's responsibility, and that absolutely extends to the cloud. The provider must protect the hardware, virtualization, VMs, and network connectivity. The consumer must protect their virtual systems (OSs, applications, and data). Sometimes this is a challenge in the real world. Where does your testing start and end? If your entire system relies on a cloud provider to remain up and secure, can you test *all* of it? And what happens if your resources are comingled somewhere inside all that cloud secret sauce? Can you really trust they're on top of things, security wise? Should you? *Can* you?

☒ **A, B,** and **D** are all incorrect statements.

18. Which tool offers penetration-test-like services for Amazon EC2 customers?

   A. CloudPassage Halo

   B. Core Cloud

   C. CloudInspect

   D. Panda Cloud Office Protection

   ☑ **C.** CloudInspect (http://www.coresecurity.com/corelabs-research/projects/core-cloudinspect) is "a tool that profits from the Core Impact & Core Insight technologies to offer penetration-testing as a service from Amazon Web Services for EC2 users." It's obviously designed for AWS cloud subscribers and runs as an automated, all-in-one testing suite specifically for your cloud subscription.

   ☒ **A** is incorrect because CloudPassage Halo (http://www.cloudpassage.com) "provides instant visibility and continuous protection for servers in any combination of data centers, private clouds and public clouds. The Halo platform is delivered as a service, so it deploys in minutes and scales on-demand. Halo uses minimal system resources, so layered security can be deployed where it counts, right at every workload—servers, instances and containers." Other tools for cloud pen testing you should know for your exam include Dell Cloud Manager and Parasoft SOAtest.

   ☒ **B** is incorrect because there is no such tool.

   ☒ **D** is incorrect because Panda Cloud Office Protection is not an automated pen test tool suite.

19. An attacker sets up a VM on the same physical cloud host as the target's VM. He then takes advantage of the shared physical resources to steal data. Which of the following describes this attack?

   A. Side channel

   B. VM flood

   C. Session riding

   D. Cybersquatting

   ☑ **A.** The side channel attack, also known as a cross-guest VM breach, occurs when a bad guy gets a virtual machine on the same host as the target. Through a variety of means for taking advantage of vulnerabilities in some shared technologies, the attacker then uses the shared physical resources to pilfer data. Providers can mitigate these attacks by using an up-to-date hypervisor provision, implementing strong virtual firewalls between guest OSs, and enforcing the use of encryption. Subscribers can help by locking down (hardening) their OSs and using good coding in their applications (especially when it comes to accessing resources such as memory).

   ☒ **B** is incorrect because VM flood may sound cool, but it is not a legitimate attack term.

   ☒ **C** is incorrect because session riding is a CSRF attack inside the cloud.

   ☒ **D** is incorrect because cybersquatting has nothing to do with this attack.

20. In the trusted computing model, what is a set of functions called that's always trusted by the computer's operating system?

    A. SOA

    B. RoT

    C. TCG

    D. VM

    ☑ **B.** Trusted computing is a simple idea: resolve a lot of computing problems through hardware enhancements and software modifications. Several vendors got together, calling themselves the Trusted Computing Group (TCG), and worked out specifications, proposals, and technologies to help protect system resources. Within all this work is the idea of Roots of Trust (RoT), which is a set of functions that is *always* trusted by the operating system. It provides a lot of the functionality the rest of the model is built on, such as real-time encryption, rootkit detection, memory curtailing, digital rights management (DRM) through hardware, and more.

    ☒ **A** is incorrect because this does not describe Service-Oriented Architecture. SOA is an architectural design effort in computer software where application components communicate with, and provide services to, other components via a network.

    ☒ **C** is incorrect because this does not describe the Trusted Computing Group.

    ☒ **D** is incorrect because this does not describe a virtual machine.

## CHAPTER 9

Trojans and Other Attacks

This chapter includes questions from the following topics:
- Describe malware types and their purpose
- Identify malware deployment methods
- Describe the malware analysis process
- Identify malware countermeasures
- Describe DoS attacks and techniques
- Identify DoS detection and countermeasure action
- Describe session hijacking and sequence prediction

Every new hobby and activity ends up with a huge learning curve, with all sorts of lingo and terminology to figure out. And, usually, it winds up costing a lot of money. For example, suppose you decide to get into photography. All of a sudden you're learning about ISO ratings and saturation—and buying insanely expensive cameras and lenses because you *need* them. What if you decide shooting is your thing? Well, now you're learning about calibers, double versus single action, trigger pull, and IWB versus OWB—and you'll wind up purchasing multiple weapons of different action and caliber to feed the need. And bass fishing? Oh, now we're talking serious addictions.

Braid versus monofilament line? Flourocarbon gets my vote for leader material, but braid's great for the back end. Baitcast versus spinning reel? I'd say that depends on the situation, but unless you can figure out the centrifugal braking systems and tension settings, with plenty of time to practice, spinning may be your best bet. Rod material and makeup? Hook style? Knots to use? And don't get me started on electronics for your boat!

And as we also know with every hobby, there are rules and expectations for the use of everything you buy. The people who have been engaging in it for a long time usually look at newcomers with a bemused derision, mocking the misuse of tools and techniques until they get with the program and do what everyone else is doing. In bass fishing, this idea kept loads of people from catching lots of fish.

For decades, the use of a particular bait known as a jig was relegated by those who knew everything to one method of presentation: flip the jig directly into really heavy cover (bushes, sticks, lily pads, and so on) and gently pop it around the bottom until a fish bites. In 1996, a bass professional named Bill Lowen was fishing a tournament with a jig the same way everyone else had been using it since the dawn of artificial bait fishing. He had tossed it in a tree that had fallen over into the water, and was slowly working it back. Deciding to move to another place, he started reeling the jig back to him and—whammo—fish on! At the next spot, he started fishing again, but decided to try reeling the jig back to him, instead of using it like everyone else did. Whammo—more fish on. He wound up winning that tournament, and in doing so created a brand-new technique called "swimming" a jig.

Why all this about bass fishing and techniques? Because it's applicable to our work here as ethical hackers. See, there are two ways to catch fish on any given lure—first, by using the lure the way it was designed, and, second, by using it in whatever way it catches fish. Whether the technique is "dead-sticking" a worm or, believe it or not, using a wrench as a lure (don't laugh— I've seen it with my own eyes), whatever works to catch fish is what should be used, right? In ethical hacking, the same thing applies. Malware certainly won't ever be confused with a "good-guy" tool, but maybe you can use it in a different way than it was intended. Your pen test tool set can be augmented by visiting the dark side yourself, wielding tools and actions that may seem a bit unsavory to you and in ways you just haven't thought about.

 STUDY TIPS   There hasn't been a whole lot of change between previous versions of the exam and version 9 when it comes to malware and other attacks. Most of the questions from the malware sections—especially those designed to trip you up—still will be of the pure memorization type. Stick with key words for each definition (it'll help you in separating good answers from bad ones), especially for the virus types. Don't miss an easy point on the exam because you forgot the difference between polymorphic and multipartite or why a worm is different from a virus. Tool identification should also be relatively straightforward (assuming you commit all those port numbers to memory, like I told you to do).

Finally, as always, get rid of the answers you know to be wrong in the first place. It's actually easier sometimes to identify the ones you downright know aren't relevant to the question. Then, from the remainder, you can scratch your gray matter for the key word that will shed light on the answer.

1. Bart receives an e-mail that appears to be from his lawyer containing a zip file named Courtdoc.zip. Bart double-clicks the zip file to open it, and a message stating "This word document is corrupt" appears. In the background, a file named Courtdoc.doc.exe runs and copies itself to the local APPDATA directory. It then begins beaconing to an external server. Which of the following best describes the malware Bart installed?

    A. Worm

    B. Virus

    C. Trojan

    D. Macro

2. You have established a Netcat connection to a target machine. Which flag can be used to launch a program?

    A. –p

    B. –a

    C. –l

    D. –e

3. Claire is surfing the Web and, after some time, a message pops up stating her system has been infected by malware, and offers a button to click for removal of the virus. After she clicks the button, another message window appears stating the system has been quarantined due to the nature of the infection and provides a link with instructions to pay in order to regain control and to clear the virus. Which of the following best describes this infection?

    A. Spyware

    B. Ransomware

    C. Trojan

    D. Adware

4. Which virus type will rewrite itself after each new infection?

    A. Multipartite

    B. Metamorphic

    C. Cavity

    D. Macro

    E. Boot sector

5. Pen test team member Amy attempts to guess the ISN for a TCP session. Which attack is she most likely carrying out?

   A. XSS

   B. Session splicing

   C. Session hijacking

   D. Multipartite attack

6. An attacker wishes to make his malware as stealthy and undetectable as possible. He employs an effort that uses compression to reduce the file size of the malware. Which of the following best describes this?

   A. Crypters

   B. Wrappers

   C. Packers

   D. Compressors

7. An attacker is attempting a DoS attack against a machine. She first spoofs the target's IP address and then begins sending large amounts of ICMP packets containing the MAC address FF:FF:FF:FF:FF:FF. What attack is underway?

   A. ICMP flood

   B. Ping of death

   C. SYN flood

   D. Smurf

   E. Fraggle

8. An attacker makes use of the Beacon implant on a target system to hijack a browser session. Which of the following best describes this attack?

   A. Man in the browser

   B. Man in the middle

   C. Man in the pivot

   D. IE hijacking

9. Claire's Windows system at work begins displaying strange activity, and she places a call to the IT staff. On investigation, it appears Claire's system is infected with several viruses. The IT staff removes the viruses, deleting several file and folder locations and using an AV tool, and the machine is reconnected to the network. Later in the day, Claire's system again displays strange activity and the IT staff is called once again. Which of the following are likely causes of the re-infection? (Choose all that apply.)

   A. Claire revisits a malicious website.

   B. Claire opens her Microsoft Outlook e-mail client and newly received e-mail is loaded to her local folder (.pst file).

C. Claire uses a system restore point to regain access to deleted files and folders.

D. Claire uses the organization's backup application to restore files and folders.

10. In regard to Trojans, which of the following best describes a wrapper?

    A. The legitimate file the Trojan is attached to

    B. A program used to bind the Trojan to a legitimate file

    C. A method of obfuscation using compression

    D. A software tool that uses encryption and code manipulation to hide malware

11. An attacker makes use of data streams already allowed by the network access controls of the target network to open a command shell on an internal machine. Communications between the target server and the attacker's machine travel on these open ports, and attacks against internal systems are launched from the internal server. Which of the following best describes the attack?

    A. BugBear

    B. CCTT

    C. RAT

    D. Botnet

12. Which of the following is a legitimate communication path for the transfer of data?

    A. Overt

    B. Covert

    C. Authentic

    D. Imitation

    E. Actual

13. In what layer of the OSI reference model is session hijacking carried out?

    A. Data link layer

    B. Transport layer

    C. Network layer

    D. Physical layer

14. A pen test team member types the following command:

```
nc222.15.66.78 -p 8765
```

Which of the following is true regarding this attempt?

    A. The attacker is attempting to connect to an established listening port on a remote computer.

    B. The attacker is establishing a listening port on his machine for later use.

    C. The attacker is attempting a DoS against a remote computer.

    D. The attacker is attempting to kill a service on a remote machine.

15. Examine the partial command-line output listed here:

```
Active Connections
Proto   Local Address            Foreign Address           State
  TCP   0.0.0.0:912              COMPUTER11:0              LISTENING
  TCP   0.0.0.0:3460             COMPUTER11:0              LISTENING
  TCP   0.0.0.0:3465             COMPUTER11:0              LISTENING
  TCP   0.0.0.0:8288             COMPUTER11:0              LISTENING
  TCP   0.0.0.0:16386            COMPUTER11:0              LISTENING
  TCP   192.168.1.100:139        COMPUTER11:0              LISTENING
  TCP   192.168.1.100:58191      173.194.44.81:https      ESTABLISHED
  TCP   192.168.1.100:58192      173.194.44.81:https      TIME_WAIT
  TCP   192.168.1.100:58193      173.194.44.81:https      TIME_WAIT
  TCP   192.168.1.100:58194      173.194.44.81:https      ESTABLISHED
  TCP   192.168.1.100:58200      bk-in-f138:http          TIME_WAIT
```

Which of the following is a true statement regarding the output?

A. This is output from a **netstat –an** command.

B. This is output from a **netstat –b** command.

C. This is output from a **netstat –e** command.

D. This is output from a **netstat –r** command.

16. You are discussing malware with a new pen test member who asks about restarting executables. Which registry keys within Windows automatically run executables and instructions? (Choose all that apply.)

A. HKEY_LOCAL_MACHINE\Software\Microsoft\Windows\CurrentVersion\RunServicesOnce

B. HKEY_LOCAL_MACHINE\Software\Microsoft\Windows\CurrentVersion\RunServices

C. HKEY_LOCAL_MACHINE\Software\Microsoft\Windows\CurrentVersion\RunOnce

D. HKEY_LOCAL_MACHINE\Software\Microsoft\Windows\CurrentVersion\Run

17. Which of the following is a true statement?

A. Sequence prediction attacks are specific to TCP.

B. Using a protocol in a way it is not intended to be used is an example of an overt channel.

C. All DoS and DDoS attacks are specific to TCP.

D. Fraggle is a TCP-based attack.

18. Which denial-of-service attack involves sending SYN packets to a target machine but never responding to any of the SYN/ACK replies?

A. SYN flood

B. SYN attack

C. Application-level flood

D. LOIC

19. Which of the following takes advantage of weaknesses in the fragment reassembly functionality of TCP/IP?

    A. Teardrop

    B. SYN flood

    C. Smurf attack

    D. Ping of death

20. IPSec is an effective preventative measure against session hijacking. Which IPSec mode encrypts only the data payload?

    A. Transport

    B. Tunnel

    C. Protected

    D. Spoofed

21. What provides for both authentication and confidentiality in IPSec?

    A. AH

    B. IKE

    C. OAKLEY

    D. ESP

22. Which of the following best describes the comparison between spoofing and session hijacking?

    A. Spoofing and session hijacking are the same thing.

    B. Spoofing interrupts a client's communication, whereas hijacking does not.

    C. Hijacking interrupts a client's communication, whereas spoofing does not.

    D. Hijacking emulates a foreign IP address, whereas spoofing refers to MAC addresses.

23. Which of the following is an effective deterrent against TCP session hijacking?

    A. Install and use a HIDS on the system.

    B. Install and use Tripwire on the system.

    C. Enforce good password policy.

    D. Use unpredictable sequence numbers.

24. Which of the following is a group of Internet computers set up to forward transmissions to other computers on the Internet without the owner's knowledge or permission?

    A. Botnet

    B. Zombie

    C. Honeypot

    D. DDoS

25. Within a TCP packet dump, a packet is noted with the SYN flag set and a sequence number set at A13F. What should the acknowledgment number in the return SYN/ACK packet be?

    A. A131

    B. A130

    C. A140

    D. A14F

26. When is session hijacking performed?

    A. Before the three-step handshake

    B. During the three-step handshake

    C. After the three-step handshake

    D. After a FIN packet

1. C	**10.** B	**19.** A
2. D	**11.** B	**20.** A
3. B	**12.** A	**21.** D
4. B	**13.** B	**22.** C
5. C	**14.** A	**23.** D
6. C	**15.** A	**24.** A
7. D	**16.** A, B, C, D	**25.** C
8. A	**17.** A	**26.** C
9. A, C, D	**18.** B	

1. Bart receives an e-mail that appears to be from his lawyer containing a zip file named Courtdoc.zip. Bart double-clicks the zip file to open it and a message stating "This word document is corrupt" appears. In the background, a file named Courtdoc.doc.exe runs and copies itself to the local APPDATA directory. It then begins beaconing to an external server. Which of the following best describes the malware Bart installed?

   A. Worm

   B. Virus

   C. Trojan

   D. Macro

   ☑ **C.** The definition of a Trojan is a non-self-replicating program that appears to have a useful purpose but in reality has a different, malicious purpose. In other words, it looks harmless but acts very naughty when activated. This is precisely what is going on in this example. E-mail is not the *only* method to spread a Trojan, but phishing certainly does seem to work well.

   ☒ **A** is incorrect because this does not describe a worm. A worm is a self-replicating, self-propagating, self-contained program that uses networking mechanisms to spread itself.

   ☒ **B** is incorrect because this does not describe a virus. A virus is a malicious computer program with self-replication capabilities that attaches to another file and moves with the host from one computer to another.

   ☒ **D** is incorrect because this does not describe a macro. A macro is a single instruction that expands automatically into several instructions to perform a specific task (usually associated with Microsoft Office products, as far as your exam is concerned).

2. You have established a Netcat connection to a target machine. Which flag can be used to launch a program?

   A. –p

   B. –a

   C. –l

   D. –e

   ☑ **D.** Netcat is often referred to as the Swiss Army knife of hacking efforts. You can use it to set up a listening port on target machines that you can then revisit to wreak all sorts of havoc. The flag associated with launching a program is –e. For example, issuing the command

   ```
   nc –L –p 12657 –t –e cmd.exe
   ```

   will open a Windows command shell on the target machine; the –t flag sets up a Telnet connection over the port you defined with the –p flag (12657).

   ☒ **A** is incorrect because the –p flag indicates the protocol port you want to use for your session.

☒ **B** is incorrect because –a is not a recognized Netcat flag.

☒ **C** is incorrect because the –l flag indicates Netcat should open the port for listening. As an aside, the –L flag does the same thing; however, it restarts listening after the inbound session completes.

3. Claire is surfing the Web and, after some time, a message pops up stating her system has been infected by malware, and offers a button to click for removal of the virus. After she clicks the button, another message window appears stating the system has been quarantined due to the nature of the infection and provides a link with instructions to pay in order to regain control and to clear the virus. Which of the following best describes this infection?

   A. Spyware

   B. Ransomware

   C. Trojan

   D. Adware

   ☑ **B.** Ransomware isn't anything new, but it sure has attracted new attention from EC-Council. The name itself gives away its purpose: the malware infects your system and then restricts access to your files and folders, demanding a ransom payment to get control back. ECC lists five different ransomware families: Cryptorbit, Cryptolocker, Cryptodefense, Cryptowall, and police-themed. Usually the online payment involves Bitcoin, but can take other avenues. In any case, never pay off the attacker—you're only signing yourself up for future terror. Cleaning off ransomware may involve booting into Safe Mode, or even using a system restore on Windows systems. You may even get away with an external AV scan as a fix action, but be sure to scrub the system for hidden files and folders the ransomware may have left behind.

   ☒ **A** is incorrect because this does not describe spyware. Spyware is type of malware that covertly collects information about a user.

   ☒ **C** is incorrect because this does not describe a Trojan. A Trojan is a non-self-replicating program that appears to have a useful purpose but in reality has a different, malicious purpose.

   ☒ **D** is incorrect because this does not describe adware. Adware is software that has advertisements embedded within it. It generally displays ads in the form of pop-ups.

4. Which virus type will rewrite itself after each new infection?

   A. Multipartite

   B. Metamorphic

   C. Cavity

   D. Macro

   E. Boot sector

☑ **B.** EC-Council defines several different virus types, depending on what the virus does, how it acts, and how it is written. In the case of a metamorphic virus, it will rewrite itself each time it infects a new file. Metamorphic viruses write versions of themselves in machine code, making them easy to port to different machines.

☒ **A** is incorrect because multipartite viruses do not rewrite themselves. They attempt to infect and spread in multiple ways and try to infect files and the boot sector at the same time. They can spread quickly and are notoriously hard to clean.

☒ **C** is incorrect because a cavity virus writes itself into unused space within a file. The idea is to maintain the file's size.

☒ **D** is incorrect because macro viruses do not rewrite themselves. Macro viruses usually attack Microsoft Office files, executing as a macro within the file itself (anyone who has ever been stuck in Excel purgatory should be familiar with macros within a spreadsheet). Melissa (a famous virus attacking Microsoft Word 97) is a classic example of a macro virus.

☒ **E** is incorrect because this does not describe a boot sector virus. A boot sector virus plants itself in a system's boot sector and infects the master boot record (MBR).

5. Pen test team member Amy attempts to guess the ISN for a TCP session. Which attack is she most likely carrying out?

A. XSS

B. Session splicing

C. Session hijacking

D. Multipartite attack

☑ **C.** The idea behind session hijacking is fairly simple: the attacker waits for a session to begin and, after all the pesky authentication gets done, jumps in to steal the session for herself. In practice, it's a little harder and more complicated than that, but the key to the whole attack is in determining the initial sequence number (ISN) used for the session. The ISN is sent by the initiator of the session in the first step (SYN). This is acknowledged in the second step of the handshake (SYN/ACK) by incrementing that ISN by 1, and then another ISN is generated by the recipient. This second number is acknowledged by the initiator in the third step (ACK), and from there on out communication can occur. Per EC-Council, the following steps describe the session hijack:

1. Sniff the traffic between the client and the server.

2. Monitor the traffic and predict the sequence numbering.

3. Desynchronize the session with the client.

4. Predict the session token and take over the session.

5. Inject packets to the target server.

For what it's worth, pulling this attack off via EC-Council's take on the whole matter requires you to do some fairly significant traffic sniffing. And if you're already positioned to sniff the traffic in the first place, wouldn't the whole scenario possibly be a moot point? You need to know it for the exam, but real-world application may be rare.

☒ **A** is incorrect because cross-site scripting is a web application attack.

☒ **B** is incorrect because session splicing is an IDS evasion method. The attacker delivers a payload that the IDS would have otherwise seen by "slicing" it over multiple packets. The payload can be spread out over a long period of time.

☒ **D** is incorrect because *multipartite* refers to a virus type, not an attack that requires ISN determination.

6. An attacker wishes to make his malware as stealthy and undetectable as possible. He employs an effort that uses compression to reduce the file size of the malware. Which of the following best describes this?

   A. Crypters

   B. Wrappers

   C. Packers

   D. Compressors

   ☑ **C.** Packers use compression to pack the malware executable into a smaller size. Not only does this reduce the file size, but it serves to make the malware harder to detect for some antivirus engines. It works much like a zip file, except that the extraction occurs in memory and not on the disk.

   ☒ **A** is incorrect because crypters are software tools that use a combination of encryption and code manipulation to render malware undetectable to AV and other security monitoring products (in Internet lingo, it's referred to as *fud*, for "fully undetectable").

   ☒ **B** is incorrect because wrappers are used to bind a Trojan and a legitimate program together so the Trojan will be installed when the legitimate program is executed.

   ☒ **D** is included merely as a distractor and is not a true term.

7. An attacker is attempting a DoS attack against a machine. She first spoofs the target's IP address and then begins sending large amounts of ICMP packets containing the MAC address FF:FF:FF:FF:FF:FF. What attack is underway?

   A. ICMP flood

   B. Ping of death

   C. SYN flood

   D. Smurf

   E. Fraggle

   ☑ **D.** A smurf attack is a generic denial-of-service (DoS) attack against a target machine. The idea is simple: have so many ICMP requests going to the target that all its resources are taken up. To accomplish this, the attacker spoofs the target's IP address and then sends thousands of ping requests from that spoofed IP to the subnet's broadcast address. This, in effect, pings every machine on the subnet. Assuming it's configured to do so, every machine will respond to the request, effectively crushing the target's network resources.

☒ **A** is incorrect because an ICMP flood does not act this way. In this attack, the hacker sends ICMP Echo packets to the target with a spoofed (fake) source address. The target continues to respond to an address that doesn't exist and eventually reaches a limit of packets per second sent.

☒ **B** is incorrect because a ping of death does not act this way. It's not a valid attack with modern systems, because of preventative measures in the OS; in the ping of death, an attacker fragments an ICMP message to send to a target. When the fragments are reassembled, the resulting ICMP packet is larger than the maximum size and crashes the system. As an aside, each OS has its own method of dealing with network protocols, and the implementation of dealing with particular protocols opens up things like this.

☒ **C** is incorrect because a SYN flood takes place when an attacker sends multiple SYN packets to a target without providing an acknowledgment to the returned SYN/ACK. This is another attack that does not necessarily work on modern systems.

☒ **E** is incorrect because in a fraggle attack, UDP packets are used. The same principle applies—spoofed IP and Echo requests sent to the broadcast address—it's just with UDP.

8. An attacker makes use of the Beacon implant on a target system to hijack a browser session. Which of the following best describes this attack?

   A. Man in the browser

   B. Man in the middle

   C. Man in the pivot

   D. IE hijacking

   ☑ **A.** Most have heard of session hijacking and man in the middle, but what about man in the browser? An MITB attack occurs when the hacker sends a Trojan to intercept browser calls. The Trojan basically sits between the browser and libraries, allowing a hacker to watch, and interact within, a browser session. Cobalt Strike creator Peiter C. Zatko (a.k.a. Mudge) added this feature a couple years back (http://www.advancedpentest.com/help-browser-pivoting). If you have his Beacon (the name of his implant) on a box, you can "browser pivot" such that all of the target's active sessions become your own. All of them. It effectively sets up a local proxy port so you can point your browser to it, and it directs all your requests through the Beacon on the target machine. Now you're browsing in your own browser as the target, without them even knowing it.

☒ **B** is incorrect because this does not necessarily describe a man-in-the-middle (MITM) attack, which is an attack where the hacker positions himself between the client and the server to intercept (and sometimes alter) data traveling between the two.

☒ **C** and **D** are incorrect because these are not legitimate terms.

9. Claire's Windows system at work begins displaying strange activity, and she places a call to the IT staff. On investigation, it appears Claire's system is infected with several viruses. The IT staff removes the viruses, deleting several file and folder locations and using an AV tool, and the machine is reconnected to the network. Later in the day, Claire's system again displays strange activity, and the IT staff is called once again. Which of the following are likely causes of the re-infection? (Choose all that apply.)

A. Claire revisits a malicious website.

B. Claire opens her Microsoft Outlook e-mail client and newly received e-mail is loaded to her local folder (.pst file).

C. Claire uses a system restore point to regain access to deleted files and folders.

D. Claire uses the organization's backup application to restore files and folders.

☑ **A, C, D.** Virus removal can be tricky, especially if nobody knows how and when it got on the system in the first place. As a matter of fact, in many places I've worked, discovering the source of the virus is as important as cleaning the system in the first place. Cleaning a virus off the system usually involves scrubbing the Microsoft registry, deleting files and folders (don't forget to check for hidden ones), and a host of other details and actions. Sometimes AV removal applications can help with this process, but sometimes it's an involved, manual process.

Even with tools to help in removal, administrators can't afford to overlook system restore points, backups, and user behavior. If a virus is on a system during a system restore copy action, then any restoration of that point will reinstall the virus. The same thing goes for data backups themselves—it should follow that an infected file while being backed up will remain infected during the restore action. As for user behavior, if the user is re-infected immediately following a specific website visit, or after using a USB (or other removable media), at least you can pinpoint the source and hopefully stop it from happening again.

☒ **B** is incorrect because new e-mail from the server wouldn't necessarily be the cause of the original infection.

10. In regard to Trojans, which of the following best describes a wrapper?

A. The legitimate file the Trojan is attached to

B. A program used to bind the Trojan to a legitimate file

C. A method of obfuscation using compression

D. A software tool that uses encryption and code manipulation to hide malware

☑ **B.** *Wrappers* are programs that allow you to bind an executable of your choice (Trojan) to an innocent file your target won't mind opening. For example, you might use a program such as EliteWrap to embed a backdoor application with a game file (.exe). A user on your target machine then opens the latest game file (maybe to play a hand of cards against the computer or to fling a bird at pyramids built by pigs) while your backdoor is installing and sits there waiting for your use later. As an aside, many wrappers themselves are considered malicious and will show up on any up-to-date virus signature list.

☒ **A** is incorrect because the wrapper is not the legitimate file the malware is bound to.

☒ **C** is incorrect because this describes a packer.

☒ **D** is incorrect because this describes a crypter.

11. An attacker makes use of data streams already allowed by the network access controls of the target network to open a command shell on an internal machine. Communications between the target server and the attacker's machine travel on these open ports, and attacks against internal systems are launched from the internal server. Which of the following best describes the attack?

   A. BugBear

   B. CCTT

   C. RAT

   D. Botnet

   ☑ **B.** In another addition of terminology for memorization purposes, EC-Council has defined an entire class of Trojan exploitation as Covert Channel Tunneling Trojan (CCTT). The idea is simple—use data streams the network already allows and run attacks and communications over those connections. In describing this attack method to us, EC-Council shows us an external "client" CCTT system connecting to a CCTT server on the inside. The attacker uses his machine to communicate with the external system, which then sends messages and instructions over the open channels to the internal server. Attacks are then launched from there against internal machines.

   Some other, specific, tunneling Trojans to keep in mind are HTTP RAT, Shttpd, and ICMPsend. HTTP RAT uses the widely open port 80, normally used for standard web traffic, for sending command and control data back and forth. Shttpd is much the same; however, it uses port 443—usually in place for HTTP over SSL traffic. ICMPsend is a Trojan that uses ICMP to send messages back and forth.

   ☒ **A** is incorrect because BugBear is a virus that propagates through network shares (and actually tries killing any resident antivirus programs).

   ☒ **C** is incorrect because RAT (Remote Access Trojan) is an acronym used to describe a host of Trojans that set up remote access for the attacker.

   ☒ **D** is incorrect because a botnet refers to a group of zombie systems controlled by an attacker.

12. Which of the following is a legitimate communication path for the transfer of data?

    A. Overt

    B. Covert

    C. Authentic

    D. Imitation

    E. Actual

    ☑ **A.** This is another one of those easy, pure-definition questions you simply can't miss on your exam. Whether the channel is inside a computer, between systems, or across the Internet, any legitimate channel used for communications and data exchange is known as an *overt channel*. And don't let the inherit risk with any channel itself make the decision for you—even if the channel itself is a risky endeavor, if it is being used for its intended purpose, it's still overt. For example, an IRC or a gaming link is still an overt channel, so long as the applications making use of it are legitimate. Overt channels are legitimate communication channels used by programs across a system or a network, whereas covert channels are used to transport data in ways they were not intended for.

    ☒ **B** is incorrect because a covert channel, per EC-Council's own definition, is "a channel that transfers information within a computer system or network in a way that violates security policy." For example, a Trojan might create a channel for stealing passwords or downloading sensitive data from the machine.

    ☒ **C, D,** and **E** are incorrect because none of these is a term for the communications channel; they are included here as distractors.

13. In what layer of the OSI reference model is session hijacking carried out?

    A. Data link layer

    B. Transport layer

    C. Network layer

    D. Physical layer

    ☑ **B.** Think about a session hijack, and this makes sense. Authentication has already occurred, so we know both computers have already found each other. Therefore, the physical, data link, and network layers have already been eclipsed. And what is being altered and played with in these hijacking attempts? Why, the sequence numbers, of course, and sequencing occurs at the transport layer. Now, for all you real-world guys out there screaming that communications can be, and truly are, hijacked at every level, let me caution your outrage with something I've said repeatedly throughout this book: sometimes the exam and reality are two different things, and if you want to pass the test, you'll need to memorize it the way EC-Council wants you to. Session hijacking is taught in CEH circles as a measure of guessing sequence numbers, and that's a transport layer entity. In the real world, your physical layer interception of a target would result in access to everything above, but on the exam just stick with "session hijacking = transport layer."

⊠ **A, C,** and **D** are incorrect because these layers are not where a session hijack attack is carried out.

14. A pen test team member types the following command:

```
nc 222.15.66.78 -p 8765
```

Which of the following is true regarding this attempt?

A. The attacker is attempting to connect to an established listening port on a remote computer.

B. The attacker is establishing a listening port on his machine for later use.

C. The attacker is attempting a DoS against a remote computer.

D. The attacker is attempting to kill a service on a remote machine.

☑ **A.** As covered earlier, Netcat is a wonderful tool that allows all sorts of remote access wizardry on a machine, and you'll need to be able to recognize the basics of the syntax. In the command example, Netcat is being told, "Please attempt a connection to the machine with the IP address of 222.15.66.78 on port 8765. I believe you'll find the port in a listening state, waiting for our arrival." Obviously at some point previous to issuing this command on his local machine, the pen tester planted the Netcat Trojan on the remote system (222.15.66.78) and set it up in a listening state. He may have set it up with command-shell access (allowing a Telnet-like connection to issue commands at will) using the following command:

```
nc -L -p 8765 -t -e cmd.exe
```

⊠ **B** is incorrect because this command is issued on the client side of the setup, not the server side. At some point previously, the port was set to a listening state, and this Netcat command will access it.

⊠ **C** is incorrect because this command is not attempting a denial of service against the target machine. It's included here as a distractor.

⊠ **D** is incorrect because this command is not attempting to kill a process or service on the remote machine. It's included here as a distractor.

15. Examine the partial command-line output listed here:

```
Active Connections
Proto   Local Address            Foreign Address        State
  TCP   0.0.0.0:912              COMPUTER11:0           LISTENING
  TCP   0.0.0.0:3460             COMPUTER11:0           LISTENING
  TCP   0.0.0.0:3465             COMPUTER11:0           LISTENING
  TCP   0.0.0.0:8288             COMPUTER11:0           LISTENING
  TCP   0.0.0.0:16386            COMPUTER11:0           LISTENING
  TCP   192.168.1.100:139        COMPUTER11:0           LISTENING
  TCP   192.168.1.100:58191      173.194.44.81:https    ESTABLISHED
  TCP   192.168.1.100:58192      173.194.44.81:https    TIME_WAIT
  TCP   192.168.1.100:58193      173.194.44.81:https    TIME_WAIT
  TCP   192.168.1.100:58194      173.194.44.81:https    ESTABLISHED
  TCP   192.168.1.100:58200      bk-in-f138:http        TIME_WAIT
```

Which of the following is a true statement regarding the output?

A. This is output from a **netstat –an** command.

B. This is output from a **netstat –b** command.

C. This is output from a **netstat –e** command.

D. This is output from a **netstat –r** command.

☑ **A.** You'll need to get to know Netstat before your exam. It's not a huge thing, and you won't get bogged down in minutiae, but you do need to know the basics. Netstat is a great command-line tool built into every Microsoft operating system. From Microsoft's own description, Netstat "displays active TCP connections, ports on which the computer is listening, Ethernet statistics, the IP routing table, IPv4 statistics (for the IP, ICMP, TCP, and UDP protocols), and IPv6 statistics (for the IPv6, ICMPv6, TCP over IPv6, and UDP over IPv6 protocols)." It's a great, easy way to see which ports you have open on your system, helping you to identify any naughty Trojans that may be hanging around. A **netstat –an** command will show all connections and listening ports in numerical form.

☒ **B** is incorrect because the –b option displays the executable involved in creating each connection or listening port. Its output appears something like this:

```
Proto   Local Address       Foreign Address  State
  TCP     127.0.0.1:5354      COMPUTER11:49155 ESTABLISHED
  [mDNSResponder.exe]
  TCP     127.0.0.1:27015   COMPUTER11:49175 ESTABLISHED
  [AppleMobileDeviceService.exe]
  TCP     127.0.0.1:49155   COMPUTER11:5354   ESTABLISHED
  [AppleMobileDeviceService.exe]
  TCP     127.0.0.1:49175   COMPUTER11:27015 ESTABLISHED
  [iTunesHelper.exe]
```

☒ **C** is incorrect because the –e flag displays Ethernet statistics for the system. The output appears something like this:

	Received	Sent
Bytes	125454856	33551337
Unicast packets	164910	167156
Non-unicast packets	570	15624
Discards	0	0
Errors	0	268
Unknown protocols	0	

☒ **D** is incorrect because the –r flag displays the route table for the system. Here's a sampling of the output:

```
IPv4 Route Table
===========================================================================
Active Routes:
Network Destination        Netmask      Gateway      Interface Metric
          0.0.0.0          0.0.0.0 192.168.1.1 192.168.1.100    25
         15.0.0.0        255.0.0.0      On-link 16.213.104.24    26
   15.195.201.216 255.255.255.255 192.168.1.1 192.168.1.100    26
   15.255.255.255 255.255.255.255      On-link 16.213.104.24   281.
```

16. You are discussing malware with a new pen test member who asks about restarting executables. Which registry keys within Windows automatically run executables and instructions? (Choose all that apply.)

    A. HKEY_LOCAL_MACHINE\Software\Microsoft\Windows\CurrentVersion\RunServicesOnce

    B. HKEY_LOCAL_MACHINE\Software\Microsoft\Windows\CurrentVersion\RunServices

    C. HKEY_LOCAL_MACHINE\Software\Microsoft\Windows\CurrentVersion\RunOnce

    D. HKEY_LOCAL_MACHINE\Software\Microsoft\Windows\CurrentVersion\Run

    ☑ **A, B, C, D.** Creating malware and infecting a machine with it is accomplishing only the basics. Getting it to hang around by having it restart when the user reboots the machine? Now we're talking. The Run, RunOnce, RunServices, and RunServicesOnce registry keys within the HKEY_LOCAL_MACHINE hive are great places to stick all sorts of executables. Because of this, it's helpful to run registry monitoring on occasion to check for anything suspicious. Sys Analyzer, Regshot, and TinyWatcher are all options for this.

17. Which of the following is a true statement?

    A. Sequence prediction attacks are specific to TCP.

    B. Using a protocol in a way it is not intended to be used is an example of an overt channel.

    C. All DoS and DDoS attacks are specific to TCP.

    D. Fraggle is a TCP-based attack.

    ☑ **A.** Sequence prediction attacks are specific to TCP because…TCP uses sequence numbers. Unlike the fire-and-forget method employed by UDP, TCP uses sequence numbers and windowing to keep track of conversations. Sequence prediction is a session hijacking procedure where the attacker guesses the next sequence number and launches himself into the data connection between client and server.

    ☒ **B** is incorrect because this is an example of a covert channel.

    ☒ **C** is incorrect because not all DoS and DDoS attacks are TCP based.

    ☒ **D** is incorrect because fraggle is a UDP-based DoS attack.

18. Which denial-of-service attack involves using multiple intermediary and secondary machines to contribute to the DoS effort?

    A. SYN flood

    B. DRDoS

    C. Application-level flood

    D. LOIC

☑ **B.** A *distributed reflection denial of service* (DRDoS) attack is also known as a "spoofed" attack and makes use of multiple intermediary and secondary machines. The bad guy sends attack information to the intermediary machines, which, in turn, send the messages out to the secondary machines. This makes tracking the real source of the attack very difficult to determine (the investigators will see and react to the secondaries, not the originator).

☒ **A** is incorrect because a SYN flood takes advantage of tons of half-open connections, and does not use intermediary systems.

☒ **C** is incorrect because an application-level flood is a DoS action that floods applications or disrupts application-database communications.

☒ **D** is incorrect because Low Orbit Ion Cannon (LOIC) is a simple-to-use DDoS tool that floods a target with TCP, UDP, or HTTP requests. It was originally written as open source to attack various Scientology websites but has since had many people voluntarily joining a botnet to support all sorts of attacks. Recently, LOIC was used in a coordinated attack against Sony's PlayStation network, and the tool has a track record of other successful hits: the Recording Industry Association of America, PayPal, MasterCard, and several other companies have all fallen victim to LOIC.

19. Which of the following takes advantage of weaknesses in the fragment reassembly functionality of TCP/IP?

   A. Teardrop

   B. SYN flood

   C. Smurf attack

   D. Ping of death

☑ **A.** ECC can be rather capricious in their choice of which malware to test and which not to, and sometimes they look far into the past for question material. In a teardrop attack, overlapping, mangled packet fragments are sent in an effort to confuse a target system, causing it to reboot or crash. Teardrop attacks exploit an overlapping IP fragment bug present in Windows 95, Windows NT, and Windows 3.1 machines, as well as some early versions of Linux—all more than ten years old. The attack was really more of an annoyance than anything because a reboot clears it all up; however, anything that was open and altered, sitting unsaved on the device, would be lost. In modern systems, finding this attack in use is virtually impossible.

☒ **B** is incorrect because a SYN flood attack exhausts connections on a device by flooding it with thousands of open SYN packets, never sending any acknowledgments to the return SYN/ACKs.

☒ **C** is incorrect because a smurf attack involves spoofing the target's address and then pinging the broadcast address with it. The resulting responses of thousands of ICMP packets kills the machine.

☒ **D** is incorrect because the ping of death attack involves sending a ping request with an unusually large payload. The ping would be fragmented and, when put together, would kill the target machine.

20. IPSec is an effective preventative measure against session hijacking. Which IPSec mode encrypts only the data payload?

   A. Transport

   B. Tunnel

   C. Protected

   D. Spoofed

   ☑ **A.** IPSec is a wonderful encryption mechanism that can rather easily be set up between two endpoints or even across your entire subnet if you configure the hosts appropriately. You won't need to know all the bells and whistles with IPSec (and thank goodness, because there's a lot to write about), but you do need the basics. Transport mode does not affect the header of the packet at all and encrypts only the payload. It's typically used as a secured connection between two endpoints, whereas Tunnel mode creates a VPN-like connection protecting the entire session. Additionally, Transport mode is compatible with conventional Network Address Translation (NAT).

   ☒ **B** is incorrect because Tunnel mode encapsulates the entire packet, including the header. This is typically used to form a VPN connection, where the tunnel is used across an untrusted network (such as the Internet). For pretty obvious reasons, it's not compatible with conventional NAT; when the packet goes through the router (or whatever is performing NAT for you), the source address in the packet changes because of Tunnel mode and, therefore, invalidates the packet for the receiving end. There are workarounds for this, generally lumped together as NAT traversal (NAT-t). Many home routers take advantage of something referred to as *IPSec passthrough* to allow just this.

   ☒ **C** and **D** are incorrect because they are invalid terms involving IPSec.

21. What provides for both authentication and confidentiality in IPSec?

   A. AH

   B. IKE

   C. OAKLEY

   D. ESP

   ☑ **D.** Encapsulation Security Payload (ESP) is a member of the IPSec protocol suite, and provides data authentication (proving it's actually from who it's supposed to be from) and confidentiality (by encrypting the data). In Transport mode, ESP doesn't provide integrity and authentication for the entirety of the packet, but it does in tunnel mode (excluding the outer IP header, of course).

   ☒ **A** is incorrect because Authentication Header (AH) provides authentication but not encryption.

   ☒ **B** is incorrect because Internet Key Exchange (IKE) is a protocol that produces the security keys.

☒ **C** is incorrect because OAKLEY is a protocol used to create a master key as well as a key specific to each session in the data transfer. It makes use of the Diffie–Hellman algorithm for this process.

22. Which of the following best describes the comparison between spoofing and session hijacking?

    A. Spoofing and session hijacking are the same thing.

    B. Spoofing interrupts a client's communication, whereas hijacking does not.

    C. Hijacking interrupts a client's communication, whereas spoofing does not.

    D. Hijacking emulates a foreign IP address, whereas spoofing refers to MAC addresses.

    ☑ **C.** Hijacking and spoofing can sometimes be confused with each other, although they really shouldn't be. *Spoofing* refers to a process where the attacking machine pretends to be something it is not. Whether by faking a MAC address or an IP address, the idea is that other systems on the network will communicate with your machine (that is, set up and tear down sessions) as if it's the target system. Generally this is used to benefit sniffing efforts. Hijacking is a totally different animal. In hijacking, the attacker jumps into an already existing session, knocking the client out of it and fooling the server into continuing the exchange. In many cases, the client will simply reconnect to the server over a different session, with no one the wiser: the server isn't even aware of what happened, and the client simply connects again in a different session. As an aside, EC-Council describes the session hijack in these steps:

    1. Sniff the traffic between the client and the server.

    2. Monitor the traffic and predict the sequence numbering.

    3. Desynchronize the session with the client.

    4. Predict the session token and take over the session.

    5. Inject packets to the target server.

    ☒ **A** is incorrect because spoofing and hijacking are different. An argument can be made that hijacking makes use of some spoofing, but the two attacks are separate entities: spoofing pretends to be another machine, eliciting (or setting up) sessions for sniffing purposes, whereas hijacking takes advantage of existing communications sessions.

    ☒ **B** is incorrect because spoofing doesn't interrupt a client's existing session at all; it's designed to sniff traffic and/or set up its own sessions.

    ☒ **D** is incorrect because spoofing isn't relegated to MAC addresses only. You can spoof almost anything, from MAC and IP addresses to system names and services.

23. Which of the following is an effective deterrent against TCP session hijacking?

    A. Install and use an HIDS on the system.

    B. Install and use Tripwire on the system.

    C. Enforce good password policy.

    D. Use unpredictable sequence numbers.

☑ **D.** As noted already, session hijacking requires the attacker to guess the proper upcoming sequence number(s) to pull off the attack, pushing the original client out of the session. Using unpredictable session IDs (or, better stated in the real world, using a modern operating system with less predictable sequence numbers) in the first place protects against this. Other countermeasures for session hijacking are fairly common sense: use encryption to protect the channel, limit incoming connections, minimize remote access, and regenerate the session key after authentication is complete. And, lastly, don't forget user education: if the users don't know any better, they might not think twice about clicking past the security certificate warning or reconnecting after being suddenly shut down.

☒ **A** is incorrect because a host-based intrusion detection system may not deter session hijacking at all.

☒ **B** is incorrect because Tripwire is a file integrity application and won't do a thing for session hijacking prevention.

☒ **C** is incorrect because system passwords have nothing to do with session hijacking.

24. Which of the following is a group of Internet computers set up to forward transmissions to other computers on the Internet without the owner's knowledge or permission?

   A. Botnet

   B. Zombie

   C. Honeypot

   D. DDoS

   ☑ **A.** A botnet is a group of systems an attacker has control over, without the owner's knowledge or permission. Each zombie system in the network sends messages and data transmissions for the botnet controller—everything from spam and e-mail to viruses and ads. They are probably best known for their roles in distributed denial of service attacks, but botnets can be used for all sorts of activities. As an aside, ECC maintains that botnets are most commonly controlled via IRC (Internet Relay Chat), but in the real world they can be controlled by a host of methods.

   ☒ **B** is incorrect because while a botnet is made up of zombie computers, a single zombie does not make up a botnet.

   ☒ **C** is incorrect because a honeypot is a system set up specifically to be hacked, so security staff can watch what an attacker is doing.

   ☒ **D** is incorrect because a distributed denial of service may be carried out by a botnet, but it does not define one.

25. Within a TCP packet dump, a packet is noted with the SYN flag set and a sequence number set at A13F. What should the acknowledgment number in the return SYN/ACK packet be?

   A. A131

   B. A130

   C. A140

   D. A14F

   ☑ **C.** We've been over the need for predicting sequence numbers before, so I won't bore you with it again other than to restate the salient point here: the ISN is incremented by 1 in the SYN/ACK return packet. Because these values were given in hex instead of decimal, all you need to know is what the next hex value after A13F is. You could split it out into binary (each hex digit is 4 bits, so this would equate to 1010000100111111) and then pick the next available number (1010000101000000) and split it back into hex (1010 = A, 0001 = 1, 0100 = 4, and 0000 = 0). Alternatively, you could convert directly to decimal (41279), add 1, and then convert back to hex. And, yes, you do need to know number conversion from decimal to binary to hex, so stop complaining.

   ☒ **A, B,** and **D** are incorrect hex equivalents for decimal 41280 (the next number acknowledgment for the ISN).

26. When is session hijacking performed?

   A. Before the three-step handshake

   B. During the three-step handshake

   C. After the three-step handshake

   D. After a FIN packet

   ☑ **C.** This question should be an easy one for you, but it's included here to reinforce the point that you need to understand session hijacking steps well for the exam. Of course, session hijacking should occur after the three-step handshake. As a matter of fact, you'll probably need to wait quite a bit after the three-step handshake so that everything on the session can be set up—authentication and all that nonsense should be taken care of before you jump in and take over.

   ☒ **A** and **B** are incorrect because session hijacking occurs after a session is already established, and the three-step handshake must obviously occur first for this to be true.

   ☒ **D** is incorrect because the FIN packet brings an orderly close to the TCP session. Why on Earth would you wait until it's over to start trying to hijack it?

Cryptography 101

This domain includes questions from the following topics:

- Describe cryptography and encryption techniques
- Define cryptographic algorithms
- Describe public and private keys generation concepts
- Describe digital signature components and use
- Describe cryptanalysis and code-breaking tools and methodologies
- List cryptography attacks

I've lived in four different states and two foreign countries, and each stop along the way in my life offered something irreplaceable, unique, and downright cool. And almost without fail, I didn't appreciate that irreplaceable, unique, and cool thing until I left for a new locale. Maybe it's just human nature to look backward and romanticize the things no longer yours, but I think it's valuable to pause where you're at right now and take stock of the things you do have available to you and to sometimes marvel at how it's all put together.

Technology is no different, and we're all guilty of taking it for granted. When you examine how nearly anything in technology works, though, it's almost a miracle to behold and something definitely not to be taken lightly or just accepted as a given, like gravity or rain. Cryptography is a prime example.

Consider the document I am typing right now. It's made up of a bunch of 1s and 0s arranged in such a way as to present the text in a readable format on the screen—not to mention all the font formats, bolding, spacing, and other goodies I type in here to make the text more pleasing to the eye. Just pause for a moment and consider the simple act of typing this sentence and how many bits it takes, properly formatted to display it onscreen or to save and transport it. Then figure out a way to encrypt it, also using a bunch of 1s and 0s.

The entire concept is mind-boggling, if you really think about it, and something we should all be grateful for. I mean, replacing a letter with a different one based on a number wheel *as you write* is one thing, and maybe replacing characters with symbols as you jot them down on a sheet of paper doesn't seem so exciting to you. But consider how this document's 1s and 0s can be altered in such a way that they make no sense to an outsider but are perfectly readable for anyone I provide the key to. It's downright magical, I tell you. Cryptography and cryptanalysis are big parts of the security world and have been ever since the earliest known communication between people. If you're going to be an ethical hacker, you're going to have to at least know the basics. The good news is, you are not required to break down the mathematics behind the algorithms. The bad news, though, is that you need to know pretty much everything else about them.

 STUDY TIPS   In previous versions, EC-Council concentrated on the minutiae of cryptography: things like questions on key lengths, categories of crypto systems (block and stream, symmetric and asymmetric, and so on), and components of crypto systems that only required rote memorization. That's changed a lot in this version.

Sure, you'll still get a few of the "normal" questions in the batch, so don't ignore the detail-oriented memorization terms. On these, characteristics of algorithms and key lengths will be hit fairly hard, so study up. And when it comes to encrypted messaging, PKI is always going to be high on the testing list. Simply remembering that you encrypt with a public key and decrypt with a private key will nab you a couple questions without fail, but you'll definitely need to have a solid understanding of the entire system and what makes it: questions on certificate authorities, trust systems, and cross-certification will undoubtedly show up. And, for goodness sake, be sure to know the difference between a digital certificate and a digital signature.

You'll also get a lot more questioning on the *application* of cryptography. Scenario-based questioning will be more the norm, and while they may seem fairly straightforward, you'll still need to pay close attention. Know your cryptographic attacks very well—you'll definitely see Heartbleed, POODLE, Shellshock, DROWN, and others on your exam.

1. An attacker employs a Metasploit auxiliary module that exploits a built-in feature of OpenSSL. In the effort, the attacker's system sends a single byte of data representing it has received 64KB. The target responds by sending back 64KB of data from its memory. Which of the following describes this attack?

   A. POODLE

   B. FREAK

   C. Heartbleed

   D. DROWN

2. Which of the following is an effort within cryptography to provide the government with wiretap-like abilities inside encrypted communications?

   A. FIPS 186-2

   B. Self-signed certificates

   C. Asymmetric algorithm

   D. GAK

3. Which of the following statements are true regarding a PKI system? (Choose two.)

   A. The CA encrypts all messages.

   B. The CA is the trusted root that issues certificates.

   C. The CA is the recovery agent for lost certificates.

   D. The RA verifies an applicant to the system.

   E. The RA issues all certificates.

   F. The RA encrypt all messages.

4. A person approaches a network administrator and wants advice on how to send encrypted e-mail from home. The end user does not want to have to pay for any license fees or manage server services. Which of the following offers a method for sending encrypted e-mail without having to pay for license fees or manage a server?

   A. IP Security (IPSec)

   B. Multipurpose Internet Mail Extensions (MIME)

   C. Pretty Good Privacy (PGP)

   D. Hypertext Transfer Protocol with Secure Socket Layer (HTTPS)

5. Which of the following is best defined as an encryption protocol commonly used for e-mail security?

   A. PGP

   B. Keyczar

   C. RSA

   D. MD5

6. You're describing a basic PKI system to a new member of the team. He asks how the public key can be distributed within the system in an orderly, controlled fashion so that the users can be sure of the sender's identity. Which of the following would be your answer?

   A. Digital signature

   B. Hash value

   C. Private key

   D. Digital certificate

   E. Nonrepudiation

7. After TLS had largely replaced SSL for secure communications, many browsers retained backward compatibility to SSL 3.0. Which vulnerability takes advantage of the degradation of service down to SSL 3.0 in the TLS handshake?

   A. Heartbleed

   B. FREAK

   C. DROWN

   D. POODLE

8. Which mode of IPSec is most often chosen for internal communications?

   A. AH

   B. ESP

   C. Tunnel

   D. Transport

9. An organization is concerned about corporate espionage and has evidence suggesting an internal employee has been communicating trade secrets to a competitor. After some investigation, the employee trading secrets was identified. Monitoring of the employee's previous communications outside the company revealed nothing out of the ordinary, save for some large unencrypted e-mails containing image files of humorous pictures to external addresses. Which of the following is the most logical conclusion based on these facts?

   A. E-mail encryption allowed the user to hide files.

   B. The user hid information in the image files using steganography.

   C. Logical watermarking of images and e-mails fed the sensitive files piece by piece to the competitor.

   D. SMTP transport fuzzing was used.

10. A hacker has gained access to several files. Many are encrypted, but one is not, and it happens to be an unencrypted version of an encrypted file. Which of the following is the best choice for possibly providing a successful break into the encrypted files?

    A. Cipher text only

    B. Known plain text

C. Chosen cipher text

D. Replay

11. Which of the following methods should be used to check for the Heartbleed vulnerability?

    A. Use the ssl-heartbleed script in nmap.

    B. Connect via TLS to each system and examine the response handshake.

    C. Use **ping -ssl** and examine the responses.

    D. Use Tripwire.

12. What is the XOR output of 01010101 and 11001100?

    A. 01100110

    B. 10101010

    C. 10011001

    D. 00110011

13. Amy and Claire work in an organization that has a PKI system in place for securing messaging. Amy encrypts a message for Claire and sends it on. Claire receives the message and decrypts it. Within a PKI system, which of the following statements is true?

    A. Amy encrypts with her private key. Claire decrypts with her private key.

    B. Amy encrypts with her public key. Claire decrypts with her public key.

    C. Amy encrypts with Claire's private key. Claire decrypts with her public key.

    D. Amy encrypts with Claire's public key. Claire decrypts with her private key.

14. Which of the following would you find in an X.509 digital certificate? (Choose all that apply.)

    A. Version

    B. Algorithm ID

    C. Private Key

    D. Public Key

    E. Key Usage

    F. PTR Record

15. Which of the following is not true regarding steganography?

    A. Steganography can use least significant bit insertion, masking, and filtering as techniques to hide messaging.

    B. Steganography only works on color images.

    C. Image files embedded with steganography may be larger in size and display strange color palettes.

    D. Character positioning, text patterns, unusual blank spaces, and language anomalies can all be symptoms of a text file embedded with steganography.

16. An SSL session requires a client and a server to pass information between each other via a handshake and agree on a secured channel. Which of the following best describes the session key creation during the setup of an SSL session?

   A. The server creates the key after verifying the client's identity.

   B. The server creates the key immediately on the client connection.

   C. The client creates the key using the server's public key.

   D. The client creates the key after verifying the server's identity.

17. Which encryption algorithm uses variable block sizes (from 32 to 128 bits)?

   A. SHA-1

   B. RC5

   C. 3DES

   D. AES

18. Which hash algorithm was developed by the NSA and produces output values up to 512 bits?

   A. MD5

   B. SHA-1

   C. SHA-2

   D. SSL

19. You are concerned about protecting data on organization laptops from loss or theft. Which of the following technologies best accomplishes this goal?

   A. Single sign-on

   B. Cloud computing

   C. IPSec tunnel mode

   D. Full Disk Encryption

20. Which of the following best describes session key creation in SSL?

   A. It is created by the server after the user's identity has been verified.

   B. It is created by the server as soon as the client connects.

   C. It is created by the client using the server's public key.

   D. It is created by the client after the server's identity has been verified.

21. In a discussion on symmetric encryption, a friend mentions that one of the drawbacks with this system is scalability. He goes on to say that for every person you add to the mix, the number of keys increases dramatically. If seven people are in a symmetric encryption pool, how many keys are necessary?

   A. 7

   B. 14

C. 21

D. 28

22. Which of the following is a true statement?

    A. Symmetric encryption scales easily and provides for nonrepudiation.

    B. Symmetric encryption does not scale easily and does not provide for nonrepudiation.

    C. Symmetric encryption is not suited for bulk encryption.

    D. Symmetric encryption is slower than asymmetric encryption.

23. The PKI system you are auditing has a certificate authority (CA) at the top that creates and issues certificates. Users trust each other based on the CA. Which trust model is in use here?

    A. Stand-alone CA

    B. Web of trust

    C. Single authority

    D. Hierarchical trust

24. A portion of a digital certificate is shown here:

```
Version                      V3
Serial Number                26 43 03 62 e9 6b 39 a4 9e 15 00 c7 cc 21 a2
20
Signature Algorithm          sha1RSA
Signature Hash Algorithm     sha1
Issuer                       VeriSign Class 3 Secure Server
Valid From                   Monday, October 17, 2011 8:00 PM
Valid To                     Wednesday, October 17, 2012 7:59:59 PM

Public Key                   RSA (2048)
.
```

    Which of the following statements is true?

    A. The hash created for the digital signature holds 160 bits.

    B. The hash created for the digital signature holds 2048 bits.

    C. RSA is the hash algorithm used for the digital signature.

    D. This certificate contains a private key.

25. Two bit strings are run through an XOR operation. Which of the following is a true statement for each bit pair regarding this function?

    A. If the first value is 0 and the second value is 1, then the output is 0.

    B. If the first value is 1 and the second value is 0, then the output is 0.

    C. If the first value is 0 and the second value is 0, then the output is 1.

    D. If the first value is 1 and the second value is 1, then the output is 0.

26. Which of the following attacks attempts to re-send a portion of a cryptographic exchange in hopes of setting up a communications channel?

A. Known plain text

B. Chosen plain text

C. Man in the middle

D. Replay

27. Within a PKI system, which of the following is an accurate statement?

A. Bill can be sure a message came from Sue by using his public key to decrypt it.

B. Bill can be sure a message came from Sue by using his private key to decrypt it.

C. Bill can be sure a message came from Sue by using her private key to decrypt the digital signature.

D. Bill can be sure a message came from Sue by using her public key to decrypt the digital signature.

28. A systems administrator is applying digital certificates for authentication and verification services inside his network. He creates public and private key pairs using Apple's Keychain and uses the public key to sign documents that are used throughout the network. Which of the following certificate types is in use?

A. Public

B. Private

C. Signed

D. Self-signed

1. C
2. D
3. B, D
4. C
5. A
6. D
7. D
8. D
9. B
10. B

11. A
12. C
13. D
14. A, B, D, E
15. B
16. D
17. B
18. C
19. D
20. D

21. C
22. B
23. C
24. A
25. D
26. D
27. D
28. D

1. An attacker employs a Metasploit auxiliary module that exploits a built-in feature of OpenSSL. In the effort, the attacker's system sends a single byte of data representing it has received 64KB. The target responds by sending back 64KB of data from its memory. Which of the following describes this attack?

   A. POODLE

   B. FREAK

   C. Heartbleed

   D. DROWN

   ☑ **C.** Heartbleed was described as the worst vulnerability found (at least in terms of its potential impact) since commercial traffic began to flow on the Internet back when it was discovered in March of 2014. Heartbleed exploits a small feature in OpenSSL that turned out to present a very big problem. OpenSSL uses a heartbeat during an open session to verify that data was received correctly, and it does this by "echoing" data back to the other system. Basically one system tells the other, "I received what you sent and it's all good. Go ahead and send more." In Heartbleed, an attacker sends a single byte of data while telling the server it sent 64KB of data. The server will then send back with 64KB of random data from its memory. Items such as user names and passwords, private keys (which is exceptionally troubling, since future communication could be decrypted), cookies, and a host of other nifty bits of information could be easily stolen.

   ☒ **A** is incorrect because this does not describe POODLE. POODLE (Padding Oracle On Downgraded Legacy Encryption) is a vulnerability in the backward-compatibility steps taken by TLS clients.

   ☒ **B** is incorrect because this does not describe FREAK. Factoring Attack on RSA-EPORT Keys (FREAK) is a man-in-the-middle attack that forces a downgrade of an RSA key to a weaker length. The attacker forces the use of a weaker encryption key length, enabling successful brute-force attacks.

   ☒ **D** is incorrect because this does not describe DROWN. DROWN (Decrypting RSA with Obsolete and Weakened eNcryption) is a serious vulnerability that affects HTTPS and other services that rely on SSL and TLS (in particular, SSLv2 connections).

2. Which of the following is an effort within cryptography to provide the government with wiretap-like abilities inside encrypted communications?

   A. FIPS 186-2

   B. Self-signed certificates

   C. Asymmetric algorithm

   D. GAK

   ☑ **D.** Government Access to Keys (GAK) is one of those things that either sounds like a really good idea, or a very bad idea, depending on your personal opinion (and trust of the government). The idea behind GAK is simple: ensure the government has a way to decrypt encrypted communications so they can wiretap the bad guys when needed to keep the public safe. For this to work, software companies must willingly provide key copies to the government, which then stores them securely and uses them *only* with a court-issued warrant. Is mandatory key disclosure a good idea? That's a discussion for another time....

☒ **A** is incorrect because this does not describe FIPS 186-2 correctly. FIPS 186-2 specifies which DSA (Digital Signature Algorithm) may be used in the generation and verification of digital signatures.

☒ **B** is incorrect because self-signed certificates are simply digital certificates used internally when certificate services are needed but external verification is neither necessary nor worth the cost.

☒ **C** is incorrect because asymmetric algorithms have nothing to do with this effort. Asymmetric encryption uses two keys—what the one key encrypts, the other key decrypts. The "public" key is the one used for encryption, whereas the "private" key is used for decryption.

3. Which of the following statements are true regarding a PKI system? (Choose two.)

   A. The CA encrypts all messages.

   B. The CA is the trusted root that issues certificates.

   C. The CA is the recovery agent for lost certificates.

   D. The RA verifies an applicant to the system.

   E. The RA issues all certificates.

   F. The RA encrypt all messages.

   ☑ **B, D**. A PKI system consists of a bunch of parts, but the certificate authority is right at the top. The CA issues, maintains, and protects all the certificates for the system and maintains the revocation list (CRL). It is the one place everything in the system can go to for protected data. The registration authority (RA) does all sorts of stuff to take the load off the CA, and verifying the identity of an applicant wanting to use the system is one of the major tasks.

   ☒ **A, C, E,** and **F** are all incorrect because they do not correctly describe a PKI environment. The CA does not encrypt messages and is not a recovery agent for lost ones. The RA does not issue certificates or encrypt messages.

4. A person approaches a network administrator and wants advice on how to send encrypted e-mail from home. The end user does not want to have to pay for any license fees or manage server services. Which of the following offers a method for sending encrypted e-mail without having to pay for license fees or manage a server?

   A. IP Security (IPSec)

   B. Multipurpose Internet Mail Extensions (MIME)

C. Pretty Good Privacy (PGP)

D. Hypertext Transfer Protocol with Secure Socket Layer (HTTPS)

☑ **C.** I'm pretty sure you understand this comment already, but I'll say it again here to reinforce it: sometimes things on your CEH exam simply don't match up with reality. This question is a prime example. EC-Council, and its documentation up through version 8, defines Pretty Good Privacy (PGP) as a free, open source e-mail encryption method available for all to use. In truth, PGP is now synonymous with a single company's offering, based on the original PGP. The true open source, free side of it now is known more by OpenPGP (http://www.openpgp.org/). OpenPGP uses a decentralized system of trusted introducers that act in the same way as a certificate authority. Basically, in this web-of-trust relationship, if User A signs User B's certificate, then anyone who trusts User A will also trust User B. You can find downloads for software still using the free, open PGP at http://www.pgpi.org/.

☒ **A** is incorrect because IPSec is not intended as an e-mail encryption standard; it creates tunnels for the secure exchange of data from one system to another.

☒ **B** is incorrect because MIME is an Internet standard that allows the text-only protocol SMTP to transport nontext entities, such as pictures and non-ASCII character sets.

☒ **D** is incorrect because HTTPS is not intended as an e-mail encryption standard. It sets up a secured means of transporting data within a session and is *usually* associated with web traffic.

5. Which of the following is best defined as an encryption protocol commonly used for e-mail security?

A. PGP

B. Keyczar

C. RSA

D. MD5

☑ **A.** Even though it's probably best known as an e-mail security protocol/application, Pretty Good Privacy (PGP) can be used for a variety of purposes. PGP is used for encryption and decryption of messaging (including e-mail), data compression, digital signing, and even whole disk encryption. It provides authentication and privacy as well as combines conventional and public-key cryptography.

Don't get this confused with S/MIME. Secure/Multipurpose Internet Mail Extensions (S/MIME) is a standards-based protocol that can also encrypt messages; however, it does not provide many of the other features PGP offers (most importantly, whole disk encryption).

☒ **B** is incorrect because Keyczar is an open source cryptographic tool kit designed to help developers to use cryptography in their applications.

☒ **C** is incorrect because RSA is an asymmetric encryption algorithm that makes use of two large prime numbers. Factoring these numbers creates key sizes up to 4096 bits. RSA can be used for encryption and digital signatures, and it's the modern de facto standard for those purposes.

☒ **D** is incorrect because MD5 is a hash algorithm, and as we all know, hash algorithms don't encrypt anything. Sure, they're great at integrity checks, and, yes, you can pass a hash of something in place of the original (sending a hash of a stored password, for instance, instead of the password itself). However, this is not true encryption.

6. You're describing a basic PKI system to a new member of the team. He asks how the public key can be distributed within the system in an orderly, controlled fashion so that the users can be sure of the sender's identity. Which of the following would be your answer?

   A. Digital signature

   B. Hash value

   C. Private key

   D. Digital certificate

   E. Nonrepudiation

☑ **D.** This one is actually easy, yet it is confusing to a lot of folks. You have to remember the goal of this little portion of a PKI system—how does one *know* this public key really belongs to User Joe and not User Mike, and how can it be delivered safely to everyone? A digital certificate is the answer because it contains the sender's public key and can be used to identify the sender. Because the CA provides the certificate and key (public), the user can be certain the public key actually belongs to the intended recipient. This simplifies distribution of keys as well, because users can go to a central authority—a key store, if you will—instead of directly to each user in the organization. Without central control and digital certificates, it would be a madhouse, with everyone chucking public keys at one another with wild abandon. And PKI is no place for Mardi Gras, my friend.

☒ **A** is incorrect because although a digital signature does provide a means for verifying an identity (encryption with your private key, which can be decrypted only with your corresponding public key, proves you are indeed you), it doesn't provide any means of sending keys anywhere. A digital signature is nothing more than an algorithmic output that is designed to ensure the authenticity (and integrity) of the sender. You need it to prove your certificate's authenticity, but you need the certificate in order to send keys around.

☒ **B** is incorrect because a hash value has nothing to do with sending public keys around anywhere. Yes, hash values are "signed" to verify authenticity, but that's it. There is no transport capability in a hash. It's just a number and, in this case, a distractor answer.

☒ **C** is incorrect for a number of reasons, but one should be screaming at you from the page right now: you never, *never* send a private key anywhere. If you did send your private key off, it wouldn't be private anymore, now would it? The private key is simply the part of the pair used for encryption. It is never shared with anyone.

☒ **E** is incorrect because nonrepudiation is a definition term and has nothing to do with the transport of keys. Nonrepudiation is the means by which a recipient can ensure the identity of the sender, and neither party can deny having sent or received the message.

7. After TLS had largely replaced SSL for secure communications, many browsers retained backward compatibility to SSL 3.0. Which vulnerability takes advantage of the degradation of service down to SSL 3.0 in the TLS handshake?

   A. Heartbleed

   B. FREAK

   C. DROWN

   D. POODLE

   ☑ **D.** POODLE (Padding Oracle On Downgraded Legacy Encryption) was discovered by Google's security team and announced to the public on October 14, 2014. This time it was a case of backward compatibility being a problem. Many browsers would revert to SSL 3.0 when a TLS connection was unavailable, and because TLS performs a handshake effort designed to degrade service until something acceptable is found, if a hacker could jump in the connection between client and server, he could interfere with these handshakes, making them all fail. This would result in the client dropping all the way to SSL 3.0.

   SSL 3.0 has a design flaw that allows the padding data at the end of a block cipher to be changed so that the encryption cipher becomes less secure each time it is passed. If the same secret—let's say a password—is sent over several sessions, more and more information about it will leak. Eventually the connection may as well be plain text, and the attacker sitting in the middle can see everything. Mitigation for POODLE is simple—don't use SSL 3.0 anywhere.

   ☒ **A** is incorrect because Heartbleed exploits the heartbeat function in OpenSSL, which allows 64KB of random memory to be transferred to the attacker.

   ☒ **B** is incorrect because Factoring Attack on RSA-EPORT Keys (FREAK) is a man-in-the-middle attack that forces a downgrade of an RSA key to a weaker length.

   ☒ **C** is incorrect because DROWN (Decrypting RSA with Obsolete and Weakened eNcryption) is a serious vulnerability that affects HTTPS and other services that rely on SSL and TLS (in particular, SSLv2 connections).

8. Which mode of IPSec is most often chosen for internal communications?

   A. AH

   B. ESP

   C. Tunnel

   D. Transport

☑ **D.** IPSec is a network layer encryption protocol that can be used in two modes: tunnel and transport. In transport mode, the data payload is encrypted but the rest of the packet (the IP header in particular) is not touched. This works well internally, between end stations or between an end station and a gateway, if the gateway is being treated as a host. NAT is not supported by transport mode, although it can be combined with other tunneling protocols.

☒ **A** is incorrect because the Authentication Header (AH) is a protocol in the IPSec suite, verifying an IP packet's integrity and determining the validity of its source.

☒ **B** is incorrect because Encapsulating Security Payload (ESP) is another protocol in the IPSec suite, and it actually encrypts each packet.

☒ **C** is incorrect because tunnel mode encrypts the entire packet, including the headers. It's not that you can't use tunnel mode inside the network; it's just not common or recommended.

9. An organization is concerned about corporate espionage and has evidence suggesting an internal employee has been communicating trade secrets to a competitor. After some investigation, the employee trading secrets was identified. Monitoring of the employee's previous communications outside the company revealed nothing out of the ordinary, save for some large unencrypted e-mails containing image files of humorous pictures to external addresses. Which of the following is the most logical conclusion based on these facts?

A. E-mail encryption allowed the user to hide files.

B. The user hid information in the image files using steganography.

C. Logical watermarking of images and e-mails fed the sensitive files piece by piece to the competitor.

D. SMTP transport fuzzing was used.

☑ **B.** In this circumstance, you know the employee has been sending sensitive documents out of the network. IDS obviously hasn't picked up on anything, and there was nothing overtly done to give away the intent. The only thing out of the ordinary turned out to be large e-mail files holding nothing but images. Steganography is the most logical choice here, and the user simply folded the sensitive data into the latest joke image he found and sent it on its merry way.

☒ **A** is incorrect because e-mail encryption isn't in place—it's specifically called out in the question and wouldn't necessarily allow external encryption or hide the information from later forensics examinations.

☒ **C** and **D** are incorrect because logical watermarking and SMTP transport fuzzing, so far as I know, don't even exist. They sound cool and may appear legitimate, but they're definitely not the answer you're looking for.

10. A hacker has gained access to several files. Many are encrypted, but one is not, and it happens to be an unencrypted version of an encrypted file. Which of the following is the best choice for possibly providing a successful break into the encrypted files?

   A. Cipher text only

   B. Known plain text

   C. Chosen cipher text

   D. Replay

   ☑ **B.** There is definitely some room for argument on this question: Who's to say all the files were encrypted in the same way? However, of the options presented, known plain text is the one that makes the most sense. In this attack, the hacker has both plain-text and cipher-text messages. Plain-text copies are scanned for repeatable sequences, which are then compared to the cipher-text versions. Over time, and with effort, this can be used to decipher the key.

   ☒ **A** is incorrect, but just barely so. I'm certain some of you are arguing that a cipher-text-only attack could also be used here because in that attack several messages encrypted in the same way are run through statistical analysis to eventually reveal repeating code, which may be used to decode messages later. Sure, an attacker might just ignore the plain-text copy in there, but the inference in the question is that he'd use both. You'll often see questions like this where you'll need to take into account the inference without overthinking the question.

   ☒ **C** is incorrect because chosen cipher text works almost exactly like a cipher-text-only attack. Statistical analysis without a plain-text version for comparison can be performed, but it's only for *portions* of gained cipher text. That's the key word to look for. As an aside, RSA is susceptible to this attack in particular (an attacker can use a user's public key to encrypt plain text and then decrypt the result to find patterns for exploitation).

   ☒ **D** is incorrect because it's irrelevant to this scenario. Replay attacks catch streams of data and replay them to the intended recipient from another sender.

11. Which of the following methods should be used to check for the Heartbleed vulnerability?

   A. Use the ssl-heartbleed script in nmap.

   B. Connect via TLS to each system and examine the response handshake.

   C. Use **ping -ssl** and examine the responses.

   D. Use Tripwire.

   ☑ **A.** An nmap scan can show you all sorts of information, and thankfully it also provides a quick means to check for Heartbleed. Using the ssl-heartbleed script will return "NOT VULNERABLE" on systems without the vulnerability. Syntax for the script use is **nmap -d -script ssl-hearbleed -script-args vulns.showall -sV *IPADDRESS*** (where *IPADDRESS* is the host, or range, you are testing).

☒ **B** is incorrect because Heartbleed has nothing to do with TLS.

☒ **C** is incorrect because there is no such thing as the **ping -ssl** command.

☒ **D** is incorrect because Tripwire is a conglomeration of tool actions that perform the overall IT security efforts for an enterprise. Tripwire provides for integrity checks, regulatory compliance, configuration management, and all other sorts of goodies, but not Heartbleed scans.

12. What is the XOR output of 01010101 and 11001100?

   A. 01100110

   B. 10101010

   C. 10011001

   D. 00110011

   ☑ **C.** XOR operations are used a lot in various encryption efforts (in addition to many other uses). In an XOR operation, two bits are compared. If the bits match, the output is a zero. If they don't, the output is a 1. In this example, put 01010101 on top of 11001100 and compare each bit, one by one. The first bit in each set is 0 and 1, respectively, so the XOR output is 1. The second bit in each set is 1 and 1 so, since they match, the output is 0. Continuing bit by bit, the output would be 10011001.

   ☒ **A, B,** and **D** are incorrect because these do not represent the output of an XOR on these two inputs.

13. Amy and Claire work in an organization that has a PKI system in place for securing messaging. Amy encrypts a message for Claire and sends it on. Claire receives the message and decrypts it. Within a PKI system, which of the following statements is true?

   A. Amy encrypts with her private key. Claire decrypts with her private key.

   B. Amy encrypts with her public key. Claire decrypts with her public key.

   C. Amy encrypts with Claire's private key. Claire decrypts with her public key.

   D. Amy encrypts with Claire's public key. Claire decrypts with her private key.

   ☑ **D.** When it comes to PKI encryption questions, remember the golden rule: encrypt with public, decrypt with private. In this instance, Amy wants to send a message to Claire. She will use Claire's public key—which everyone can get—to encrypt the message, knowing that only Claire, with her corresponding private key, can decrypt it.

   ☒ **A** is incorrect because you do not encrypt with a private key in a PKI system. Yes, you *can* encrypt with it, but what would be the point? Anyone with your public key—which everyone has—could decrypt it! Remember, private = decrypt, public = encrypt.

   ☒ **B** is incorrect because, in this case, Amy has gotten her end of the bargain correct, but Claire doesn't seem to know what she's doing. PKI encryption is done in key pairs—what one key encrypts, the other decrypts. So, her use of her own public key to decrypt something encrypted with Amy's key—a key from a completely different pair—is baffling.

☒ **C** is incorrect because there is no way Amy should have anyone's private key, other than her own. That's kind of the point of a private key—you keep it to yourself and don't share it with anyone. As a note here, the stated steps would actually work—that is, one key encrypts, so the other decrypts—but it's completely backward for how the system is supposed to work. It's an abomination to security, if you will.

14. Which of the following would you find in an X.509 digital certificate? (Choose all that apply.)

    A. Version

    B. Algorithm ID

    C. Private Key

    D. Public Key

    E. Key Usage

    F. PTR Record

    ☑ **A, B, D, E.** You are definitely going to need to know the digital certificate and what it contains. A *digital certificate* is an electronic file that is used to verify a user's identity, providing nonrepudiation throughout the system. The certificate contains standard fields used for specific purposes. Those fields are Version, Serial Number, Subject, Algorithm ID (or Signature Algorithm), Issuer, Valid From and Valid To, Key Usage, Subject's Public Key, and Optional.

    ☒ **C** is incorrect because a private key is never shared. The certificate usually is "signed" with an encrypted hash by the private key, but the key itself is never shared.

    ☒ **F** is incorrect because a PTR record is a part of the Domain Name System (DNS), not a digital certificate. A PTR record provides a reverse DNS lookup as a pointer to a canonical name.

15. Which of the following is not true regarding steganography?

    A. Steganography can use least significant bit insertion, masking, and filtering as techniques to hide messaging.

    B. Steganography only works on color images.

    C. Image files embedded with steganography may be larger in size and display strange color palettes.

    D. Character positioning, text patterns, unusual blank spaces, and language anomalies can all be symptoms of a text file embedded with steganography.

    ☑ **B.** Steganography is the practice of concealing a message inside another medium (such as another file or an image) in such a way that only the sender and recipient even know of its existence, let alone the manner in which to decipher it. It can be as simple as hiding the message in the text of a written correspondence or as complex as changing bits within a huge media file to carry a message. Steganography can be embedded in color or grayscale images, text files, audio files, and even in video.

In grayscale images, steganography is usually implemented via masking (also known as filtering, which hides the data in much the same way as a watermark on a document).

☒ **A, C,** and **D** are incorrect because these are true statements regarding steganography.

16. An SSL session requires a client and a server to pass information between each other via a handshake and agree on a secured channel. Which of the following best describes the session key creation during the setup of an SSL session?

   A. The server creates the key after verifying the client's identity.

   B. The server creates the key immediately on the client connection.

   C. The client creates the key using the server's public key.

   D. The client creates the key after verifying the server's identity.

☑ **D.** In the CEH world, SSL has six major steps (others claim seven or more, but we're studying for the CEH certification here, so we'll stick with theirs). The six steps are (1) Client hello, (2) Server hello and certificate, (3) Server hello done message, (4) Client verifies server identity and sends Client Key Exchange message, (5) Client sends Change Cipher Spec and Finish message, and (6) Server responds with Change Cipher Spec and Finish message. The session key is created by the client after it verifies the server's identity (using the certificate provided in step 2).

☒ **A** is incorrect because the server does not create the session key.

☒ **B** is incorrect for the same reason—the client creates the key, not the server.

☒ **C** is incorrect because the client does not use a "public key" for an SSL session. It's a great distractor, trying to confuse you with PKI terms in an SSL question.

17. Which encryption algorithm uses variable block sizes (from 32 to 128 bits)?

   A. SHA-1

   B. RC5

   C. 3DES

   D. AES

☑ **B.** Questions on identifying encryption algorithms really come down to memorization of some key terms. Rivest Cipher (RC) encompasses several versions, from RC2 through RC6. It is an asymmetric block cipher that uses a variable key length up to 2040 bits. RC6, the latest version, uses 128-bit blocks, whereas RC5 uses variable block sizes (32, 64, or 128).

☒ **A** is incorrect because SHA-1 is a hash algorithm, not an encryption algorithm. If this question were about verifying integrity, this would be a good choice. However, in this case, it is a distractor.

☒ **C** is incorrect because although 3DES is a symmetric block cipher, it does not use variable block sizes. 3DES (called *triple* DES) uses a 168-bit key and can use up to three keys in a multiple-encryption method. It's much more effective than DES but is much slower.

⊠ **D** is incorrect because AES, another symmetric block cipher, uses key lengths of 128, 192, or 256 bits. It effectively replaces DES and is much faster than either DES or its triplicate cousin (3DES).

18. Which hash algorithm was developed by the NSA and produces output values up to 512 bits?

    A. MD5

    B. SHA-1

    C. SHA-2

    D. SSL

    ☑ **C.** Both SHA-1 and SHA-2 were developed by the NSA; however, SHA-1 produced only a 160-bit output value. SHA-2 was developed to rectify the shortcomings of its predecessor and is capable of producing outputs of 224, 256, 384, and 512 bits. Although it was designed as a replacement for SHA-1 (which was supposed to have been phased out in 2010), SHA-2 is still not as widely used.

    ⊠ **A** is incorrect because MD5 produces 128-bit output. It was created by Ronald Rivest for ensuring file integrity; however, serious flaws in the algorithm, and the advancement of other hashes, have resulted in this hash being rendered obsolete (U.S. CERT, August 2010). Despite this, you'll find MD5 is still used for file verification on downloads and, in many cases, to store passwords.

    ⊠ **B** is incorrect because SHA-1 produces a 160-bit value output. It was created by NSA and used to be required by law for use in U.S. government applications. However, serious flaws became apparent in late 2005, and the U.S. government began recommending the replacement of SHA-1 with SHA-2 after 2010 (see FIPS PUB 180-1).

    ⊠ **D** is incorrect because SSL isn't even a hash algorithm. If you picked this one, you have some serious studying to do.

19. You are concerned about protecting data on organization laptops from loss or theft. Which of the following technologies best accomplishes this goal?

    A. Single sign-on

    B. Cloud computing

    C. IPSec tunnel mode

    D. Full Disk Encryption

    ☑ **D.** Data at rest (DAR) protection is a security technology tailor-made for loss and theft protection, with one tiny little catch: Full Disk Encryption in DAR sets up a preboot session that requires valid credentials to unlock the machine. However, it's important to note the preboot session will only engage after a full system power down: if the user just closes the lid and puts the machine into sleep mode, DAR protection does nothing. Assuming the user does power off the machine before taking it on a trip, preboot protects everything—including the Master Boot Record—and ensures that even if the laptop is stolen or lost, the data inside is protected. If the user doesn't power off, then DAR is just another security tool that provides the illusion of security—which may be even worse than having nothing at all.

☒ **A** is incorrect because single sign-on—a method of authentication allowing a user to access multiple resources with one set of credentials—has nothing to do with loss or theft protection.

☒ **B** is incorrect because while cloud computing may provide some data storage and protection efforts, it does nothing to protect against loss or theft of the laptop, and leaves everything on it vulnerable.

☒ **C** is incorrect because, although IPSec tunnel mode will protect data in transit from the laptop back into the remote network, it doesn't provide any protection for the laptop itself.

20. Which of the following best describes session key creation in SSL?

   A. It is created by the server after the user's identity has been verified.

   B. It is created by the server as soon as the client connects.

   C. It is created by the client using the server's public key.

   D. It is created by the client after the server's identity has been verified.

   ☑ **D.** Depending on the book you're reading, an SSL session can have anywhere from five to ten steps. For our purposes, there are six defined steps, starting with an exchange of hello packets to allow the server to authenticate itself to the client (using public-key techniques and providing the SSL version, session ID, and certificate). After these three handshake messages are exchanged, the client verifies the certificate and generates a secret key, which it then encrypts using the server's public key. Finally, a finish message from the client is sent, and the server compares hashes, sending its own finish message to start the session. The session key itself is used to encrypt the data.

   ☒ **A** and **B** are incorrect because the server does not create the secret key.

   ☒ **C** is incorrect because the public key is used to *encrypt* the key, not to *create* it.

21. In a discussion on symmetric encryption, a friend mentions that one of the drawbacks with this system is scalability. He goes on to say that for every person you add to the mix, the number of keys increases dramatically. If seven people are in a symmetric encryption pool, how many keys are necessary?

   A. 7

   B. 14

   C. 21

   D. 28

☑ **C.** Symmetric encryption is really fast and works great with bulk encryption; however, scalability and key exchange are huge drawbacks. To determine the number of keys you need, use the formula $N (N - 1) / 2$. Plugging 7 into this, we have $7 (7 - 1) / 2 = 21$.

☒ **A** is incorrect because although symmetric key does use the same key for encryption and decryption, each new node requires a different key. Seven keys simply isn't enough.

☒ **B** is incorrect because 14 keys isn't enough.

☒ **D** is incorrect because 28 keys is too many. Stick with the formula $N (N - 1) / 2$.

22. Which of the following is a true statement?

    A. Symmetric encryption scales easily and provides for nonrepudiation.

    B. Symmetric encryption does not scale easily and does not provide for nonrepudiation.

    C. Symmetric encryption is not suited for bulk encryption.

    D. Symmetric encryption is slower than asymmetric encryption.

☑ **B.** Symmetric encryption has always been known for strength and speed; however, scalability and key exchange are big drawbacks. Additionally, there is no way to provide for nonrepudiation (within the confines of the encryption system). Symmetric encryption is good for a great many things when you don't want all the overhead of key management.

☒ **A** is incorrect because symmetric encryption does not scale easily and does not provide for nonrepudiation. The single key used for each channel makes scalability an issue. Remember, the formula for number of keys is $N (N - 1) / 2$.

☒ **C** is incorrect because symmetric encryption is perfectly designed for bulk encryption. Assuming you can find a way to ensure the key exchange is protected, speed makes this the best choice.

☒ **D** is incorrect because one of the benefits of symmetric encryption is its speed. It is much faster than asymmetric encryption but doesn't provide some of the benefits asymmetric provides us (scalability, nonrepudiation, and so on).

23. The PKI system you are auditing has a certificate authority (CA) at the top that creates and issues certificates. Users trust each other based on the CA. Which trust model is in use here?

    A. Stand-alone CA

    B. Web of trust

    C. Single authority

    D. Hierarchical trust

☑ **C.** Trust models within PKI systems provide a standardized method for certificate and key exchanges. The valid trust models include web of trust, single authority, and hierarchical. The single authority system has a CA at the top that creates and issues certs. Users then trust each other based on the CA at the top vouching for them. Assuming a single authority model is used, it's of vital importance to protect it. After all, if it is compromised, your whole system is kaput.

☒ **A** is incorrect because *stand-alone CA* doesn't refer to a trust model. It instead defines a single CA that is usually set up as a trusted offline root in a hierarchy or when extranets and the Internet are involved.

☒ **B** is incorrect because *web of trust* refers to a model where users create and manage their own certificates and key exchange and multiple entities sign certificates for one another. In other words, users within this system trust each other based on certificates they receive from other users on the same system.

☒ **D** is incorrect because although a hierarchical trust system also has a CA at the top (which is known as the *root CA*), it makes use of one or more intermediate CAs underneath it—known as *RAs*—to issue and manage certificates. This system is the most secure because users can track the certificate back to the root to ensure authenticity without a single point of failure.

24. A portion of a digital certificate is shown here:

```
Version                      V3
Serial Number                26 43 03 62 e9 6b 39 a4 9e 15 00 c7 cc 21 a2
20
Signature Algorithm          sha1RSA
Signature Hash Algorithm     sha1
Issuer                       VeriSign Class 3 Secure Server
Valid From                   Monday, October 17, 2011 8:00 PM
Valid To                     Wednesday, October 17, 2012 7:59:59 PM
.
Public Key                   RSA (2048)
.
```

Which of the following statements is true?

A. The hash created for the digital signature holds 160 bits.

B. The hash created for the digital signature holds 2048 bits.

C. RSA is the hash algorithm used for the digital signature.

D. This certificate contains a private key.

☑ **A.** Questions on the digital certificate are usually easy enough, and this is no exception. The algorithm used to create the hash is clearly defined as Signature Hash Algorithm (SHA-1), and, as we already know, SHA-1 creates a 160-bit hash output. This will then be encrypted by the sender's private key and decrypted on the recipient's end with the public key, thus verifying identity.

☒ **B** is incorrect because it is a distractor: the RSA key size of 2048 is listed in the public key section of the certificate.

☒ **C** incorrect because RSA is not a hash algorithm. It is, without doubt, used as an encryption algorithm with this certificate (and uses a 2048-bit key to do so) but does not hash anything.

☒ **D** is incorrect because (as I'm certain you are already aware) a private key is *never* shared. The public key is retained for recipients to use if they want to encrypt something to send back to the originator, but the private key is never shared.

25. Two bit strings are run through an XOR operation. Which of the following is a true statement for each bit pair regarding this function?

A. If the first value is 0 and the second value is 1, then the output is 0.

B. If the first value is 1 and the second value is 0, then the output is 0.

C. If the first value is 0 and the second value is 0, then the output is 1.

D. If the first value is 1 and the second value is 1, then the output is 0.

☑ **D.** An XOR operation requires two inputs, and in the case of encryption algorithms, this would be the data bits and the key bits. Each bit is fed into the operation—one from the data, the next from the key—and then XOR makes a determination: if the bits match, the output is 0; if they don't, it's 1.

☒ **A** is incorrect because the two values being compared are different; therefore, the output would be 1.

☒ **B** is incorrect because the two values being compared are different; therefore, the output would be 1.

☒ **C** is incorrect because the two values being compared are the same; therefore, the output should be 0.

26. Which of the following attacks attempts to re-send a portion of a cryptographic exchange in hopes of setting up a communications channel?

A. Known plain text

B. Chosen plain text

C. Man in the middle

D. Replay

☑ **D.** Replay attacks are most often performed within the context of a man-in-the-middle attack and not necessarily just for communications channel setup. They're also used for DoS attacks against a system, to feed bad data in hopes of corrupting a system, to try to overflow a buffer (send more encrypted data than expected), and so on. The hacker repeats a portion of a cryptographic exchange in hopes of fooling the system into setting up a communications channel. The attacker doesn't really have to know the actual data (such as the password) being exchanged; he just has to get the timing right in copying and then replaying the bit stream. Session tokens can be used in the communications process to combat this attack.

☒ **A** is incorrect because known plain text doesn't really have anything to do with this scenario. Known plain text refers to having both plain-text and corresponding cipher-text messages, which are scanned for repeatable sequences and then compared to the cipher-text versions.

☒ **B** is incorrect because it simply doesn't apply to this scenario. In a chosen plain-text attack, a hacker puts several encrypted messages through statistical analysis to determine repeating code.

☒ **C** is incorrect because, in this instance, replay refers to the attack being described in the question, not man in the middle. I know you think this is confusing, and I do understand. However, this is an example of the CEH wordplay you'll need to be familiar with. Man in the middle is usually listed as an attack by every security guide; however, within the context of the exam, it may also refer solely to where the attacker has positioned himself. From this location, he can launch a variety of attacks—replay being one of them.

27. Within a PKI system, which of the following is an accurate statement?

   A. Bill can be sure a message came from Sue by using his public key to decrypt it.

   B. Bill can be sure a message came from Sue by using his private key to decrypt it.

   C. Bill can be sure a message came from Sue by using her private key to decrypt the digital signature.

   D. Bill can be sure a message came from Sue by using her public key to decrypt the digital signature.

   ☑ **D.** Remember, a digital signature is a hash value that is encrypted with the user's private key. Because the corresponding public key can decrypt it, this provides the nonrepudiation feature we're looking for. This is the only instance on the exam where the private key is used for encryption. In general, public encrypts, and private decrypts. The steps for creating an encrypted message with a digital signature are as follows:

     1. Create a hash of the body of the message.

     2. Encrypt that hash with your private key (adding it to the message as your signature).

     3. Encrypt the entire message with the public key of the recipient.

☒ **A** is incorrect because not only does this have nothing to do with proving identity, but it also cannot work. Bill can't use his own public key to decrypt a message sent to him. The keys work in pairs—if the message is encrypted with his public key, only his private key can decrypt it.

☒ **B** is incorrect because this has nothing to do with proving Sue's identity. Sure, Bill will be using his own private key to decrypt messages sent to him by other users; however, it doesn't provide any help in proving identity.

☒ **C** is incorrect because there is no way Bill should have Sue's private key. Remember, private keys are not shared with anyone, for any reason. This is why encrypting a hash with it works so well for the digital signing process.

28. A systems administrator is applying digital certificates for authentication and verification services inside his network. He creates public and private key pairs using Apple's Keychain and uses the public key to sign documents that are used throughout the network. Which of the following certificate types is in use?

   A. Public

   B. Private

   C. Signed

   D. Self-signed

☑ **D.** Security certificates are used for all sorts of things in networking: for example, applications and network services might use them for authentication. If you are doing business across the Internet, your clients will want to ensure a trusted third party signs your certificates, so they can verify you are indeed legitimate. Internally, though, due to cost and speed of deployment/maintenance, self-signed certificates are the way to go. A self-signed certificate is simply one that is signed by the same entity that created it. Because most of your internal certificate needs can be served without going to an external CA to verify identity, using self-signed certificates may be the best bet.

☒ **A** and **B** are incorrect because these are not certificate types.

☒ **C** is incorrect because regular signed certificates are signed and verified by a third-party certificate authority (CA).

Low Tech: Social Engineering and Physical Security

This chapter includes questions from the following topics:

- Define social engineering
- Describe different types of social engineering techniques and attacks
- Describe identity theft
- List social engineering countermeasures
- Describe physical security measures

I know a lot of people will pick up books like this in an effort to train themselves to be a "hacker," but I've got some news for you: you were *already* partway there. You're a born social engineer, and you've most likely been doing some of this stuff since you could walk. In fact, I'll bet serious cash you'll probably employ at least some manipulation of your fellow human beings *today*, maybe without even thinking about it.

Don't believe me? I guarantee if you search your memory banks there was at least once in your childhood where you talked your way into another piece of candy or few minutes playing with a toy, just because you were cute. If you had siblings, I bet all of you conspired—at least once—to cover up something bad or to convince Mom you really need more ice cream. And the technique of employing "Well, Dad said it was okay," pitting Mom versus Dad? Oldest trick in the book.

We all work the system every day because it's how we are wired, and there's not a person reading this book who doesn't try to influence and manipulate the people around them to gain an advantage or accomplish a goal. You've been doing it since you were born, and you will continue to do so until you shuffle off this mortal coil. All we're doing with pen testing and ethical hacking is bringing those same thoughts and actions to influence our virtual workplace and adding one slight twist: while most of your manipulation of others isn't consciously purposeful, it *has to be* in the virtual world. There's a lot of acting, a lot of intuition, and a lot of lying involved, and to be successful in this area you have to be *convincing* to pull it off.

The entire subject is fascinating, and there are endless articles, studies, and books devoted to it. A Kaspersky blog dubbed it "Hacking the Human OS," which is about as apt a description as I could ever come up with myself. Social engineering and physical security measures are those obvious and simple solutions you may accidentally overlook. Why spend all the effort to hack into a system and crack passwords offline when you can just call someone up and ask for them? Why bother with trying to steal sensitive business information from encrypted shares when you can walk into the building and sit in on a sales presentation? Sure, you occasionally almost get arrested shuffling around in a dumpster for good information, and you might even get the pleasure of seeing how powerful a dog handler is, as he keeps the vicious, barking animal held tight on the leash while you cower in the corner (our esteemed technical editor can attest to both of these), but a lot of social engineering is just worth it. It's easy, simple, and effective, and not an area of your pen testing you can afford to ignore.

 STUDY TIPS EC-Council lumps social engineering and physical security into the "Security" segment of the exam. Because the exam is 150 questions and the Security segment comprises 25 percent of the overall questions, that means 37.5 questions will be directly related to the Security segment. And how many of those 37 or so questions will be related to social engineering and physical security? I can't say for sure, but given the breakdown of the rest of the Security segment (including firewalls, cryptography, wireless, and so on), you can probably count on ten or so.

There hasn't been a lot of change between previous versions to the current one: most questions you'll see about social engineering and physical security are of the straightforward, definition-based variety, and they cover the same areas and topics you'd think would be part of this discussion. Areas of focus will still include various social engineering attacks (shoulder surfing, dumpster diving, impersonation, and so on), security controls (physical, operational and technical), and biometrics. Anything new in this section will probably be in the mobile realm (using SMS texting and cell phones for social engineering, for example).

One note of caution, though: be careful with the wording in some of these questions. For example, *tailgating* and *piggybacking* mean the same thing to us in the real world, but there's a significant difference when it comes to your exam. It's true that most of these are fairly easy to decipher, but EC-Council sometimes likes to focus on minutiae.

1. While observing a target organization's building, you note the lone entrance to the building has a guard posted just inside the door. After entering the external door, you note the lobby of the building is separated from the external door by a small glass-paneled room, with a closed door facing the exterior and a closed door to the interior. There appears to be an RFID scanning device and a small keyboard with video display in the room. Which of the following best defines this physical security control?

   A. Guard shack

   B. Turnstile

   C. Man shack

   D. Man trap

2. In your social engineering efforts, you call the company help desk and pose as a user who has forgotten a password. You ask the technician to help you reset your password, which they happily comply with. Which social engineering attack is in use here?

   A. Piggybacking

   B. Reverse social engineering

   C. Technical support

   D. Halo effect

3. Which of the following is a true statement regarding biometric systems?

   A. The lower the CER, the better the biometric system.

   B. The higher the CER, the better the biometric system.

   C. The higher the FRR, the better the biometric system.

   D. The higher the FAR, the better the biometric system.

4. A pen tester sends an unsolicited e-mail to several users on the target organization. The e-mail is well crafted and appears to be from the company's help desk, advising users of potential network problems. The e-mail provides a contact number to call in the event a user is adversely affected. The pen tester then performs a denial of service on several systems and receives phone calls from users asking for assistance. Which social engineering practice is in play here?

   A. Technical support

   B. Impersonation

   C. Phishing

   D. Reverse social engineering

5. A pen test member has gained access to a building and is observing activity as he wanders around. In one room of the building, he stands just outside a cubicle wall opening and watches the onscreen activity of a user. Which social engineering attack is in use here?

   A. Eavesdropping

   B. Tailgating

   C. Shoulder surfing

   D. Piggybacking

6. A recent incident investigated by the local IR team involved a user receiving an e-mail that appeared to be from the U.S. Postal Service, notifying her of a package headed her way and providing a link for tracking the package. The link provided took the user to what appeared to be the USPS site, where she input her user information to learn about the latest shipment headed her way. Which attack did the user fall victim to?

   A. Phishing

   B. Internet level

   C. Reverse social engineering

   D. Impersonation

7. Which type of social engineering attacks uses phishing, pop-ups, and IRC channels?

   A. Technical

   B. Computer based

   C. Human based

   D. Physical

8. An attacker identifies a potential target and spends some time profiling her. After gaining some information, the attacker sends a text to the target's cell phone. The text appears to be from her bank and advises her to call a provided phone number immediately regarding her account information. She dials the number and provides sensitive information to the attacker, who is posing as a bank employee. Which of the following best defines this attack?

   A. Vishing

   B. Smishing

   C. Phishing

   D. Tishing

9. Which of the following constitutes the highest risk to the organization?

   A. Black-hat hacker

   B. White-hat hacker

   C. Gray-hat hacker

   D. Disgruntled employee

10. After observing a target organization for several days, you discover that finance and HR records are bagged up and placed in an outside storage bin for later shredding/recycling. One day you simply walk to the bin and place one of the bags in your vehicle, with plans to rifle through it later. Which social engineering attack was used here?

    A. Offline

    B. Physical

    C. Piggybacking

    D. Dumpster diving

11. An attacker waits outside the entry to a secured facility. After a few minutes an authorized user appears with an entry badge displayed. He swipes a key card and unlocks the door. The attacker, with no display badge, follows him inside. Which social engineering attack just occurred?

    A. Tailgating

    B. Piggybacking

    C. Identity theft

    D. Impersonation

12. Tim is part of a pen test team and is attempting to gain access to a secured area of the campus. He stands outside a badged entry gate and pretends to be engaged in a contentious cell phone conversation. An organization employee walks past and badges the gate open. Tim asks the employee to hold the gate while flashing a fake ID badge and continuing his phone conversation. He then follows the employee through the gate. Which of the following best defines this effort?

    A. Shoulder surfing

    B. Piggybacking

    C. Tailgating

    D. Drafting

13. Which of the following may be effective countermeasures against social engineering? (Choose all that apply.)

    A. Security policies

    B. Operational guidelines

    C. Appropriately configured IDS

    D. User education and training

    E. Strong firewall configuration

14. Which of the following are indicators of a phishing e-mail? (Choose all that apply.)

    A. It does not reference you by name.

    B. It contains misspelled words or grammatical errors.

    C. It contains spoofed links.

    D. It comes from an unverified source.

15. You are discussing physical security measures and are covering background checks on employees and policies regarding key management and storage. Which type of physical security measures are being discussed?

    A. Physical

    B. Technical

    C. Operational

    D. Practical

16. Which of the following resources can assist in combating phishing in your organization? (Choose all that apply.)

    A. Phishkill

    B. Netcraft

    C. Phishtank

    D. IDA Pro

17. An attacker targets a specific group inside the organization. After some time profiling the group, she notes several websites the individual members of the group all visit on a regular basis. She spends time inserting various malware and malicious codes into some of the more susceptible websites. Within a matter of days, one of the group member's system installs the malware from an infected site, and the attacker uses the infected machine as a pivot point inside the network. Which of the following best defines this attack?

    A. Spear phishing

    B. Whaling

    C. Web-ishing

    D. Watering hole attack

18. Which type of social engineering makes use of impersonation, dumpster diving, shoulder surfing, and tailgating?

    A. Physical

    B. Technical

    C. Human based

    D. Computer based

19. In examining the About Us link in the menu of a target organization's website, an attacker discovers several different individual contacts within the company. To one of these contacts, she crafts an e-mail asking for information that appears to come from an individual within the company who would be expected to make such a request. The e-mail provides a link to click, which then prompts for the contact's user ID and password. Which of the following best describes this attack?

    A. Trojan e-mailing

    B. Spear phishing

    C. Social networking

    D. Operational engineering

20. A security admin has a control in place that embeds a unique image into e-mails on specific topics, which verifies the message as authentic and trusted. Which anti-phishing method is being used?

    A. Steganography

    B. Sign-in seal

    C. PKI

    D. CAPTCHA

21. Which of the following should be in place to assist as a social engineering countermeasure? (Choose all that apply.)

    A. Classification of information

    B. Strong security policy

    C. User education

    D. Strong change management process

22. Joe uses a user ID and password to log into the system every day. Jill uses a PIV card and a PIN. Which of the following statements is true?

    A. Joe and Jill are using single-factor authentication.

    B. Joe and Jill are using two-factor authentication.

    C. Joe is using two-factor authentication.

    D. Jill is using two-factor authentication.

23. A system owner has implemented a retinal scanner at the entryway to the data floor. Which type of physical security measure is this?

    A. Technical

    B. Single factor

    C. Computer based

    D. Operational

24. Which of the following is the best representation of a technical control?

    A. Air conditioning

    B. Security tokens

    C. Automated humidity control

    D. Fire alarms

    E. Security policy

1. D	**9.** D	**17.** D
2. C	**10.** D	**18.** C
3. A	**11.** B	**19.** B
4. D	**12.** C	**20.** B
5. C	**13.** A, B, D	**21.** A, B, C, D
6. A	**14.** A, B, C, D	**22.** D
7. B	**15.** C	**23.** A
8. B	**16.** B, C	**24.** B

1. While observing a target organization's building, you note the lone entrance to the building has a guard posted just inside the door. After entering the external door, you note the lobby of the building is separated from the external door by a small glass-paneled room, with a closed door facing the exterior and a closed door to the interior. There appears to be an RFID scanning device and a small keyboard with video display in the room. Which of the following best defines this physical security control?

   A. Guard shack

   B. Turnstile

   C. Man shack

   D. Man trap

   ☑ **D.** If you took a test on college football history, you know it would contain a question about Alabama. If you took one on trumpet players, there'd be one about Dizzy Gillespie. And if you take a test on physical security measures for Certified Ethical Hacker, you're going to be asked about the man trap. They love it that much.

   A *man trap* is nothing more than a locked space you can hold someone in while verifying their right to proceed into the secured area. It's usually a glass (or clear plastic) walled room that locks the exterior door as soon as you enter. Then there is some sort of authentication mechanism, such as a smartcard with a PIN or a biometric system. Assuming the authentication is successful, the second door leading to the interior of the building will unlock, and the person is allowed to proceed. If it's not successful, the doors will remain locked until the guard can check things out. As an aside, in addition to authentication, some man traps add all sorts of extra fun, such as checking your weight to see if you've mysteriously gained or lost 20 pounds since Friday.

   A few other notes here may be of use to you: First, I've seen a man trap defined as either manual or automatic, where *manual* has a guard locking and unlocking the doors, and *automatic* has the locks tied to the authentication system, as described previously. Second, a man trap is also referred to in some definitions as an *air lock*. Should you see that term on the exam, know that it is referring to the man trap. Lastly, man traps in the real world can sometimes come in the form of a rotating door or turnstile, locking partway around if you don't authenticate properly. And, on some of the really fancy ones, sensors will lock it if you're trying to smuggle two people through.

   ☒ **A** is incorrect because this question is not describing a small location at a gate where guards are stationed. Traditionally, these are positioned at gates to the exterior wall or the gate of the facility, where guards can verify identity and so on before allowing people through to the parking lot.

   ☒ **B** is incorrect because a turnstile is not being described here and, frankly, does absolutely nothing for physical security. Anyone who has spent any time in subway systems knows this is true: watching people jump the turnstiles is a great spectator sport.

☒ **C** is incorrect because, so far as I know, *man shack* is not a physical security term within CEH. It's maybe the title of a 1970s disco hit, but not a physical security term you'll need to know for the exam.

2. In your social engineering efforts, you call the company help desk and pose as a user who has forgotten a password. You ask the technician to help you reset your password, which they happily comply with. Which social engineering attack is in use here?

   A. Piggybacking

   B. Reverse social engineering

   C. Technical support

   D. Halo effect

   ☑ **C.** Although it may seem silly to label social engineering attacks (because many of them contain the same steps and bleed over into one another), you'll need to memorize them for your exam. A technical support attack is one in which the attacker calls the support desk in an effort to gain a password reset or other useful information. This is a valuable method because if you get the right help desk person (that is, someone susceptible to a smooth-talking social engineer), you can get the keys to the kingdom.

   ☒ **A** is incorrect because *piggybacking* refers to a method to gain entrance to a facility— not to gain passwords or other information. Piggybacking is a tactic whereby the attacker follows authorized users through an open door without any visible authorization badge at all.

   ☒ **B** is incorrect because *reverse social engineering* refers to a method where an attacker convinces a target to call him with information. The method involves marketing services (providing the target with your phone number or e-mail address in the event of a problem), sabotaging the device, and then awaiting for a phone call from the user.

   ☒ **D** is incorrect because *halo effect* refers to a psychological principle that states a person's overall impression (appearance or pleasantness) can impact another person's judgment of them. For example, a good-looking, pleasant person will be judged as more competent and knowledgeable simply because of their appearance. The lesson here is to look good and act nice while you're trying to steal all the target's information.

3. Which of the following is a true statement regarding biometric systems?

   A. The lower the CER, the better the biometric system.

   B. The higher the CER, the better the biometric system.

   C. The higher the FRR, the better the biometric system.

   D. The higher the FAR, the better the biometric system.

☑ **A.** The crossover error rate (CER) is the point on a chart where the false acceptance rate (FAR) and false rejection rate (FRR) meet, and the lower the number, the better the system. It's a means by which biometric systems are calibrated—getting the FAR and FRR the same. All that said, though, keep in mind that in certain circumstances a client may be more interested in a lower FAR than FRR, or vice versa, and therefore the CER isn't as much a concern. For example, a bank may be far more interested in preventing false acceptance than it is in preventing false rejection. In other words, so what if a user is upset they can't log on, so long as their money is safe from a false acceptance?

☒ **B** is incorrect because this is exactly the opposite of what you want. A high CER indicates a system that more commonly allows unauthorized users through and rejects truly authorized people from access.

☒ **C** is incorrect because the false rejection rate needs to be as low as possible. The FRR represents the amount of time a true, legitimate user is denied access by the biometric system.

☒ **D** is incorrect because the false acceptance rate needs to be as low as possible. The FAR represents the amount of time an unauthorized user is allowed access to the system.

4. A pen tester sends an unsolicited e-mail to several users on the target organization. The e-mail is well crafted and appears to be from the company's help desk, advising users of potential network problems. The e-mail provides a contact number to call in the event a user is adversely affected. The pen tester then performs a denial of service on several systems and receives phone calls from users asking for assistance. Which social engineering practice is in play here?

   A. Technical support

   B. Impersonation

   C. Phishing

   D. Reverse social engineering

   ☑ **D.** This may turn out to be a somewhat confusing question for some folks, but it's actually pretty easy. Reverse social engineering involves three steps. First, in the marketing phase, an attacker advertises himself as a technical point of contact for problems that may be occurring soon. Second, in the sabotage phase, the attacker performs a denial of service or other attack on the user. Third, in the tech support phase, the user calls the attacker and freely hands over information, thinking they are being assisted by company's technical support team.

   As an aside, there are two things to remember about employing this in the real world. First, be sure to market to the appropriate audience: attempting this against IT staff probably won't work as well as the "average" user and may get you caught. Second, and perhaps more important, you'll need to remember that the more lies you tell, the more things you have to make true. Complexity is risky, and reverse social engineering involves a lot of complexity. It's best used in special cases, and then only if you can't find something else to do.

- [X] **A** is incorrect because a technical support attack involves the attacker calling a technical support help desk, not having the user calling back with information.

- [X] **B** is incorrect because this is not *just* impersonation—the attack described in the question revolves around the user contacting the attacker, not the other way around. Impersonation can cover anybody, from a "normal" user to a company executive. And impersonating a technical support person can result in excellent results; just remember if you're going through steps to have the user call you back, you've moved into reverse social engineering.

- [X] **C** is incorrect because a phishing attack is an e-mail crafted to appear legitimate but in fact contains links to fake websites or to download malicious content. In this example, there is no link to click—just a phone number to call in case of trouble. Oddly enough, in my experience, people will question a link in an e-mail far more than just a phone number.

5. A pen test member has gained access to a building and is observing activity as he wanders around. In one room of the building, he stands just outside a cubicle wall opening and watches the onscreen activity of a user. Which social engineering attack is in use here?

   A. Eavesdropping

   B. Tailgating

   C. Shoulder surfing

   D. Piggybacking

- [✓] **C.** This one is so easy I hope you maintain your composure and stifle the urge to whoop and yell in the test room. Shoulder surfing doesn't necessarily require you to actually be on the victim's shoulder—you just have to be able to watch their onscreen activity. I once shoulder surfed *in front of* someone (a mirror behind her showed her screen clear as day). You don't even really need to be close to the victim—there are plenty of optics that can zoom in a field of vision from a very long distance away. As an aside, in the real world, if you are close enough to see someone's screen, you're probably close enough to listen to them as well. EC-Council puts the emphasis of shoulder surfing on the visual aspect—eavesdropping would be auditory.

- [X] **A** is incorrect because *eavesdropping* is a social engineering method where the attacker simply remains close enough to targets to overhear conversations. Although it's doubtful users will stand around shouting passwords at each other, you'd be surprised how much useful information can be gleaned by just listening in on conversations.

- [X] **B** is incorrect because *tailgating* is a method for gaining entrance to a facility by flashing a fake badge and following an authorized user through an open door.

- [X] **D** is incorrect because *piggybacking* is another method to gain entrance to a facility. In this effort, though, you don't have a badge at all; you just follow people through the door.

6. A recent incident investigated by the local IR team involved a user receiving an e-mail that appeared to be from the U.S. Postal Service, notifying her of a package headed her way and providing a link for tracking the package. The link provided took the user to what appeared to be the USPS site, where she input her user information to learn about the latest shipment headed her way. Which attack did the user fall victim to?

A. Phishing

B. Internet level

C. Reverse social engineering

D. Impersonation

☑ **A.** Phishing is one of the most pervasive and effective social engineering attacks on the planet. It's successful because crafting a legitimate-looking e-mail that links a user to an illegitimate site or malware package is easy to do, is easy to spread, and preys on our human nature to trust. If the source of the e-mail looks legitimate or the layout looks legitimate, most people will click away without even thinking about it. Phishing e-mails can often include pictures lifted directly off the legitimate website and use creative means of spelling that aren't easy to spot: www.regions.com is a legitimate bank website that could be spelled in a phishing e-mail as www.regi0ns.com.

When it comes to real-world use of phishing by ethical hackers and pen testers, there are a couple of notes our beloved tech editor begged me to include. First is that phishing has an extreme liability aspect to it when spoofing a legitimate business. If you're pen testing an organization and phish using a variant of a real business name, you could be opening yourself up to some serious costs: the first time someone calls the *real* Regions bank to complain is the moment that the attacker just became liable for the costs associated with the attack. Second is the risk involved with people simply forwarding your phishing attempt to recipients you never intended, allowing it to take on a life of its own. In short, the pen tester will certainly limit the bait (malware or website link embedded in the phishing attempt), but they will have no control over what a user decides to do with the e-mail. Suppose the pen tester doesn't know the exact IP range, or makes a simple mistake in configuration of the malware, and a user sends it home. Or to a banking friend. Or to the FBI. Or to a friend who works on a DoD system. Now you've not only hooked the wrong fish, but maybe infected something in the government. That's nothing to joke about, and may be a lot worse than a simple mistake. The bottom line is, in the real world, phishing is dangerous if not planned and implemented almost perfectly, and pen test teams need to use extreme caution in implementing it.

☒ **B** is incorrect because *Internet level* is not a recognized form of social engineering attack by this exam. It's included here as a distractor.

☒ **C** is incorrect because *reverse social engineering* is an attack where the attacker cons the target into calling back with useful information.

☒ **D** is incorrect because this particular description does not cover impersonation. *Impersonation* is an attack where a social engineer pretends to be an employee, a valid user, or even an executive (or other VIP). Generally speaking, when it comes to the exam, any impersonation question will revolve around an in-person visit or a telephone call.

7. Which type of social engineering attack uses phishing, pop-ups, and IRC?

   A. Technical

   B. Computer based

   C. Human based

   D. Physical

☑ **B.** All social engineering attacks fall into one of two categories: human based or computer based. Computer-based attacks are those carried out with the use of a computer or other data-processing device. Examples include, but are not limited to, fake pop-up windows, SMS texts, e-mails, and chat rooms or services. Social media sites (such as Facebook and LinkedIn) are consistent examples as well, and spoofing entire websites isn't out of the realm here either.

☒ **A** is incorrect because *technical* is not a social engineering attack type and is included here as a distractor.

☒ **C** is incorrect because *human-based* social engineering involves the art of human interaction for information gathering. Human-based social engineering uses interaction in conversation or other circumstances between people to gather useful information.

☒ **D** is incorrect because *physical* is not a social engineering attack type and is included here as a distractor.

8. An attacker identifies a potential target and spends some time profiling her. After gaining some information, the attacker sends a text to the target's cell phone. The text appears to be from her bank and advises her to call a provided phone number immediately regarding her account information. She dials the number and provides sensitive information to the attacker, who is posing as a bank employee. Which of the following best defines this attack?

   A. Vishing

   B. Smishing

   C. Phishing

   D. Tishing

☑ **B.** Aren't you excited to have another memorization term added to your CEH vocabulary? In smishing (for SMS text-based phishing), the attacker sends SMS text messages crafted to appear as legitimate security notifications, with a phone number provided. The user unwittingly calls the number and provides sensitive data in response.

☒ **A** is incorrect because vishing is an attack using a phone call or voice message. In vishing, the attacker calls the target or leaves them a voicemail with instructions to follow.

☒ **C** is incorrect because phishing makes use of specially crafted e-mails to elicit responses and actions.

☒ **D** is incorrect because this term does not exist.

9. Which of the following constitutes the highest risk to the organization?

   A. Black-hat hacker

   B. White-hat hacker

   C. Gray-hat hacker

   D. Disgruntled employee

   ☑ **D.** When considering security measures, most of the attention is usually aimed outside, because that's where all the bad guys are, right? Unfortunately this line of thinking leads to all sorts of exposure, for a whole lot of reasons, and is more common than you might think. A disgruntled employee is *still* an employee, after all, which leads to the main reason they're so dangerous: location. They are *already* inside the network. Inside attacks are generally easier to launch, are more successful, and are harder to prevent. When you add the human element of having an axe to grind, this can boil over quickly—whether the employee has the technical knowledge to pull it off or not. The idea that someone wanting to do harm to our organization's network not only already has the access to do so but has it because *we gave it to them* and *we're not watching them* should be frightening to us all.

   ☒ **A** is incorrect because black-hat hackers aren't necessarily already inside the network. They have a lot of work to do in getting access and a lot of security levels to wade through to do it.

   ☒ **B** is incorrect because a white-hat hacker is one of the good guys—an ethical hacker, hired for a specific purpose.

   ☒ **C** is incorrect because a gray-hat (or grey-hat) hacker falls somewhere between white and black. They may be hacking without express consent, but doing so with good intentions (not that good intentions will keep one out of jail). Supposedly they're not hacking for personal gain; they just don't bother to get permission and occasionally dance on the dark side of legality.

10. After observing a target organization for several days, you discover that finance and HR records are bagged up and placed in an outside storage bin for later shredding/recycling. One day you simply walk to the bin and place one of the bags in your vehicle, with plans to rifle through it later. Which social engineering attack was used here?

   A. Offline

   B. Physical

C. Piggybacking

D. Dumpster diving

☑ **D.** Dumpster diving doesn't necessarily mean you're actually taking a header into a dumpster outside. It could be any waste canister, in any location, and you don't even have to place any more of your body in the canister than you need to extract the old paperwork with. And you'd be amazed what people just throw away without thinking about it: password lists, network diagrams, employee name and number listings, and financial documents are all examples. Lastly, don't forget that EC-Council defines this as a passive activity. Sure, in the real world, you run a real risk of discovery and questioning by any number of the organization's staff, but on your exam it's considered passive.

☒ **A** is incorrect because *offline* is not a social engineering attack and is used here as a distractor.

☒ **B** is incorrect because *physical* is not a social engineering attack type.

☒ **C** is incorrect because *piggybacking* is a social engineering attack that allows entry into a facility and has nothing to do with digging through trash for information.

11. An attacker waits outside the entry to a secured facility. After a few minutes an authorized user appears with an entry badge displayed. He swipes a key card and unlocks the door. The attacker, with no display badge, follows him inside. Which social engineering attack just occurred?

A. Tailgating

B. Piggybacking

C. Identity theft

D. Impersonation

☑ **B.** This is one of those questions that just drives everyone batty—especially people who actually perform pen tests for a living. Does knowing that gaining entry without flashing a fake ID badge of any kind is called piggybacking make it any easier or harder to pull off? I submit having two terms for what is essentially the same attack, separated by one small detail, is a bit unfair, but there's not a whole lot we can do about it. If it makes it easier to memorize, just keep in mind that pigs wouldn't wear a badge—they don't have any clothes to attach it to.

☒ **A** is incorrect because a tailgating attack requires the attacker to be holding a fake badge of some sort. I know it's silly, but that's the only differentiation between these two items: tailgaters have badges, piggybackers do not. If it makes it any easier, just keep in mind a lot of tailgaters at football games should have a badge on them—to prove they are of legal drinking age.

☒ **C** is incorrect because this attack has nothing to do with identity theft. Identity theft occurs when an attacker uses personal information gained on an individual to assume that person's identity. Although this is normally thought of in the context of the criminal world (stealing credit cards, money, and so on), it has its uses elsewhere.

☒ **D** is incorrect because impersonation is not in play here. The attacker isn't pretending to be anyone else at all—he's just following someone through an open door.

12. Tim is part of a pen test team and is attempting to gain access to a secured area of the campus. He stands outside a badged entry gate and pretends to be engaged in a contentious cell phone conversation. An organization employee walks past and badges the gate open. Tim asks the employee to hold the gate while flashing a fake ID badge and continuing his phone conversation. He then follows the employee through the gate. Which of the following best defines this effort?

    A. Shoulder surfing

    B. Piggybacking

    C. Tailgating

    D. Drafting

    ☑ **C.** This type of question is so annoying I added it twice, back to back, in this chapter: almost as if I was nearly certain you'll see it on your exam. Tailgating involves following someone through an open door or gate just like piggybacking does; however, in tailgating, a fake identification badge of some sort is used. As an aside, if your exam question does not include both terms—tailgating and piggybacking— but the effort is the same (an attacker following a badged employee through a gate or door), you won't have to choose between them. Usually, in this case, tailgating will be used more frequently than piggybacking.

    ☒ **A** is incorrect because shoulder surfing isn't about following someone anywhere; instead, it's about positioning yourself in such a way as to be able to observe the keystrokes and activities of someone at their system.

    ☒ **B** is incorrect because piggybacking does not involve the use of a badge or identification of any sort.

    ☒ **D** is incorrect because drafting is a cool term used in NASCAR, but has nothing to do with physical pen testing.

13. Which of the following may be effective countermeasures against social engineering? (Choose all that apply.)

    A. Security policies

    B. Operational guidelines

    C. Appropriately configured IDS

    D. User education and training

    E. Strong firewall configuration

☑ **A, B, D.** The problem with countermeasures against social engineering is they're almost totally out of your control. Sure you can draft strong policy requiring users to comply with security measures, implement guidelines on everything imaginable to reduce risks and streamline efficiency, and hold educational briefings and training sessions for each and every user in your organization, but when it comes down to it, it's the user who has to do the right thing. All countermeasures for social engineering have something to do with the users themselves because they are the weak link here.

☒ **C** and **E** are both incorrect for the same reason: a social engineering attack doesn't target the network or its defenses; it targets the users. Many a strongly defended network has been compromised because a user inside was charmed by a successful social engineer.

14. Which of the following are indicators of a phishing e-mail? (Choose all that apply.)

   A. It does not reference you by name.

   B. It contains misspelled words or grammatical errors.

   C. It contains spoofed links.

   D. It comes from an unverified source.

☑ **A, B, C, D.** One of the objectives of CEH version 7 is, and I quote, to "understand phishing attacks." Part of the official curriculum to study for the exam covers detecting phishing e-mail in depth, and all of these answers are indicators an e-mail might not be legitimate. First, most companies now sending e-mail to customers will reference you *by name* and sometimes by account number. An e-mail starting with "Dear Customer" or something to that effect may be an indicator something is amiss. Misspellings and grammatical errors from a business are usually dead giveaways because companies do their best to proofread things before they are released. There are, occasionally, some slip-ups (Internet search some of these; they're truly funny), but those are definitely the exception and not the rule. Spoofed links can be found by hovering a mouse over them (or by looking at their properties). The link text may read www.yourbank.com, but the hyperlink properties will be sending you to some IP address you don't want to go to.

As an aside, while these are all great answers to a question on an exam, don't let them dictate your day-to-day Internet life outside of your exam. A perfectly written, grammatically correct e-mail containing real links and originating from someone you trust could *still* be part of a phishing campaign. Never click a link in an e-mail without knowing exactly what it is and where it's taking you—no matter who you think the message is from or how well written it is. Finally, if you get a phishing e-mail that is accurate, references you by name, has real links, and truly appears to be accurate, you probably have a real problem on your hands. Everyone gets the annoying "spam" e-mails with "Click here for free stuff." However, if you get one that is delivered to you, with your name and identifying details in it, you have someone who spent the time to target you specifically, not randomly.

15. You are discussing physical security measures and are covering background checks on employees and policies regarding key management and storage. Which type of physical security measure is being discussed?

   A. Physical

   B. Technical

   C. Operational

   D. Practical

   ☑ **C.** Physical security has three major facets: physical measures, technical measures, and operational measures. Operational measures (sometimes referred to as *procedural* controls) are the policies and procedures you put into place to assist with security. Background checks on employees and any kind of written policy for operational behaviors are prime examples.

   ☒ **A** is incorrect because physical measures can be seen or touched. Examples include guards (although you probably would want to be careful touching one of them), fences, and locked doors.

   ☒ **B** is incorrect because technical measures include things such as authentication systems (biometrics anyone?) and specific permissions you assign to resources.

   ☒ **D** is incorrect because, although these may seem like practical measures to put into place, there is simply no category named as such. It's included here as a distractor, nothing more.

16. Which of the following resources can assist in combating phishing in your organization? (Choose all that apply.)

   A. Phishkill

   B. Netcraft

   C. Phishtank

   D. IDA Pro

   ☑ **B, C.** For obvious reasons, there are not a lot of questions from these objectives concerning tools—mainly because social engineering is all about the human side of things, not necessarily using technology or tools. However, you can put into place more than a few protective applications to help stem the tide. There are innumerable e-mail filtering applications and appliances you can put on an e-mail network boundary to cut down on the vast amount of traffic (spam or otherwise) headed to your network. Additionally, Netcraft's phishing toolbar and Phishtank are two client-side, host-based options you can use (there are others, but these are pointed out specifically in EC-Council's official courseware).

   Netcraft's (http://toolbar.netcraft.com/) and Phishtank's (http://www.phishtank.com/) toolbars are like neighborhood watches on virtual steroids, where eagle-eyed neighbors can see naughty traffic and alert everyone else. From the Netcraft site: "Once the first recipients of a phishing mail have reported the target URL, it is blocked for community members as they subsequently access the URL."

These tools, although useful, are not designed to completely protect against phishing. Much like antivirus software, they will act on attempts that match a signature file. This, sometimes, makes it even easier on the attacker—because they know which phishing will *not* work right off the bat.

☒ **A** is incorrect because phishkill is not an anti-phishing application.

☒ **D** is incorrect because IDA Pro is a debugger tool you can use to analyze malware (viruses).

17. An attacker targets a specific group inside the organization. After some time profiling the group, she notes several websites the individual members of the group all visit on a regular basis. She spends time inserting various malware and malicious codes into some of the more susceptible websites. Within a matter of days, one of the group member's system installs the malware from an infected site, and the attacker uses the infected machine as a pivot point inside the network. Which of the following best defines this attack?

A. Spear phishing

B. Whaling

C. Web-ishing

D. Watering hole attack

☑ **D.** Have you ever watched nature documentaries on the Discovery Channel? It seems predators frequently hang out in places the prey tends to show up at. For example, a pride of lions might just hang out near a watering hole—knowing full well their prey will eventually just come to them. This attack uses the same principle, except we're talking about the virtual world. And none of us are lions (at least not outside our imaginations, anyway).

In a watering hole attack, the bad guy spends a lot of time profiling the group that is being targeted (note the key wording in this is a *group* is targeted, not an individual). The attacker can observe or even guess websites that the group would visit, and then infect those sites with some sort of malware or malicious code. Eventually someone from the group will visit the virtual watering hole and—*voilà*—success.

☒ **A** is incorrect because spear phishing involves phishing (sending specially crafted e-mails that include links to malicious code) being targeted at a specific group of people. In this question, there was no phishing involved.

☒ **B** is incorrect because whaling is a special type of spear phishing targeting high-level employees.

☒ **C** is incorrect because this term doesn't exist.

18. Which type of social engineering makes use of impersonation, dumpster diving, shoulder surfing, and tailgating?

   A. Physical

   B. Technical

   C. Human based

   D. Computer based

   ☑ C. Once again, we're back to the two major forms of social engineering: human based and computer based. Human-based attacks include all the attacks mentioned here and a few more. Human-based social engineering uses interaction in conversation or other circumstances between people to gather useful information. This can be as blatant as simply asking someone for their password or pretending to be a known entity (authorized user, tech support, or company executive) in order to gain information.

   ☒ A is incorrect because social engineering attacks do not fall into a physical category.

   ☒ B is incorrect because social engineering attacks do not fall into a technical category.

   ☒ D is incorrect because computer-based social engineering attacks are carried out with the use of a computer or other data-processing device. These attacks can include everything from specially crafted pop-up windows for tricking the user into clicking through to a fake website, to SMS texts that provide false technical support messages and dial-in information to a user.

19. In examining the About Us link in the menu of a target organization's website, an attacker discovers several different individual contacts within the company. To one of these contacts, she crafts an e-mail asking for information that appears to come from an individual within the company who would be expected to make such a request. The e-mail provides a link to click, which then prompts for the contact's user ID and password. Which of the following best describes this attack?

   A. Trojan e-mailing

   B. Spear phishing

   C. Social networking

   D. Operational engineering

   ☑ B. Yes, sometimes you'll get an easy one. Phishing is using e-mail to accomplish the social engineering task. Spear phishing is actually targeting those e-mails to specific individuals or groups within an organization. This usually has a much higher success rate than just a blind-fire phishing effort.

   ☒ A, C, and D are incorrect because they are all added as distractors and do not match the circumstances listed. *Trojan e-mailing* and *operational engineering* aren't valid terms in regard to social engineering attacks. A social networking attack, per EC-Council, is one that involves using Facebook, LinkedIn, Twitter, or some other social media to elicit information or credentials from a target.

20. A security admin has a control in place that embeds a unique image into e-mails on specific topics, which verifies the message as authentic and trusted. Which anti-phishing method is being used?

A. Steganography

B. Sign-in seal

C. PKI

D. CAPTCHA

☑ **B.** Sign-in seal is an e-mail protection method in use at a variety of business locations. The practice is to use a secret message or image that can be referenced on any official communication with the site. If you receive an e-mail purportedly from the business but it does not include the image or message, you're aware it's probably a phishing attempt. This sign-in seal is kept locally on your computer, so the theory is that no one can copy or spoof it.

☒ **A** is incorrect because steganography is not used for this purpose. As you know, steganography is a method of hiding information inside another file—usually an image file.

☒ **C** is incorrect because PKI refers to an encryption system using public and private keys for security of information between members of an organization.

☒ **D** is incorrect because a CAPTCHA is an authentication test of sorts, which I am sure you've seen hundreds of times already. CAPTCHA (actually an acronym meaning Completely Automated Public Turing test to tell Computers and Humans Apart) is a challenge-response-type method where an image is shown, and the client is required to type the word from the image into a challenge box. An example is on a contest entry form—you type in your information at the top and then see an image with a word (or two) in a crazy font at the bottom. If you type the correct word in, it's somewhat reasonable for the page to assume you're a human (as opposed to a script), and the request is sent forward.

21. Which of the following should be in place to assist as a social engineering countermeasure? (Choose all that apply.)

A. Classification of information

B. Strong security policy

C. User education

D. Strong change management process

☑ **A, B, C, D.** All of the answers are correct, but let's get this out of the way up front: you'll never be able to put anything whatsoever into place that will effectively render *all* social engineering attacks moot. You can do some things to limit them, and those on this list can definitely help in that regard, but a security organization that responds to social engineering concerns with "We have a strong policy and great user education" is probably one that'll see a high turnover rate.

Classification of information is seen as a strong countermeasure because the information—and access to it—is stored and processed according to strict definitions of sensitivity. In the government/DoD world, you'd see labels such as Confidential, Secret, and Top Secret. In the commercial world, you might see Public, Sensitive, and Confidential. I could write an entire chapter on the difference between DoD and commercial labels and have all sorts of fun arguing the finer points of various access control methods, but we'll stick just to this chapter and what you need here. As a side note, classification of information won't do you a bit of good if the enforcement of access to that information, and the protection of it in storage or transit, is lax.

Strong security policy has been covered earlier in the chapter, so I won't waste much print space here on it. You must have a good one in place to help prevent all sorts of security failures; however, you can't *rely* on it as a countermeasure on its own.

According to EC-Council, user education is not only a viable social engineering countermeasure but it's the best measure you can take. Anyone reading this book who has spent any time at all trying to educate users on a production, enterprise-level network is probably yelling right now because results can sometimes be…spotty at best. However, the weak point in the chain *is* the user, so we must do our best to educate users on what to look for and what to do as they see it. There simply is no better defense than a well-educated user (and by "well-educated" I mean a user who absolutely refuses to participate in a social engineering attempt). There's just not that many of them out there.

A change management process helps to organize change to a system or organization by providing a standardized, reviewable process to any major change. In other words, if you allow changes to your financial system, IT services, HR processes, or *fill-in-the-blank* without any review or control process, you're basically opening Pandora's box. Change can be made on a whim (sometimes at the behest of a social engineer, maybe?), and there's no control or tracking of it.

22. Joe uses a user ID and password to log into the system every day. Jill uses a PIV card and a PIN. Which of the following are true?

    A. Joe and Jill are using single-factor authentication.

    B. Joe and Jill are using two-factor authentication.

    C. Joe is using two-factor authentication.

    D. Jill is using two-factor authentication.

    ☑ **D.** When it comes to authentication systems, you can use three factors to prove your identity to a system: something you *know*, something you *have*, and something you *are*. An item you know is, basically, a password or PIN. Something you have is a physical token of some sort—usually a smartcard—that is presented as part of the authentication process. Something you are relates to biometrics—a fingerprint or retinal scan, for instance. Generally speaking, the more factors you have in place, the better (more secure) the authentication system. In this example, Joe is using only something he knows, whereas Jill is using something she has (PIV card) *and* something she knows (PIN).

☒ **A** is incorrect because Jill is using two-factor authentication.

☒ **B** is incorrect because Joe is using single-factor authentication.

☒ **C** is incorrect because Joe is using single-factor authentication.

23. A system owner has implemented a retinal scanner at the entryway to the data floor. Which type of physical security measure is this?

    A. Technical

    B. Single factor

    C. Computer based

    D. Operational

☑ **A.** Physical security measures are characterized as physical (door locks, guards), operational (policies, procedures), and technical (authentications systems, permissions). This example falls into the technical security measure category. Sure, the door itself is physical, but the question centers on the biometric system, which is clearly technical in origin.

☒ **B** is incorrect because *single factor* refers to the method the authentication system uses, not the physical security measure itself. In this case, the authentication is using something you are—a biometric retina scan.

☒ **C** is incorrect because *computer based* refers to a social engineering attack type, not a physical security measure.

☒ **D** is incorrect because an *operational* physical security measure deals with policy and procedure.

24. Which of the following is the best representation of a technical control?

    A. Air conditioning

    B. Security tokens

    C. Automated humidity control

    D. Fire alarms

    E. Security policy

☑ **B.** All security controls are put into place to minimize, or to avoid altogether, the probability of a successful exploitation of a risk or vulnerability. Logical controls (*logical* is the other term used for *technical*) do this through technical, system-driven means. Examples include security tokens, authentication mechanisms, and antivirus software.

☒ **A, C, D,** and **E** are incorrect because they are not logical (technical) controls. Air conditioning, fire alarms, and a humidity control fall under physical controls. A policy would fall under procedural controls.

## CHAPTER 12

The Pen Test: Putting It All Together

This chapter includes questions from the following topics:

- Describe penetration testing, security assessments, and risk management
- Define automatic and manual testing
- List pen test methodology and deliverables

I've been exceedingly blessed in my life, in a great many ways I don't have the time or print space here to cover. I have had opportunities to travel the world and experience things many people just flat out don't get to. In one of my travels I wound up in Florence, Italy, and decided to go see the statue of David. Even if you're not familiar with the background of this sculpture, I'll bet you've seen a replica of it somewhere—from garden art re-creations and store displays to one very cool episode of *SpongeBob SquarePants*, where he had to "*BE the marble!*" David was carved by Michelangelo sometime between 1501 and 1504 and is universally acclaimed as one of the greatest sculptures of all time. The statue now sits in a domed atrium within the Galleria dell'Accademia in Florence. It is truly an unbelievable experience to see this work of art, displayed in all its glory in a perfect setting within a beautiful gallery, and is definitely a highlight of any visit to Florence.

What made as big an impression on me, though, were the other, *unfinished* works of art from Michelangelo you had to pass by in order to get to the statue of David. There's a giant hallway leading to the atrium that is literally packed, on the right and left, with sculptures he started but, for whatever reason, never finished. Walking down the hallway (at least in your imagination anyway), we're surrounded by stonework that is simply amazing. Here, on the right, is a giant marble stone with half a man sticking out of the left side and chisel marks leading downward to something as yet unfinished. On the left we see the front half of a horse exploding out of a rough-hewn block of granite; the rest of the beautiful animal still buried in the story Michelangelo never got to finish telling with the sculpture. Traveling down this long hallway, we see other works—a battle raging in one boulder, a face clearly defined and nearly expressionless looking out of a little, almost leftover piece of rock—all displayed left and right for us to gape at.

These unfinished works weren't crude by any means; quite the opposite. I stood there among the crowds racing to get a glimpse of monumental talent, marveling at how a man could take a big chunk of rock and shape and smooth it into something that looked so *real*. But these pieces weren't finished, and it showed. There were giant scratch marks over areas that should have been smooth, and a few sculptures simply broke off because the rock itself cracked in two.

What has this got to do with this book, you may be asking? The answer, dear reader, is because we've all put a lot of work into this. We've chipped away at giant boulders of knowledge and are on the verge of finishing. No, I'm not making some crazed corollary to this book being some work of art (anyone who really knows me can attest that's not my bag, baby), but I am saying we, you and I, are on the verge of something good here. Keep hacking away at that stone. Keep sanding and polishing. Sooner or later you'll finish and have your statue to display—just don't forget all the work you put into it, and don't throw any of it away. I promise, you'll want to go back, sometime later, and walk through your own hallway of work to see how far you've come.

This chapter is, admittedly, short and sweet. The questions and answers are easier (if memorizing terms is easy for you, that is), and the write-ups on what's correct and what's false will reflect that as well. Sure, I might sneak in a question from earlier in the book—just to see if you're paying attention, and to wrap up terms EC-Council throws into this section—but these are all supposed to be about the pen test itself. We've already covered the nuts and bolts, so now we're going to spend some time on the finished product. And, of course, you will see most of this stuff on your exam. I just hope that you'll be so ready for it by then it'll be like Michelangelo wiping the dust off his last polishing of the statue of David.

 STUDY TIPS This chapter is, by design, a little bit of a wrap-up. There are things here that just don't seem to fit elsewhere, or that needed special attention, away from the clutter of the original EC-Council chapter they were stuck in. Most of this generally boils down to basic memorization. While that may sound easy enough to you, I think you'll find that some of these terms are so closely related that questions on the exam referencing them will be confusing at the very least—and most likely rage-inducing by the time the exam ends. Pay close attention to risk management terminology—you'll definitely see a few questions on it in your exam. Another area you'll probably see at least a couple questions on is the ethics of being a professional, ethical hacker. Admittedly, some of these will be tough to answer, as real-world and EC-Council CEH definitions don't always coincide, but hopefully we'll have enough information here to get you through.

Lastly, and I think I've said this before, it's sometimes easier to eliminate wrong answers than it is to choose the correct one. When you're looking at one of these questions that seems totally out of left field, spend your time eliminating the choices you know aren't correct. Eventually all that's left must be the correct answer. After all, the mechanism scoring the test doesn't care *how* you got to the answer, only that the right one is chosen.

1. Incident response (IR) is an important part of organizational security. In what step of the incident-handling process would IR team members disable or delete user accounts and change firewall rules?

   A. Detection and Analysis

   B. Classification and Prioritization

   C. Containment

   D. Forensic Investigation

2. A software company puts an application through stringent testing and, on the date of release, is confident the software is free of known vulnerabilities. An organization named BigBiz purchases the software at a premium cost, with a guarantee of service, maintenance, and liability. Which risk management method is in use by the BigBiz organization?

   A. Accept

   B. Transfer

   C. Avoid

   D. Mitigate

3. Which of the following provide automated pen test–like results for an organization? (Choose all that apply.)

   A. Metasploit

   B. Nessus

   C. Core Impact

   D. CANVAS

   E. SAINT

   F. GFI Languard

4. Which of the following best describes an assessment against a network segment that tests for existing vulnerabilities but does not attempt to exploit any of them?

   A. Penetration test

   B. Partial penetration test

   C. Vulnerability assessment

   D. Security scan

5. You are a member of a pen test team conducting tests. Your team has all necessary scope, terms of engagement, and nondisclosure and service-level agreements in place. You gain access to an employee's system and during further testing discover child pornography on a hidden drive folder. Which of the following is the best course of action for the ethical hacker?

   A. Continue testing without notification to anyone, but ensure the information is included in the final outbrief report.

   B. Continue testing without interruption, but completely remove all hidden files and the folder containing the pornography.

   C. Stop testing and notify law enforcement authorities immediately.

   D. Stop testing and remove all evidence of intrusion into the machine.

6. In which phase of a pen test is scanning performed?

   A. Pre-attack

   B. Attack

   C. Post-attack

   D. Reconnaissance

7. Which of the following describes risk that remains after all security controls have been implemented to the best of one's ability?

   A. Residual

   B. Inherent

   C. Deferred

   D. Remaining

8. Which of the following statements are true regarding OSSTMM? (Choose all that apply.)

   A. OSSTMM is a non-profit, international research initiative dedicated to defining standards in security testing and business integrity testing.

   B. OSSTMM recognizes ten types of controls, which are divided into two classes.

   C. ISECOM maintains the OSSTMM.

   D. OSSTMM defines three types of compliance.

9. Which of the following is an open source project produced by OISSG (Open Information Systems Security Group) intended to provide security testing assistance?

   A. OSSTMM

   B. OWASP

   C. COBIT

   D. ISSAF

10. NIST SP 800-30 defines steps for conducting a risk assessment. Which of the following statements is true regarding the process?

    A. Threats are identified before vulnerabilities.

    B. Determining the magnitude of impact is the first step.

    C. Likelihood is determined after the risk assessment is complete.

    D. Risk assessment is not a recurring process.

11. In which phase of a pen test will the team penetrate the perimeter and acquire targets?

    A. Pre-attack

    B. Attack

    C. Post-attack

    D. None of the above

12. An organization participates in a real-world exercise designed to test all facets of their security systems. An independent group is hired to assist the organization's security groups, assisting in the defense of assets against the attacks from the attacking group. Which of the following statements is true?

    A. The group assisting in the defense of the systems is referred to as a blue team.

    B. The group assisting in the defense of the systems is referred to as a red team.

    C. The group assisting in the defense of the systems is known as a white-hat group.

    D. The team attacking the systems must provide all details of any planned attack with the defense group before launching to ensure security measures are tested appropriately.

13. Which of the following best describes the difference between a professional pen test team member and a hacker?

    A. Ethical hackers are paid for their time.

    B. Ethical hackers never exploit vulnerabilities; they only point out their existence.

    C. Ethical hackers do not use the same tools and actions as hackers.

    D. Ethical hackers hold a predefined scope and agreement from the system owner.

14. Sally is part of a penetration test team and is starting a test. The client has provided a network drop on one of their subnets for Sally to launch her attacks from. However, they did not provide any authentication information, network diagrams, or other notable data concerning the systems. Which type of test is Sally performing?

    A. External, white box

    B. External, black box

    C. Internal, white box

    D. Internal, black box

15. Your pen test team is discussing services with a potential client. The client indicates they do not see the value in penetration testing. Which of the following is the correct response from your team?

   A. Run a few tests and display the results to the client to prove the value of penetration testing.

   B. Provide detailed results from other customers you've tested, displaying the value of planned testing and security deficiency discovery.

   C. Provide information and statistics regarding pen testing and security vulnerabilities from reliable sources.

   D. Perform the penetration test anyway in case they change their mind.

16. In which phase of a penetration test would you compile a list of vulnerabilities found?

   A. Pre-attack

   B. Attack

   C. Post-attack

   D. Reconciliation

17. Which of the following has a database containing thousands of signatures used to detect vulnerabilities in multiple operating systems?

   A. Nessus

   B. Hping

   C. LOIC

   D. SNMPUtil

18. Cleaning registry entries and removing uploaded files and tools are part of which phase of a pen test?

   A. Covering tracks

   B. Pre-attack

   C. Attack

   D. Post-attack

19. Which of the following are true statements regarding a pen test? (Choose all that apply.)

   A. Pen tests do not include social engineering.

   B. Pen tests may include unannounced attacks against the network.

   C. During a pen test, the security professionals can carry out any attack they choose.

   D. Pen tests always have a scope.

   E. A list of all personnel involved in the test is not included in the final report.

20. Which of the following causes a potential security breach?

    A. Vulnerability

    B. Threat

    C. Exploit

    D. Zero day

21. Which Metasploit payload type operates via DLL injection and is difficult for antivirus software to pick up?

    A. Inline

    B. Meterpreter

    C. Staged

    D. Remote

22. Metasploit is a framework allowing for the development and execution of exploit code against a remote host and is designed for use in pen testing. The framework consists of several libraries, each performing a specific task and set of functions. Which library is considered the most fundamental component of the Metasploit framework?

    A. MSF Core

    B. MSF Base

    C. MSF Interfaces

    D. Rex

23. Which of the following may be effective countermeasures against an inside attacker? (Choose all that apply.)

    A. Enforce elevated privilege control.

    B. Secure all dumpsters and shred collection boxes.

    C. Enforce good physical security practice and policy.

    D. Perform background checks on all employees.

1. C	**9.** D	**17.** A
2. B	**10.** A	**18.** D
3. A, C, D	**11.** B	**19.** B, D
4. C	**12.** A	**20.** B
5. C	**13.** D	**21.** B
6. A	**14.** D	**22.** D
7. A	**15.** C	**23.** A, B, C, D
8. B, C, D	**16.** C	

1. Incident response (IR) is an important part of organizational security. In what step of the incident-handling process would IR team members disable or delete user accounts and change firewall rules?

   A. Detection and Analysis

   B. Classification and Prioritization

   C. Containment

   D. Forensic Investigation

   ☑ **C.** In a refrain you've heard over and over again throughout this book, sometimes real life and EC-Council don't see eye to eye. However, when it comes to IR, ECC kind of gets it right. Almost. Lots of organizations define the incident-handling response in different ways, with different phases for actions taken. Generally speaking, though, all incident handling falls into four sets of actions: Identify, Contain, Eradicate, and Recover. Most organizations will define a Preparation phase beforehand and a Lessons Learned phase at the end for a full incident process. ECC defines eight phases:

   - **Preparation** Defining rules, processes, and toolsets, and testing them (usually with some regularly scheduled exercises at a minimum).

   - **Detection and Analysis** This is where alerting functions (toolsets, IDS, IPS, users notifying of strange events, and so on) and initial research into the event take place.

   - **Classification and Prioritization** Decision making on whether to elevate as an incident and at what level to elevate is made here (ramping up an IR event for a false alarm serves no one). Levels of categorization vary from organization to organization, but usually assign response time frames to levels.

   - **Notification** Alerting appropriate teams and organizations to assist in the event occurs here.

   - **Containment** Steps to contain the incident occur here. This may include steps to revoke or suspend user accounts and blocking system or even subnet access via firewall or other methods.

   - **Forensic Investigation** In this stage, if possible, pull live memory and disk captures for evaluation and analysis. This does not have to wait until the conclusion of the event but, depending on the assets involved and the nature of the incident, forensics may have to wait.

   - **Eradication and Recovery** This encompasses all steps taken to remove the incident cause (malware, malicious code, backdoors, rootkits, viruses, and so on) and to return the assets involved to baseline standards before putting them back into production.

   - **Post-Incident** This is where reporting, follow-up analysis, and lessons learned are put together. Evaluation from this step is fed into the preparation phase for the next event.

Questions on incident response and incident handling can be pretty vague. For the most part, common sense should guide you on anything truly weird, but most questions will be like this one: fairly easy to figure out on your own.

☒ **B, C,** and **D** are incorrect because the actions listed in the question do not occur in these incident-handling phases.

2. A software company puts an application through stringent testing and, on the date of release, is confident the software is free of known vulnerabilities. An organization named BigBiz purchases the software at a premium cost, with a guarantee of service, maintenance, and liability. Which risk management method is in use by the BigBiz organization?

   A. Accept

   B. Transfer

   C. Avoid

   D. Mitigate

   ☑ **B.** Depending on who you talk to, there are as many as seven different methods in risk management. Of primary concern for you and EC-Council, however, are these four: Accept, Avoid, Transfer, and Mitigate. In this example, the organization has paid a cost to the software developer, trusting them that they've tested the software and that they will assume responsibility and liability for it. In effect, the organization has *transferred* the risk to the software company for this application. Transferring risk is all about finding a different entity to take responsibility for managing the risk, and accepting the liability of an exploitation or loss resulting from the risk.

   ☒ **A** is incorrect because this does not describe acceptance. Acceptance of a risk means the organization is aware a risk is present but due to a variety of reasons (such as cost of mitigation or the unlikeliness the risk can ever be exploited), they decide to do nothing about it. Basically, the owner decides they will just deal with the fallout if the risk is ever realized.

   ☒ **C** is incorrect because this does not describe risk avoidance. In risk avoidance, the organization recognizes the risk and eliminates anything and everything that has to do with it. If a particular service, application, or technology is useful to an organization but the cost and effort to deal with the risks involved in its use are too high, they can simply choose to not use the service or application altogether.

   ☒ **D** is incorrect because this does not describe mitigation. Risk mitigation is exactly what it sounds like: the organization needs the technology or service despite the risk involved, so they take all steps necessary to lower the chance it will ever be exploited. Purchasing and using antivirus and practicing strong patch management are examples.

3. Which of the following provide automated pen test–like results for an organization? (Choose all that apply.)

   A. Metasploit

   B. Nessus

C. Core Impact

D. CANVAS

E. SAINT

F. GFI Languard

☑ **A, C, D.** Automated tool suites for pen testing can be viewed as a means to save time and money by the client's management, but (in my opinion and in the real world, at least) these tools don't do either. They do not provide the same quality results as a test performed by security professionals and are extremely expensive. Automated tools *can* provide a lot of genuinely good information but are also susceptible to false positives and false negatives and don't necessarily care what your agreed-upon scope says is your stopping point. Metasploit has a free, open source version and an insanely expensive "Pro" version for developing and executing exploit code against a remote target machine. Metasploit offers an autopwn module that can automate the exploitation phase of a penetration test.

Core Impact is probably the best-known, all-inclusive automated testing framework. Per its website (http://www.coresecurity.com/content/core-impact-overview), Core Impact "takes security testing to the next level by safely replicating a broad range of threats to the organization's sensitive data and mission-critical infrastructure— providing extensive visibility into the cause, effect, and prevention of data breaches." Core Impact tests everything from web applications and individual systems to network devices and wireless.

Per the Immunity Security website (http://www.immunitysec.com), CANVAS "makes available hundreds of exploits, an automated exploitation system, and a comprehensive, reliable exploit development framework to penetration testers and security professionals." Additionally, the company claims CANVAS's Reference Implementation (CRI) is "the industry's first open platform for IDS and IPS testing."

For you real-world purists out there and for those reading this who don't have any experience with any of this just quite yet, it's important to note that no automated testing suite provides anything close to the results you'd gain from a real pen test. Core Impact provides a one-step automated pen test result feature (and probably offers the best result and report features), Metasploit offers autopwn, and CANVAS has a similar "run everything" mode; however, all lack the ability to provide results that a true pen test would provide. In the truest sense of "automated pen test," you simply can't do it in the real world (for your exam, stick with the three listed here).

☒ **B, E,** and **F** are incorrect for the same reason: they are all vulnerability assessment tool suites, not automated pen test frameworks. Nessus is probably the most recognizable of the three, but SAINT and GFI Languard are both still listed as top vulnerability assessment applications.

4. Which of the following best describes an assessment against a network segment that tests for existing vulnerabilities but does not attempt to exploit any of them?

   A. Penetration test

   B. Partial penetration test

   C. Vulnerability assessment

   D. Security audit

   ☑ **C.** A vulnerability assessment is exactly what it sounds like: the search for and identification of potentially exploitable vulnerabilities on a system or network. These vulnerabilities can be poor security configurations, missing patches, or any number of other weaknesses a bad guy might exploit. The two keys to a vulnerability assessment are that the vulnerabilities are identified, not exploited, and the report is simply a snapshot in time. The organization will need to determine how often they want to run a vulnerability assessment. Lastly, it's important to note that there are some vulnerabilities that simply can't be confirmed without exploiting them. For example, the act of infecting SQL statements to expose a SQL injection vulnerability may very well constitute an exploit action, but it's the only way to prove it exists. For your exam, though, stick with no exploitation during this assessment and move on with your life.

   ☒ **A** is incorrect because team members on a pen test not only discover vulnerabilities but also actively exploit them (within the scope of their prearranged agreement, of course).

   ☒ **B** is incorrect because this is not a valid term associated with assessment types and is included as a distractor.

   ☒ **D** is incorrect because a security audit is designed to test the organization's security policy itself. It should go without saying the organization must have a security policy in place to begin with before a security audit can take place.

5. You are a member of a pen test team conducting tests. Your team has all necessary scope, terms of engagement, and nondisclosure and service-level agreements in place. You gain access to an employee's system and during further testing discover child pornography on a hidden drive folder. Which of the following is the best course of action for the ethical hacker?

   A. Continue testing without notification to anyone, but ensure the information is included in the final outbrief report.

   B. Continue testing without interruption, but completely remove all hidden files and the folder containing the pornography.

   C. Stop testing and notify law enforcement authorities immediately.

   D. Stop testing and remove all evidence of intrusion into the machine.

   ☑ **C.** If you've ever taken any philosophy studies in high school or college, you've undoubtedly read some of the ethical dilemmas presented to challenge black-and-white thinking on a matter. For example, theft is undoubtedly bad and is recognized as a crime in virtually every law system on the planet, but what if it's the only way to save a child's life? In ethical hacking, there are fine lines on actions to take when you discover something, and sometimes hard edges where there is no choice in the matter. Possession of child porn is a crime, so this case would seem relatively easy to discern. To be fair, and to make the assumption you'll need to on questions like this on the exam, your course of action is straightforward and simple: notify the authorities and let them handle it.

In the real world, things might be a little more difficult. How do you really know what you're looking at? Are you positive that what you see is illegal in nature (regardless of what it is—pornography, documentation, letters, and so on)? If you're not and you falsely accuse someone, what kind of liability do you have now? What about your team? It's not an easy question to answer in the real world, and you'll have to largely depend on good, solid pen test agreements up front. Let the client know what actions will be taken when suspected *fill-in-the-blank* is discovered, and agree upon actions both sides will take. Otherwise you, and your client, could be in for very difficult times.

☒ **A** is incorrect because the discovery of child porn automatically necessitates the cessation of test activities and contacting the authorities. Waiting until the outbrief is not the appropriate course of action and can get you in hot water.

☒ **B** is incorrect because this is not only unethical behavior and outside the scope and test agreement bounds, but it's against the law. You've tampered with evidence and obstructed justice *at a minimum*.

☒ **D** is incorrect because removing evidence of your actions is not the correct action to take and is unethical in the least (and can actually be considered illegal, depending on the circumstances).

6. In which phase of a pen test is scanning performed?

   A. Pre-attack

   B. Attack

   C. Post-attack

   D. Reconnaissance

   ☑ **A.** I know you're sick of CEH definitions, terms, and phases of attacks, but this is another one you'll just need to commit to memory. Per EC-Council, there are three phases of a pen test: pre-attack, attack, and post-attack. The pre-attack phase is where you'd find scanning and other reconnaissance (competitive intelligence, website crawling, and so on).

   ☒ **B** is incorrect because scanning is completed in the pre-attack phase. The attack phase holds four areas of work: penetrate the perimeter, acquire targets, execute attack, and escalate privileges.

☒ **C** is incorrect because scanning is completed long before the post-attack phase. Actions accomplished in post-attack include removing all uploaded files and tools, restoring (if needed) to the original state, analyzing results, and preparing reports for the customer.

☒ **D** is incorrect because reconnaissance is not a phase of pen testing.

7. Which of the following describes risk that remains after all security controls have been implemented to the best of one's ability?

   A. Residual

   B. Inherent

   C. Deferred

   D. Remaining

   ☑ **A.** Risk management has all sorts of terminology to remember, and identifying risk before and after security control implementation is what this question is all about. The *inherent risk* of the system is that which is in place if you implement no security controls whatsoever: in other words, there are risks inherent to every system, application, technology, and service. After you recognize these inherent risks and implement security controls, you may have some *residual risks* remaining. In other words, residual risk is what is left in the system after you implement security controls.

   ☒ **B** is incorrect because inherent risk is what was on the system before you started implementing security controls.

   ☒ **C** and **D** are incorrect because these terms are included merely as distractors.

8. Which of the following statements are true regarding OSSTMM? (Choose all that apply.)

   A. OSSTMM is a non-profit, international research initiative dedicated to defining standards in security testing and business integrity testing.

   B. OSSTMM recognizes ten types of controls, which are divided into two classes

   C. ISECOM maintains the OSSTMM.

   D. OSSTMM defines three types of compliance.

   ☑ **B, C, D.** The Open Source Security Testing Methodology Manual (OSSTMM) provides a methodology for a thorough security test (also known as an OSSTMM audit). It's maintained by ISECOM (Institute for Security and Open Methodologies; http://www.isecom.org/) and is a peer-reviewed manual of security testing and analysis that results in fact-based actions that can be taken by an organization to improve security. OSSTMM recognizes ten types of controls, split into two different classes:

   - **Class A: Interactive**   Authentication, Indemnification, Resilience, Subjugation, and Continuity

   - **Class B: Process**   Nonrepudiation, Confidentiality, Privacy, Integrity, and Alarm

   An OSSTMM audit tests for three different types of compliance: legislative, contractual, and standards-based compliance.

☒ **A** is incorrect because this is actually the description of ISECOM—the group responsible for the creation and maintenance of OSSTMM.

9. Which of the following is an open source project produced by OISSG (Open Information Systems Security Group) intended to provide security testing assistance?

   A. OSSTMM

   B. OWASP

   C. COBIT

   D. ISSAF

   ☑ **D.** The following is from OISSG's site: "The Information Systems Security Assessment Framework (ISSAF) is produced by the Open Information Systems Security Group, and is intended to comprehensively report on the implementation of existing controls to support IEC/ISO 27001:2005(BS7799), Sarbanes Oxley SOX404, CoBIT, SAS70 and COSO, thus adding value to the operational aspects of IT related business transformation programmes. It is designed from the ground up to evolve into a comprehensive body of knowledge for organizations seeking independence and neutrality in their security assessment efforts."

   ☒ **A** is incorrect because OSSTMM is a peer-reviewed manual of security testing and analysis maintained by ISECOM that results in fact-based actions that can be taken by an organization to improve security.

   ☒ **B** is incorrect because OWASP (Open Web Application Security Project) is an open source web application security project.

   ☒ **C** is incorrect because COBIT (Control Objectives for Information and Related Technologies) is a good-practice governance framework and supporting toolset created by ISACA for information technology (IT) management and governance.

10. NIST SP 800-30 defines steps for conducting a risk assessment. Which of the following statements is true regarding the process?

    A. Threats are identified before vulnerabilities.

    B. Determining the magnitude of impact is the first step.

    C. Likelihood is determined after the risk assessment is complete.

    D. Risk assessment is not a recurring process.

    ☑ **A.** NIST 800-30 Guide for Conducting Risk Assessments (http://nvlpubs.nist .gov/nistpubs/Legacy/SP/nistspecialpublication800-30r1.pdf) describes in detail how to perform a risk assessment. The publication defines four overall steps for an assessment, as shown in the following illustration.

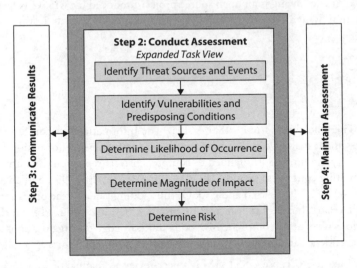

Step 1: Prepare for Assessment
Derived from Organizational Risk Frame

Step 2: Conduct Assessment
Expanded Task View

Identify Threat Sources and Events

Identify Vulnerabilities and Predisposing Conditions

Determine Likelihood of Occurrence

Determine Magnitude of Impact

Determine Risk

Step 3: Communicate Results

Step 4: Maintain Assessment

Even if you knew nothing about this publication, though, you could probably work your way into the correct answer here. Of the choices provided, only answer A makes any sense.

☒ **B** is incorrect because you can't possibly determine the magnitude of anything until you define what it is.

☒ **C** is incorrect because the likelihood of risk exploitation is a key part of the risk assessment effort and equation.

☒ **D** is incorrect because assessing your risk level is a recurring, always ongoing process.

11. In which phase of a pen test will the team penetrate the perimeter and acquire targets?

   A. Pre-attack

   B. Attack

   C. Post-attack

   D. None of the above

   ☑ **B.** EC-Council splits a pen test into three phases: pre-attack, attack, and post-attack. In the attack phase, the team will attempt to penetrate the network perimeter, acquire targets, execute attacks, and elevate privileges. Getting past the perimeter might take into account things such as verifying ACLs by crafting packets as well as checking the use of any covert tunnels inside the organization. Attacks such as XSS, buffer overflows, and SQL injections will be used on web-facing applications and sites. After specific targets are acquired, password cracking, privilege escalation, and a host of other attacks will be carried out.

☒ **A** is incorrect because these actions do not occur in the pre-attack phase. Per EC-Council, pre-attack includes planning, reconnaissance, scanning, and gathering competitive intelligence.

☒ **C** is incorrect because these actions do not occur in the post-attack phase. Per EC-Council, post-attack includes removing all files, uploaded tools, registry entries, and other items installed during testing of the targets. Additionally, your analysis of findings and creation of the pen test report will occur here.

☒ **D** is incorrect because there is an answer for the question listed.

12. An organization participates in a real-world exercise designed to test all facets of their security systems. An independent group is hired to assist the organization's security groups, assisting in the defense of assets against the attacks from the attacking group. Which of the following statements is true?

A. The group assisting in the defense of the systems is referred to as a blue team.

B. The group assisting in the defense of the systems is referred to as a red team.

C. The group assisting in the defense of the systems is known as a white-hat group.

D. The team attacking the systems must provide all details of any planned attack with the defense group before launching to ensure security measures are tested appropriately.

☑ **A.** Many organizations run full "war game" scenarios, including defense and attack groups, to test security measures. Generally speaking, the group doing the attacking is known as a red team, while the group assisting with the defense is known as a blue team. The red team is the offense-minded group, simulating the bad guys in the world, actively attacking and exploiting everything they can find in the environment. In a traditional war game scenario, the red team is attacking "black-box" style, given little to no information to start things off. A blue team, on the other hand, is defensive in nature. They're not out attacking things; rather, they're focused on shoring up defenses and making things safe. Unlike red teams, blue teams are responsible for defense against the bad guys, so they usually operate with full knowledge of the internal environment.

Blue teams are almost always independent in terms of the target, but their goal is to assist the defenders and to do so with whatever information is available. The difference between blue and red in this scenario is in the cooperative versus adversarial nature: red is there to be the bad guys, do what they would do, look for the impacts they would want to have, and to test the organization's defense/response, whereas blue is there to help.

☒ **B, C,** and **D** are incorrect because these are not true statements. The attacking group is known as a red team. I suppose an argument could be made that members of the blue team are all, in effect, white hats, but there is no such term as a "white-hat group." And if you're really testing the true security of a system, alerting the defense teams of everything you plan to do and when you plan on doing it makes little sense.

13. Which of the following best describes the difference between a professional pen test team member and a hacker?

    A. Ethical hackers are paid for their time.

    B. Ethical hackers never exploit vulnerabilities; they only point out their existence.

    C. Ethical hackers do not use the same tools and actions as hackers.

    D. Ethical hackers hold a predefined scope and agreement from the system owner.

    ☑ **D.** This one is a blast from the book's past and will pop up a couple of times on your exam. The only true difference between a professional pen test team member (an ethical hacker) and the hackers of the world is the existence of the formally approved, agreed-upon scope and contract before any attacks begin.

    ☒ **A** is incorrect because although professional ethical hackers are paid for their efforts during the pen test, it's not necessarily a delineation between the two (ethical and nonethical). Some hackers may be paid for a variety of illicit activities. For one example, maybe a company wants to cause harm to a competitor, so they hire a hacker to perform attacks.

    ☒ **B** and **C** are incorrect for the same reason. If a pen test team member never exploited an opportunity and refused to use the same tools and techniques that the hackers of the world have at their collective fingertips, what would be the point of an assessment? A pen test is designed to show true security weaknesses and flaws, and the only way to do that is to attack it just as a hacker would.

14. Sally is part of a penetration test team and is starting a test. The client has provided a network drop on one of their subnets for Sally to launch her attacks from. However, they did not provide any authentication information, network diagrams, or other notable data concerning the systems. Which type of test is Sally performing?

    A. External, white box

    B. External, black box

    C. Internal, white box

    D. Internal, black box

    ☑ **D.** Sally was provided a network drop inside the organization's network, so we know it's an internal test. Additionally, no information of any sort was provided—from what we can gather, she knows nothing of the inner workings, logins, network design, and so on. Therefore, this is a black-box test—an internal black-box test.

    ☒ **A** and **B** are incorrect because this is an internal test, not an external one.

    ☒ **C** is incorrect because a white-box test would have included all the information Sally wanted about the network—designed to simulate a disgruntled internal network or system administrator.

15. Your pen test team is discussing services with a potential client. The client indicates they do not see the value in penetration testing. Which of the following is the correct response from your team?

   A. Run a few tests and display the results to the client to prove the value of penetration testing.

   B. Provide detailed results from other customers you've tested, displaying the value of planned testing and security deficiency discovery.

   C. Provide information and statistics regarding pen testing and security vulnerabilities from reliable sources.

   D. Perform the penetration test anyway in case they change their mind.

   ☑ **C.** Ethical behavior will definitely find its way to your exam, and this cheesy question is an example. Your potential client may or may not be convinced when presented with the undeniable proof of pen test value from industry leaders (and possibly the U.S. government), but as the saying goes, "you can lead a horse to water, but you can't make him drink." An ethical hacker does not proceed without authorization, and doing so not only calls your integrity into question but also makes you a criminal. Documentation for an ethical test team will include scope (of what you can touch, how far you can go with testing, and how much time you'll spend doing it), terms of engagement, nondisclosure, liability statements, and all sorts of other goodies.

   ☒ **A** and **D** are incorrect because an ethical hacker does not proceed without prior, written permission.

   ☒ **B** is incorrect because ethical hackers do not disclose findings, procedures, or any other information about a test to anyone not specified in the agreement without authorization. This is usually covered in the nondisclosure agreement portion of the test team documentation.

16. In which phase of a penetration test would you compile a list of vulnerabilities found?

   A. Pre-attack

   B. Attack

   C. Post-attack

   D. Reconciliation

   ☑ **C.** This is another simple definition question you're sure to see covered on the exam. You compile the results of all testing in the post-attack phase of a pen test so you can create and deliver the final report to the customer.

   ☒ **A** and **B** are incorrect because this action does not occur in the pre-attack or attack phase.

   ☒ **D** is incorrect because reconciliation is not a phase of a pen test as defined by EC-Council.

17. Which of the following has a database containing thousands of signatures used to detect vulnerabilities in multiple operating systems?

   A. Nessus

   B. Hping

   C. LOIC

   D. SNMPUtil

   ☑ **A.** Nessus is probably the best-known, most utilized vulnerability assessment tool on the planet—even though it's not necessarily free anymore. Nessus works on a server-client basis and provides "plug-ins" to test everything from Cisco devices, Mac OS, and Windows machines to SCADA devices, SNMP, and VMware ESX (you can find a list of plug-in families here: http://www.tenable.com/plugins/index.php?view=all). It's part of virtually every security team's portfolio, and you should definitely spend some time learning how to use it.

   As an aside—not necessarily because it has anything to do with your test but because I am all about informing you on how to become a good pen tester—Openvas (http://www.openvas.org) is the open source community's attempt at a free vulnerability scanner. Nessus was a free scanner for the longest time. However, once Nessus was purchased by Tenable Network Security, it, for lack of a better term, angered a lot of people in the security community because Nessus became a for-profit entity instead of a for-security one. Don't get me wrong—Nessus is outstanding in what it does; it just costs you money. Openvas is attempting to do the same thing for free because the community wants security over profit.

   Just keep in mind that most vulnerabilities that are actually capable of causing harm to your systems probably won't be found by any scanner. The recent Heartbleed vulnerability, which takes advantage of an SSL issue, is a prime example: scanners simply can't find vulnerabilities we don't already know about.

   ☑ **B** is incorrect because Hping is not a vulnerability assessment tool. Per Hping's website (http://www.hping.org), it is "a command-line-oriented TCP/IP packet assembler/analyzer" used to test firewalls, to fingerprint operating systems, and even to perform man-in-the-middle (MITM) attacks.

   ☒ **C** is incorrect because Low Orbit Ion Cannon (LOIC) is a distributed interface denial-of-service tool. It's open source and can be used, supposedly legitimately, to test "network stress levels."

   ☒ **D** is incorrect because SNMPUtil is an SNMP security verification and assessment tool.

18. Cleaning registry entries and removing uploaded files and tools are part of which phase of a pen test?

   A. Covering tracks

   B. Pre-attack

   C. Attack

   D. Post-attack

☑ **D.** Cleaning up all your efforts occurs in the post-attack phase, alongside analyzing the findings and generating the final report. The goal is to put things back exactly how they were before the assessment.

☒ **A** is incorrect because "covering tracks" is part of the phases defining a hacking attack, not a phase of a pen test.

☒ **B** and **C** are incorrect because these steps do not occur in the pre-attack or attack phase.

19. Which of the following are true statements regarding a pen test? (Choose all that apply.)

   A. Pen tests do not include social engineering.

   B. Pen tests may include unannounced attacks against the network.

   C. During a pen test, the security professionals can carry out any attack they choose.

   D. Pen tests always have a scope.

   E. A list of all personnel involved in the test is not included in the final report.

   ☑ **B, D.** Pen tests are carried out by security professionals who are bound by a specific scope and rules of engagement, which must be carefully crafted, reviewed, and agreed on before the assessment begins. This agreement can allow for unannounced testing, should upper management of the organization decide to test their IT security staff's reaction times and methods.

   ☒ **A, C,** and **E** are incorrect because these are false statements concerning a pen test. Unless expressly forbidden in the scope agreement, social engineering is a big part of any true pen test. The scope agreement usually defines how far a pen tester can go— for example, no intentional denial-of-service attacks and so on. Clients are provided a list of discovered vulnerabilities after the test, even if the team did not exploit them: there's not always time to crack into every security flaw during an assessment, but that's no reason to hide it from the customer. Lastly, the final report includes a list of all personnel taking part in the test.

20. Which of the following causes a potential security breach?

   A. Vulnerability

   B. Threat

   C. Exploit

   D. Zero day

   ☑ **B.** So which came first—the chicken or the egg? This question is right along those same lines and can be really confusing, but if you key on the "cause" portion of the question, you should be okay. Sure, a vulnerability would need to be present; however, a vulnerability on its own doesn't cause anything. A *threat* is something that could potentially take advantage of an existing vulnerability. Threats can be intentional, accidental, human, or even an "act of God." A hacker is a threat to take advantage of an open port on a system and/or poor password policy. A thunderstorm is a threat to exploit a tear in the roof, leaking down into your systems. Heck, a rhinoceros is a threat to bust down the door and destroy all the equipment in the room. Whether those threats have intent, are viable, and are willing/able to take up the vulnerability is a matter for risk assessment to decide; they'll probably beef up password policy and fix the roof, but I doubt much will be done on the rhino front.

☒ **A** is incorrect because a vulnerability is a weakness in security. A vulnerability may or may not necessarily be a problem. For example, your system may have horribly weak password policy or even a missing security patch, but if it's never on the network and is locked in a guarded room accessible by only three people who must navigate a biometric system to even open the door, the existence of those vulnerabilities is moot.

☒ **C** is incorrect because an exploit is what is or actually can be done by a threat agent to utilize the vulnerability. Exploits can be local or remote, a piece of software, a series of commands, or anything that actually uses the vulnerability to gain access to, or otherwise affect, the target.

☒ **D** is incorrect because a zero-day exploit is simply an exploit that most of us don't really know much about at the time of its use. For instance, a couple years back some bad guys discovered a flaw in Adobe Reader and developed an exploit for it. From the time the exploit was created to the time Adobe finally recognized its existence and built a fix action to mitigate against it, the exploit was referred to as *zero day*.

21. Which Metasploit payload type operates via DLL injection and is difficult for antivirus software to pick up?

   A. Inline

   B. Meterpreter

   C. Staged

   D. Remote

   ☑ **B.** For those of you panicking over this question, relax. You do not have to know all the inner workings of Metasploit, but it does appear enough—in the variety of study materials available for the version 7 exam—that EC-Council wants you to know some basics, and this question falls in that category. There are a bunch of different payload types within Metasploit, and *meterpreter* (short for meta-interpreter) is one of them. The following is from Metasploit's website: "Meterpreter is an advanced payload that is included in the Metasploit Framework. Its purpose is to provide complex and advanced features that would otherwise be tedious to implement purely in assembly. The way that it accomplishes this is by allowing developers to write their own extensions in the form of shared object (DLL) files that can be uploaded and injected into a running process on a target computer after exploitation has occurred. Meterpreter and all of the extensions that it loads are executed entirely from memory and never touch the disk, thus allowing them to execute under the radar of standard anti-virus detection."

☒ **A** is incorrect because inline payloads are single payloads that contain the full exploit and shell code for the designed task. They may be more stable than other payloads, but they're easier to detect and, because of their size, may not be viable for many attacks.

☒ **C** is incorrect because staged payloads establish a connection between the attacking machine and the victim. Once the connection is established, the payload is revisited to execute on the remote machine.

☒ **D** is incorrect because "remote" isn't a recognized payload type.

22. Metasploit is a framework allowing for the development and execution of exploit code against a remote host and is designed for use in pen testing. The framework consists of several libraries, each performing a specific task and set of functions. Which library is considered the most fundamental component of the Metasploit framework?

    A. MSF Core

    B. MSF Base

    C. MSF interfaces

    D. Rex

☑ **D.** Once again, this is another one of those weird questions you may see (involving any of the framework components) on your exam. It's included here so you're not caught off guard in the actual exam room and freak out over not hearing it before. Don't worry about learning all the nuances of Metasploit and its architecture before the exam—just concentrate on memorizing the basics of the framework (key words for each area will assist with this), and you'll be fine.

Metasploit, as you know, is an open source framework allowing all sorts of automated (point-and-shoot) pen test methods. The framework is designed in a modular fashion, with each library and component responsible for its own function. The following is from Metasploit's development guide (http://dev.metasploit.com/ redmine/projects/framework/wiki/DeveloperGuide#12-Design-and-Architecture): "The most fundamental piece of the architecture is the *Rex* library, which is short for the Ruby Extension Library. Some of the components provided by Rex include a wrapper socket subsystem, implementations of protocol clients and servers, a logging subsystem, exploitation utility classes, and a number of other useful classes." Rex provides critical services to the entire framework.

☒ **A** is incorrect because the MSF Core "is responsible for implementing all of the required interfaces that allow for interacting with exploit modules, sessions, and plugins." It interfaces directly with Rex.

☒ **B** is incorrect because the MSF Base "is designed to provide simpler wrapper routines for dealing with the framework core as well as providing utility classes for dealing with different aspects of the framework, such as serializing module state to different output formats." The Base is an extension of the Core.

☒ **C** is incorrect because the MSF interfaces are the means by which you (the user) interact with the framework. Interfaces for Metasploit include Console, CLI, Web, and GUI.

23. Which of the following may be effective countermeasures against an inside attacker? (Choose all that apply.)

   A. Enforce elevated privilege control.

   B. Secure all dumpsters and shred collection boxes.

   C. Enforce good physical security practice and policy.

   D. Perform background checks on all employees.

   ☑ **A, B, C, D.** All of the answers are correct. Admittedly, there's nothing you can really do to completely prevent an inside attack. There's simply no way to ensure every single employee is going to remain happy and satisfied, just as there's no way to tell when somebody might just up and decide to turn to crime. It happens all the time, in and out of Corporate America, so the best you can do is, of course, the best you can do.

   Enforcing elevated privilege control (that is, ensuring users have only the amount of access, rights, and privileges to get their job done, and no more) seems like a commonsense thing, but it's amazing how many enterprise networks simply ignore this. After all, a disgruntled employee with administrator rights on his machine can certainly do more damage than one with just plain user rights. Securing dumpsters and practicing good physical security should help protect against an insider who wants to come back after hours and snoop around. And background checks on employees, although by no means a silver bullet in this situation, can certainly help to ensure you're hiring the right people in the first place (in many companies a background check is a requirement of *law*). Other steps include, but are not limited to, the following:

   - Monitoring user network behavior

   - Monitoring user computer behavior

   - Disabling remote access

   - Disabling removable drive use on all systems (USB drives and so on)

   - Shredding all discarded paperwork

   - Conducting user education and training programs

Pre-assessment Test

This pre-assessment test is designed to help you prepare to study for the CEH Certified Ethical Hacker examination. You should take this test to identify the areas where you should focus your study and preparation.

The pre-assessment test includes 60 questions that are similar in style and format to the questions on the exam. As you prepare to take this test, try to simulate the actual exam conditions as closely as possible. Go to a quiet place and be sure that you will not be interrupted for the full length of time it will take to complete the test. You should give yourself 1 hour and 45 minutes. Do not use any reference materials or other assistance while taking the pre-assessment—remember, the idea is to help you determine what areas you need to focus on during your preparation for the actual exam.

The pre-assessment test contains questions divided in proportion to the CEH exam. Here is a breakdown of the exam content:

Chapter	Exam Weight	Number of Pre-assessment Questions
1: Getting Started: Essential Knowledge	10%	6
2: Reconnaissance: Information Gathering for the Ethical Hacker	10%	6
3: Scanning and Enumeration	10%	6
4: Sniffing and Evasion	10%	6
5: Attacking a System	15%	9
6: Web-Based Hacking: Servers and Applications	10%	6
7: Wireless Network Hacking	10%	6
8: Security in Cloud Computing	5%	3
9: Trojans and Other Attacks	5%	3
10: Cryptography 101	5%	3
11: Low Tech: Social Engineering and Physical Security	5%	3
12: The Pen Test: Putting It All Together	5%	3

Complete the entire pre-assessment test before checking your results. Once you have finished, use both the "Quick Answer Key" and the "Answers" sections to score your test. Use the table in the "Analyzing Your Results" section to determine how well you performed. The objective map at the end of the appendix will help you identify those areas that require the most attention while you prepare for the exam.

Are you ready? Set your clock for 1 hour and 45 minutes and begin!

1. A vendor is alerted of a newly discovered flaw in its software that presents a major vulnerability to systems. While working to prepare a fix action, the vendor releases a notice alerting the community of the discovered flaw and providing best practices to follow until the patch is available. Which of the following best describes the discovered flaw?

   A. Input validation flaw

   B. Shrink-wrap vulnerability

   C. Insider vulnerability

   D. Zero day

2. A security professional applies encryption methods to communication channels. Which security control role is she attempting to meet?

   A. Preventive

   B. Detective

   C. Defensive

   D. Corrective

3. Bob is working with senior management to identify the systems and processes that are critical for operations. As part of this business impact assessment, he performs calculations on various systems to place value on them. On a certain server he discovers the following:

   The server costs $2500 to purchase.

   The server typically fails once every five years.

   Salary for the repair technician for a server failure is at $40 hourly, and it typically takes two hours to fully restore a failure.

   The accounting group has five employees paid at $25 an hour who are at a standstill during an outage.

   What is the ALE for the server?

   A. 20 percent

   B. $2830

   C. $566

   D. $500

4. You've discovered a certain application in your environment that has proven to contain vulnerabilities. Which of the following actions best describes avoiding the risk?

   A. Remove the software from the environment.

   B. Install all known security patches for the application.

   C. Install brand-new software guaranteed by the publisher to be free of vulnerabilities.

   D. Leave the software in place.

5. James is a member of a pen test team newly hired to test a bank's security. He begins searching for IP addresses the bank may own, using public records on the Internet, and also looks up news articles and job postings to discover information that may be valuable. What phase of the pen test is James working?

   A. Reconnaissance

   B. Pre-attack

   C. Assessment

   D. Attack

   E. Scanning

6. Enacted in 2002, this U.S. law requires every federal agency to implement information security programs, including significant reporting on compliance and accreditation. Which of the following is the best choice for this definition?

   A. FISMA

   B. HIPAA

   C. NIST 800-53

   D. OSSTMM

7. Which of the following is true regarding MX records?

   A. MX records require an accompanying CNAME record.

   B. MX records point to name servers.

   C. MX record priority increases as the preference number decreases.

   D. MX record entries are required for every namespace.

8. Which Google operator is the best choice in searching for a particular string in the website's title?

   A. intext:

   B. inurl:

   C. site:

   D. intitle:

9. An ethical hacker begins by visiting the target's website and then peruses social networking sites and job boards looking for information and building a profile on the organization. Which of the following best describes this effort?

   A. Active footprinting

   B. Passive footprinting

   C. Internet footprinting

   D. Sniffing

10. Internet attackers—whether State sponsored or otherwise—often discover vulnerabilities in a service or product but keep the information quiet and to themselves, ensuring the vendor is unaware of the vulnerability, until the attackers are ready to launch an exploit. Which of the following best describes this?

    A. Zero day

    B. Zero hour

    C. No day

    D. Nada sum

11. The organization has a DNS server out in the DMZ and a second one internal to the network. Which of the following best describes this DNC configuration?

    A. Schematic DNS

    B. Dynamic DNS

    C. DNSSEC

    D. Split DNS

12. Search engines assist users in finding the information they want on the Internet. Which of the following is known as the hacker's search engine, explicitly allowing you to find specific types of computers (for example, routers or servers) connected to the Internet?

    A. Whois

    B. Shodan

    C. Nslookup

    D. BurpSuite

13. Which of the following methods correctly performs banner grabbing with Telnet on a Windows system?

    A. telnet <IPAddress> 80

    B. telnet 80 <IPAddress>

    C. telnet <IPAddress> 80 -u

    D. telnet 80 <IPAddress> -u

14. Which TCP flag instructs the recipient to ignore buffering constraints and immediately send all data?

    A. URG

    B. PSH

    C. RST

    D. BUF

15. Which of the following correctly describes the TCP three-way handshake?

    A. SYN, ACK, SYN/ACK

    B. SYN, SYN/ACK, ACK

    C. ACK, SYN, ACK/SYN

    D. ACK, ACK/SYN, SYN

16. You are examining results of a SYN scan. A port returns a RST/ACK. What does this mean?

    A. The port is open.

    B. The port is closed.

    C. The port is filtered.

    D. Information about this port cannot be gathered.

17. You want to run a reliable scan but remain as stealthy as possible. Which of the following nmap commands accomplishes your goal best?

    A. nmap -sN *targetIPaddress*

    B. nmap -sO *targetIPaddress*

    C. nmap -sS *targetIPaddress*

    D. nmap -sT *targetIPaddress*

18. You are examining a host with an IP address of 65.93.24.42/20, and you want to determine the broadcast address for the subnet. Which of the following is the correct broadcast address for the subnet?

    A. 65.93.24.255

    B. 65.93.0.255

    C. 65.93.32.255

    D. 65.93.31.255

    E. 65.93.255.255

19. Angie captures traffic using Wireshark. Which filter should she apply to see only packets sent from 220.99.88.77?

    A. ip = 220.99.88.77

    B. ip.src == 220.99.88.77

    C. ip.equals 220.99.88.77

    D. ip.addr == 220.99.88.77

20. A systems administrator notices log entries from a host named MATTSYS (195.16.88.12) are not showing up on the syslog server (195.16.88.150). Which of the following Wireshark filters would show any attempted syslog communications from the machine to the syslog server?

   A. tcp.dstport==514 && ip.dst==195.16.88.150

   B. tcp.srcport==514 && ip.src==195.16.88.12

   C. tcp.dstport==514 && ip.src==195.16.88.12

   D. udp.dstport==514 && ip.src==195.16.88.12

21. What does the following Snort rule accomplish?

   `alert tcp any any -> any 23(msg: "Telnet Connection Attempt")?`

   A. The rule logs any Telnet attempt over port 23 to any internal client.

   B. The rule logs any Telnet attempt over port 23 leaving the internal network.

   C. The rule alerts the monitor of any Telnet attempt to an internal client.

   D. The rule alerts the monitor of any Telnet attempt leaving the internal network.

22. A pen tester connects a laptop to a switch port and enables promiscuous mode on the NIC. He then turns on Wireshark and leaves for the day, hoping to catch interesting traffic over the next few hours. Which of the following is true regarding this scenario? (Choose all that apply.)

   A. The packet capture will provide the MAC addresses of other machines connected to the switch.

   B. The packet capture will provide only the MAC addresses of the laptop and the default gateway.

   C. The packet capture will display all traffic intended for the laptop.

   D. The packet capture will display all traffic intended for the default gateway.

23. Which of the following best describes ARP poisoning?

   A. In ARP poisoning, an attacker floods a switch with thousands of ARP packets.

   B. In ARP poisoning, an attacker uses ARP to insert bad IP mappings into a DNS server.

   C. In ARP poisoning, an attacker continually inserts forged entries into an ARP cache.

   D. In ARP poisoning, an attacker continually deletes an ARP cache.

24. Which of the following best describes port security?

   A. It stops traffic sent to a specified MAC address from entering a port.

   B. It allows traffic sent to a specific MAC address to enter a port.

   C. It stops traffic from a specific MAC from entering a port.

   D. It allows traffic from a specific MAC address to enter to a port.

25. Where is the SAM file found on a Windows 7 machine?

    A. C:\windows\config

    B. C:\windows\system32

    C. C:\windows\system32\etc

    D. C:\windows\system32\config

26. Which of the following commands would be useful in adjusting settings on the built-in firewall on a Windows machine?

    A. The netstat command

    B. The netsh command

    C. The sc command

    D. The ntfw command

27. Which SID indicates the true administrator account on the Windows machine?

    A. S-1-5-31-1045337334-12924807993-5683276715-1500

    B. S-1-5-31-1045337334-12924807993-5683276715-1001

    C. S-1-5-31-1045337334-12924807993-5683276715-501

    D. S-1-5-31-1045337334-12924807993-5683276715-500

28. Which of the following is true regarding LM hashes?

    A. If the left side of the hash begins with 1404EE, the password is less than eight characters.

    B. If the right side of the hash ends with 1404EE, the password is less than eight characters.

    C. There is no way to tell whether passwords are less than eight characters because hashes are not reversible.

    D. There is no way to tell whether passwords are less than 8 characters because each hash is always 32 characters long.

29. Which password-cracking method usually takes the most time and uses the most resources?

    A. Hybrid

    B. Dictionary

    C. Brute force

    D. Botnet

30. Which of the following is the best choice for protection against privilege escalation vulnerabilities?

    A. Ensure drivers are appropriately signed.

    B. Set admin accounts to run on least privilege.

    C. Make maximum use of automated services.

    D. Ensure services run with least privilege.

31. During a pen test, you notice VoIP traffic is traversing the subnet. Which of the following tools could be used to decode a packet capture and extract voice conversations?

    A. Black Widow

    B. Netcat

    C. Nmap

    D. Cain

32. A pen tester gains access to a Windows application server and enters the following command:

    `netsh firewall show config`

    What should be displayed in return?

    A. Settings of the built-in firewall

    B. An authentication screen for firewall configuration access

    C. Route mapping to nearest firewall

    D. None of the above

33. Which of the following statements is true regarding Kerberos?

    A. Kerberos makes use of UDP as a transport protocol.

    B. Kerberos makes use of TCP as a transport protocol.

    C. Kerberos uses port 88 for transmission of data.

    D. Kerberos makes use of both symmetric and asymmetric encryption techniques.

    E. All the above.

34. The < character opens an HTML tag, and the > character closes it. In some web forms, input validation may deny these characters to protect against XSS. Which of the following represents the HTML entities used in place of these characters? (Choose two.)

    A. <

    B. >

    C. &

    D. ®

    E.

35. An attacker discovers a form on a target organization's website. He interjects some simple JavaScript into one of the form fields, instead of the username. Which attack is he carrying out?

    A. XSS

    B. SQL injection

    C. Buffer overflow

    D. Brute force

36. An attackers enters the following into a web form: **' or 1=1 --**. Which attack is being attempted?

    A. XSS

    B. Brute force

    C. Parameter manipulation

    D. SQL injection

37. OWASP releases several Top Ten lists. On their top security priorities, one entry includes flaws that allow attackers to compromise passwords, encryption keys, and session tokens. Which of the following matches this description best?

    A. Broken Authentication and Session Management

    B. Injection

    C. Insecure Direct Object References

    D. Security Misconfiguration

38. After a recent attack, log files are reviewed by the IR team to determine attack scope, success or failure, and lessons learned. Consider the following entry:

```
SELECT username, password FROM users;
```

Which of the following best describes the result of this command query?

    A. The command deletes username and password fields from a table named "users."

    B. The command adds username and password fields to a table named "users."

    C. The command displays the contents of the username and password fields stored in the table named "users."

    D. The command will not produce any results.

39. Which jailbreaking method does not retain the patched kernel after reboot, but does leave the software on the device, allowing for future jailbreak activities?

    A. Tethered jailbreaking

    B. Semi-tethered jailbreaking

    C. Untethered jailbreaking

    D. Rooting

40. Which of the following statements best defines smishing?

    A. It is sending SMS texts to a user in an effort to trick them into downloading malicious code.

    B. It is sniffing Bluetooth connections.

    C. It is hijacking Bluetooth connections to send text messages.

    D. It is rooting an Android device.

41. XenMobile, MaaS360, AirWatch, and MobiControl are all examples of which kind of security solution?

    A. 802.1x

    B. BYOD

    C. MDM

    D. CCMP

42. Which of the following is a passive wireless discovery tool?

    A. NetStumbler

    B. Aircrack

    C. Kismet

    D. Netsniff

43. Which of the following provides the integrity method for WPA2?

    A. RC4

    B. CCMP

    C. AES

    D. 802.1x

44. An attacker performs reconnaissance and learns the organization's SSID. He places an access point inside a closet, which tricks normal users into connecting, and begins redirecting them to malicious sites. Which of the following categorizes this attack?

    A. Replay attack

    B. Evil twin attack

    C. Closet AP attack

    D. WEP nap attack

45. Which attack can be mitigated by configuring the web server to send random challenge tokens?

    A. XSS

    B. Buffer overflow

    C. CSRF

    D. Form field manipulation

46. You deploy cloud services such that services are provided over a network open for public use. Which of the following best describes your deployment of cloud?

    A. Private

    B. Community

    C. Public

    D. Hybrid

47. In NIST cloud architecture, which role acts as the organization that has the responsibility of transferring the data?

    A. Cloud carrier

    B. Cloud consumer

    C. Cloud auditor

    D. Cloud broker

48. Which of the following provides visibility and security controls for servers in a cloud?

    A. Cloud Passage Halo

    B. Metasploit

    C. AWSExploit

    D. CloudInspect

49. Which of the following best describe crypters?

    A. Software tools that use a combination of encryption and code manipulation to render malware as undetectable to antivirus software

    B. Software tools that use compression to pack the malware executable into a smaller size

    C. Software that appears to perform a desirable function for the user prior to running or installing it but instead performs a function that steals information or otherwise harms the system

    D. Software that hides data in other files

50. Which command displays all connections and listening ports in numerical form?

    A. netstat -a localhost -n

    B. netstat -an

    C. netstat -r

    D. netstat -s

51. Which virus type overwrites otherwise empty areas within a file?

    A. Polymorphic

    B. Cavity

    C. Macro

    D. Boot sector

52. Which of the following best matches the POODLE attack?

    A. MITM

    B. DoS

    C. DDoS

    D. XSS

53. An attacker uses a Metasploit auxiliary exploit to send a series of small messages to a server at regular intervals. The server responds with 64 bytes of data from its memory. Which of the following best describes the attack being used?

    A. POODLE

    B. Heartbleed

    C. FREAK

    D. DROWN

54. Which of the following would most likely be used to encrypt an entire hard drive?

    A. PGP

    B. TLS

    C. SSH

    D. SSL

55. Which of the following could be a potentially effective countermeasure against social engineering?

    A. User education and training

    B. Strong security policy and procedure

    C. Clear operational guidelines

    D. Proper classification of information and individuals' access to that information

    E. All of the above

56. Which of the following represents the highest risk to an organization?

    A. Black hat

    B. Gray hat

    C. White hat

    D. Disgruntled employee

57. Jill receives an e-mail that appears legitimate and clicks the included link. She is taken to a malicious website that steals her login credentials. Which of the following best describes this attack?

    A. Phishing

    B. Javelin

    C. Wiresharking

    D. Bait and switch

58. Bill is asked to perform an assessment but is provided with no knowledge of the system other than the name of the organization. Which of the following best describes the test he will be performing?

   A. White box

   B. Gray box

   C. Black box

   D. None of the above

59. OWASP provides a testing methodology. Which of the following is provided to assist in securing web applications?

   A. COBIT

   B. A list of potential security flaws and mitigations to address them

   C. Web application patches

   D. Federally recognized security accreditation

60. Which of the following best describes a red team?

   A. Security team members defending a network

   B. Security team members attacking a network

   C. Security team members with full knowledge of the internal network

   D. Security team members dedicated to policy audit review

1. D	31. D
2. A	32. A
3. C	33. E
4. A	34. A, B
5. B	35. A
6. A	36. D
7. C	37. A
8. D	38. C
9. B	39. B
10. A	40. A
11. D	41. C
12. B	42. C
13. A	43. B
14. B	44. B
15. B	45. C
16. B	46. C
17. C	47. A
18. D	48. A
19. B	49. A
20. D	50. B
21. C	51. B
22. A, C	52. A
23. C	53. B
24. D	54. A
25. D	55. E
26. B	56. D
27. D	57. A
28. B	58. C
29. C	59. B
30. D	60. B

Total Score: _____

1. ☑ **D.** *Zero day* means there has been no time to work on a solution. The bad thing is that the discovery by security personnel of the existing vulnerability doesn't mean it just magically popped up—it means it has been there without the good guys' knowledge and could have already been exploited.

   ☒ **A, B,** and **C** are incorrect. Input validation refers to verifying that a user's entry into a form or field contains only what the form or field was designed to accept. The terms *shrink-wrap vulnerability* and *insider vulnerability* are not valid so far as your exam is concerned.

2. ☑ **A.** Controls fall into three categories: preventive, detective, and corrective. In this instance, encryption of data is designed to prevent unauthorized eyes from seeing it. Depending on the encryption used, this can provide for confidentiality and nonrepudiation and is most definitely preventive in nature.

   ☒ **B, C,** and **D** are incorrect. Detective controls are designed to watch for security breaches and detect when they occur. Corrective controls are designed to fix things after an attack has been discovered and stopped. Defensive controls do not exist as a category.

3. ☑ **C.** ALE = ARO × SLE. To find the correct annualized loss expectancy, multiply the percentage of time it is likely to occur annually (annual rate of occurrence—in this case, 0.2 [1 failure / 5 years = 20%]) by the amount of cost incurred from a single failure (single loss expectancy—in this case, $80 [for the repair guy] + $250 [5 employees at $25 an hour for 2 hours] + $2500 (replacement of server) = $2830). ALE = 0.2 × $2830, so the ALE for this case is $566.

   ☒ **A, B,** and **D** are incorrect: 20 percent is the ARO for this scenario (1 failure / 5 years); $2830 is the SLE for this scenario (repair guy cost + lost work from accounting guys + replacement of server, or $80 + $250 + $2500); $500 would be the ALE if you did not take into account the technician and lost work production.

4. ☑ **A.** Removing the software or service that contains a vulnerability is described as avoiding the risk—if it's not there to be exploited, there's no risk.

   ☒ **B, C,** and **D** are incorrect. Installing patches (or a new versions) is an attempt to mitigate risk. Installing different software without vulnerabilities is called transferring risk (however, I don't care what the publisher says, the community will determine if there are vulnerabilities). Leaving the software in place is an example of accepting the risk: maybe there are security controls in place to where the chance of it being exploited is so small you're willing to just accept the vulnerabilities exist.

5. ☑ **B.** The pre-attack phase (a.k.a. the preparation phase) is where all this activity takes place—including the passive information gathering performed by James in this example. This would be followed by the attack and post-attack phases.

   ☒ **A, C,** and **D** are incorrect. Reconnaissance and scanning are part of ethical hacking phases (reconnaissance, scanning/enumeration, gaining access, maintaining access, and clearing tracks). Assessment is akin to the attack phase.

6. ☑ **A.** FISMA has been around since 2002 and was updated in 2014. It gave certain information security responsibilities to NIST, OMB, and other government agencies, and declared the Department of Homeland Security (DHS) as the operational lead for budgets and guidelines on security matters.

   ☒ **B, C,** and **D** are incorrect. These do not match the description.

7. ☑ **C.** MX records have a preference number to tell the SMTP client to try (and retry) each of the relevant addresses in a list in order, until a delivery attempt succeeds. The smallest preference number has the highest priority, and any server with the smallest preference number must be tried first. If there is more than one MX record with the same preference number, all of them must be tried before moving on to lower-priority entries.

   ☒ **A, B,** and **D** are incorrect. MX records do not require an alias (CNAME), they do not point to name servers, and not every namespace absolutely requires an e-mail server.

8. ☑ **D.** Google hacking refers to manipulating a search string with additional specific operators to search for valuable information. The intitle: operator will return websites with a particular string in their title. Website titles contain all sorts of things, from legitimate descriptions of the page or author information to a list of words useful for a search engine.

   ☒ **A, B,** and **C** are incorrect. The intext: operator looks for pages that contain a specific string in the text of the page body. The inurl: operator looks for a specific string within the URL. The site operator limits the current search to only the specified site (instead of the entire Internet).

9. ☑ **B.** Footprinting competitive intelligence is a passive effort because of competitive intelligence being open and accessible to anyone. Passive footprinting is an effort that doesn't usually put you at risk of discovery.

   ☒ **A, C,** and **D** are incorrect. This is not active footprinting, because no internal targets have been touched and there is little to no risk of discovery. Internet footprinting isn't a legitimate term to commit to memory, and sniffing is irrelevant to this question.

10. ☑ **A.** A zero-day attack is one carried out on a vulnerability the good guys didn't even know existed. The true horror of these attacks is that you do not known about the vulnerability until it's far too late.

    ☒ **B, C,** and **D** are incorrect. These answers are not legitimate terms.

11. ☑ **D.** Split DNS is recommended virtually everywhere. Internal hosts may need to see everything internal, but external hosts do not. Keep internal DNS records split away from external ones, as there is no need for anyone outside your organization to see them.

    ☒ **A, B,** and **C** are incorrect. These answers are all distractors.

12. ☑ **B.** Shodan allows users to search for very specific types of hosts, which can be very helpful to attackers—ethical or not.

    ☒ **A, C,** and **D** are incorrect. Whois provides registrar and technical POC information. Nslookup is a command-line tool for DNS lookups. BurpSuite is a website/application hacking tool.

13. ☑ **A.** Telnetting to port 80 will generally pull a banner from a web server. You can telnet to any port you want to check, for that matter, and ideally pull a port; however, port 80 just seems to be the one used on the exam the most.

☒ **B, C,** and **D** are incorrect. These are all bad syntax for Telnet.

14. ☑ **B.** It really does sound like an urgent request, but the PSH flag is designed for these scenarios.

☒ **A, C,** and **D** are incorrect. The URG flag is used to inform the receiving stack that certain data within a segment is urgent and should be prioritized (not used much by modern protocols). The RST flag forces a termination of communications (in both directions). BUF is not a TCP flag.

15. ☑ **B.** This is bedrock knowledge you should already have memorized from networking 101 classes. TCP starts a communication with a synchronize packet (with the SYN flag set). The recipient acknowledges this by sending both the SYN and ACK flags. Finally, the originator acknowledges communications can begin with an ACK packet.

☒ **A, C,** and **D** are incorrect. These answers do not have the correct three-way handshake order.

16. ☑ **B.** Think about a TCP handshake—SYN, SYN/ACK, ACK—and then read this question again. Easy, right? In a SYN scan, an open port is going to respond with a SYN/ACK, and a closed one is going to respond with a RST/ACK.

☒ **A, C,** and **D** are incorrect. The return response indicates the port is closed. An open port would respond with a SYN/ACK, and a filtered one likely wouldn't respond at all.

17. ☑ **C.** A full-connect scan would probably be best, provided you run it slowly. However, given the choices, a half-open scan, as defined by this nmap command line, is the best remaining option.

☒ **B, C,** and **D** are incorrect. A null scan probably won't provide the reliability asked for because it doesn't work on Windows hosts at all. The -sO (operating system) scan would prove too noisy here. The full scan (-sT) would provide reliable results, but without a timing modifier to greatly slow it down, it will definitely be seen.

18. ☑ **D.** If you view the address 65.93.24.42 in binary, it looks like this: 01000001.010 11101.00011000.00101010. The subnet mask given (/20) tells us only the first 24 bits count as the network ID (which cannot change if we are to stay in the same subnet), and the remaining 12 bits belong to the host. Turning off all the host bits (after the 20th) gives us our network ID: 01000001.01011101.00010000.00000000 (52.93.16.0/20). Turning on all the host bits gives us our broadcast address: 01000001.01011101.000111 11.11111111 (65.93.31.255/20).

☒ **A, B,** and **C** are incorrect. These answers do not match the broadcast address for this subnet.

19. ☑ **B.** The ip.src== xxxx filter tells Wireshark to display only those packets with the IP address xxxx in the source field.

☒ **A, C,** and **D** are incorrect. These are incorrect Wireshark filters.

20. ☑ **D.** This Wireshark filter basically says, "Show all packets with a destination port matching syslog (which is, by default, UDP 514) coming from MATTSYS (whose IP address is 195.16.88.12).

☒ **A, B,** and **C** are incorrect. They do not match the correct syntax.

21. ☑ **C.** This rule alerts on Telnet in only one direction—into the internal network. It states that any IP address on any port attempting to connect to an internal client will generate the message "Telnet Connection Attempt."

☒ **A, B,** and **D** are incorrect. Answers A and B are incorrect because they reference log-only rules. Answer D is incorrect because the arrow is in only one direction.

22. ☑ **A, C.** Switches are designed to filter traffic—that is, they send traffic intended for a destination MAC—to only the port that holds the MAC address as an attached host. The exception, however, is broadcast and multicast traffic, which gets sent out every port. Because ARP is broadcast in nature, all machines' ARP messages would be viewable.

☒ **B** and **D** are incorrect. The switch will filter traffic to the laptop, and MAC addresses will be available from the broadcast ARPs.

23. ☑ **C.** In ARP poisoning, the bad guy keeps injecting a bad IP-to-MAC mapping in order to have traffic intended for the target go somewhere else.

☒ **A, B,** and **D** are incorrect. None of these answers correctly describes ARP poisoning. Yes, it's true an attacker may be sending thousands of ARP packets through a switch to the target, but that in and of itself does not ARP poisoning make.

24. ☑ **D.** This is exceedingly confusing on purpose—because it's how you'll see it on the exam. "Port security" refers to a security feature on switches that allows an administrator to manually assign MAC addresses to a specific port; if the machine connecting to the port does not use that particular MAC, it isn't allowed to even connect. Port security works on source addresses, so you're automatically looking at "from," not "to." In other words, it is specifically allowing access (entering a port) to a defined MAC address— think of it as a whitelist.

In truth, this type of implementation turns out to be a bit of a pain for the network staff, so most people don't use it that way. In most cases, port security simply restricts the number of MAC addresses connected to a given port. Suppose your Windows 7 machine runs six VMs for testing, each with its own MAC. As long as your port security allows for at least seven MACs on the port, you're in good shape.

☒ **A, B,** and **C** are incorrect. Port security works on source addressing, so you can throw out answers A and B. Answer C is incorrect because it's not stopping a specific MAC from connecting; it's only allowing a specific one to do so.

25. ☑ **D.** The SAM file, holding all those wonderful password hashes you want access to, is located in the C:\Windows\system32\config folder. You may also find a copy sitting in repair, at c:\windows\repair\sam.

☒ **A, B,** and **C** are incorrect. These folders do not contain the SAM file.

26. ☑ **B.** Netsh is "a command-line scripting utility that allows you to, either locally or remotely, display or modify the network configuration of a computer that is currently running." Typing **netsh** at the command line then allows you to step into various "contexts" for adjusting all sorts of network configuration options, including the firewall. Typing a question mark shows all available commands at the context you are in. You can also execute the command without stepping into each context. For example, typing **netsh firewall show config** will show the configuration of the firewall.

☒ **A, C,** and **D** are incorrect. Netstat is a great tool for viewing ports and what's happening to them on the device. Sc is service control. Ntfw isn't a valid command-line tool.

27. ☑ **D.** A security identifier (SID) has five components, each one providing specific information. The last component—the relative identifier (RID)—provides information on the type of account. The RID of 500 indicates the true administrator account on the machine.

☒ **A, B,** and **C** are incorrect. The RID values starting at 1000 refer to standard user accounts, so answers A and B can be thrown out. The 501 RID indicates the built-in guest account.

28. ☑ **B.** In a password less than eight characters, LM hashes will always have the right side of the hash the same, ending in 1404EE, because of the method by which LM performs the hash.

☒ **A, C,** and **D** are incorrect. The left side of each hash will always be different and indicates nothing. Answers C and D are incorrect because the hash value can tell you password length.

29. ☑ **C.** Brute-force attacks attempt every conceivable combination of letters, numbers, characters, and length in an attempt to find a match. Given you're starting from scratch, it follows you'd need a lot of time and a lot of resources. As an aside, the increase in processing power of systems and the ability to combine multiple systems together to work on problems cuts down on the time portion of this in modern cracking technique fairly significantly.

☒ **A, B,** and **D** are incorrect. Both hybrid and dictionary attacks have a word list to work with and can run through it fairly quickly (in computing time, that is). A botnet is a series of zombie systems set up by an attacker to carry out duties.

30. ☑ **D.** Ensuring your services run with least privilege (instead of having all services run at admin level) can help in slowing down privilege escalation.

☒ **A, B,** and **C** are incorrect. Ensuring drivers are in good shape is good practice but doesn't have a lot to do with privilege escalation prevention. Admin accounts don't run with least privilege; they're admin accounts for a reason. Automating services may save time but don't slow down hacking efforts.

31. ☑ **D.** Cain (and Abel) can do all sorts of great stuff, including extracting voice from VoIP captures.

☒ **A, B,** and **C** are incorrect. These answers do not perform the task listed. Black Widow copies websites to your system for later review. Netcat can be used for all sorts of things but is mostly known for its use in creating backdoor access to compromised systems. Nmap is probably the best known port scanner in the world.

32. ☑ **A.** The netsh command can show all sorts of goodies. In this example, it is used to display the Windows firewall settings.

    ☒ **B, C,** and **D** are incorrect. These answers do not accurately reflect the command.

33. ☑ **E.** Kerberos makes use of both symmetric and asymmetric encryption technologies to securely transmit passwords and keys across a network. The entire process consists of a key distribution center (KDC), an authentication service (AS), a ticket granting service (TGS), and the ticket granting ticket (TGT). It can make use of both TCP and UDP and runs over port 88 by default.

    ☒ **A, B, C,** and **D** are incorrect. Because all these are true statements, none can individually be the correct answer.

34. ☑ **A, B.** Whether attempting to bypass input validation or just having things appear the way you want them to on a web page, HTML entities can be useful. The less-than sign (<) equates to <, whereas the greater-than sign (>) equates to >. You can also use their respective numbered equivalents (< and >).

    ☒ **C** and **D** are incorrect. & equates to the ampersand (&), and ® equates to the Registered symbol, ®.   is a nonbreaking space.

35. ☑ **A.** Using a script entry in a web form field is cross-site scripting.

    ☒ **B, C,** and **D** are incorrect. This entry does not indicate SQL injection or buffer overflow. Brute force refers to a password-cracking effort.

36. ☑ **D.** If you missed this one, please consider taking a break or just starting your study process over again—you're obviously too tired to concentrate or you've never seen this before and are attempting to memorize your way to exam success. This question displays the classic SQL injection example that you'll see on every single practice test you'll take on the subject.

    ☒ **A, B,** and **C** are incorrect. XSS is cross-site scripting and involves inserting a script into a web form entry field to produce an outcome. Brute force is a password cracking technique, using all possible variants to match the encrypted value. Parameter manipulation refers to any parameter within communications being manipulated to force a desired outcome and is most likely displayed on the exam within the URL.

37. ☑ **A.** Broken Authentication and Session Management is second on the list of security priorities in OWASP's 2013 list, and best matches the question parameters. The following is taken directly from the list: "Application functions related to authentication and session management are often not implemented correctly, allowing attackers to compromise passwords, keys, or session tokens, or to exploit other implementation flaws to assume other users' identities."

    ☒ **B, C,** and **D** are incorrect. The site states the following on Injection (#1): "Injection flaws, such as SQL, OS, and LDAP injection, occur when untrusted data is sent to an interpreter as part of a command or query. The attacker's hostile data can trick the interpreter into executing unintended commands or accessing data without proper authorization." The site states the following about Insecure Direct Object References (#4):

"A direct object reference occurs when a developer exposes a reference to an internal implementation object, such as a file, directory, or database key. Without an access control check or other protection, attackers can manipulate these references to access unauthorized data." And, finally, the website has this to say about Security Misconfiguration (#5): "Good security requires having a secure configuration defined and deployed for the application, frameworks, application server, web server, database server, and platform. Secure settings should be defined, implemented, and maintained, as defaults are often insecure. Additionally, software should be kept up to date."

38. ☑ **C.** Walking through this command, we see that SELECT retrieves information from a database, and the username and password fields are designated as what to select. Then, using the FROM command, the table holding the fields is identified.

☒ **A, B,** and **D** are incorrect. DROP TABLE would be used to delete an entire table. ALTER TABLE can add or remove individual fields (columns), among other things.

39. ☑ **B.** In semi-tethered jailbreaking, a reboot no longer retains the patched kernel; however, the software has already been added to the device. Therefore, if admin privileges are required, the installed jailbreaking tool can be used.

☒ **A, C,** and **D** are incorrect. A reboot removes all jailbreaking patches in tethered mode, and in untethered mode, the kernel will remain patched (that is, jailbroken) after reboot, with or without a system connection. Rooting is associated with Android devices, not iOS.

40. ☑ **A.** Smishing comes from cramming SMS (texting) and phishing together. "Smishing," get it? The idea is the same as with phishing, except you use text messaging to trick users into downloading stuff.

☒ **B, C,** and **D** are incorrect. These terms do not apply to smishing.

41. ☑ **C.** Mobile Device Management is an effort to provide at least some organizational security thought to the maddening problem of mobile devices on the network. It attempts to monitor, manage, and secure the mobile devices (and associated service providers and mobile operating systems) in use in the organization. Much like group policy and such in the Microsoft Windows world, MDM helps in pushing security policies, application deployment, and monitoring of mobile devices. Solutions include, but are not limited to, XenMobile, MaaS360, AirWatch, and MobiControl.

☒ **A, B,** and **D** are incorrect: 802.1x is the wireless standards family. BYOD sounds like fun, but it's really "Bring Your Own Device" (a policy allowing personal mobile devices on organizational networks). CCMP is a function inside WPA2.

42. ☑ **C.** Kismet works as a passive network discovery tool, without using packet interjection to gather information. Kismet also works by channel hopping to discover as many networks as possible and has the ability to sniff packets and save them to a log file, readable by Wireshark or TCPDump.

☒ **A, B,** and **D** are incorrect. NetStumbler is an active discovery tool. Aircrack is a WEP cracking program. Netsniff is a false choice.

43. ☑ **B.** As good as WPA was, there were tiny flaws to be exploited in TKIP. Counter Mode with Cipher Block Chaining Message Authentication Code Protocol (CCMP) was created to fix those and is the integrity method used by Wi-Fi Protected Access 2 (WPA2).

☒ **A, C,** and **D** are incorrect. RC4 and AES are encryption algorithms (AES is used in WPA, by the way); 802.1x is the standards family wireless comes from.

44. ☑ **B.** A rogue access point is also known as an evil twin. Usually they're discovered quickly; however, there are lots of organizations that don't regularly scan for them.

☒ **A, C,** and **D** are incorrect. A replay attack occurs when communications (usually authentication related) are recorded and replayed by the attacker. Closet AP and WEP nap aren't legitimate terms.

45. ☑ **C.** In a CSRF attack, a user is already on a validated session with the target server. He then opens a link sent by the attacker to a malicious site. If things are set appropriately, the attacker can then send requests to the user's valid server connection. Using random challenge tokens ensures each request is actually coming from the user's already-established session.

☒ **A, B,** and **D** are incorrect. These attack will not be affected by random challenge tokens.

46. ☑ **C.** A public cloud model is one where services are provided over a network that is open for public use (like the Internet). Public cloud is generally used when security and compliance requirements found in large organizations isn't a major issue.

☒ **A, B,** and **D** are incorrect. Private clouds are…private, and used for a single tenant. Community is deployment model where the infrastructure is shared by several organizations, usually with the same policy and compliance considerations. Hybrid is another deployment model containing two or more methods of deployment.

47. ☑ **A.** The cloud carrier is the organization that has the responsibility of transferring the data, akin to the power distributor for the electric grid.

☒ **B, C,** and **D** are incorrect. The cloud consumer is the individual or organization that acquires and uses cloud products and services. The cloud auditor is the independent assessor of cloud service and security controls. The cloud broker acts to manage the use, performance, and delivery of cloud services as well as the relationships between providers and subscribers.

48. ☑ **A.** CloudPassage Halo (https://www.cloudpassage.com/products/) "provides instant visibility and continuous protection for servers in any combination of data centers, private clouds, and public clouds."

☒ **B, C,** and **D** are incorrect. Metasploit is a framework for delivering exploits. AWSExploit is not a legitimate tool. CloudInspect was designed for AWS cloud subscribers and runs as an automated, all-in-one testing suite specifically for your cloud subscription.

49. ☑ **A.** Crypters are software tools that use a combination of encryption and code manipulation to render malware as undetectable to AV and other security-monitoring products (in Internet lingo, it's referred to as *fud,* for "fully undetectable").

☒ **B, C,** and **D** are incorrect. Packers are a variant of crypters and use compression to pack the malware executable into a smaller size. Trojans look innocent but turn naughty after installation. Steganography tools hide data in existing image, video, or audio files.

50. ☑ **B.** Netstat provides all sorts of good info on your machine. The -a option is for all connections and listening ports. The -n option puts them in numerical order.

☒ **A, C,** and **D** are incorrect. netstat -a localhost -n is incorrect syntax. netstat -r displays the route table. netstat -s displays per-protocol statistics.

51. ☑ **B.** One thing all malware writers attempt to do is find ways to hide their work. By finding empty spaces in a file and writing to them, a cavity virus can infect a file and not change its size so far as the system is concerned.

☒ **A, C,** and **D** are incorrect. Polymorphic viruses try mutating themselves to avoid detection. Macro viruses use macros built in to various programs (such as Microsoft Excel). A boot sector virus is exceedingly difficult to get rid of and, obviously, installs on the boot sector of the disk.

52. ☑ **A.** In a POODLE attack, the man in the middle interrupts all handshake attempts by TLS clients, forcing a degradation to a vulnerable SSL version. Because many browsers would revert back to SSL 3.0 for backward compatibility and TLS handshakes "walked down" the connection until a usable one was found, attackers could interrupt the handshake and make it go all the way down to SSL 3.0

☒ **B, C,** and **D** are incorrect. POODLE is not a denial-of-service attack of any kind, and cross-site scripting has nothing to do with it.

53. ☑ **B.** Heartbleed takes advantage of the data-echoing acknowledgement heartbeat in SSL. OpenSSL version 1.0.1 through version 1.0.1f are vulnerable to this attack.

☒ **A, C,** and **D** are incorrect. The original variant of POODLE was a man-in-the-middle attack, where the bad guy exploits vulnerabilities in the TLS security protocol fallback mechanism. Factoring Attack on RSA-EXPORT Keys (FREAK) is a technique used in man-in-the-middle attacks to force the downgrade of RSA keys to weaker lengths. DROWN (Decrypting RSA with Obsolete and Weakened eNcryption) allows attackers to break SSLv2 encryption (left on sites for backward compatibility) and read or steal sensitive communications.

54. ☑ **A.** Pretty Good Privacy (PGP) uses an asymmetric encryption method to encrypt information. Although generally associated with e-mail, it can encrypt virtually anything. PGP uses public/private key encryption.

☒ **B, C,** and **D** are incorrect. TLS and SSL are encryption algorithms for network traffic. SSH is an encrypted version of Telnet.

55. ☑ **E.** Social engineering can't ever be fully contained—after all, we're only human. However, these options present good steps to take in slowing it down. A properly trained employee, who not only knows the policies and guideline but agrees with and practices them, is a tough nut to crack. Assigning classification levels helps by restricting access to specific data, thereby limiting (ideally) the amount of damage of a successful social engineering attack.

☒ **A, B, C,** and **D** are incorrect individually because they all apply.

56. ☑ **D.** It's bad enough we have to worry about the external hackers trying to break their way into a network, but what about all the folks we already let onto it? Disgruntled employees are serious threats because they already have connectivity and, depending on their job, a lot of access to otherwise protected areas.

☒ **A, B,** and **C** are incorrect. A black hat is an external, malicious attacker. A white hat is an ethical hacker. A gray hat doesn't work under an agreement but might not be malicious.

57. ☑ **A.** Phishing is the act of crafting e-mails to trick recipients into behavior they would not otherwise complete. Usually the phishing e-mail contains a link to a malicious site or even an embedded piece of malware.

☒ **B, C,** and **D** are incorrect. These answers are not legitimate attacks and do not apply here.

58. ☑ **C.** While there may be some argument about the real-world version of a black-box test, as far as your exam goes it is an assessment without any knowledge provided about the target.

☒ **A, B,** and **D** are incorrect. White-box and gray-box tests both provide information about the target (white is all of it, gray some of it).

59. ☑ **B.** OWASP provides an inside look at known web application vulnerabilities to assist developers in creating more secure environments. The following is from the site: "Everyone is free to participate in OWASP and all of our materials are available under a free and open software license. OWASP does not endorse or recommend commercial products or services, allowing our community to remain vendor neutral with the collective wisdom of the best minds in software security worldwide."

☒ **A, C,** and **D** are incorrect. COBIT is a framework for IT governance and control provided by ISACA. (Previously known as the Information Systems Audit and Control Association, ISACA now goes by its acronym only to reflect the broad range of IT governance professionals it serves.) The remaining answers are included as distractors.

60. ☑ **B.** Red teams are on offense. They are employed to go on the attack, simulating the bad guys out in the world trying to exploit anything they can find. They typically have little to no knowledge of the target to start.

☒ **A, C,** and **D** are incorrect. Blue teams work on the defensive side and have internal knowledge of the environment. Policy audit review is nothing more than a distractor here.

Analyzing Your Results

Congratulations on completing the CEH pre-assessment. You should now take the time to analyze your results with these two objectives in mind:

- Identifying the resources you should use to prepare for the exam
- Identifying the specific topics you should focus on in your preparation

Use this table to help you gauge your overall readiness for the CEH examination:

Number of Answers Correct	Recommended Course of Study
1–25	I recommend you spend a significant amount of time reviewing the material in the *CEH Certified Ethical Hacker All-in-One Exam Guide, Third Edition* before using this practice exams book.
26–37	I recommend you review the following objective map to identify the particular areas that require your focused attention and use *CEH Certified Ethical Hacker All-in-One Exam Guide, Third Edition* to review that material. Once you have done so, you should proceed to work through the questions in this book.
38–55	I recommend you use this book to refresh your knowledge and prepare yourself mentally for the exam.

Once you have identified your readiness for the exam, use the following table to identify the specific objectives that require your focus as you continue your preparation:

Chapter	Weight	Objective	Question Number in Pretest
1: Getting Started: Essential Knowledge	10%	Identify essential terminology associated with ethical hacking	1
		Understand basic elements of information security	2, 3, 4
		Describe the five stages of ethical hacking	5
		Identify laws, acts, and standards affecting IT Security	6
2: Reconnaissance: Information Gathering for the Ethical Hacker	10%	Describe DNS record types	7, 11
		Understand the use of social networking, search engines, and Google hacking in information gathering	8, 12
		Define active and passive footprinting	9
		Identify methods and procedures in information gathering	10

Chapter	Weight	Objective	Question Number in Pretest
3: Scanning and Enumeration	10%	Understand enumeration and enumeration techniques	13
		Describe TCP communication (three-way handshake and flag types)	14, 15
		Understand the use of various scanning and enumeration tools	17
		Describe scan types and the objectives of scanning	16
		Understand basic subnetting	18
4: Sniffing and Evasion	10%	Describe sniffing concepts, including active and passive sniffing and protocols susceptible to sniffing	22, 23
		Describe sniffing tools and understand their output	19, 20
		Describe sniffing countermeasures	24
		Describe signature analysis within Snort	21
5: Attacking a System	15%	Identify basics of Windows and Linux file structure, directories, and commands	25, 26, 27, 28, 32, 33
		Describe methods used to escalate privileges	30
		Describe methods used to gain access to systems	29, 31
6: Web-Based Hacking: Servers and Applications	10%	Identify web server and application vulnerabilities	34, 35, 37
		Describe web server and web application attacks	36, 45
		Identify features of common web server architecture	38
7: Wireless Network Hacking	10%	Identify wireless hacking methods and tools	42, 44
		Identify wireless network architecture and terminology	43
		Identify Mobile Device Management	41
		Describe mobile platform attacks	39, 40

Chapter	Weight	Objective	Question Number in Pretest
8: Security in Cloud Computing	5%	Understand basic elements of cloud security	46
		Identify cloud computing concepts	47
		Identify cloud security tools	48
9: Trojans and Other Attacks	5%	Identify malware deployment methods	49
		Identify malware countermeasures	50
		Describe malware types and their purpose	51
10: Cryptography 101	5%	List cryptography attacks	52, 53
		Define cryptographic algorithms	54
11: Low Tech: Social Engineering and Physical Security	5%	List social engineering countermeasures	55
		Describe different types of social engineering techniques and attacks	56, 57
12: The Pen Test: Putting It All Together	5%	Define automatic and manual testing	58
		Describe penetration testing, security assessments, and risk management	59, 60

About the CD-ROM

The CD-ROM included with this book comes with Total Tester customizable practice exam software with 300 practice exam questions and a free PDF copy of the book. The software can be installed on any Windows computer and must be installed to access the Total Tester practice exams.

System Requirements

The software requires Windows Vista or higher and 30 MB of hard disk space for full installation. To run, the screen resolution must be set to 1024 × 768 or higher. The PDF copy of the book requires Adobe Acrobat Reader, which is available for installation from a link on the CD-ROM.

Installing and Running Total Tester

From the main screen you can install the Total Tester by clicking the Install Total Tester Practice Exams button. This will begin the installation process and place an icon on your desktop and in your Start menu. To run the Total Tester, navigate to Start | (All) Programs | Total Seminars or double-click the icon on your desktop.

To uninstall the Total Tester software, go to Start | Control Panel | Programs And Features and then select the Total Tester program. Select Remove and Windows will completely uninstall the software.

About Total Tester

Total Tester provides you with a simulation of the Certified Ethical Hacker exam. Exams can be taken in either Practice Mode, Exam Mode, or Custom Mode. Practice Mode provides an assistance window with hints, references to the book, an explanation of the answer, and the option to check your answer as you take the test. Exam Mode is set with the same number of questions and time allowance as the real certification exam. Custom Mode allows you to create custom exams from selected domains or chapters, and you can further customize the number of questions and time allowed.

To take a test, launch the program and select Certified Ethical Hacker from the Installed Question Packs list. You can then select Practice Mode, Exam Mode, or Custom Mode. All exams provide an overall grade and a grade broken down by domain.

PDF Copy of the Book

The contents of this book are provided in secured PDF format on the CD-ROM. This file is viewable on your computer and many portable devices. Adobe Acrobat Reader is required to view the file on your PC. A link to Adobe's website, where you can download and install Adobe Acrobat Reader, has been included on the CD-ROM.

NOTE For more information on Adobe Reader and to check for the most recent version of the software, visit Adobe's website at http://www.adobe .com and search for the free Adobe Reader or look for Adobe Reader on the product page.

To view the book PDF on a portable device, copy the PDF file to your computer from the CD-ROM and then copy the file to your portable device using a USB or other connection. Adobe offers a mobile version of Adobe Reader, the Adobe Reader mobile app, which currently supports iOS and Android. The Adobe website also has a list of recommended applications.

Technical Support

For questions regarding the Total Tester software or operation of the CD-ROM, visit http://www .totalsem.com or e-mail support@totalsem.com.

For questions regarding the PDF copy of the book, e-mail techsolutions@mhedu.com or visit http://mhp.softwareassist.com.

For questions regarding book content, e-mail hep_customer-service@mheducation.com. For customers outside the United States, e-mail international_cs@mheducation.com.

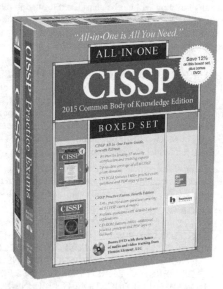

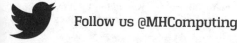